U. Mc. G. S.

GREEN
SUEDE
SHOES

Feb. 2006

To Mr. J.S.
Feb. 3, 2006

GREEN
SUEDE
SHOES

An Irish–American Odyssey

LARRY KIRWAN

THUNDER'S MOUTH PRESS
NEW YORK

GREEN SUEDE SHOES
AN IRISH-AMERICAN ODYSSEY

Published by
Thunder's Mouth Press
An Imprint of Avalon Publishing Group Inc.
245 West 17th St., 11th Floor
New York, NY 10011

AVALON
publishing group incorporated

Copyright © 2005 by Larry Kirwan
All photos used by courtesy of the author unless otherwise noted.

Library of Congress Cataloging-in-Publication Data is available.

ISBN 1-56025-644-3

9 8 7 6 5 4 3 2 1

Book design by Maria Elias
Printed in the United States of America
Distributed by Publishers Group West

GREEN
SUEDE
SHOES

1

LIFE'S LIKE THAT, ISN'T IT?

The boy is holding his mother's hand
In a seaside station
The streets are silent in the rain
Naked and dead in their small-town pain
When the train pulls in, a man alights
Lugging a suitcase, battered but bright
With labels from the Argentines
He pulls down his hat, flexes his knees
Swaggers up the platform, Bogart on ice
Winks at the boy, kisses his wife
For a moment they're lost in their ardor
The boy is suddenly jealous of his father.

The young couple walk hand in hand up the town
The boy just keeps his head down
Past the furniture store
Owned by a comrade from the Spanish Civil War
Looks in the window, to his surprise
An apparition in maple catches his eye
A Loyalist guitar from the Siege of Madrid
He presses his nose up to the windowsill
His father says, "¿Como estás, Señor?
The boy is entranced by your guitar
Here's a couple of quid down
You'll get the rest next Saturday
Life's like that, isn't it?"

Back in the house his parents disappear
To the bedroom they go, but all the boy can hear
Are the strings echoing off the maple,
His father shouts out, "Hey son, soon you'll be able
To play me a tango, knock spots off the sound"
Then he grabs his wife, twirls her around.
The boy watches in wonder as the couple cavort
Outside the rain and thunder drown out
The chill of the devotional bell
While inside their small kitchen the father and mother
Are sublimely going to hell.

The boy is religious, serves Mass at the friary
He's got a crush on St. Anthony
Got a hot date with him when he gets to heaven,
But it's still hard to get up at twenty to seven
On a gale force morning, slates hitting the streets
Exploding in smithereens all around him.
He runs in fear past the deserted garden where a man hung himself
His soul ever after sentenced to roam in search of salvation
But that morning his father leaves from the station
Six months on the banana run down to West Africa
It's up to him now he's got to look after
His tango-less, Bogarted broken-hearted mother,
"Later for you, Dad, it was nice while it lasted but
Life's like that, isn't it?"

The boy plays guitar, reads voraciously
About sex and revolution in the County Library
And in bed he tunes in Radio Sofia
Gets it on with the sister comrade from Bulgaria
The librarian is worried she visits his mother
"All he wants is James Connolly and Patrice Lumumba."
The Friars don't know what to do with this Communist
"If he don't look out he'll end up poor as St. Francis
Them auld books is drivin' the poor chap crazy,

It's time he got a job, he's far too lazy,
Go out into the real world, meet a nice girl."

He meets the girl but she is not so nice
She wears micro dresses has stormy black eyes
He no longer has time for the County Library
Learning about life in the back of a mini
Her dress is so soft but it's nothing compared to
Her silky white thighs, oh how he'd like to
Go much further so they run off to Dublin
He's drinking too much, getting in trouble
With Mao's little red book, he's ready for action
But Black Eyes wants a house not Satisfaction
In Terenure, but he's heard Bernadette Devlin
So it's—take to the streets—Rock & Roll revolution!

Black Eyes is gone on the boat to London
And Connolly Youth is explodin'
So he hops a plane to New York
He's down on the Deuce hustling work
And recreation when she rings him,
In a Richmond accent, "My only darling,
It would never work out, here is the reason:
I've fallen head over heels for an English policeman."

So he plays the tango, remembers his father
Resolves to live life like Bogart
Turn pain to music, sorrow to laughter
Live for today, to hell with tomorrow
It started at the station waiting for his father,
One moment affects everything thereafter, but
Life's like that, isn't it?

From Kilroy Was Here, *Gadfly Records, 2001*
Published by Starry Plough Music (BMI)

IT WAS EITHER raining back then or about to rain, although most of my memories are backlit by the sparkle of sunny days. Memory tends to do that, doesn't it? Reinvent and rearrange the past by spinning it in the positive glow of childhood. And even if it wasn't raining, it had been very recently. I know that for a fact, because even memory can't deny the deepness of the damp green, gleaming from the mossy-backed walls that meander through the back alleys and gardens of Wexford. The town itself doesn't give a damn about memory. Wexford has seen it all and goes its brooding melancholy way without even a thought for its current burghers, let alone apostates like myself who jumped ship years back but still dream about her. Ptolemy charted this port in the third century, Henry II sank to his knees in Selskar Abbey petitioning forgiveness for the murder of Thomas à Becket, Cromwell's roundheads sacked it, the Pikemen of 1798 won it and lost it; while a local Kennedy despaired of it and set sail for faraway Boston where he built a dynasty.

Growing up on its narrow streets and laneways in the early '60s, we were rarely more than peripherally aware of such matters, although from my bedroom, across the wet slate rooftops, I could glimpse the nearby spire and towers of Henry's Selskar Abbey. But that was only "auld history," as the locals called it. It was far more interesting to watch the crowds traipse up George's Street to the spanking new emporium of dreams, the Abbey Cinema. There we could link visions with Bogart, Cagney, and Audie Murphy, while measuring and memorizing the curves of goddesses the likes of Ava Gardner, Grace Kelly, and Rita Hayworth, not to forget our own dear Marilyn. Wexford was crazy for the "pictures" and mad for Monroe's silky femininity. Some went every night and could recite whole films by heart; it was a rare person who didn't go at least twice a week. We spoke and acted like gangsters and cowboys: our accents a mélange of Brooklyn and Wyoming. Our Abbey endings were all positive. The "Chap," as we called the hero, despite taking the inevitable hammering, always triumphed by the final reel and won the beautiful, ever chaste heroine (what they did after they rode off into the sunset was a matter of much speculation). *Casablanca* was troubling to us.

Although, it was greatly admired, something about its ending lurked in the brain, and didn't inspire you to get up and get on with it the following morning. And that's what life was all about, wasn't it?

The Abbey is long gone now. Replaced by a block of boxy flats that wouldn't so much as inspire a dry dream. But what of all those visions of Bogie and Marilyn? Do they still swirl through the cobbled laneways bumping into fanatical Crusader, jack-booted Cromwellian, Croppy republican, or returning deep-sea sailor? My father was one of the latter. Six months away with the White Star Line cruising down the coast of South America, then home to idle for three months, driving my mother crazy with his insistence on constant hot water and daily showering. No central heating back then, just a gas stove in the kitchen and an open fire in the sitting room. Hot water was expensive and a fierce drain on a subsistence budget. And wasn't a bath on a Saturday night good enough for everyone else? These sailors, with their airs and graces, their foreign clothes and ways, caused all sorts of bother—budgetary and otherwise—to the wives and mothers saddled with them.

Wexford was a town apart. Cut off from the rest of the country, it had its own accent, slang, and way of looking at things. A melting pot of Viking, Gael, Norman, Flemish, and English spiced by a healthy dose of the riffraff common to all British Empire barracks towns; it was incestuous, narrow-minded, and up to its arse in everyone else's business. Before they self-destructed, it was run tighter than any Thomas Hardy novel by a theocratic Catholic clergy convinced of its own infallibility, and unafraid to self-righteously kick the bejaysus out of anyone with the least aspiration for freedom or self-expression. Don't get me wrong. We had been well conditioned down the centuries to live under this religious dictatorship and, for the most part, we accepted our lot with the same good grace that the citizens of Karbala or the Holy City of Qum accord their ayatollahs. Unless you were a rebel in the soul, Wexford was a wonderful spot to grow up in: warm, womblike, and still reeking of a fading genteel Victorianism, a town where everyone knew their station and rejoiced in this implicit divine system.

In the midst of this benevolent uniformity, the deep-sea sailors and their foreign notions came and went in a standoff, if not a truce, with the Third Order of Saint Francis, the Holy Family Confraternity, and various other apparatchiks of the Catholic infrastructure. The sailors had little time for these religious Johnny-Stay-At-Homes; they had been out in the world and knew that there were many ways of living and seeing things. They murmured in the pubs and shook their heads about the sacred con job that was being foisted on the rest of us. They smirked behind their pints when the whole town marched to Our Lady's statue out in the grotto at Rocklands, filling the air with incense and hymns to the Mother of God who would surely intervene for us with her Son, if no one else cared to listen. But what did we know? The farthest most of us had ever been was to the bright lights of Dublin for a big hurling game. And that was rare enough.

And yet, I was happy in Wexford. There was a certainty to life that I've never experienced since. Medieval it might have been, but as long as you toed the party line, you could grow up, get married, grow old, and die in its cozy surety without facing many of the nagging questions and fears that haunt those of us who left; but, most important, Catholicism—this faith of our fathers, this most mathematically precise and pragmatic of religions—made perfect sense to me. As a boy, I didn't question it. Indeed, I exulted in its confident certitude. Go to enough Masses, say enough rosaries, stay pious, pure, and far away from sex—whatever that was—and you were guaranteed a place in heaven nestled close to the blue veil of the Blessed Virgin, and within hailing distance of the handsome, Aryan, golden-haired Redeemer Himself.

Puberty and dreams of revolution were years, if not worlds, away from me then. I was the eldest boy. I adored and loved my mother. She was all warmth and beauty. She married her dashing mariner at twenty-one, and had three children by twenty-five, with still two to come. What doubts and insecurities she must have had, longing for a husband halfway around the globe. I have an early memory of her in a rose-print swimsuit, standing on the rocks of Kilmore Quay, staring out to sea; what was she thinking of, I've often wondered? Dark and shyly glamorous, she reminded me so much of Ava Gardner at the pictures. Even then, I knew I'd never lose that seaside image, and would dig it out of the back of my mind for reassurance in times of stress and impending disaster.

Weeks before my father's arrival home, she would begin the preparations. The house would be turned upside down, inside out, every stray speck of dust and dampness banished or scorched to high heaven. And as the great day grew nearer, she would spend more time straying toward the mirror, microscopically examining and heightening her looks, making sure everything was just so, in case he blew in early, as sometimes happened. And then, at six o'clock on the morning of the day—always a summer morning, I don't recall winter ones, though there must have been many— she would rouse me from the warmth of my bed, tame my unruly hair with great globs of Brylcreem, dress me in my reluctant Sunday best, and haul me down to the North Station, where we would stare at the railway signal and jump with excitement when its indicator dropped, meaning the boat train from Rosslare Harbour would soon be shunting up the quay. We would hear its whistle before it turned Redmond's Bend, and watch it trundle toward us in a squeal of brakes and anticipation.

He always seemed to be at the back of the train, and we would peer anxiously through the locomotive steam, for occasionally he didn't show. And there were heart-stopping days when it seemed that he wasn't there and she would dig her nails into my palms, squeezing until I would almost cry out; and then just when all hope had fled, he'd emerge from the crowd of returning emigrants, bidding good-bye to some other tar or drinking companion, homburg cocked sportily to one side, Sam Spade white raincoat belted carelessly, battered suitcase (which was later stolen by a junky from my East Village apartment) covered with decals from cities only viewed on atlases by the rest of us. He'd let the case drop to the platform, throw out his arms, and she'd melt into them, still holding my hand. At first, I'd hold back for fear I wasn't being included, before throwing inhibitions to the wind and clinging on for dear life to his wide-trousered leg. When their embrace was over, he'd lean down and tug on my ear, smelling of aftershave, yesterday's booze, and the dry sweat of all-night travel. He always laid his hand upon my head and measured me—at first to just above his knee, then thigh, later waist and chest, until eventually I was grown up and self-conscious and too much of a teenage moron to attend his returns.

But that was long before I aspired to coolness. And on those summer mornings, we'd walk hand in hand down Main Street of the old town. Is it fancy now, or did we once hear the sound of an Eddie Calvert trumpet from an upstairs window, because when I came to record this song, nothing would suit me to but to have such a horn oozing melody and melancholia all across the track. Then again, I suppose any song about Wexford could profit with a trumpet; for Wexford was a town of brass players. Clattering guitars might have been all right for Dublin gurriers and the like, but in the Sunny South-East, the horn player was the man and Satchmo was king.

I always marveled at my father's self-confidence. Nothing seemed to faze him, and all emergencies, both great and small, were greeted civilly with a muttered oath, then summarily dealt with. Of course, he'd already cut his teeth on the doings of the world by the time I got to know him. He'd bolted to sea at fourteen—away from his own father's rich farms and proprietorial anger—and celebrated his fifteenth birthday in Russia; he'd been torpedoed and given up for lost, landed troops at Anzio under Nazi fire, smuggled microfilm into Argentina and butted heads with Peron's goons. He rarely mentioned any of it. But he could, and would, name a string of saloons in any port city, and when knocking back glasses of Jameson's down the pub with the other salts, the air would be thick with strange faraway names like Valetta, Singapore, Rio, and Montevideo. He was an unreconstructed atheist and annoyed the local clergy by democratically addressing them all as *Padre,* with a rare hint of sarcasm that made both bishop and brother uneasy. During the rosary, he would kneel down, but only after carefully spreading the newspaper in front of him, and when my mother couldn't hear he would wink at me and whisper, "Hail Mary full of grace, little Johnny won the race." He looked up sharply the day I announced my intention of becoming a Franciscan altar boy, but in the end he just shrugged his shoulders and returned to the racing page. Men tended to stay out of the raising of children back then. Still, he never came to see me strut about my sacred duties during Mass. This rankled, because I was quite proud of myself and of my elevated stature in the community. Now, I understand his absence.

My mother often complained that he had no imagination but, like many men, he rarely chose to articulate his deeper thoughts. There was no denying, however, that he was a wonderful dancer who especially excelled at the tango and cha-cha. Had he had his way, he would have moved us lock, stock, and barrel to Argentina, for he loved that country and its people. Wexford's damp solipsistic ways got to him, though he rarely complained. "Not a lot of point, is there?" he once uncharacteristically confided in me.

Still, after a couple of weeks at home, he would get bored and restless. He never cared for idleness and could be prevailed upon to dig up the hallway and put in a new floor, add a sunroom to the kitchen—anything to stay busy. I wonder now was this activity designed to keep his mind off the world waiting outside. Eventually, the time would tick down to departure, and it would be two weeks, then one, then the last day, and then the good-bye again at the North Station, full to the brim of weeping wives and children, as the men of Wexford headed back to sea, or returned to lonely London and Birmingham to dig ditches and make cars and the hard-earned money that would provide food and shelter for those who stayed at home.

And then, once more, I'd be king of the castle. My mother would be in a daze for the first few days after he'd gone, silent and lost in thoughts or dreams or wherever grown-ups went when they were no long focused upon you. And my life would slip back into the comforting routine of school at the Christian Brothers, and Mass at the friary, and the Beatles on Radio Caroline, and celluloid dreams at the abbey, and the seeping rain, and the chill of the east wind, and the sooty comforting smell of burning coal that drifted from every chimney and saturated us unquestioning all, who were surrounded by the apostolic comfort and security of the mossy-backed walls of Wexford.

2

BIG FELLAH

Mo chara is mo lao thu, Is aisling trí néallaibh
Do deineadh aréir dom I gCorcaigh go déanach
Ar leaba im aonar
My friend and my calf, a vision in a dream
Was revealed to me last night in Cork of a late hour
In my solitary bed

I remember you back in the GPO with Connolly and Clarke
Laughing with McDermott through the bullets and the sparks
Always with a smart remark, your eyes blazing and blue
But when we needed confidence, we always turned to you.
When they shot our leaders up against Kilmainham wall
You were there beside us in that awful Easter dawn.

Hey Big Fellah
Where the hell are you now
When we need you the most?
Big Fellah, c'mon,
Tabhair dom do lámh

Back on the streets of Dublin when we fought the Black & Tans
You were there beside us, a towering mighty man
God help the informer or the hated English spy
By Jaysus, Mick, you'd crucify them without the blinking of an eye
Still you had a heart as soft as the early morning dew
Every widow, whore and orphan could always turn to you.

Hey we beat them in the country, we whipped them in the streets
The world hailed Michael Collins, our commander and our chief
They sent you off to London to negotiate a deal
Gain us a republic, united, boys, and real.
But the women and the drink, Mick, they must have got to you
For you came back with a country divided up in two.

We had to turn against you, Mick, there was nothing we could do
'Cause we couldn't betray the Republic like Arthur Griffith and you
Fought against each other, two brothers steeped in blood
But I never doubted that your heart was broken in the flood
Though we had to shoot you down at golden *Béal na Bláth*
I always knew that Ireland lost her greatest son of all.

From Home of the Brave, *EMI Records, 1994*
Published by Starry Plough Music/EMI Blackwood Music (BMI)

I MOVED IN with my grandfather when I was ten years of age. The arrangement seems strange now, but it wasn't unusual for the time. My grandmother had died some years previously and I was considered mature enough to keep the old man company. My mother's house was but a mile distant in Corish Park, and I would still return there for dinner at one o'clock every day. Breakfast and tea, however, would be at the big house in George's Street. Although he was somewhat solitary by nature, my grandfather was far from alone. His eldest son, my Uncle Paddy, shared the house; and all three of us were looked after by Miss Codd, a formidable lady who had until recently been employed as a priest's housekeeper.

Perhaps because of this drop in stature, Miss Codd took upon herself the unenviable mission of bringing some semblance of order to this odd household while, at the same time, instilling some manners in me. The first task was the more difficult, as my grandfather and his son had not spoken in many years. They tended to communicate, only when absolutely necessary, by a series of grunts and gestures that I soon picked up on, but never ceased to baffle our intrepid housekeeper. I was never totally sure of the reason for their familial fissure but gathered that it had something to do with a perceived lack of initiative and endeavor on the part of my uncle, coupled with his fondness for drink. This latter was quite puzzling, for my grandfather was an alcoholic himself, although he only hit the bottle once or twice a year. On these occasions his failure to appear for his normally punctual six o'clock tea would lead to a nail-biting vigil, during which I would await his slurred and stumbling return, usually at the ungodly hour of half past eleven.

My uncle, not coincidentally, would arrive at roughly the same time bearing a bellyful of Guinness and the surfeit of filial grudges he had accumulated over the years. My brief was to ensure that these two pickled and prickly individuals passed like ships in the night. No mean task, given that all pubs closed on the dot of eleven, with a strict ten minutes' grace for the draining of glasses and dreams. Things came to a head one winter's night, when the grunts and gestures matriculated to full-scale roars, recriminations, and threats, whereupon my grandfather delivered an uppercut, worthy of Rocky Marciano, that sent my uncle careening across a table full of crockery to be lodged arse over elbow in the crevice next to the wall. I know this because I was cowering underneath, bawling my eyes out, for fear of getting struck by one or other of their haymakers.

I was rescued by Miss Codd who arrived downstairs like an avenging angel in flannel nightgown, hair curlered and netted in place, informing them "to go ahead and kill yourselves but you'll answer to me and the good God in heaven, if you harm so much as a hair on the head of this poor innocent child." This divine threat occasioned somewhat of a standoff, and was accompanied by the groans and curses of Paddy as he tried to extricate himself from the space between the table and the wall. My grandfather pitilessly watched his efforts from behind a pugilistic stance he had copied from pictures of Jack Dempsey, the Manassas Mauler. Eventually, Paddy tottered off upstairs to his frigid room threatening to never bother his arse with the old man again. To which

Miss Codd rejoined, "a fine thing indeed to be troubling," as Paddy's bare posterior winked at us from behind the shreds of his ripped trousers.

But I was happy—in my own way. For Thomas Hughes, my grandfather, was a remarkable man. Built like a lump of granite, he was a monumental sculptor by trade. He worked mostly with marble, but it was limestone that defined him; indeed, he was usually covered in its gray dust from head to toe. It made little difference that he meticulously scoured himself over the kitchen sink every evening: the dust seemed to have established a permanent and independent presence in his pores. This gave him a wan, unhealthy look; yet he was rarely sick, never missed a day of work, and lived until he was ninety-four years of age, though by then, his once keen brain had been ravaged by dementia, and dust, too, no doubt.

He wasn't from Wexford and always remained just a shade removed from the town. Born in Carlow in 1880, he left school at fourteen to apprentice in his father's stone yard. The youngest of many sons, in 1898 he borrowed ten guineas from a maiden aunt, loaded up a "pony and trap with tools and a sufficiency of stone," and drove the fifty miles to Wexford. There, he set up his own stonecutting business across the street from the North Station. He never had a lesson in drafting or sculpting but he had an eye like a hawk and could handily turn out copies of the masters. He kept a picture of Michelangelo's beautiful David—gray as himself with dust and time—over his desk. He stared at this in brooding affection during times of trial, which were many, for he had a large family to provide for and was "always mindful of the bailiff's rap upon the door." His favorite customers were the tinkers, Ireland's traveling people, for he said that they alone had an "appreciation of the majesty of death." Or in plain speak, which he never used, they allowed him a stab at the artistic grandiosity that he cherished, much to my Uncle Paddy's chagrin, for these ornate headstones and statues invariably led to a financial loss for the business. It was from their seething disagreements that I first learned of the complicated relationship between art and commerce.

If my grandfather and uncle differed over artistic matters, they formed a staunch united front on politics. Ours was an Irish republican household. My uncle faithfully bought the proscribed *United Irishman* newspaper in the pub every Saturday night, and it had pride of place on our breakfast table the following morning. Our walls were graced with the obligatory pictures of the heroes of the 1916 Uprising—Pearse, Connolly, and McDermott. Their steely doomed glares followed our every move in both sitting room and kitchen. Religious pictures, however—the norm for Wexford—were banished upstairs to draughty bedrooms, as Thomas Hughes had an uneasy relationship with Mother Church. While he depended on the good graces of the bishop and clergy for work in chapels and graveyards, he never forgot that in a spiritual class action he, as a member of the republican movement, had been excommunicated from the fold.

He adored the memory of the martyred Sean McDermott who had initiated him into the clandestine Irish Republican Brotherhood. According to my grandfather, McDermott bade him remain on the shadowy fringes because of his eight children; while my uncle one stormy evening sneeringly suggested the reason had more to do with an inability "to keep your bloody mouth shut with the drink in you!" McDermott had a certain allure to me, but there was something about his narrow-eyed, demagogic intensity that I could never totally warm to.

No, I was a Michael Collins man to the core. Collins was the dashing leader of the resistance to the British forces in the War of Independence. This affection of mine caused my grandfather no small amount of discomfort. To his way of thinking, Collins had "turned" and become a traitor to the Cause by accepting self-government for the twenty-six southern counties of Ireland. In return for this, the big Corkman had settled for an Oath of Allegiance to the hated British Crown and betrayed the aspirations of hundreds of thousands of Catholic Nationalists left trapped behind a sectarian Unionist curtain in the northern six counties.

But Collins was handsome, intelligent, and remained forever young—having been shot by his former colleagues—no small thing to a bookish adolescent. He had fought the British to a stand-still, impressed the redoubtable Churchill, matched brains with the crafty Lloyd George, and been betrayed by his comrade, the Machiavellian DeValera. I was certain that, had he lived, he would never have allowed the senseless partition of our country to stand. My grandfather listened to my thesis, but shook his head in dismay. Thomas Hughes might have suffered heartbreak and betrayal on account of his principles, but his life would never be complicated by such ignoble traits as pragmatism and compromise. I now see that he feared the worst for me down all the days to come, when he would no longer be there for counsel and advice.

We lived in a big old barracks on George's Street that had once been a town house of the landed gentry. Cold, creaky, and drafty, many ghosts floated around its long-faded elegance. It was, in short, a palace for a child with a fevered imagination. The second floor was given over to a large gracious room, seldom used, which had once functioned as a drawing room-cum-library. My grandfather had never received more than a primary education, but like many of his generation, he was an avid reader. He had restocked this room with volumes of books ferreted out of the great old houses around the country. Thus, we had the obvious Shelley, Keats, Wordsworth, Browning, and much of the theologically questionable Blake and Milton. Shakespeare was there in his entirety; the forbidden Gibbon strutted his stuff, along with tomes on anatomy, physiology, botany, and the wild and wooly Bible. This latter presence was unusual in a Catholic household: the practice of reading the unabridged Word of God was not encour-aged by our clergy. They much preferred that the faithful limit themselves to the well-vetted party line of the rather tame and anemic four evangelists.

Pride of place was given over to books on history. Thomas Hughes had no fear of this subject. He had lived through it, sur-vived it, and cherished its lessons. Like many republicans who abhor royalty, he had a fascination with the characters of kings and princes, not to mention princesses. Thus my mother was called Anastasia, after Tsar Nicholas's assassinated daughter. My

Uncle Paddy was lucky not to have been named in honor of Bonaparte, another obsession. Napoleon Hughes would have been a hard name to hump around the pubs of Wexford. The shame might have killed him long before the drink did.

Not surprisingly, my grandfather was most fascinated with the history of the times in which he'd lived. He had a treasured collection of books devoted to the War of Independence against the British, and the even bloodier, ensuing civil war between republicans and Free Staters. Within these volumes was entombed every argument both for and against Collins and his decision to accept a partitioned Ireland. Thomas Hughes knew all the facts by heart, and I regularly had to run upstairs and pore over one of these dusty books to counter his theses and theories. Our arguments continued over the years: in the winter before an open coal fire sputtering out blue and red flames, while in the summer, exhilarated and unaware, our discussions would spill out onto the streets. It always seemed as if he was one step ahead of me, had one extra parry or rebuttal up his sleeve that could catch me flat-footed and feeling slightly foolish.

On those long, lovely summer evenings, we would stroll down to the quayside and watch the fishing boats unload their catch. Oblivious to those around us, we would argue the merits of Cathal Brugha or Arthur Griffith, how Ireland would have been different if Rory O'Connor or Liam Mellows had survived the fraternal butchery, and a thousand other maybes and what ifs. I mined his brain for all manner of information and he gave gladly and in any way that he could, for he was an embodiment of the history and politics of his time. Through him, I could stretch back and touch his own father's memories of the horror of the famine year of Black '47: the cries of the people eating grass on the sides of roads, dumbfounded that their God had deserted them, bitter over their government's betrayal. And through him I learned that history, politics, and a desire for positive change are ineluctably intertwined.

The narrow streets of Wexford teemed with people back then; everyone walked or gawked or stood and stared, as in a scene by Breughel. Strolling along the quayside, my grandfather's hand would shoot up like a piston to tip his hat at the approach of any lady of his acquaintance. He would bow slightly from the waist and murmur a greeting or some solicitation, thereby upsetting my concentration as I marshaled slippery facts and suppositions with no less dedication than the fishermen unloading their shining slippery mackerel and eels. Messenger boys rode by on their broad-basket bikes, whistling arias from Gilbert and Sullivan or stuttering through Elvis's "Jailhouse Rock." Priests and paupers, bookies and poets, last-chance spinsters and slimy bachelors, wide-eyed culchies and know-it-all townies made the best of the fine evenings. None had any idea that change was just around the corner and would soon barrel in, forever destroying their sense of place and pride of belonging. Very few gave a thought to Mick Collins, the Big Fellah, lying in his cold hero's grave up in Glasnevin, icily fuming over the mess his followers had made of the country. But the old man and the boy did and, delighting in their own company, they argued on and on . . .

3

FIRE OF FREEDOM

Darlin', darlin' you put up with so much
Betrayed by your leaders, abandoned by your church
I watched you suffer, now you're older than your years
But you still look beautiful, though you're fighting back the tears

You can break down my door, you can even strip search me
Never going to take away my human dignity
Beat me, shoot me, flame keep on burnin'
Never goin' to put out the fire of freedom.

When we were children we thought we would be
God's anointed, but the joke was on you and me
Ten years later, we're still searching for the sun
But I want you to know that our day will come

So many hopes and dreams lying in pieces
All of us betrayed by politician speeches
I want you to know, I'll love you forever
Our dreams will continue in the eyes of our children.

Out in the street all I hear is violence
But the authorities react with silence
One law for you, for me it's another
Things got to change, oh my sisters and brothers

O ró 'se do bheatha 'bhaile
O ró 'se do bheatha 'bhaile
O ró 'se do bheatha 'bhaile
Anois ar theacht an tsamhraidh

Don't use the color of my skin as an issue
Hey politician your lies are going to get you
Chickens comin' home to roost in the White House
Blood on the streets if you don't shut your big mouth!

Power to the people sang Johnny Lennon
Twenty years later we're back at the beginnin'
Sick of hangin' round for divine intervention
Take to the streets if you're lookin' for redemption.

From Fire of Freedom, *EMI Records, 1993*
Published by Starry Plough Music/EMI Blackwell Music (BMI)

AROUND ABOUT THE time the priest came home from the Philippines I began to change. I must have been about fourteen at the time and going through what is commonly known as puberty, although this stage in life might better be known as "the endless embarrassment." This was definitely the case in Wexford, where morals were tight, mores rigid, and the whole town watched and waited on tenterhooks for the least deviation from either.

There was great anticipation in George's Street concerning the return of Father Jim. It had been almost ten years since his last visit and by all accounts he was a real character. He was my grandfather's youngest son, and a strange bird by any stretch of the imagination. Imprisoned by Mao's army in Shanghai in the late '40s, in the understated words of the family, he was "never the better for it." He had spent most of his life toiling in the Catholic missions of the Orient and was now back for an unspecified "rest."

Unlike many priests, Father Jim didn't talk a lot and wasn't one for some of the more recognized small-town social graces either, although both in manner and manners he was courtly and refined. He'd obviously seen a bit of the world and gazed out at it with a bruised understanding, curried by a somewhat existential amusement. It's obvious to me now that he had absorbed some lessons from the Zen masters but, in the Wexford of the time, he just seemed plain old odd, for want of a better word. God only knows what he thought about us, as he wasn't one for sharing confidences. People, in general, were wary of him because he was unpredictable and had an iron will; thus, you could often find yourself being set to a task for which you had neither taste nor inclination—it being a well-known fact that when the humor was on this man, he could charm the very birds down out of the trees.

When he officiated at my sister's wedding, instead of delivering the standard, wittily officious speech that preceded the giving of toasts, he raised himself up, looked around guardedly at friends and family, the tongues hanging out of them for a drink; then, in an almost inaudible voice he delivered the following to the bride and groom, word for dragged-out word: "There will be many mountains ahead of you in life. Instead of trying to climb them all, you might try walking around one or two." With that he winked knowingly, then slid back down into his chair, leaving the guests to ponder his words in slack-jawed, thirsty silence.

I should, of course, have asked his advice on "the endless embarrassment." Judging by what he said at the wedding, it would have been short, if not to the point. For puberty was causing me no end of problems, particularly in relation to religion and its many calls upon me. Most outsiders see Catholicism as monolithic and autocratic. Indeed, it can be both of those but, in practice, most believers tend to emphasize those aspects of the One True Faith that appeal to them, while conveniently downplaying the rest. My own brand ran to an odd concoction of pragmatic hucksterism and intense spirituality. After much calculation, I had divined that if I fulfilled the Nine First Fridays, regularly trekked around the Stations of the Cross, and fulfilled an array of novenas guaranteeing plenary indulgences, I would be long ensconced in heaven before the devil even had an inkling that I had vacated the planet Earth. However, I rounded out this rather mercenary outlook on salvation with a deep abiding mysticism inspired by John of the Cross and various Franciscan aesthetes including Anthony (whose main function is the miraculous retrieval of lost objects) and Francis of Assisi (he of the bird and flowers). Such ridiculous ideas as papal infallibility never cost me a thought, and I didn't give a fiddler's fart if the pope in Rome held the keys to Paddy Carey's pub, let alone those of the Kingdom of Heaven.

Sex had raised its confusing head. No one had taken the trouble to inform me of the facts of life. My mother seemed to think that was my father's job; he, no doubt, would have been willing to share in great detail what he had discovered as a boy on Boogey Street in Singapore, but I was far from ready for the degree of graphic detail such a disclosure might entail. And anyway, he was somewhere down around Tierra del Fuego at the time and not a whole lot of use to me. Nature herself, however, awaited neither time nor tide, but slyly introduced me to her pleasures by way of some startlingly erotic dreams. Marilyn Monroe, Jacqueline Kennedy, and some unwitting members of the local sodality of the Legion of Mary had starring roles in these romping epics. I'm not even sure I knew what was transpiring, but I felt little doubt that I would burn in hell for my sexual gymnastics. It was indeed as Mister Dickens had proclaimed, the best of times and the worst of times.

Because of my nocturnal, and now increasingly daily, activities, I had ceased availing myself of the sacrament of confession. I had experienced some rather uncomfortable interviews with various clergymen; some merely shrugged off my indiscretions, while others seemed a little too interested in the raw details and, to my horror, insisted on a blow-by-blow account of what I was up to between my solitary sheets. As chance would have it, the Redemptorists came to town around then to deliver one of their Parish Missions. These spiritual purgings were held every seven years and the Catholic populations—which was just about everybody—was expected to attend evening diatribes over a three-week period. The sexes were separated, and we men and boys were sequestered to Rowe Street Church.

The Redemptorists, members of the Congregation of the Most Holy Redeemer, were the storm troopers of the Catholic hierarchy. Their mission in Wexford was to root out all iniquity, face it head on, and vaporize it, leaving the town cleansed and fortified enough to not only talk the talk, but walk the walk, against Protestants, perverts, Freemasons, miniskirts, Socialists, Communists, horse thieves, wankers, spankers, and cross-dressers, and anyone else with even the remotest spark of individuality in them. And, by God, did these boyos mean business! Not only would they roam the streets and surrounding country lanes seeking out any kind of horseplay, hand-holding, or innocent fornication; they also roared and screamed threats, supplications, and invocations in the most persuasive and horrifying manner every night of those three weeks. Their *pièce de résistance,* however, was kept under wraps until the final night, when their leader, a thin-lipped redheaded termagant, flew into a paroxysm in the pulpit while luridly describing the perils of hell. As he goaded himself into frenzy, he appeared to think that his words were being lost on us, although to a man and pup we were shaking with fear in the pews. Without warning, he leaped from the pulpit and raced up to the high altar bedecked with flaring candles. He seized a branch of these, and shook it in front of him, the wax pouring down onto the crimson carpet. Then he bellowed at the top of his lungs in a strangled ecclesiastical accent, "Send up the strongest among you!"

There wasn't the rustle of a movement. Even the toughest of the cornerboys did not shift a limb, for the man seemed genuinely unhinged. He cast his fiery eyes all over us and waited a good minute, the silence building almost to a roar. "I see," he sneered at the cowardice or, perhaps, pragmatism of the men of Wexford. There were still no takers. "All the better," he said, his voice rising again in virtuous certainty, "for if I was to hold his finger over this little flame, he would scream out and faint within ten seconds." Having received no argument on this issue, he then dropped his voice to a maniacal whisper. "Then think what would happen if your entire body was to be cast into the blazing fires of hell for the remainder of eternity!" Those were his final words and we filed out of Rowe Street Chapel in shaken, ashen-faced silence, but resolved, once and for all, to change our bestial ways.

All very well for him, but I was left in a quandary. On the one hand, I could almost feel the flames licking at my eternal soul. On the other, I knew that in the confessional, I would be keenly interrogated on the number and quality of times I had committed my indiscretions. On a long sleepless night, I finally confronted the unconfessed total, now stretching back over a three-month period. Given that I was engaged in my nefarious pursuit anything from one to three times a day—the Lord between us and all harm—I figured that the grand total could be approaching, or even beyond, a whopping one hundred and eighty times. I was aghast at my degradation and could not bring myself to admit this figure to any man of God, let alone one of these Redemptorists to whom innocent hand-holding seemed a problem. And supposing the good father was to ask the names of the ladies I had mentally frolicked with, and I was forced to compromise not only the divine Marilyn and the wife of the martyred president of the United States, but any number of my friends and neighbors in the local Legion of Mary. My palms grew sweaty and the hair stood out on the back of my neck at the mere prospect.

But as the dawn leaked in over the slate roofs, I remembered that Henry II had been forgiven his murder of à Becket over in Selskar Abbey. God, from all accounts, was indeed good, and, not even the dirty black Protestant, Martin Luther, his bloated sinful body crawling with worms, would have been denied absolution, had he so requested it. My tortured brain suddenly jolted into action, in a manner that, to me at any rate, suggested divine intervention. A veil lifted and a solution was offered unto me. Why not divide my transgressions into three equal parts: confess sixty a man to three different servants of God. None need be shocked overduly and, by the time the moon arose that night, I too would be restored to purity in the sight of Our Lord God in Heaven.

And so, I set out that evening and made my penitential way to the three different houses of the Almighty in Wexford. To my surprised relief, the first priest didn't even raise a sweat at my disclosure. In fact, I wondered about his hearing, so lah-de-dah was his manner; still I refrained from tempting providence with a rerun. My penance completed in no time at all, I moved on in rising spirits. In the second confessional, I equivocated and slyly declared that it "had not been very long since my last confession." This was accepted in good faith, but the figure of sixty times in a three-month period caused the good father some concern. He desired to know, in excruciating detail, "the nature of these impure actions" and wished to discuss the matter at some length. We encountered a bit of a problem when he inquired if all the actions were committed with one lady. He was staggered when this fourteen-year-old confessed that, on the contrary, many were involved. After much to and fro, it was established that the ladies in question all resided in my imagination; thus was I able to protect the identities and reputations of Miss Monroe, Mrs. Kennedy, and the wives, mothers, and sisters of various of my friends.

He sighed in relief, and took a little time to gather himself after this misunderstanding had been cleared up. Then, he confessed to me in mournful terms, that he was very concerned at what appeared to be "the gathering moral torpor" of my character. I kept my cool and assured him that I was far along in the process of finding my spiritual bearings and would never again stoop to such depravity. Instead, I was silently congratulating myself that I had made the right decision in concealing from this innocent the fact that I had risen to the occasion thrice that many times. The poor man might have keeled over from a heart attack had I favored him with the hard facts. He would not hear of me leaving until I repeated to him a number of times that "all women are vessels of God and should be treated in such a manner." I was becoming delirious at this point, and almost confessed to him that the mental image he was invoking was having an opposite effect to the one he desired. Luckily, he dismissed me before I muddied the water further.

My penance was considerable (ten rosaries, five stations of the cross, and an ongoing novena to Saint Teresa of Avila for a speedy return of my tarnished purity). My confidence had taken a considerable blow and I paused in the nave of the church for a quick prayer to Saint Jude, who, I had been assured, was a good man to turn to in the direst of cases. He must have been on duty, for I felt a burst of energy and resolved to press on to the third church. With that final encounter behind me, I would combine the two penances in one great cathartic cleansing of the soul.

I had kept the Franciscans for last, and particularly the invariably jolly Father Justin, who I knew would forgive me were I to tell him that I had engaged in congress with John Wilson's dray horse. But to my horror, when I entered his confessional and the slatted window flew back, my squinted eyes beheld not the comforting rotund face of my friend, but rather the hawk-headed visage of some visiting friar. My adolescent courage evaporated, my mouth went dry, and I could barely speak. I began to tremble for fear, because only then did it truly dawn on me that, though I might wash away the hundred and eighty mortal sins by subterfuge, I would be committing one new almighty humdinger, namely, the making of a bad confession, something even more horrendous than buggering John Wilson's bag-of-bones, muck-to-the-eyes, auld gelding.

The visiting father was kindness itself as he nonchalantly inquired how long since my last confession, along with the name, nature, and number of times I had sinned since that blessed day. I looked at my watch and figured it had been less than twenty minutes since my visit to Rowe Street Church; I would therefore, were I truthful, have to account for sixty mortal sins, meaning that I had been indecent with myself at the rate of once every twenty seconds, a feat that Mick Jagger himself—who rumor had it possessed two mickeys—could not even have contemplated. I hemmed and hawed, but the more I tried to explain, the deeper was my grave dug. The aquiline friar grew incensed and turned to look at me in a mixture of disgust and fascination, before inquiring in a West Brit accent, at a decibel or two above decency, "Do you have the least idea of God's punishment for making a bad confession?" I did have such a notion, but chose not to elaborate. It would have made little difference, for he continued in a rising bray, "And to add insult to injury, you have polluted yourself on sixty different occasions." I could see that this interview would have no good end, and bolted at a gallop that would have put John Wilson's hauler of a coal cart to shame. The other penitents looked up from their prayers to witness this adolescent anti-Christ tear down the aisle, while behind him the aggrieved friar cried in muffled tones from within the confessional, "Come back here, sir, this instant!"

I remained indoors for some days feigning an illness. Stripped now of all spiritual armor, I was disconsolate and needed time to consider my dilemma. I also feared getting knocked down by a car, or other such calamity, that might hasten an interview with my Redeemer. I was full certain that heaven was no longer an option for a sinner of my proportions, and even a stiff sentence of a million or so years roasting in purgatory seemed to be beyond my aspirations. From time to time, I felt the eyes of Father Jim upon me. Despite his otherworldliness, he was an astute man and probably caught an echo of the existential terror that was rattling around my soul.

It seemed too much of a coincidence, therefore when, a couple of days later, my mother informed me that I would be accompanying him on a trip to our relatives in far-off Donegal. Almost as an afterthought, she added that Father Jim was very keen on taking in a bit of sightseeing through the British-occupied Six Counties—this traitorous diversion to be kept a secret from my grandfather. At this point, I would have gone willingly to the Gulag in Siberia to escape Wexford, for it could only be a matter of time before the word got back to my family of my confessional debacle. Given the normal rumor and exaggeration rampant in a small Irish town, I had little fear that I was soon to be elevated into the company of such sinners as Karl Marx, Christine Keeler, and, the divil himself, Oliver Cromwell.

And so, Father Jim and I set off in my grandfather's powder blue Morris Minor on the meandering journey to the wilds of Donegal. I remember little of the visit, except that my relatives remarked often that I seemed on the quiet side and out of sorts. Little did they know the depraved specimen of humanity they had sheltering under their roof. But the days slipped by and, away from the accusing sacramental spires of Wexford, nature reasserted herself and I began to perk up again, so to speak. On the morning of our departure, my uncle, too, had a new spring in his step. To my apprehensive eye, he was obviously a man on a mission. Upon inquiring the nature of his quest, I was informed through a sequence of nods, smiles, and Zenlike winks that all would be unfolded in due course. My suspicions should have been aroused at the border crossing into the rogue state of Northern Ireland, when Father Jim managed to surreptitiously hum a full verse of "A Nation Once Again," while answering a couple of cursory questions from an officer of Her Majesty's Royal Ulster Constabulary.

We were well beyond Limavady, cruising through the Union Jacked buckle of the Bible Belt, when my uncle sprang the news on me that, in actual fact, we were on a mission to Belfast to take in a service of the Reverend Ian Paisley. I was used to his sly humor and sniggered along in empathy. But when he didn't return my laughter, I grew alarmed. I was already in danger of burning in hell forever, but I was no fool and intended to stay alive long enough to figure out a way of reconciling the demands of nature and religion. I knew, from chat around the school yard, that marriage gave one license to commit any act of debauchery on the lucky lady. On the other hand, at fourteen years of age, my face aglow with pimples and freckles, and never having had so much as a conversation with a girl, my matrimonial prospects seemed dim, at best. But I had heard the Reverend Ian Paisley on the radio denouncing the Holy Father in Rome as being no better than the Whore of Babylon, whoever she was; thus, I had little doubt that attending his Free Presbyterian Kirk in East Belfast in the company of a papist priest would prove nothing short of suicidal.

But Father Jim was on a roll. He had somehow got it into his head that the Reverend Ian was the reincarnation of Saint Paul descended upon Sandy Row, and should be given full opportunity to explain and, if possible, redeem himself. I knew from experience that there was no talking to my uncle once a bee had invaded his bonnet. The more one argued, the more stubborn he became.

Perhaps, he had picked up this trait in Mao's prisons, but, to my mind, one should tread very carefully when proselytizing militant Protestants in the heart of their sacred homeland. To add to my alarm, he now insisted on stopping at any statue or monument bedecked by the British Union Jack. He seemed to think we were both in need of familiarization with the customs and beliefs of our Protestant brethren. Luckily for us, it was raining steadily, and the damp chill was getting to him after his years in the Orient; this caused him to button up his long black coat so that his Roman collar remained well concealed. Happy as a lark, he perused his map and puffed on Sweet Afton cigarettes, while propelling the Morris Minor up the middle of the road at a stately thirty miles an hour, democratically blocking those of all faiths from over-taking us. Upon spotting a sought-for road sign, without warning he would swerve off down some country byway, leaving a long caravan of honking cars, tractors, and lorries in our wake.

By late Saturday afternoon, with the skies darkening, according to the map we should have been within striking distance of the town of Ballymena. Instead, we had reached the butt end of some farmer's rutted track. I was in relatively good spirits, since I calcu-lated that our chances of making the Reverend Ian's sermon on the following morning were now fairly slim. And so I sat there and hummed the chorus of Jagger's "Satisfaction," while my uncle climbed a ditch to get the lay of the land. Like a great black crow he surveyed the windswept fields of County Antrim, sheltering his eyes from the drenching rain. Then he slithered back down and hopped into the car.

"Lights up ahead," he murmured and kicked the blue jalopy into gear. "And not a second too soon," thought I, as the last rays of twilight slipped into the gloomy northern night. Then with a great roar of the engine—he had yet to master the art of manipu-lating both clutch and accelerator—we shot off down the lane, the car huffing and puffing over the bumps and through the pools of rain. The aurora of the lights came into view and finally we rounded a bend to find a group of men, bearing torches and lamps some thirty yards ahead of us. They seemed to have set up strategic camp in the middle of a crossroads. One of the lights detached itself, moved toward us, and waved in a threatening manner. At first, I thought we were not going to slow down; the burly man signaling with his torch seemed to share my conviction, for he cocked one leg like an ostrich, ready to leap for his life. As we neared him, Father Jim jammed his foot on the brakes; he must not have put his foot full down on the clutch, for the car cut off with a great roaring shudder, leaving only the sound of the rain fingering the roof.

"Oh Jesus," I whimpered. For the burly man had pulled himself to his knees in the ditch and was pointing some kind of a large revolver at us. His companions had dropped their lights and were strewn across the road, having abandoned all pretense at military formation. Nonetheless, they appeared to be pointing long sticks in our direction; when my eyes adjusted to the light, I recognized these as rifles.

"Why didn't you slow down?" I demanded.

"Silence!" He hushed me imperiously and sat stock-still, staring straight ahead. Then, as if he was commenting on the price of turnips or something equally inconsequential, he noted that the gentlemen we had almost annihilated were, in fact, B Specials.

"Out of that car!" the burly one shouted.

I was not sure my uncle heard the command, for he didn't so much as bat an eyelash, though I lifted an inch or two from my seat. This order seemed even more threatening delivered in the flat Northern accent. My terror was far removed from that of the confessional: mere feet from my face stood a unit of the armed and dreaded Protestant militia entrusted with the security of the border and all other areas of the Northern Ireland statelet. And here were we: a Catholic priest and his carrot-topped Fenian nephew staring out at their drawn weapons, with night closing in around the wilds of County Antrim.

If this bothered my uncle, he betrayed not a whit of fear, but continued to stare straight ahead as if this was the most natural of encounters, though he must have had eyes in the side of his head, because when I reached for the door to obey the order, he laid a restraining hand on my arm. I was of two minds to jump out and lick the boots of these bigots, beg forgiveness, and assure them that my Catholic brogues would never again defile their sacred soil. But the burly B Special had already thrown open my uncle's door and was gesturing to him with his pistol, to which the priest replied in the courtliest manner, "Thank you, I'm sure."

This seemed not to be what was expected. The Special shoved his torch in my uncle's face and minutely examined him, while impatiently motioning to his more cautious comrades to step forward.

"What's your business in these parts?" he inquired.

"Myself and the boy," my uncle replied very evenly, never taking his eyes off the other's face, "are on our way to Belfast."

The Special beamed his light in the car and inspected me in a manner that suggested that such a monster as James Connolly or Padraig Pearse might have reincarnated their seditious selves in my frightened, fourteen-year-old personage. When he had apparently satisfied himself on this matter, he returned the torch to my uncle's face. "To Belfast?" he stated in a mixture of wonder and disbelief. My uncle might as well have stated that we were en route to Bali or Baghdad.

This question did not appear to require an answer on the priest's part. Nor did it elicit one. But the other Specials had now moved forward in a threatening manner, their ears cocked at the unexpected sound of the priest's polyglot accent. There were six, or perhaps seven, of them; all wore long black raincoats and some form of sou'wester hat. A motley bunch of farmers and shop clerks, red faced and weather-beaten or pale and undistinguished, with bigotry the only bond linking them, they stared in the window at us, suspicious and unforgiving. One had his coat open, and I could see a dark uniform underneath, belted and buckled against the elements. The rain sparkled in the headlights and beat tattoos on the roof and hood of our insignificant little car. It was black night and we were far from home. I now came to understand instinctively what my grandfather had been telling me for years: that we in the South had committed a grave travesty in abandoning the Nationalist people to the sectarian mercies of these fascist bastards.

"It's a Free State vehicle, Billy," a voice from behind the car said with some excitement. The others tensed as though a battalion of Uncle Joe Stalin's tanks had just been identified.

Billy, the burly one, nodded an *I might have known.* "And I suppose you have a Free State license upon you?"

"International, actually," my uncle stated matter-of-factly, as if sipping a pink gin in some ex-pat club in Singapore.

"International?" Billy squinted back at him, the plot obviously thickening behind his broad forehead.

A long silence ensued, broken only, as I thought, by the drumbeat of my pounding heart. My uncle appeared to have no more to say on the subject, and now stared off into the stormy night with the equanimity of Mahatma Gandhi.

"What part of international would we be talking about?" Billy persisted, his lips tightening. I noticed, for the first time, that a small blue vein was pulsing over his right eyebrow.

"Mindanao, the Philippine Islands," Father Jim replied, and magisterially swept his arm out to the horizon, for all the world, as if this sunny isle might be just over yonder hill nestled next to grim Ballymena.

This disclosure engendered considerable interest from the other Specials. But Billy was all business now. "Where are you from, lad?" The torch beamed again on my face, this time momentarily blinding me. I raised my arm to block the light before replying in a whine barely above a whisper, "Wexford, sir."

My answer seemed to be far closer to Billy's general comprehension of the universe, for he nodded sagely. The pieces of this particular County Antrim jigsaw puzzle were swiftly falling into place around him.

"He's not your son then?" The question was as harsh and flat as the accent, and the beam of light was flush again on my uncle's face. It hovered there for what seemed like ages before the priest reached up and unbuttoned his coat to reveal his Roman collar. Billy nodded once more, but now a tight little joyless smile creased his face. "It's nay because of that collar, Reverend," and there was a viciousness in his voice when he enunciated the priest's title. "We wouldn't put that beyond you," he sneered, "but he doesn't look the least like your kith or kin."

He turned to me then, and the hatred distorted his features. It's a cold dread thing to be despised in your own country, and I recoiled from the shock. The rain had drenched my hair; a drop fell from my oily quiff and coursed down my forehead. I was struck dumb with shyness and a fear of these wild men with their guns. I looked around, but the only consoling sight was my uncle and his silent defiance. We were in this together—on a back road where this auxiliary's sectarian word was the only law. Then the oily drop fell down into my eyes and something snapped inside of me. More than anything in my life, I did not want this bigot to think I was crying. I did not have either the courage or the foolishness to take his hatred and shove it back in his face, but, at the least, I would not be seen with tears and, at the best, I would confuse them with my studied nonchalance as the priest was surely doing.

I did not cry. Nor do I remember how the encounter ended. I'm sure they tried to humiliate us further; but even B Specials rarely laid a finger on priests, no matter how much they might despise them. Though shaken by the experience, it burned a hole in my consciousness and gave me an even deeper regard for my grandfather's opinions. My uncle never mentioned the incident again, but I looked on him and his Zen ways in a different light also.

We made Belfast the next morning, but didn't attend Reverend Ian's service. A drive through that city on the Sabbath with its streets deserted and playgrounds padlocked in honor of their killjoy Lord was sobering enough. Perhaps, Father Jim, too, didn't want to risk the ire of my mother by exposing me to any more sectarian abuse.

We didn't know it then, but the storm was already gathering, and would soon explode over the North. The B Specials would be disbanded, no longer allowed to officially prowl the roads in search of Taigs or Fenians to intimidate and humiliate. New and worse horrors would take their place. But one callow fourteen-year-old learned a life's lesson from the priest: there are many ways to resist tyranny—some are small, all are important.

4

ELVIS MURPHY

I'll never forget that day back in 1969 at my sister's wedding reception
I was still wearing corduroy short pants hadn't had my first erection
The band was playing waltzes
The crowd was getting bored
When this teddy boy materialized on the floor
He jumped up on the stage like a tiger from a cage
He changed my whole life direction.

Oh, Elvis Murphy, "Jailhouse Rock" knocked me out that day
"Love Me Tender" almost melted me away
And my Blue Suedes were here to stay
The crowd was goin' crazy, all dancin' and then
I knew I'd never be the same again.

When I left school, I got a job in a bank be a real successful person
I'd work all day in my three-piece suit but at night I'd be guitar rehearsin'
My boss said, "Young man,
Concentrate on your work,"
But Elvis said, "Hey kid, I got this gig in Hamburg
For fifty quid a week," I was so thrilled I couldn't speak
I told my boss to shove his dumb occupation.

I hear his song but I still think of you
Oh man, I'd give anything just to have a drink with you
The way you moved and played your guitar
Oh Elvis baby, you just showed me the way.

The years flew past, some slow some fast, many a short-lived sensation
I got a job with a band in the States had to find my own generation.
So, come on Elvis don't you be no square
Just 'cause you got six kids don't mean you don't care.
The Sixties is gone but the party goes on
Rock & Roll is your only salvation.

From Elvis Murphy's Green Suede Shoes, *Gadfly Records, 2005*
Published by Starry Plough Music (BMI)

WEXFORD WAS MAD for music and if you cocked an ear you could hear it everywhere. Music ricocheted around the streets like errant hailstones, bouncing off the slated rooftops, tattooing cobblestones and concrete alike, dissolving in the gurgling gutters that clung haphazardly to the eaves of the houses; you could hear it careen down rickety drainpipes and flush through sewers to the ever-waiting Slaney River. Sit on a bollard by the edge of the crumbling wooden quay, and you could catch melodies as they tumbled into the harbor, slicing their way through the silty channels to the sea where they would evaporate and dance across the rainbows that followed every shower.

Every house seemed to burst with sound. Silence was a rarity. Were we afraid to be alone with our thoughts? I don't believe we ever stopped to think about it. And who cared anyway, with such magic leaking from cloth-covered wirelesses out open doorways onto the narrow echoing streets? It wasn't rare to see people trapped in freeze frame on busy thoroughfares, their faces wreathed with concentration, while wrestling with the identity of a vaguely familiar tune or scrap of lyric. Strangers would sympathetically step aside or, perhaps, stop and offer a clue or word of help. Music was important in Wexford. It greased the wheels of commerce, love, and life.

And it wasn't just the sheer quantity, but the teeming variety that still impresses. Where did all this music come from? The deep-sea sailors definitely contributed. My own house swayed to tango, calypso, and big-band rhythms oozing from scratched 78s. There was the proximity to London, too. The boat train left from the North Station every night and chugged back every morning with returning emigrants, their heads full of the tunes they'd heard in Camden Town and Cricklewood. Or was it something particular to the town itself—was there a need for music to help us get through our days?

Whatever it was, every citizen seemed to have his or her own individual and quite delineated taste. One might adore Schubert, but wouldn't travel to the corner to listen to Schumann. Those who lived and died for the stone-deaf Beethoven wouldn't be caught dead listening to the wistful, tubercular Chopin. Devotees of grand opera could effortlessly scat Verdi's arias, but would crinkle their noses at the most tasty morsels from *The Magic Flute*. Not to mention that there were admirers of light opera who would call down a plague on all that "auld Italian codswallop" beloved of snobs and poseurs; no, they would sooner live, die, and whistle Gilbert and Sullivan while feeling far superior into the bargain. I even remember my grandfather reaching a crisis of conscience over music. He was a devotee of Count John McCormack and had heard the great tenor sing on many occasions. Yet, one evening when in his cups, he tearfully admitted that, while McCormack might have had no rival this side of the Pyrenees, yet, on his best day he was only in the penny stalls next to Enrico Caruso.

Lest you might think that Wexford's musical tastes were all of the egghead variety, fear not. The town was also awash in Dixieland, pop, ballads, old time, country, blues, jigs, reels, polkas, and any manner of a thing that could get your feet tapping or, even better, hitting the boards. Wexford people truly loved to dance. They could fox-trot, waltz, tango, jive, and boogie-woogie with the best of them. And little wonder why; after all, if you were a good dancer, the fair sex would not dare refuse you a twirl around the boards; and while you were spinning one of these frosty virgins along the light fantastic, who was to stop you weaving tall tales about your many accomplishments and dropping the most delicate of hints that your twinkle-toed skill might also carry over to more private pursuits in the bedroom?

Up until the early '60s all manner of musical influences melded effortlessly into one big wash of melody and rhythm. While each enthusiast had his or her own particular favorite and field of expertise, yet it was not uncommon for a classical buff to have a soft spot for a pop tune or even a "come-all-ye" Irish ballad. A devotee of Duke Ellington might, too, belt out "The White Cliffs of Dover" or even "Danny Boy" should he be so called on, when the whiskey was flowing. Whatever your private tastes, one always made a show of civility and acceptance of another's likings while at a public gathering. This was the sign of a cultured person. The mark of a boor, or just a plain old garden-variety gobshite, was he or she who, when proposed, would not attempt some kind of song. This refusal to add to the spirit of the event was considered very poor form and would be greeted by an embarrassed silence. But it rarely happened. Music was the lifeblood of the community, and community was everything back then.

Rock 'n' roll changed all this. It hit Wexford like a ton of bricks, and little has been the same since. Wexford might have been a backwater in many ways, but it was ever vigilant and superhip to the changing styles of popular entertainment. Eddie Cochran, Gene Vincent, Buddy Holly, and many others now lost in the mists of rockabilly legend were already household names in Maudlintown, Wolfe Tone Villas, and Selskar before the ink had dried on their record contracts. A riot broke out in the Capitol Cinema when the movie *Rock Around the Clock* was shown in 1956. The action spilled out onto Main Street where teddy boys and girls continued to jive and gyrate to the strains of Bill Haley and His Comets. Flick knives and broken bottles were waved in the faces of the *Garda Síochána* (police) who tried to restore order. The town's elders wrung their hands in despair, while questions were asked in the local papers about this new generation and the music that was driving them mad.

It's no mystery, in retrospect. Many of these misfits had quit school at fourteen and hung around the town for a couple of years before moving to London in search of work. There they dug tunnels for Mr. McAlpine or built cars for Mr. Ford until the loneliness

got to them. Then they would take their savings and swagger down
to Soho where they would purchase technicolor drapes, drainpipe
trousers, and winklepicker shoes, and return by the boat train,
bringing also stacks of new American 45s. They filled Nolan's
jukebox with their choices and lounged around this ice-cream
parlor à la Jimmy Dean, while the strains of Eddie, Gene, and
Buddy ripped through the open door onto Main Street. These
echo-drenched, bass-throbbing, rockabilly anthems were far too
angular and aggressive to mix in and be subsumed by the old-
timey, permissive Wexford musical culture. Indeed, in time, they
would destroy it.

The teds were frowned upon by the town elders; the priests
couldn't even come up with a name to describe their form of
deviancy. Even the deep-sea sailors didn't know what to make of
them. But what a sight these peacocks provided the little boys
who licked ice-cream cornets and sipped sundaes among them in
Nolan's back room. I'm not even sure when I first became
entranced, but I do have an early memory of hiding in Johnny
Hore's doorway across the street and gazing at their lounging,
rebellious ways. They were so different: the first sign that the gray
dingy postwar era was passing and youth was about to have its day.
The little boy felt an odd kinship to their attitude and adored their
music. There was something about the twang of Eddie's souped-
up guitar, Buddy's plaintive cry, and the perverse echoplectic
rhythms of Blue Gene that touched me to the quick. The first two
flamed out almost instantly, while Vincent burned out slowly in
addled seclusion. Still, I never hear their voices without thinking
of the Wexford teds and their heralding of the coming teenage
revolution.

As often happens in changing times, uneasy truces rule the day;
different ideas are forced to coexist. BBC Radio, despite its ability
to ignore the institutionalized sectarianism and discrimination in
the North of Ireland, was a paragon of populism and democracy
when it came to music. If there was a program director, he was
either an anarchist or too soused from long martini lunches to
worry about the choices of his musical staff. Thus, one could hear

Stravinsky next to Chuck Berry, Mario Lanza following Fats Domino, or Peggy and Brenda Lee tripping over each other in a glorious multicultural jambalaya. What an education as well as a movable feast for the ears!

But rock 'n' roll was gaining ground and would not be denied. The sedate halls, where only recently dance cards had been de rigueur, now began to reflect the new reality. On my short-pantsed way home from evening devotions in the friary, I would push my way through teds and their petticoated girls practicing lindy and jive steps outside the town hall. Sometimes I would stop to gaze adoringly as the ladies flipped over shoulders to the clanging music in a naked display of knees and knickers. I wasn't yet even sexually aware, but there was something of the fetishistic unknown that I was exposed to on those effervescent summer nights.

It's often said that boys get into music for sex, but I, on the other hand, entered professional music through sex. At around the age of sixteen, my school friends, TJ Grant, Ritchie Lynn, Tony Crosbie, Dick Keane, Albert Leacy, and I had begun attending dances at the diocesan supervised parish hall. Being somewhat late developers, we were continually outmaneuvered in the ladies' stakes by the more experienced lads who had left school at fourteen. But we six were of an enterprising nature and hit upon a brainwave. Why not run our own dances, invite every girl of our fancy and desire, along with a couple of the lame, the near blind, and other generally uncompetitive males for ballast. We formed a company, Teendance Promotions, and hired the town hall. This ballroom fortress had long been closed for dancing because of teddy boy rumbles and general rowdiness.

This was how I first came to be introduced to Elvis Murphy. Among other endeavors, Elvis ran a dance band under many different names and guises. Should one desire entertainment for a formal event, such as a hunt ball or reunion, he would turn out an orchestra with horns and female singers; a duo or trio could be provided for pubs of varying sizes and budgets; while a rock 'n' roll outfit was available for functions peopled by old teds, the young at heart, and other deviants. We had no need of musicians, but a sound system of sorts was necessary for our first record hop. I had heard that Elvis had a corner on this market. When I telephoned him, he informed me that he had everything I needed and a price would be arranged to my liking.

He duly showed up on the first night with a small amp that in his words could "blow the shit out of the Albert Hall." We had arrived with my old hi-fi set and fifty or sixty of the latest 45s that we had scrounged from big sisters, young uncles, and other acquaintances. Elvis looked on this setup with some dismay but, to his credit, he managed to get the affair up and indeed blowing the hell out of the place, though not without some world class distortion. He was at somewhat of a loose end, he informed me, and would stay on as technical adviser for a few shillings extra; this position would entail, but not be confined to, keeping an eye on both his amplifier and the general proceedings. It seemed less of an offer than a statement of intent, so there I let matters stand.

Our plan backfired. The more experienced lads showed up and made short shrift of all our prospective girlfriends, and we were left twiddling our collective thumbs at the end of the night. Over the next week we came up with a solution. Despite the various changes occurring in the outside world, the modus operandi of dances in Wexford—be they Victorian soirees or rock 'n' roll bloodbaths—consisted of consecutive sets of three fast songs followed by three smooches. Generations dating back to the mists of time had met, danced, and courted to that formula. All that tradition would have to go out the window, we reckoned, if we were ever to get our hands on a woman.

And so at our second hop, we played a dozen fast songs in a row, with no break, until the hard chaws were dropping to the floor with exhaustion and the mascara of the ladies was running in streams down their faces from the huffing and puffing. Upon a given signal we halted the carnage in midsong, announced "next dance please," and moved in on our perspiring crushes before they had even gathered their senses, let alone departed the floor. While they clung to us from sheer exhaustion, the dripping dehydrated lads would troop down the stairs and out the door to Molly Mythen's public house for much needed alcoholic sustenance. This worked like a charm for a couple of weeks until it dawned on our rivals exactly what our game was. After a number of threats and recriminations, they decided to boycott us en masse. Teen-dance Promotions went under, but we each had gained girlfriends, and were too busy dealing with the benefits and rigors of relation-ships to care about running record hops anymore.

Elvis had watched this caper with some amusement, and not a little admiration. On the last night while settling up financial mat-ters, he even appeared a tad sentimental. He had already shaken hands with me a number of times when he noted backhandedly, "You're a musician too, Kirwan?" I told him I dabbled in guitar and could make a fair fist at most songs from the Top Twenty, should the notion strike me.

"Is that so?" He nodded in wonder, as if I had just pronounced that I was the bastard son of the Queen Mother. "That's a good one," he then remarked gravely, "because I'm in the market for a good man to play the bass guitar." He must have deciphered a cer-tain apprehension on my part, for he hastened to assure me that "the bass has only four strings and should be no bother to someone who can handle six. If you want it, the job is yours." This, I felt, was a singular honor as, to the best of my knowledge, he'd never heard me play; somehow or other, he must have got wind of my prowess. I was to find out over the course of our acquain-tance, however, that Elvis was unafraid to roll the dice in the game of life and placed much importance on his own judgment of char-acter. He told me to report to the CYMS dance hall on the fol-lowing Friday night at 8 P.M. sharp.

The Catholic Young Men's Society, despite its name, was a notorious dive where one could easily get one's teeth kicked in for looking the wrong way at the right person. It was not the kind of spot that the likes of me—a studious and well brought up schoolboy—was ever likely to frequent. I wasn't quite sure how to put this to Elvis. But he was already rounding the corner. He shouted back that on Friday I would be presented with a bass guitar and installed as a fully fledged member of the Liars Show-band, an auspicious name, as it would turn out. The upshot of this was: my newly found girlfriend ditched me before I had even got the tip of my tongue past her tightly pursed lips, which pleasure I had been assured was akin to nirvana itself and almost worth turning Protestant for. Added to this, my former partners in Teen-dance Promotions said I was out of my bloody skull and would get myself killed. After a week of troubled foreboding, I was forced to sneak out the door on Friday night, without my grandfather, Uncle Paddy, or Miss Codd witnessing my departure.

I was crossing many the Rubicon with my entrée to the world of showbands, not the least of which was class. Wexford, in those days, would have left Calcutta breathless in its devotion and adherence to an ironclad caste system. The only comfort was that everyone had someone else to look down on. The lowest of the low were the tinkers; but even tinkers were afforded lower breeds of their group upon whom to shower disdain. I can't even imagine what these semilarval, lowest of the low raised their noses to, but you can be sure they did. I had an unusual upbringing myself, in that I straddled many of these caste lines. My paternal grandfather was a big landowner; my maternal grandfather, if not in the same league, occupied a large town house; while my parents lived on a corporation housing estate. Though I might have a leisurely lunch with my grandmother at the swanky Talbot Hotel on a Sunday, yet I would report to the Christian Brothers School on Monday morning cheek by jowl with the children of shop clerks, agricul-tural laborers, and receivers of the state's dole.

I gave this little thought. I had enough things to worry about, not the least of which was that I hadn't as yet been kissed, at least nothing like Bogie up at the Abbey Cinema, and I wasn't con-vinced that I might not explode into a shower of lustful particles if a woman such as Ava Gardner were to so favor me. Still, I was aware, at least on a subconscious level, that I was breaking social taboos of a major nature by joining a showband. Although there were exceptions, musicians in those days tended toward the unwashed and unschooled. Thus, I did not think that news of my recruitment to the Liars Showband would go down too well with my dowager grandmother the next time we partook of high tea together down at the Talbot.

If I felt I was crossing boundaries, my new bandmates did not disagree. To a man, they ignored me, not in any specifically hostile manner, but as if I was Duncan's ghost, present but invisible. Apart from any class divide my arrival might have sparked, the bass player, a very popular man and a great player, had been fired for falling dead drunk off the stage. One could, apparently, drink to one's heart's content in Elvis's various combos, but failure to stand erect was considered a grievous breach of protocol. To make matters worse, I had never before held a bass guitar in my hand, let alone played any kind of amplified instrument. I didn't even know how to plug the bloody thing in and was in mortal fear of getting fried by 220 volts of good old Irish electricity. To add insult to injury, my drunken predecessor had only just slunk out the door and was, I heard it whispered, ready to "kill the bollocks who takes my place."

With that in mind, Elvis had strategically delayed my arrival until minutes before the first tune was called. He now hurriedly slung over my shoulders a battered bass of dubious make. After my acoustic Yamaha, I couldn't believe the sheer weight of this electric lump of painted timber. Elvis shook my hand for good luck and advised me that the four strings were the equivalent to the bottom four on my six-string. I had little time to chew on this piece of information, for the drummer counted in "one, two, three, four" and we were off into the first song. Within the opening twelve bars I recognized its name and even knew who had written and recorded this masterpiece, but scream as much as I liked, no one would tell me in what key we were supposed to be playing.

The evening proceeded in this nightmarish fashion: I could usually decipher, in or around, where we were chordally by the first chorus; from then on I would try to lay down some rudimentary pattern of chords, while hitting some string or other on the first and third beat of the bar. Paul McCartney need have lost no sleep over this new threat from Wexford. The other musicians must have been hard set to ignore my many and appalling mistakes, but while they might raise their eyes to the good God in heaven for deliverance, they still never deigned to look my way or inform me of the next choice of song or its key.

When he wasn't belting out some tune or blaring away on a battered trumpet, Elvis watched all things—me included—like a hawk. As well he might, for the crowded hall was a roiling bed of tension, testosterone, open-ended harassment of women, drunkenness, vomiting, and balls-to-the-wall debauchery in the shaded corners and doorways. None of this seemed to trouble him to any great degree, but still he scanned the crowd like a lighthouse beacon. I soon realized that he had a bouncer positioned in each corner. Not only did they look after their particular sector, like the allies in Berlin, but they also watched him for signs in the heavens of trouble to come. He had merely to nod to an area, for all four to descend on some group of unfortunates and either beat the living shit out of them then and there, or else drag them by the collars of their suit jackets outside for an even more thorough shellacking.

At times, though, these behemoths were too late and some dispute over love or money—usually fueled by drink—would flare open and spread like a wave throughout the room. Women would flatten against the wall, raise elbows and fists over breasts and faces, and wait for better days, which arrived remarkably quickly, given the blood and gore that I saw spilled on that gelatinous floor. Our job was to continue playing even though chairs and bodies might be flying through the air in front, and occasionally on top, of us. My colleagues were past masters at defending themselves in such circumstances. They could play and sing effortlessly, with one foot kicking out at the head of any offender, and the other planted firmly on the floor for balance. Nor did they change expression or exhibit the least concern in the course of this mayhem. It appeared to be all in a night's work.

I was terrified and frequently retreated behind the sneering drummer who amused himself by flinging broken sticks at any moving target. Then all would quiet down again during the slow songs while several hundred bodies—melded together in pairs—shuffled past the bandstand before my virginal, popping eyes. Their own eyes glazed and lips slightly parted, young working-class Wexford was oblivious to all past sermons and hectoring of priest, nuns, or Redemptorists. Is it any wonder that sex and music are forever intertwined in my mind?

After four such hours, the fingers of both my hands were shredded, and blood flowed down the wine-dark face of the bass. Agony, shame, embarrassment, and the fear of a real arse-kicking after the dance surged within me and I would gladly have slunk off to my big barracks of a home on George's Street. But Elvis would have none of that: he stuck a pound note in one hand and an opened bottle of Harp in the other, put his arm around my shoulder, and led me into the dressing room. No one spoke, but I think that the flowing blood impressed my bandmates as I sat there in the corner and listened to Elvis joke, banter, and rattle off the names and dates of our next gigs.

That was my first beer and I've never tasted a sweeter one. A full night's music was reverberating through my head in one big tangled loop; chordal mistakes reran in flash frame and musical strategies that I had agonized over for years became totally obvious. I had learned more in four hours on that stage than in hundreds of nights spent practicing on the side of my bed. Vistas of the dancers crowded my consciousness, pretty girls—many from the wrong side of the tracks—had looked on me with interest, suspicion, hostility, or pure indifference; but they had looked and I had stared back for the first time in my life. My foot was still tapping from the combined rhythms of a hundred songs. I had been put through more than a musical blender. I might have entered that ballroom a boy, but I would leave it as the makings of a man. I looked around at the others. This was a different world. Women of all sorts flitted in and out of the small steamy room. Men, who I knew were married with children, attended church, and were weekly communicants, balanced young women on their knees and casually felt their breasts. Others passed around a pint of whiskey, and snapped off the caps of bottles of stout and lager. Everyone smoked and a blue haze shrouded our heads, uniting us. We were a band.

Then some shop girls from Woolworths entered and the room filled to overflowing with their scent, giggles, and sexual bantering. They plopped down on every available knee. One girl remained standing. She was very pretty—younger than I but so much older in many ways. The previous Christmas, she had sold me a bottle of perfume for my mother. I had blushed mightily back then when she smiled at me. This time I blushed less. One of her older friends squealed, "Would you ever sit down on his knee, Mary, before the poor chap dies of shame." And Mary did, and I put my arms around her slender waist, and smelled her hair, and felt the softness of her face and neck, and the drummer winked at me and I had been accepted into the world of rock 'n' roll, and all was well within that world.

5

JAMES CONNOLLY

Marching down O'Connell Street with the starry plough on high
There goes the Citizen Army with their fists raised in the sky
Leading them is a mighty man with a mad rage in his eye,
"My name is James Connolly, I didn't come here to die . . ."

But to fight for the rights of the workingman, the small farmer too
Protect the proletariat from the bosses and their screws
So hold on to your rifles, boys, don't give up your dreams
Of a republic for the working class, economic liberty.

Then Jem yelled out, "Oh citizens, this system is a curse
An English boss is a monster, an Irish one even worse
They'll never lock us out again and here's the reason why
My name is James Connolly, I didn't come here to die . . ."

And now we're in the GPO with the bullets whizzing by
With Pearse and Sean McDermott kissing each other good-bye
Up steps our citizen leader, he roars out to the sky,
"My name is James Connolly, I didn't come here to die . . ."

"Oh, Lillie, I don't want to die, we've got so much to live for
And I know we're all going out to get slaughtered
But I just can't take any more
Just the sight of one more child screaming from hunger in a Dublin slum
Or his mother slaving fourteen hours a day for the scum

Who exploit her, take her youth, throw it on a factory floor
Oh, Lillie, I just can't take any more
They've locked us out, they've banned our unions
They even treat their animals better than us
No, it's far better to die like a man on your feet
Than to live forever—some slave always down on your knees
But I don't want to die, Lillie, I don't want to die
Don't let them wrap any green flag around me
And for Christ's sake, don't let them bury me in some field full of harps
and shamrocks
And whatever you do, Lillie, don't let them make a martyr out of me
No rather, raise the starry plough on high! Sing a song of freedom!
Here's to you, Lillie, the rights of man, and international revolution!"

We fought them to a standstill while the flames lit up the sky
'Til a bullet pierced our leader and we gave up the fight.
They shot him in Kilmainham Jail but they'll never stop his cry
My name is James Connolly, I didn't come here to die . . .

From Black 47, *independent 1991, and* Fire of Freedom, *EMI Records 1993*
Published by Starry Plough Music/EMI Blackwell Music (BMI)

JAMES CONNOLLY CAME to Wexford in 1911. His visit was still remembered by many while I was growing up. As a leader of the Irish Transport and General Workers Union, he took part in what was known around town as the Great Lockout. The owners of Pierce's Foundry and the Star Ironworks had refused to deal with the workers' unions; after a number of stoppages they let all the men go and imported scabs to take their places. Violence broke out and riots ensued. An innocent man, Michael O'Leary, was killed in a baton charge. In a number of mass meetings, Connolly and his immediate superior, the great Jim Larkin, called for reinstatement of the workers, their right to organize into unions, and the granting of a fair and living wage. This clash was a precursor to the Dublin Lockout of 1913 that led to the formation of Connolly's Irish Citizen Army. The workers lost both battles, but the conflict sent the country hurtling irrevocably toward the Insurrection of 1916 and eventual freedom; the Wexford Lockout led to a polarization of the classes that continued to reverberate through the town fifty years later.

One has only to look at the pictures in the local papers to get a feel for those times: silent masses of laid-off foundry workers lurking down the back lanes of Wexford, their faces tense but expectant; you can almost hear their seditious murmurings. And at the fetes and garden parties of the Anglo-Irish, you see young men, home from Eton and Harrow, preen before the flash cameras, with no idea that they'll be blown to smithereens a couple of years later on the Somme and Passchendaele, my paternal granduncle among them. It's also hard to ignore the stilted self-importance of the Catholic middle classes promenading down the quayside, ever fearful of their clergy, ever mindful of their coveted place in the fading Edwardian Empire. Connolly and Larkin stepped into this sepia-toned freeze-frame and changed the town forever.

Thomas Hughes did not care for Connolly. Like Sean O'Casey the playwright, however, he had much time for Larkin. Interestingly enough, both leaders were born outside Ireland: Connolly in dour Edinburgh and Larkin in lively Liverpool. Could that have something to do with the general perception of their personalities? Larkin was seen as a champion of the people who not only demanded a loaf of bread, but a rose on every table; Connolly was more doctrinaire and taken with ideology. Not that Connolly didn't burn with passion; after all, when the cards were down, he gave his life for his principles. Perhaps it was the fact that Larkin was a charismatic giant of a man and a tremendous orator, while Connolly was smaller, more retiring, and preferred the pen to the podium. It doesn't really matter. They'll always be linked now—in both their successes and their failures—and there's no doubt that they electrified Ireland and changed it for the better. Larkin's day has yet to come. His shy comrade is still very much in the ascendancy. Martyrdom is a tough card to trump, it adds a veneer that's hard to chip away, and myth overtakes the man. One of Connolly's descendants informed me that, in family lore, he was considered "a wonderful person but a royal-sized pain in the arse who was always getting you to do things you didn't want to." Does that not sum him up better than all the platitudes from history books and his apologists?

He stares out determinedly from the old photographs in his suit and waistcoat; but there's usually a hint of foreboding in his expression. Perhaps he already had an inkling of the task ahead of him and his eventual fate. He definitely had a vision of the Ireland he wanted. For he was the main force behind the Proclamation read outside the General Post Office at the outset of the Easter Rising. This document made no bones about the fact that women would be treated equally in the new republic, and that each citizen would be encouraged in the pursuit of their individual happiness. Because of his leadership of this quixotic—and, at the time, unpopular—uprising, he has become an icon, appropriated by Irish people in general and by republicans in particular. But was he a democrat in the sense that we now recognize the term? When you peel off the shamrocks, it's much easier to place him in the spectrum of European revolutionary politics. He would have fit right into Moscow and Petersburg of the 1917 Revolution. Would he, like his Russian comrades, also have felt that democracy should grant more than just the right to vote? You bet he would! His aims were always very class-based: at the very least, the raising up of the poor and the workers to a respectable partnership with the other tiers of society. Might he not also have gone a step or two further and tried to emulate the Bolsheviks? Maybe he would have mellowed if he had lived. But it's hard to imagine the leader of the Irish Citizen Army fitting back into the grind of union politics after his taste of battle in 1916.

My grandfather never trusted him. He was a small businessman himself and considered Connolly a troublemaker and a Communist. To the boy who was secretly tuned in at night to Radio Moscow, these credentials were far from a turnoff. And so, in our arguments, I championed Connolly. It wasn't easy to be more rebellious than my grandfather—a republican subversive. I had to work hard and the only way to outflank him was to head left. That led to uproar in the house. Then it emerged that my grandfather never bought into Connolly's late-blooming republicanism. Contrary to popular belief, Connolly spent much of his time up until late 1915 making fun of Irish nationalists and had a sudden conversion to the cause only months before the Easter Rising. However, no one—not even Thomas Hughes—doubted the man's courage and leadership abilities during the Rising, and his subsequent martyrdom.

And so Connolly was a beacon to me, as I became more interested in the world outside Wexford. He was our own Trotsky/Che/Allende wrapped up in one. Perhaps it was the idealism of youth or simply an unawareness of how the actual wheels turn, but there was a sense of possibility back in those heady days of the late '60s and early '70s. Conservatism was on the run and a new world appeared to be just around the corner. Left-wing egalitarian ideals might not rule the new order, but they would certainly fuel it. It mattered little that this utopia could not have been other than anarchistic and unstable; there was a surefire feeling that things could be put right, that old wrongs could be redressed, and that a new beginning would soon be available for all. In tandem, there was the gypsy side, where everyone could sing, dance, and spout poetry and politics while marching along to their own different drummer. Sound like a recipe for disaster? Well, eventually it was, but what times and hopes and dreams there were in between.

Even staid Wexford was opening up. As ever, London returnees led the way with their Carnaby Street finery: bell-bottoms, flowered shirts, and John Lennon's granny glasses. Up until then, most Irish men and boys dressed in dark suits and white shirts; many even wore this outfit to the beach. There was nothing quite like lying on the wet sand listening to "Good Vibrations," and looking for all the world like an undertaker on vacation. But now the streets became a riot of color and old teddy boys sniggered at all the newly converted peacocks. The deep-sea sailors just shook their heads and returned to their pints, convinced that the whole world was going to hell in a breadbasket.

If many in Wexford looked to London, my own focus was on Dublin. I had begun hitching up there in my midteens. Just hit Wexford's new bridge at seven in the morning, stick out your thumb, and you could be strolling around Stephen's Green well before noon. Dublin was then a very manageable city. Actors, poets, politicians, writers, musicians, and television announcers promenaded by; the pubs were chockablock with characters only awaiting their own turn to become celebrities. On my first shy foray inside the infamous Bailey on Duke Street, a whiskey glass was fired down the length of the bar and crashed into the wall behind me. A gangly bespectacled man waved his fist above his head and called down God's damnation on all present. No one else even turned to look at this bedraggled anti-Christ. When I finally summoned the nerve to ask for a bottle of lemonade, my neighbor—noticing my timidity—advised, "Ah, will you don't be mindin' that auld bollocks—if he could only write half as well as he can drink." I'd almost been cleft in two by the poet Patrick Kavanagh, out on a skite.

Poetry was one thing, but there were more serious issues on my mind. I had heard wind of the nascent Connolly Youth Movement—a Marxist/Trotskyite group—and scoured Dublin searching for comrades. Although Wexford was home to many Socialists, Marxists were thin on the ground. Besides, who knew? Were I to convince the movement of my loyalty and usefulness, might not I be appointed party secretary for the Sunny South-East in the coming revolution? And with that important post under my belt, who was to say where I might end up: perhaps, even a balcony in the Kremlin, watching the Red Army parade by?

Finding my Marxist brethren was easier said than done. The Dublin comrades were obviously devotees of Chairman Mao's theories of ongoing revolution. It appeared that their beliefs also extended to the ongoing relocation of party headquarters, for it was nigh impossible to pinpoint a permanent address. However, after taking part in a potpourri of a march up O'Connell Street protesting everything from poor housing to the illegality of condoms, I was taken to a small room in the back of a shabby tenement

somewhere just north of the Liffey. After a series of knocks and signals that would have done credit to a spastic Freemason, we were
admitted to a smoke-filled office; there, beneath a naked lightbulb,
a sallow, tubercular-looking individual—the butt of a Woodbine
cigarette dangling from his lip—surveyed me. As the silence gathered I wondered if I might not be undergoing some form of initia-
tion beyond the comprehension of a rural comrade. Finally, I could
take the suspense no longer and blurted out my desire to join the
one true Party and contribute to the unstoppable revolution of
workers and small farmers. I thought that, given my country background, the mention of the farmers was a nice touch, although I
had never met any tiller of the soil, rich or poor, who would even
consider voting for the bourgeois Labor Party, let alone volunteer
away their hard-won acres to collectivization.

The comrade studied me for some moments and even went to
the rare extreme of removing the butt from his mouth. Then he
took one more long slow drag, and I winced, for the burning ash
appeared to merge with his nicotine-yellow fingers. He exhaled
mightily and his cough was like the bark of an asthmatic greyhound. Then he shook his head in disgust before declaiming in
spitfire Dublinese: "Are you the only gobshite in Ireland who don't
know that we're riddled by the Special Branch? Will you go home
to your mammy, you half-arsed culchie eejit!" With that, he lit
another fag and returned to his perusal of *The News of the World,*
leaving me to blush and back down that dank tenement hall with
whatever little dignity I had left. So much for world revolution
and the secretary-generalship of the Communist Party of County
Wexford!

But if my small efforts to agitate the nation were failing down
South, the North of Ireland was in turmoil. The Catholic popula-
tion had watched with admiration the rise of the American civil
rights movement and the striving of its messianic leader, Dr. Martin
Luther King. Beaten down by years of discrimination in jobs and
housing, most older Catholics could scarcely dream by this stage.
But with the introduction of affordable university education in the
UK, Catholic youth, eager for advancement and recognizing a way

out of their ghettos, flooded the college system. Cut free from their parochial teachers, they were exposed to all manner of left-wing thought and infected by the new air of possibility sweeping the world. They began to question the sectarian system that had beaten down their parents. They wondered why, if black Americans were attempting to overthrow segregation in the United States, they should accept the role of second-class citizens in Northern Ireland. Led by Michael Farrell, Eamonn McCann, and Bernadette Devlin, they formed Peoples Democracy and became a spearhead of the broader Northern Ireland Civil Rights Association.

They were attacked and brutalized by loyalist mobs that were often aided by the RUC and various auxiliary police forces. But by now the sectarian state of Northern Ireland had become part of the international stage. The faces of battered and bleeding young people were flashed all over the world's TV screens and, when pogroms broke out in Belfast and order totally broke down, Britain was finally forced to face up to its dirty little backyard secret. Troops were sent in to restore order and were, at first, greeted as liberators by the Catholic population of Belfast and Derry.

None of us could have realized back then that the Troubles would continue for thirty or more years and that nearly four thousand people would be killed, not to mention the many who were maimed both physically and emotionally. Those who believed in nonviolent protests were soon swept to one side. Old ghosts, both orange and green, were resurrected and their words often used out of context. Such things happen when violence becomes the currency of the day.

Connolly would turn in his grave at the thought of any of his words being used for sectarian purposes. He had tried his best to unite the workers of all religions in bitterly divided Belfast. That was the Connolly I tried to capture. I wanted to restore the man and reduce the myth, return him to his Socialist and populist roots. I wondered why this most practical person would rise up against the might of the British Empire, when it was obvious that there was little chance of success. Why a family man who loved his wife and children was willing to subject them to deep personal loss and consequential poverty.

People often ask my best memory of Black 47. They want to hear about the crowds or celebrities, but there's really no contest. It was the silence that greeted our first performance of "James Connolly" on a rowdy summer night in Reilly's. For a sparkling moment the past fused with the present. I would never have had that, if James Connolly had not come to Wexford in 1911.

6

FUNKY CÉILÍ

Bridie was teaching out in Carysfort
I was working in the bank
Two paychecks every Friday
And a Morris Minor out in the back.
But I was mad for jigs and reels
Drinking dirty big pints of stout
When the Bank of Ireland gave me the boot
They said, "Don't let the door hit your arse on the way out."

Fiddleee, diddleee, deidely-dee
I was born to play the Funky Céilí
Over the seas and far away
Off to Amerikay
Fiddleee, diddleee, deidely-dee
Where the wild, wild women are waiting for me.
Think of me, Bridie, whenever you see me there on your MTV
I love you, *a cushla,* but how could I be
Without me punky Funky Céilí?

Bridie broke down and started to bawl
When I told her about me divorce from the bank
She said, "I've got news of me own, *a stór,*
I'm two months late, it's not with the rent."
She said I'd have to be tellin' her Da
So we drove the Morris Minor to Cork

The auld fellah said, "You've got two choices
Castration or a one-way ticket to New York."

So, here I am up on Bainbridge Avenue
Still in one piece but glad I'm alive
Drinking dirty big glasses of porter
Playing me jigs and me reels and me slides
I think of you, Bridie, whenever I'm sober
Which isn't too often I have to confess
Take good care of the Morris Minor
Bad luck to your Da and give the baby a great big kiss
From his Daddy in the Bronx.

Oh, Bridie, I'm still crazy about you, girl,
Does the baby look like me, Bridie?
Has he got red hair and glasses?
Bridie, sell the Morris Minor
Come on out to America
The pubs never close over here
I got a penthouse on Bainbridge Avenue
I got the biggest bed in the world, girl,
We can stay in it and make babies forever and ever and ever. . . .

From Black 47, *independent 1991, and* Fire of Freedom,
EMI Records, 1993
Published by Starry Plough Music/EMI Blackwood Music (BMI)

BRIDIE WAS A country girl, pure and simple, with all the tastes, inclinations, traditions, and prejudices of the damp stony fields she grew up in. She was a farmer's daughter, but had received a convent education, and was not raised to labor away on the farm like many of her friends. No, she was set on course, from an early age, for life as a civil servant, a secretary, or, as she ended up—a schoolteacher. All the women of her family before her had worked their hands to the bone on their boggy acres, transforming them into pliant fields that could deliver reasonable harvests of tillage, and grass succulent enough to feed a herd of cows, some small undistinguished bullocks, and a flock of black-faced sheep. Bitter about the cost of this virtual slavery, her mother had decided that her only daughter would keep smooth hands, and end up the mistress of a semidetached palace in some small town or city. And yet, you could take Bridie from the land, but the land still lay heavy on the young woman. Though she was bright and vivacious, you could feel its somber influence informing her every mood, even in the concrete heart of Dublin.

I met her at a dance in the Television Club on Harcourt Street. I must have been there to see a particular band, but for the life of me I can't remember which one. It was during the last gasp of the great showband era. Since the mid-'50s, these traveling groups had dominated the musical scene in Ireland. Almost all sported the same patented lineup: a three-piece rhythm section, three horns, and a singer out front. They played the current Top Twenty songs, it didn't matter what style or genre, as long as they could be danced to. Accordingly, members had to be fairly nifty musically and have at least a passing acquaintance with pop, funk, Motown, jazz, folk, Dixie, and hard rock, among others. In some ways this showband ethic influenced the early days of Black 47.

I had watched Bridie from a distance. It wasn't so much that she was beautiful, but there was a definite air about her; besides she was blessed with that translucent, soft-as-rain, skin that only Irish girls seem to have. Her hair was brown, somewhat oily, with a tendency to curl; this latter she considered an affliction and battled every day I knew her. She had eyes of the palest blue I've ever seen; they would light up instantly at a joke or perceived insult. Although I didn't notice it at the time, I suppose her nose was ever so slightly too big for her face; but that was offset by lips full and sensuous that had a vague promise about them. She was slim, and fit nicely into a dusty rose-pink dress, the hem swirling just below her knees. But what really attracted me were the seamed stockings that clung to her shapely legs. These had gone out of style many years previously; all the more surprising to see them on a fashion-conscious young woman.

Even more startling, though, was that she danced with most of the young men who asked. This was highly unusual. Back then, accepting a dance meant that you considered that the suitor was, at least, in with a shot for a second set of dances. And if that hurdle was cleared, then the lady might be intimating that she would accept an offer to sit in the balcony and share a lemonade. The relationship might then progress to an exchange of telephone numbers; that familiarity, of course, could be preempted by the woman allowing herself to be walked or transported home in some fashion or other. It all seems so quaint and formal now, but it was a rare person back then who would even think of casting aside this socially proven formula.

Bridie, to the contrary, seemed to have no trouble dancing a set and then quite cordially rebuffing the next step. I had even stalked her to the balcony on two separate occasions and observed her sipping lemonade and chatting away happily with potential suitors before courteously seeing them off on their way. This was a singular young woman, indeed, and one worthy of the height of consideration. To those of us of a sensitive nature, the warmth that she displayed was almost bliss in itself, for dance hall etiquette could be crude to the extreme. I remember asking one comely maiden for the honor of a second dance, to which she replied without raising her voice, "Would you ever fuck off!" And once, when I asked another charmer for a first dance, she looked at me quizzically, up, down, and then sideways before inquiring, "Dance is it? And do you think you could find me a partner?"

And so I approached Bridie for a slow set. I was straight off surprised at her confidence, for she laid her head on my shoulder and leaned into me. I had held a number of women closely before while dancing—somewhat loose girls (or so it was rumored) who did not shy from physical contact, but I had never had the nerve to take matters any further. This was different. Our bodies fitted so well together, there was almost a shock of recognition. It was nearly too much for me and, as a cover, I immediately began a monologue about whatever song we were dancing to. She moved her head back and examined me with those very frank, lovely pale eyes. Then she smiled. She had taken my measure and, somehow or other, felt reassured. When my monologue had finally run its course, she moved close against me again and asked me my age. I was so surprised, I told her the date, hour, the name of the midwife who had delivered me, and everything else pertaining to this magical event; she just murmured back, "I'm six months older so." My heart dropped to my heels for this was another social taboo rarely broken.

At the end of the set, we were still holding hands. She made no move to leave. I couldn't imagine losing her but couldn't figure out what to say. She shrugged and led me to the balcony without even mention of the obligatory lemonade. It was so easy to talk to her. I realize now that she had much more experience of romance and relationships, and knew full well how to put a boy at his ease. I walked her to her flat, off Merrion Square, and kissed her chastely, expecting the tight lips I had become accustomed to. Her mouth, however, opened; then her tongue touched mine for just a moment and she was gone. I hadn't had the nerve to ask her for a date, but had promised her a record of Leonard Cohen's. She had never heard of him, and I wished to impress her with my worldliness. She had told me she was in a habit of sitting on Patrick Kavanagh's memorial bench on the banks of the Grand Canal on warm evenings. (The great man who had almost decapitated me in the Bailey had obviously one too many stirring evenings and departed this mortal coil.) I bashfully mentioned that if she had time on her hands, I'd meet her there the following night around eight—rain, hail, or snow.

It must have been almost summer, for Dublin's cherry trees were coming into bloom. Unwilling to take any chances, I got there half an hour early and twiddled my thumbs until the stroke of nine o'clock when I saw her strolling toward me down the canal. I was so relieved she'd actually shown up, I couldn't even begin to get mad at her. She seemed lost in her own thoughts and I felt she might pass me by. Then she smiled and I silently swore I'd love her forever. In the years to come, she never gave a reason for being late and she often was. Perhaps she felt that her six months' seniority gave her the right. At times, I'd grow seriously jealous for, occasionally, she saw other men. Later on in our relationship, she told me she'd been breaking up with someone else that cherry-blossomed evening, and it had taken longer than expected to get to Kavanagh's bench. She could say these things so casually, even though she must have known that they cut me to the bone. There was always that friction between us. But perhaps she was just seizing the upper hand for, though I loved her dearly, I saw other people, too. They meant nothing to me, and I assumed she knew that. I was full of assumptions back then. It always surprised me that I could hurt her.

She loved Kavanagh and it's easy to see why. He's an alchemist who transmutes the stubbly fields of his youth into words of hope and regret, while his poems reflect an uncommon rural longing for those trapped in cement cities of the soul. And so we sat on his bench and she recited the one about arising on a Christmas morning. I can still remember the sound of her voice exulting in, and caressing, the rhymes. The plangent words seemed to blot out all preconceptions between the townie and the country girl; in fact, they coiled around the bench and brought us closer than I could ever have imagined. When she was finished I asked for more, but she just shook her head; and so I sang very softly Leonard's "Hey That's No Way to Say Good-Bye" while two swans carried on about their business up by the far lock. I wished so hard that they'd swim down and complete the picture—but they never did.

I was mad for life back then. Mad for experience, for the new, for the unexplored, for any and all possibilities. I was like the times, I suppose, perhaps a reflection of them, or was it just my age? She was open, too, or maybe she was bored with the life that was expected of her. I filled her head with books and music and politics and all sorts of the wild speculations of youth. She taught me how to kiss and a lot of other things. Later in our relationship, I began to wonder how she had attained such knowledge. I sulked and moaned and demanded to know everything. She would always reply, "Aren't we doing grand? Why can't you just leave well enough alone?" Sometimes when I'd persist, she'd tell me the plain devastating truth, and I was never able for it. It would then take hours of reassurance for her to persuade me that I was the only one who mattered. But the scars of revelation would remain fresh and turn bloody in subsequent fights.

She was right. I couldn't leave well enough alone. I had to get to the bottom of all her problems. I was sure that there was an answer for everything. That if we could get to the root of the matter, any hurt could be assuaged, any quandary resolved. I had no idea that girls of that age need the space to grow and come to terms with their own issues, that a mood is just that: something that will pass and shouldn't be needlessly delved into for deeper reasons. I didn't understand women. Perhaps I still don't. But now I know enough to know what I don't know and can let things be: what is cloudy, if left to its own device, may well become sunshine again in a couple of hours.

I learned a lot from Bridie. She had a soft, easy wisdom and a way of looking at the world that was novel to me. She taught me that love will always outweigh intellectual understanding, that more things can be settled in bed than by words or argument. But, on reflection, I think that I unwittingly introduced her to something of equal value: the boundaries of her own personality. She began to overload from all my ideas, silly fashions, political thoughts, and music. Her own natural country conservatism and practicality emerged as a counterweight and led her to question these obvious excesses. Once good sense begins to call out coolness and the flippant ideas of the day, it's only a matter of time until it takes over and restores personal equilibrium. Back in those days, many of us never discovered our natural boundaries. Everything seemed open and we rushed in to fill a perceived void, regardless of the cost. The era led to great strides in creativity and human understanding, but it also left many casualties in its wake. There were few safety nets and only those with a strong sense of self came through unscathed. Bridie was one.

I should have seen a lot of things coming. But I was consumed with our relationship. I didn't realize that Bridie was different than the person I was idealizing. She was Bridie the country girl, not an

Irish Suzanne or Marianne, sprung from Leonard's songs. While running away to a Greek island might have sounded like a great option on a rainy midnight in bed, our reality was to trudge off to boring jobs on dismal Dublin mornings. Only the really brave and committed, like James and Nora, can make the great break together. I didn't either have the drive or the lack of convention to upend my world, and she didn't have that overriding faith in me to overcome her own conservative background.

I should have known this when I visited her farmhouse for a weekend. Her family couldn't have been kinder. They had that innate dignity and shyness of country stock the world over. It didn't take them long to see through my bluster. I mistook their quietness for a lack of intelligence and curiosity. As it was, they were more than curious about me. Both father and mother wished to be convinced that I was the right person to bring happiness to their daughter. They could tell I loved her and that she loved me; but what is love alone in the face of the relentless world? In the end, compatibility, a mutual set of interests, and the ability to see things through are equal ingredients for a lasting relationship. It came to a silent head when we dressed in our best and attended Mass at the local church on Sunday morning. The old parish priest gave a long and rambling sermon about archangels and other enochian arcana that could have put a speed freak asleep. I ranted about his failure to mention the social issues of the day and sneered about archangels all the way back to the farm. It was only around the dinner table that I realized that no one was laughing with me. If Bridie was ashamed of her parish priest, she was even more mortified by me. We survived that weekend but it remained a watershed for us—never really mentioned again but always there—a silent ache in the dark between us.

Because I was different from those she grew up with, I served to focus her on the things she ultimately wanted from life. Because many of the walls of propriety had come tumbling down, girls, not yet women, slept with men who were still boys. But still, at the back of her mind, Bridie assumed that anyone she took to bed for a couple of years must be contemplating marriage. I'm not sure how I kept it from her, but the very thought of marriage froze the blood in my veins. Marriage meant a mortgage, incompatible in-laws, children, and a sacrifice of the self for the next generation. I loved her deeply, but I also wanted to be free, unencumbered, and ultimately away from the gray death that was Ireland at the time. I had oceans to cross and many things to do, even though I had no idea what they were. Eventually, she recognized this with a deep sadness and, at times, the inevitability of our breakup seemed crushing.

One night while listening to *Nashville Skyline* by Dylan, she said that someday I'd hear "I Threw It All Away," think of her, and break down crying. For that reason I kept my distance, whether consciously or otherwise, from that album for many years. Then one night in a bar in Milwaukee, the song sneaked out at me through the speakers. I was standing there with another woman, full to the gills with whiskey and swagger. I didn't even recognize the intro, though it stopped me dead in my tracks. Then Bob's mournful voice began the line about once holding her in his arms and I almost staggered from the sadness. My companion asked me what was wrong. I couldn't find the words to tell her that I had once hurt someone who loved me dearly. But I didn't cry, Bridie.

When the end came it was sudden. As it happened, I was working in a building overlooking the Grand Canal and the sunlight was glinting on its garbage-strewn waters. I was in an office with a group of young men. When the phone rang one of them picked it up and, after listening for a moment, smirked and handed it to me. It was a tightly run firm and we were not encouraged to receive personal calls, unless in an emergency. He must have signaled to the others, for the room went unaccustomedly silent. I tried to move the phone over to the window but the cord didn't quite reach. She was ringing from London and she seemed happy at first, almost breezy. But her voice gradually deepened and I recognized concern for me. She told me that I still meant so much to her and that she'd always care for me, but she now had new responsibilities and life had to go on. I must have seemed dumbstruck and I was; but, for once, I was too embarrassed by the oppressive silence in the office to get to the bottom of things. She asked me a number of times if I was going to be okay. And each time I mumbled an unconvincing yes. Finally, the silences between us got longer and she was forced to say, "Well, I suppose, that's that."

I couldn't say yes. Just couldn't let her go. I also didn't have the courage or the understanding of life to come up with any kind of meaningful answer or solution to our problem. I could tell that she wanted to get this over with, that she'd already gone the extra mile and done more than her obligation to our years together. Then it occurred to me that there might be someone else in the room with her, someone who was now of more importance to her. Finally, she said with some emphasis and not a little closure, "Then you're sure you're going to be okay, love?" I gave my last stumbling, mumbling yes. I don't remember if she said anything else. I had the phone glued to my ear; there was a click, and then the dial tone. I couldn't bear to put the phone down. But I must have because, when I turned around, I can remember every head in the room bent down attentively to whatever task was at hand.

I couldn't stay there, couldn't even bear to enter the elevator. I climbed down all those stairs of the Goulding Building and crossed the street to the canal without thinking. I was unmoored and suddenly cut free from more than Bridie. Whatever I was going to do in life, it had to be now. There was no going back, but I wasn't sure where forward was either. I knew one thing, though: Dublin and even Ireland was desolate without her. And then I stopped at a familiar bench and was about to sit down from the sheer weariness, but just in time remembered where I was; because in my head, I heard Leonard's voice, all sleepy and sad, sing about the morning and warm kisses and her hair upon the pillow. And so I kept on walking.

7

LAND OF DEVALERA

Sittin' out in Ranelagh, drinkin' Guinness in a bar
Heavy metal on the box, must have been Top of the Pops
Lizzie's on the road to London, left us all alone and wonderin'
Paddy Kavanagh on my mind, bitterness and wastin' time

Jemmy said, "I think I'll split, dig some ditches for a bit
London ladies they be waitin', try my hand at emigratin'."
No one gave a damn until we kicked the bar in, robbed the till
The barman said, "I'll see you later, hey don't forget to tip the waiter."

Got to get out of the Land of DeValera!

Seven nights on the road, join a showband see the world
Wear a suit, be a fake, but all the speed you want to take
Broken heart in Belgrave Square, culchie woman in despair
Accused of causin' future shock, but all I want to do is rock.

RTE won't play my song, said the content is all wrong
"Why don't you stick to old-time waltzes, give the public what it wants?"
Couldn't take another bit, had it up to there with shit
Bought a ticket to Manhattan—need a fix of somethin' different.

Got to get out of the Land of DeValera!

Fianna Fail, Fine Gael, Labour's got me on the rails

It never seemed to make no sense, I couldn't tell the difference
Stay married, hate her guts, no, no, no divorce
Little girls all end up pregnant, hypocrites in every convent.

Drunk and rowdy on the bus, take me to the terminus
Another exile on the run, soon to be a Bowery bum
Say good-bye to pessimism, sterile years and religion
No ifs or buts and no more maybes, I'll be back in the '80s.

From Black 47, independent 1991
Published by Starry Plough Music (BMI)

WITH BRIDIE GONE, life was bleaker, if simpler; so I did what any normal Irishman would do. I hit the bottle. Up until then, I had been a little leery of drink. I had seen its consequences up close: the rows, the spilling of old secrets, coupled with the shame, hangovers and conveniently lapsed memories of the following morning. But now I devoted myself to demon alcohol as if making up for lost time.

If you want to do some serious drinking, Dublin is the town. You'll always find someone ready to go on a tear with you. I was living in a coldwater flat in Rathmines on the South Side of the river, now a very upscale yuppie neighborhood. Back then it was the heart of culchie land. We, unsophisticated, uncouth country people, congregated there by the thousands and infested the old town houses of loyal Protestant and Castle Catholic like so many rats in a sewer. My furnished bed-sitter perched on the third floor of the building, while my kitchen was in the damp basement where servants had once slaved and lived in a warren of tiny rooms. Hot water was not part of the deal, so in order to shave, wash dishes, or do any of those things one takes for granted, you first had to boil a pot full of water. Toilets were available throughout the musty house, but the large stately bathroom, in which a battalion of troops could have been billeted, inhabited much of the the second floor. This shrine to antiquity was kept under lock and key by the owners—two old maids straight out of

Dickens—who lived a couple of blocks away. In order to take a bath in the evening, one had to notify these two tottering relics of Victoriana on one's way to work in the morning. You were then allowed to drop by again on the stroke of 6 P.M., when you would be provided with a large key that we called the hernia-giver. With this ornate piece of iron in hand, one could gain entry to the holy of holies, carrying on one's person a towel and some shillings. The coins were to be fed into a meter that would provide enough Dublin Corporation gas to heat the water. The pilot light of this heater was, in theory, supposed to remain aflame. The reality was often otherwise.

Thus maintaining the basics of physical hygiene was a scary and quite complicated proposition. I managed to survive without too much incident, but I can't say I was ever totally at my ease while lying there in the scalding water, with at least one eye on the exposed blue ring of fire that was heating the cistern. I was often reminded of the patrons of Pompeii's baths who must have similarly gazed out upon smoldering Vesuvius. My paranoia was confirmed when, one evening, I was aroused from a nap by a thunderous explosion from downstairs. Thinking that the revolution had finally begun and I was unconscionably late, I scampered downstairs brandishing Mao's little red book, ready to browbeat any and all fascists, but I was almost knocked over by a near-naked man clutching a white towel to his genitalia as he headed for the roof. "I'm fuckin' blinded," he roared, his eyebrows and moustache burned to a cinder.

He looked vaguely familiar, but without hair and uniform it was hard to recognize the *Garda Síochána* who had recently moved into the flat next door. After vainly inserting five shillings in the meter and receiving no hot water, he had stuck a lit match in to take a look, thereby igniting some cubic feet of free-flowing gas.

If life was primitive in flatland, the gargle eased a lot of the pain. Successive governments obviously felt that booze should be available at a reasonable price to keep society's ever-jutting lid firmly attached. On account of this benign policy, even poor students and workers could manage to get soused on a regular basis. Of course, when you're nineteen and there comes the choice between food or drink, it's really no contest. I might have resisted the temptation toward outright indulgence, but my brother arrived in Dublin around the time of Bridie's departure. Jemmy had gone to sea at seventeen and followed my father's watery way through West Africa and all points due east of Suez, but he soon tired of the life. To my parents' consternation he decided to change careers in midstream, as it were. Since he appeared to have few ideas about how to become a reliable cog in the workforce, they enrolled him in Atlantic College where he was to learn the trade of radio operator. With this diploma secured, he could then return to sea or, failing that, get a job in an airport or somewhere else on terra firma. At least, that was the plan in their minds.

Within days he had bonded with the greatest crowd of drinkers, dossers, and ne'er-do-wells that I've ever come across. Most of these youths and men seemed to have failed at every other known profession and were attending Atlantic College as a last resort. No one from this circle showed the least interest in any kind of formal learning and none graduated; but they could drink, smoke, borrow, gamble, whore around, and get bounced out of bars like there was no tomorrow. They gathered in whatever pub in Rathmines or Ranelagh that would allow them entry, and when each had consumed enough alcohol to kill a small pony, they danced at the hops in the Leinster Cricket or the Ranelagh Tennis club. Actually, their turns on the floor were quite few and far between, as none but the brave would take to the boards with them. But they did manage to attract a bunch of wild, nihilistic women of all shapes, sizes, and degrees of beauty who cared little for convention and even less for reputation. This was the set that I flung in my lot with.

The lads, as they were somewhat euphemistically called, had perfect loyalty to one another, except in the matter of girlfriends. Steady relationships were frowned on anyway, and it would be considered doing your friend a favor if you were to seduce the love of his life. While this betrayal might cause some initial heartbreak, it could ultimately save the poor sod from the obvious horrors of a long-term commitment, or dare one mention the proscribed word, *marriage*. And though each member of the circle would cheat, steal, borrow, or embezzle to provide cash for the evening's debauch, yet none would deny an impecunious brother the right to get blasted with them. We took to gathering at my place, pure unabated luxury compared to the oft-thrashed, ill-lit warren Jemmy and his mates inhabited on Leinster Place. We would begin with a two-gallon plastic barrel of rotgut cider. After siphoning off a round of pints, we would then replenish the remains of the barrel with a couple of bottles of cheap wine, gin, vodka, whiskey, or whatever hooch we had managed to lay our hands on during the course of the day's foraging. It's a wonder we didn't add strychnine. This brew, as one might imagine, had a taste and smell unto its own, but did it do the trick! Within an hour or so we would be on the floor, or more than likely acting out the lines of *Jesus Christ Superstar,* which unaccountably, along with Black Sabbath's debut, was one of our favorite recordings. We knew every phrase and hiccup from Lloyd Webber's double album, and it's a wonder none of us were actually nailed to a cross, such was our commitment to the score and story in the heat of our delirium.

When we were, as we decided, in good enough form, we would venture forth to the Hideaway Lounge at the top of Rathmines Road. Oddly enough, though one of our number had once fallen through a second-floor plate-glass window, causing both physical and financial pain, we were usually welcome in that establishment; and if not, we would fan off down toward the Portobello Bridge until entrance was gained in some pub, club, or shebeen. After squandering our remaining resources, we would then, uninvited, gate-crash a party and attempt to relieve the hosts of whatever liquor they had so graciously provided. All in a night's work, as they say.

Dublin had a great notion of itself in those days. And why wouldn't it? It was still only heartbeats away from the city of Joyce's *Ulysses* and you could almost touch the shadows of Bloom and Blazes promenading by. The whole place reeked of an ineluctable air of horniness that would have done Molly proud. For every year, thousands of fresh-faced convent girls—newly recruited civil servants, university students, trainee teachers and the like—descended on its bars and dance halls, many fighting fit and beyond eager to lose their rural restraints and inhibitions. Country lads and city slickers alike lined up, ever ready to volunteer their services for this perennially joyous task. It was a city of great wit and banter and it took a brave person to risk raising one's head too high for fear of ridicule. Dubliners were past masters in the art of the put-down and had invented and then perfected the Irish art of slagging. This acidic, and often mean-spirited, practice tended to stunt many very talented people, but those who could rise above it tended to be world-beaters.

Philip Lynott of Thin Lizzy was a case in point. He may have been the most charismatic person I ever set eyes on. He roamed the streets of Dublin like a pied piper, followed at the heels by a crowd of adoring ragamuffins. Dressed like Hendrix and, rumor had it, just as well endowed, everyone knew him and was on speaking terms with the man, for you had only to nod in his direction and he would bowl you over with a beaming smile that came straight from his troubled heart. If you spoke to him, he would stop and not only bid you the time of day, but find out what you were about yourself, before giving you a sound piece of advice, or a helping hand, if it was asked for.

Michael MacLiammoir and Hilton Edwards were two others who regularly made the rounds and were inured to gossip or back-biting; in fact, if anything, they cultivated it. They were the premier theatrical couple in Dublin and affected the dress, gait, and manners of a couple of Oscar Wildes out on the town for a ramble. One could always catch their roving eyes across a teeming bar, and it was a thrill to be addressed as "my dear boy" by these two amazing actors and directors who seemed, even then, to have dropped in from a different era. The city was awash in drink and come eleven at night all inhibitions would flush off down the rain-soaked streets into the Liffey, while the ghosts of fey Oscar, sunny Jim, acerbic Jonathan, and black-cloaked Bram would arise from their slumbers and hold sway. It must have tickled the hearts of Michael and Hilton that their city, dear old dirty Dublin, had finally outlasted the bishops and their stifling European Jansenism, and was now head over heels embroiled in sexual and social revolution.

It was an idyllic time but not for the faint of heart, and even less so for the sensitive of stomach or liver. The news up North was not comforting. Internment against Catholics and republicans had been introduced and the social order was disintegrating. Young men of my acquaintance were joining both the Provisional and Official IRA. The era of the peace march was over; the gun and plastic explosive ruled. And yet, south of the border, there was an air of unreality. Dublin's pubs were roaring and the dance halls bounced to a new and harder beat. T. Rex and David Bowie pounded the airwaves and glitter sparkled around every young dude's eyes; but I felt like a child rolling down a grassy hill, gathering speed with every turn. Despite the partying and the joys of my Gingerman existence, with Bridie gone, Dublin seemed empty, especially in the gray hungover mornings. And as the summer approached, the Atlantic boys were making plans for an exodus. Most were London bound. One had a brother-in-law high up in a construction company: navvying jobs were to be had for all.

I couldn't bring myself to go to England. There are aspects of British culture that I feel particularly close to; after all, it is the land of Graham Greene, John Lennon, and Shakespeare. But I felt that British policy toward Northern Ireland was pigheaded in the extreme and would harvest nothing but blood and tears until Orange intransigence was finally faced up to. Besides, I had no intention of being strip-searched every time I crossed the channel. Nor was I keen on being treated like a bomb-throwing Paddy while being granted the privilege of eking out an existence over there. So I looked the other way—westward toward far-off Amerikay.

The U.S. government, in its wisdom and compassion, had offered the use of temporary social security numbers to impoverished Irish students. The idea was that we would work for the summer in Boston or New York, and make enough money to fund the next year's education back home. All one needed was a student card to avail of this Holy Grail. The word spread like wildfire through the flatlands of Rathmines. Hundreds of drinkers, dossers, dreamers, and delinquents showed up at the American embassy with fake and, even occasionally, valid cards. So many were leaving that one wag in the Hideaway, waving a visa above his head, was heard to roar: "Last one out the door, turn out the lights!"

Our going-away party was a riot of boisterousness and bonhomie; we were too young to realize that we'd never all meet together again. Some were bent on settling in the States, and others knew instinctively that they'd never escape from the gray concrete of Camden Town or Cricklewood. But all were filled with the optimism or derring-do of the times, and my brother—who was heading to London—stated that men the like of us didn't change countries, we merely changed pubs. I don't even remember leaving Dublin Airport although I'm told that I arrived ossified and by taxi, bearing my father's battered suitcase and a guitar. I do remember the flight, however, as an obstreperous fellow student had to be pinioned to the floor and subdued by the crew when the beer ran out. The plane landed in Hartford and I got my first glimpse of the American justice system, when the unconscious partier was dragged from the plane by the local constabulary.

We endured a two-day orientation course at the University of Hartford where—after we learned that a dollar was made up of one hundred cents and could be broken down into nickels, dimes, and quarters—we received our treasured social security numbers. A black pall of smoke and clouds hovered over the city, and we were warned not to set foot off campus as some kind of riot was going on in the nearby slums. From what I could gather, this was a common occurrence and only a minor source of discomfort to those who lived in the suburbs, it being explained that "the bastards can burn down their own pigsty any time they want to." With that sterling advice under our hats, we boarded buses and sped off to New York City. It was an overcast, muggy day and I still remember the driver sweeping his hand off toward a brooding mass of buildings stretching to the horizon and flatly stating, "Das de Bronx!" The only borough on the mainland looked remote and threatening; I made a mental note to steer well clear of it. It never, in a million years, occurred to me that I'd someday come to know it's grainy streets so well.

The bus finally pulled up to the corner of Thirty-fourth Street and Eighth Avenue in Manhattan. The driver pointed out the gigantic New Yorker Hotel and announced that Irish students had been known to find shelter within. It seemed like a good enough recommendation, and anyway, I wasn't aware of any alternatives. The lobby was a scene of utter chaos. This was nothing like the reserved foyers of hotels back home; it more resembled a frantic twenty-four-hour Third World bazaar. Everything in New York City could be had there, it appeared, including the immoral and the illegal, as well as floor space at $7 a night. I angled my way past the hubbub and found the desk. The legal price of a room, I was informed, was $40. With only $114 remaining to my name, I told the nonchalant clerk that there seemed to be better offers on tap, and beat my way back to the center of the bazaar. A greasy-looking Irish guy, who looked vaguely familiar from the Hideaway, caught my eye and said that for the stated $7, there were also three beds in the room to choose from; and if one was of a sober nature, and arrived home early, the chances were that one of these could be shared with some other man of a similar disposition. I peeled off my bills and was directed to a room on the twenty-first floor. I later found out that security did not venture beyond the tenth and that anarchy reigned above the twentieth, with keys being counterfeited, and even better deals struck with cleaning and maintenance people.

That night, I arrived home at the stroke of ten and did share a bed with a man from Donegal who snored horrendously, but did not, to the best of my knowledge, rob or bugger me. However, the night was not without incident for Irish-born and other stragglers arrived until well after dawn in all states of noisy inebriation. Many lay where they fell on the floor, and by the time I arose the carpet was full of writhing, sweating bodies, for the central air-conditioning had gone down in the night.

Now that we had become intimate, so to speak, and sensing a business opportunity, the Donegal man and I hightailed it to the desk and reserved our own room for $20 each. We then joined the bazaar, hung out our shingle next to the greasy Irishman, and peddled our own sweet share of the New Yorker. The idea was to sell twelve spots—six in the bed and six on the floor—thus netting ourselves over $20 a man and our own reserved bed to boot. We furthermore resolved that if more should arrive and needed the room, no guests would be turned away from this inn; a courting couple of either sex, for instance, could share the large bath, if they were so inclined. In one day, despite my rigidly held Socialist beliefs, I had become a capitalist, a landlord, a lawbreaker, and a huckster. In other words, I had arrived.

My lodging situation thus solved, I spent the nights combing the Village for Bob Dylan. I figured that if I did not manage an actual sighting, then the very streets on which he walked might provide fodder for my own songwriting. But, alas, no Bobby and little inspiration; nighttime would find me wearing out precious shoe leather on my fatigued way back to my overcrowded room, all the while hoping that the Donegal man had reserved my side of the pillow.

The New York I perceived then is a blur to me now, full of unimaginably tall buildings and stacked to the limit with possibilities. Although it was often out of control, it never seemed un-navigable, especially after my years scrounging around Dublin; indeed, many parts of it were familiar because of the movies I'd seen, the books I'd read, and the music I'd listened to. *Midnight Cowboy* sent me tracking down the sleaze of Midtown, although Ratso was a very saccharine character compared to some of the denizens I would later become acquainted with. I could almost close my eyes in the Village and find my way around from reading Kerouac and listening to Dylan. But, in some way, I wasn't quite ready for the city yet.

It didn't matter for, within a week of arrival, I spotted an ad in the lobby of the New Yorker and auditioned for an Irish band that was being formed in the Pocono Mountains. These might have been the foothills of the Himalayas for all I knew, but I was wearing down rapidly from my rambling in search of Dylan and lack of a decent night's sleep. I passed the audition with flying colors; indeed, the interviewer, a man by name of Jim Mitchell, seemed mightily impressed that I could sing, stand, and play three chords all at the same time. He gave me a bus ticket and an address of his pub, and told me if I hurried I might yet get in a couple of sets that evening.

I bade farewell to my Donegal business partner and headed up to the bus terminal on Forty Deuce, this time not dallying to watch Sweet Nancy and the other ladies of the afternoon. I had never seen such forests as we wound our way over the Delaware Water Gap and into the hills of Pennsylvania. Was this whole state covered in trees? Mitchell was as good as his word. Five hours later I was playing in a band with Seamus Maguire, a top traditional fiddle player from Sligo, and Oliver Sweeney, a button accordionist who later became a noted Irish music critic. The hours were long and the drink flowed, but we were getting well into our stride by the third night when two crew-cut men in suits, flashing FBI identification, made their presence known. They demanded to be told the whereabouts of one Fritz Mitzelli. Our man, Mitchell, had seen them arrive, however, and had left through a bathroom window. He was last seen striking out through the woods, never to be witnessed in those parts again.

I had liked Mitchell. Although an obvious rogue with a rich past, he never broke his word to me. Indeed, he had paid some weeks in advance for our rooms in a local boarding house cum brothel. This was not your stereotypical New Orleans/Creole Madam type of institution, much less the smack/crack bare-walled rooms familiar to New York City. Instead, our establishment had an aura of small-town respectability where married women would arrive by twilight and sit around the small bar, making themselves available for an ever-changing cast of truck drivers and commercial travelers. This arrangement seemed to be a long-standing tradition in this one-horse town, and there was no apparent moral opprobrium associated with the profession. Nor did these ladies ply their wares with the "young college boys," which is how they referred to us, as out of a scene from a Tennessee Williams play. We were sequestered down at the end of a corridor where the nocturnal moans and rattling of bedsprings would not interrupt our supposedly virginal slumbers. I've often wondered if this all-American cathouse has survived the Moral Majority and the suffocating strictures of the Christian Right.

With Fritz on the lam, however, economic equilibrium soon reasserted itself: business was brisk, the rooms in demand, and the madam regretfully dispersed us to the four winds. We took jobs as busboys, waiters, and dishwashers, whatever provided shelter and any kind of remuneration. We three musicians stayed in touch and eventually took over the cellar of an Italian restaurant where we ruled triumphantly through the summer under the imaginative name of the Irish Band.

One night while working a shift as a waiter, I spilled a dish of pasta into the lap of a midlevel Mafioso. Instead of putting out a contract on me, he graciously cleaned himself off and came downstairs later to listen to the music. When leaving, he handed me a card and bade me call the number in the morning. It was an agent in Harrisburg. The word of my talent had preceded me; they urged me to hop a bus and come see them straight away. Since Seamus and Oliver were heading back to Ireland and respectability, it seemed worth a shot. I should have smelled a rat because all they wanted to hear was "Danny Boy," which I knocked off with considerable aplomb. They signed me up on the spot; before I knew it I was on the road crossing the state from one Holiday Inn to another billed as the Great Irish Tenor, Lorenzo Kerwin. When I phoned them in great dudgeon about this, they informed me that they'd been in the business a lot longer than I, that no one could spell my name anyway, and what was the problem with a touch of Italian if I was a tenor? They added that a little misspelling and exaggeration might be the least of my problems.

There was the hint of an unspoken threat implied that caught my attention; but they were definitely right. Crowds turned out everywhere to witness the coming of the new Count John McCormack. I did four sets a night with "Danny Boy" the opening and closer to each. I would have learned the full repertoire of McCormack and his rival, Caruso; but this was in the days before Napster, and small-town Pennsylvania had few outlets for recordings of grand, or even not so highfalutin, opera. Instead I interpreted Dylan in a manner that caused eyeballs to wobble and reached for my high Cs and even Ds on every imaginable Irish folk song. It was all for naught and by the second set I would be tossing back whiskey for the courage to go out there and continue this charade. The disappointed crowd would have long dwindled by the time the fourth set and I both stumbled to an end.

To make matters worse, my Mafioso called me at the beginning of each week's engagement to inquire about my health and mental well-being. This caused me no end of worry, until the agents informed me that my don had "points in the enterprise;" yet, they hastened to add, that because he had much time for me, my protector was only taking 10 instead of his usual 15 percent. They, however, had no such affection, had a pain in their asses listening to my complaints, and would continue to take their customary 15.

It was now nearing October; a chill wind was blowing across Pennsylvania and the leaves were already turning. This countryside had a promise of tough winters about it. I weighed up the pros and cons. I had a fistful of money, a dearth of confidence, and a certainty that I was pursuing the wrong line of business, and besides, my visa was almost expired. After a particularly gruesome night playing for a reunion of prison guards in Lewisburg, I crept from the Holiday Inn at dawn and snuck aboard a Greyhound bus to New York City, half expecting my don to materialize and plug me for my disloyalty. I didn't relax until I entered the lobby of the New Yorker Hotel.

My Donegal friend was still in business. He was overjoyed to see me and had apparently missed my entrepreneurial chops; in fact, there was a certain longing in his eyes as if he might have missed my head next him on the pillow, too. He suggested that if we rejoined forces, we could lease out a floor of the hotel and make our fortune into the bargain. Instead I stayed late with the bartender at the Emerald on Thirty-fourth Street and later that day, on impulse, hailed a taxi for Kennedy. The streets of Midtown were deserted and the driver informed me that it was, appropriately enough, the feast of Yom Kippur when all of God's chosen retreat into the womb. I arrived back in dear old dreary dependable Dublin the following morning a wiser, if somewhat chastened, person than the one who had left five months previously.

8

NEW YORK, NEW YORK 10009

Got in town on a Saturday night with a Fender guitar
And I checked out the sights
Worked my way down to the Lower East Side
'Cause I was nuts about Thunders and Suicide
Formed a band called the Major Thinkers
With a couple of musicians and some heavy drinkers
Went up to Max's and I said, "Hey man,
I'm gonna blow this club right off the map."

New York, New York what have you done
You've wrecked me till I have become
Half the man I might have been
Half the hero of my dreams
New York, New York it's over now
You beat me still I wish somehow
Just for once I could have proved you wrong
Ah, but you knew best all along.

I met Sheila down in Blanche's bar
She was dressed all in black but her heart was a scar
Took me home to Avenue B
We were happy there, her and me
'Til a man from the Black Rock saw the band
And he said, "Hey you dudes are just sizzling hot
Gonna cut a record make you all stars
But first things first, sign your souls away here."

Well, we cut a song about Avenue B
And the boxes boomed it all over the streets
But the record company messed us all up
And Sheila went off, joined the Scientology Church
Then Mike stopped a bullet in Staten Island
And my whole world turned ultra violent
But there's one last thing I just got to see through
There's one last thing I've got to say to you

Sheila, baby, give me one last chance
I've just gone and formed Black 47
I don't care about the money, you can keep the fame
I just want to beat this city at its own dumb game.

New York, New York what have you done
You've wrecked me till I have become
Half the man I might have been
Half the hero of my dreams
New York, New York it's over now
You beat me still I wish somehow
Just for once I could have proved you wrong
Ah, but you knew best all along.

From Fire of Freedom, *EMI Records 1993*
Published by Starry Plough Music/EMI Blackwell Music (BMI)

PIERCE TURNER AND I were the hottest duo since Cain and Abel. Or so we liked to think when stoned, which was often enough. But we did have a certain something: a loose blend of passion, originality, self-deprecating humor, and a unique mix of voices. We were also saddled with one of the most awkward names in the history of pop music. Turner and Kirwan of Wexford. Even the most devout of fans found this moniker almost impossible to repeat. It often emerged as some version of Kerner and Turwin, Turwin and Kerner, you name it. We must have had our own rationale for sticking with this gobstopper, but if so it has disappeared into the mists of time and marijuana. For Turner and Kirwan of Wexford obeyed no law but Murphy's, and even then, very reluctantly. Tactically and organizationally we seemed to get everything wrong. Depending on one's point of view, we were either a couple of hops ahead of everyone or one giant step behind. Even now, I can't be sure.

We had only one interest—music. All else would provide for itself. We never gave a damn about tomorrow. That was a concept for the straight and the bored—two things we were most definitely not. On the plus side, we both could write, sing, play, arrange, produce, and go totally nuts onstage. I suppose we may have cancelled each other out somewhat; but we were oblivious as to how the world perceived us. If there was magic in the moment, then the moment was what we were all about.

We grew up a couple of blocks apart in the North End of Wexford town. We knew each other by reputation and sight, everyone in Wexford did, but we weren't particularly friends. Pierce's mother, Molly, was a musician and had her own band. She was a formidable lady and a total character. You could talk to her about gigs and music, the way you would to another teenager. She recognized no generation gaps and hadn't a hint of patronization about her. She ran a secondhand store right on the quay that, even now, I think of as a great curiosity shop. It was full of oddities and the smell of Jeyes Fluid. It was one of my stops on rambles around the old town, and I loved to hear Molly haggle with small farmers and their wives over Sunday suits already shiny with wear and secondhand bras that were bought at face value and without the benefit of a fitting. Much to her eventual regret, Pierce persuaded his mother to give up this proven moneymaker for a record/photography store.

This latter enterprise was never profitable, but became a gathering place for the musical-minded youth of the town. That's when Pierce and I really began to take the measure of each other. Any differences we had melted away, when we discovered that we shared a passion for deconstructing hit songs that bordered on the ferocious. We both owned tape recorders—old Grundigs, if I remember—and it was only a matter of time before we began experimenting above the shop in the family sitting room. We were much influenced by *Sergeant Pepper* and *Pet Sounds,* and were fearless experimenters. The seagulls that hovered by the window, however, seemed to be the only ones impressed by our echo-drenched paeans to the beautiful teenage girls of Wexford. The subjects of these songs were, in general, mortified by our attention and ran a mile at the sight of us, for fear we might proclaim our harmonic affection in front of their tittering friends. This hurt but made little difference. Achingly chaste but forever innovative, we soldiered on and sang our songs to no one but ourselves.

Pierce was a tremendously gifted natural musician and could improvise with abandon. He was also quite out there in manner and dress, leaving himself open to ridicule by the straight section of town; this included many of the established local musicians who wouldn't be caught dead associating their molecules with "the likes of that eejit." When I mentioned him as a possibility for the Liars Showband, his name was greeted with a cacophony of groans and imprecations. Elvis, however, was a great believer in musical pedigree and had worked with Molly in the past; so the deal was done, without the benefit of an audition. This was to lead to a problem. For Pierce, like many of us, was self-taught, and had not as yet stumbled on the concept of minor chords. It probably says a lot about me that I had never noticed this lack in our sitting room experimentations; and so, for a couple of weeks, the Liars Showband hit new levels in atonality. Aggressive major chords, when slammed down on top of melancholy minors, can have a very jarring effect, especially on male dancers who are trying to sweet-talk their way into bed with members of the fair sex.

But Pierce was a quick learner and soon graduated to better bands. At one point, he even went off to Germany for a stint with Paul Raven a.k.a. Gary Glitter. When he returned to Ireland, he moved into my Dublin flat. Soon thereafter, he became the organist of the Arrows Showband. This position enabled him to live in a state of near slavery—traveling six nights a week to country dance halls for the princely sum of 25 pounds and the promise of imminent stardom.

I couldn't seem to fit back in Ireland and was fast dissipating my hard-earned Irish-tenor money. I felt aimless and was consumed by the oddest feeling that I was missing out on something. At first, I assumed it had to do with Bridie: there were streets that I could no longer bring myself to walk down, and should I chance to stray by her old flat, the bittersweetness was almost overwhelming. Besides, most of the lads had not returned and the partying seemed strained and without purpose. But it was more than that. Ireland now felt like a mold; there was a distinct way to fit in, but I no longer had the inclination to do so. I wanted something different. I wasn't even sure what, but I'd caught a glimpse of it in New York City. I decided to return and find out once and for all. Pierce, on impulse, decided to jack in the showband life and give the duo a whirl. We figured we'd scope the whole scene out in a year, and then see where we stood.

The best-laid plans of mice and musicians! We arrived in Greenwich Village on a frigid gray January morning. Being illegal made matters more complex than when I had come alone as a student. We were ever mindful of being seen not to break the law. At bus stops we were perplexed by the sign NO STANDING and the impunity with which New Yorkers idly congregated beneath this stern warning where they would even chat and smoke cigarettes. For our part, we would move a good ten to fifteen yards down the block and wait for the bus to pull up; then while the common lawbreakers were mounting the steps we would race up and join the line at the last moment before jumping aboard.

Despite our law-abiding ways, within days our money was gone and our prospects slim. We got wind that a bar called the Pig and Whistle on Forty-seventh Street was looking for a band. As it turned out they weren't. But our desperation was so apparent, that the owner, John Mahon, offered us an audition. I can still see and even smell that pub, its dark interior, candlelit tables, sawdust-strewn floor, bowls of monkey nuts and shells; I even remember that "American Pie" was the last song on the jukebox before we played. We stayed onstage for over two hours, afraid to take a break in case they told us we had failed. The crowd of happy-hour drunks was transfixed by our energy and commitment.

We did posses a hidden weapon: we had all their harmonies down to a tee and could do Simon and Garfunkel songs in a way that Paul and Artie could never dream of. Pedal to the metal, full steam ahead eye-popping intensity and none of your laconic hippie introspection. When we sang "The Boxer," it was like the whores on Seventh Avenue came shimmying right through the room. And when we performed "Bridge Over Troubled Water," it was as though we were tightrope walking in harmony across Niagara Falls. "That Silver Girl" never got such a serenading as she sailed on by, forever awaiting her dreams. I'm sure we were missing some of the sensitivity that Paul intended. But when you don't know where your next dollar, or floor to crash on, is coming from, delicacy is wont to take a backseat.

The word spread around the Times Square bar circuit about these two Irish head cases, and we were soon filling the Pig and Whistle as many nights a week as we pleased. Leggy Rockettes fawned over us and almost overnight we become a Midtown sensation. We were even offered a spot on the Radio City variety show for a staggering grand a week each. Within a month of hitting Kennedy Airport, we had arrived. Or so we thought, until the general manager of Radio City asked for a peep at our green cards.

It was to be the first of many star-crossed disappointments. But we shrugged it off, as we did all the others. We were young, didn't give a continental hoot, and, in the long pub nights, we were beginning to find our own voices. It's such a revelation, not to mention relief, when you feel that you not only have something worth saying, but that you have an audience who'll sit there and listen to it. However, the times were all about freedom and experimentation and we had two minds, as warped as the best of them, ready to follow our own visions wherever they would take us. We were never interested in honing our ideas and making them more suitable for the commercial marketplace. In our lexicon, that would have been selling out. And so, there was no master plan, no guiding hand, just do what thou wilt and go wherever the flow takes you.

And yet what glorious nights when nothing seemed to matter except squeezing out twenty-minute synthesizer/feedback guitar

versions of Ewan MacColl's "The Traveling People," the traditional "Foggy Dew," or others of our own large repertoire of originals. If Pink Floyd, Peter's Genesis, and Fripp's King Crimson
could transmute English sensibility into distinctive sonic quaint-
ness, why couldn't Turner and I do the same for wild Irish folk
music? New York was the perfect seeding ground for such a venture. It was only a matter of time, we figured; just do enough gigs
and the break was bound to come.

We never refused a paying job, although perhaps we should have,
for there was a vast cultural divide in the country at the time. Long
hair, of which we had plenty and were gaining more by the day,
was not welcome on the other side of straightness, and that
included most Irish settings. I remember we were hired for a
number of weddings before the word got out that not only did
these oddballs not know such standards as "Daddy's Little Girl" or
"The Bride Cuts the Cake," but we had never even heard of them.

We were therefore under some pressure at an Irish-American
wedding when Pierce broke a string on his clavinette—the same
instrument used by Stevie Wonder on such hits as "Superstition,"
although I'm sure Stevie never had to change his own strings. This
extremely tricky maneuver required lifting up the back of the
instrument, disentangling the broken string, then replacing it and
tuning the bloody thing and its immediate neighbors with a
screwdriver. You had to be as much a hawkeyed mechanic as a
musician to master this ax.

We had, some moments before, been experiencing a lot of
stares, pointed fingers, and sniggers from the various crew cuts
and shaved heads in attendance. On top of this, many dancers
were stranded on the floor, for the music, not surprisingly, had
ground to a halt. The father of the bride, an annoying but harmless old idiot, had just been attempting to fox-trot with a young
lady, while trumpeting his knowledge of music into her unimpressed ears. To further his suit, he now took the opportunity to
sashay over to Pierce, who was up to his eyes in his mechanical
labors. "Was that in E or in G?" he nasally inquired of the song we
had just been performing.

Pierce, stressed to the max, the sweat pouring down his face, screwdriver clenched tightly in his fist, looked up at his braying interrogator and snarled back, "Do you want me to take out me fuckin' prick and show it to you?"

The gentleman and his companion jumped back about three paces in alarm, and then ran from pillar to post informing the guests to beware of this long-haired pervert who was even now ripping the guts out of the good piano.

"What did you do that for?" I demanded with some justification. Things were going bad enough without insulting the man who would be paying us.

"What did you want me to do?" Pierce replied, equally aggrieved. "Didn't the auld bollocks ask me if I was a he or a she?"

Mixed messages were always a problem and matters were rarely easy or simple for Turner and Kirwan of Wexford. They were to get decidedly more complicated.

9

GIRL NEXT DOOR

Your bedroom blackmail has worked real good
You've gone and left home like you said you would
The note you scribbled on the kitchen wall
Said, "So long stupid!" and that was all
I suppose that I should be relieved
Even act just a little pleased
But since you've gone, life has been such a bore
Why did you leave me for the girl next door?

My bar room buddies think it's rather strange
They laugh at me and call you funny names
My mother said she knew all along
Always said that you would do me wrong
Still I wish you would consider, dear,
Leaving her and returning here
'Cause since you've gone, life has been such a bore
Why did you leave me for the girl next door?

Wish that I could be like Bogie
Hey, I'd sweep you off your feet.
But now you tell me that she can give you
Everything you need.

You've wrecked my head, I really must confess
You've left me in the most dreadful mess

I always thought you were so super straight
But I found out about you too late.
I suppose that I should be relieved
Even act just a little pleased
But since you've gone life has been such a bore
Why did you leave me for the girl next door?

From Elvis Murphy's Green Suede Shoes, *Gadfly Records*
2005 and Absolutely & Completely, *Turner & Kirwan of Wexford,*
Peter's International 1977
Published by Menapia Music (BMI)

IT'S ALMOST HARD to imagine now what New York was actually like in the '70s. Suffice it to say that it bears little resemblance to the sanitized Giuliani/Bloomberg version. The social order had broken down. As long as you didn't murder someone, you could do pretty much as you pleased. The streets were teeming and alive with all manner of dissident thought and behavior. If the Revolution had run out of steam, mere anarchy not only had been unleashed but was all the rage: in fact, you were quite welcome to go your own way and do your own thing, without raising an eyebrow. Every manner of national liberation or revolutionary group mixed, drank, fucked, danced, and made unrealistic plans down in the Village. Every gender, race, and cult had seen its own individual light and was dead bent on shining this beacon on the world at large. Talk about a universe of strobe-lit, flashing mirrors. No one seemed to arise before noon, and there was little need to turn on the city's lights in the morning, for no one had switched them off the night before.

The East Village was a world unto its own. It was filthy, fast, and furious, with apartments so available and inexpensive we wouldn't bother to sign the slightly more expensive two-year leases, more where that came from and, if times took a turn for the worse, you could always move closer to the projects on D for even cheaper rents. It was rare to see a cop east of Avenue A, save for a riot or an occasional show of force. The Fire Department came and went frequently though, for a gentleman by the name of Gasoline Gomez was torching both Alphabet City and the South Bronx with abandon. Drums were omnipresent, conga players gathered on the main corners, adding bottom and percolating rhythms to the howling of the sirens. The air reeked of sulfur and pot. The street, a perpetual carnival in the summer, morphed into a freezing netherworld of emaciated junkies who huddled in doorways waiting for their man, through the long, awful winter months. Remnants of the Young Lords ran the avenues around the projects, while Angels, Panthers, and ever-shifting coalitions of drug dealers ran whole city blocks all the way up to the Bowery. Violence was commonplace and retribution swift, but if you were perceived to be cool, unconnected with authority, and kept your head down, it was possible to live in relative harmony with the most psychotic of neighbors in this anarchistic paradise.

The lifestyle couldn't have been more different from lace curtain, small-town Ireland. The freedom to reinvent oneself was intoxicating. The area was a cauldron of varying and competing lifestyles, any of which you could adopt or discard as the humor struck. We settled into a routine of doing a couple of paid gigs a week. This kept the landlord at bay, the bodega owner happy, and enough beer on the table and food for the head as was needed. The rest of the time we wrote songs, rehearsed, did benefits, or just hung out, which seemed to be the main occupation of the time.

We had established a foothold out in the Bay Ridge area of Brooklyn, in Tomorrow's Lounge, a saloon frequented by off-duty cops, firemen, MTA workers, Norwegians, Italians, Scottish Catholics, and their Protestant drinking buddies, all watched over by both wings of the Provisional and Official IRA. An odd mix, it's true, but we broadened it even further by drawing a contingent of local freaks and their attendant drug dealers. The presence of firearms did lend an edge to the place. Throw in gallons of whiskey and you were guaranteed a combustible situation. On one notable evening, two well-oiled off-duty cops pulled guns, each suspecting the other of being the "bad guy." A passing man in blue happened to look through the window and assumed it was a stickup. While the rest of us were frozen in horror, he burst through the door, drew his gun, kicked aside chairs, and screamed, "Freeze!" With the whole bar in silence, the first "perp" whispered, "I'm a cop." The second echoed him: "I'm a cop, too." The on-duty policeman, unwilling to give up his advantage, kept them both covered. The barman, never losing his cool, verified all identities. We drinkers trembled in suspended animation, until all parties were satisfied and guns reholstered; the bartender then bought a round of shots for the house, declared that he needed a raise for putting up with this kind of malarkey, and things returned to their jittery normal.

If guns and drugs were common in Tomorrow's, sex also played a large part in the equation. During our residency, people came from far and near to this hole-in-the-wall, as it was common knowledge around New York City that none but the totally bombed could fail to get laid there. Thus, one evening, I fell in with an Irish comrade sister, worn out from her revolutionary pursuits and in the need of letting her Marxist hair down. We hit it off like the proverbial house on fire, humming bars of the "L'Internationale," in lieu of sweet nothings, in each other's ears.

She was not, however, too keen on coming back to the East Village to partake of "a cup of tea," with my roommates present. Jemmy had arrived from London and was now living with Pierce and me and our dear friend Bob Schwenk, which made for a cozy foursome in a couple of small rooms. When I suggested that these gentlemen could sleep through any manner of "cup of tea" that we cared to brew, she looked at me as if I was half cracked, and flat out stated that "them three fellahs would hear the grass grow, if they thought there was a bit of the other involved." She intimated instead that we take a taxi to Flatbush Avenue where we could brew our tea in privacy. She knew a man there of sound revolutionary pedigree, who had many empty rooms in his janitor's apartment and was a great *craic* himself into the bargain.

There was something instantly familiar, but hard to identify, about this janitor. It was even more difficult to get him to sit still or shut up, although it was now going on five in the morning. In fact, such was his energy that he not only had my life totally sorted within minutes, but my immediate future goals outlined and only awaiting his direct orders to be executed. He told me he had already heard volumes about me, and that I was essentially a somewhat talented dosser wasting my time on women, drink, and drugs. There was a greater scheme that it behooved me to become a part of; coincidentally, he possessed all the relevant information regarding this crusade, and would, at the appropriate time, provide any answers that I might desire.

His resume was impressive. At one point in San Francisco, he had delivered the same message to Carlos Santana and given the great guitarist his first decent break. I was mesmerized by the wild eyes of this janitor and listened intently, for at that time of the morning who doesn't have need of a life-changing plan? His monologue was deep and detailed, and continued as I found myself loading out great sacks of garbage onto Flatbush Avenue, with the first rays of the sun warming the streets. Long forgotten was my comrade lady friend who had some hours previously slunk off to her loveless bed. After the last sack had been placed on the sidewalk, Brian Heron casually mentioned that he was a grandson of James Connolly's and intended to set up an Irish Arts Center in New York City that would revolutionize Irish America. This organization was to be known as *An Claidheamh Soluis* or the Sword of Light and I, apparently, had been plucked from obscurity and degradation to be his right-hand man in this venture. As an added inducement, he tossed in the promise of an introduction to his friend, John Lennon, were I to join the cause. He had his man.

This union led to many adventures, including a gig with Elephant's Memory before an entire audience of Hell's Angels and the eventual procurement of a green card. I never met John Lennon, but that was my own fault. The last I heard, Brian had become a crack uilleann piper domiciled on the West Coast. He is also a lawyer; his briefs include representing both Bloods and Crips in their various excursions through the Los Angeles justice system. Mister Lennon is long gone, too, but the Irish Arts Center still occupies the building on West Fifty-first Street that James

Connolly's grandson managed to finagle from the City Council for pennies a year in perpetuity. It's no longer a Marxist haven, but what can you do? Neither is the Kremlin.

Brian was one of those characters who epitomized New York in the '70s. He was bright, articulate, forceful, and full to the gills with dreams; if he'd happened on a couple of reliable people, he could have changed the world. Alas, such helpers—myself included—while thin enough on the ground, were even more difficult to pin down for any long-term commitment. Each of us had our own burning vision, even if we lacked Brian's intricate plan of campaign. Besides, it's notoriously difficult to jump-start a revolution when you don't arise from your slumbers until early in the afternoon.

Such was not the case with Malachy McCourt who was a fountain of energy and, to this day, never seems to sleep. This volatile but lovely man was already a celebrity when I met him. A shock-jock on WMCA before the term had even been coined, he was well to the left of most Irish-Americans and was reputed to be on Richard Nixon's Enemies List. No small wonder, for he regularly devoted the first fifteen minutes of his show to a scabrously comic attack on the thirty-seventh president. The phones would light up like the Rockefeller's Christmas tree, as crazed right-wingers, holy Marys, and just the plain enraged and crazy sought to get in their shots at this formidable Limerick man. At the end of some hours of frenzied political debate, during which Malachy would do his level best to persuade sundry conservatives that they did not deserve to call the noble ape their predecessor, he would invite everyone to come finish off the evening at the Bells of Hell, his saloon on Thirteenth Street.

The Bells had its roots in the fabled Lion's Head on Sheridan Square. That is to say that many of its core drinkers had once frequented the latter establishment but now, for varying reasons, chose to bend their elbows a little further uptown. Refugees from the Head included many alcoholics with aspirations to be novelists, hard-bitten journalists, rowdy lawyers, Communist seamen, contrary folksingers and the just plain horny. The Bells added to this stew some very smart—if often masochistic—women, music critics, rockers, Vietnam vets, Bronx Irish, visiting anarchists, devotees of Aleister Crowley, gay ex–Christian Brothers and married priests, nurses from St. Vincent's, and a regularly rotating cast of adventurous young ladies from the Evangeline Residence some doors up the street. This jambalaya mixed with surprising ease and good grace under the watchful, taciturn eye of the manager and eventual owner, Peter Myers. The fact that there was a huge cellar given over to the smoking of various herbs did not hurt matters. How the place never burned down, I have no idea, for Malachy was notoriously hostile to Con Edison and rarely paid their bills. In these blackout periods, patrons often wandered the back rooms like so many Florence Nightingales with candles and lamps, searching for toilets and other comforts while endeavoring not to trip over fornicating couples. This so infuriated Jimmy Gavin, a grumpy carpenter from Mayo, he cut a hole in the wall and jacked into the power of the apartment building next door. Malachy, ever the blasphemer, was heard to mutter, "Let there be light," as the electricity returned.

Turner and Kirwan of Wexford became the house band for this set and played every Friday and Saturday night for years, aided and abetted by Niall Crumpet-Stocker on Taurus foot-pedals, harmonica, and laughs. The Bells' beer-soaked rooms became an extension of my apartment—kitchen, parlor, and occasional bedroom. I rarely paid for a drink and would not consider leaving the premises until one of the bartenders roared out the signature Bells dismissal: "Go home to your beds, there are novels to be written!"

It took some time to be accepted within this milieu; but once in, you were never "eighty-sixed," no matter how scandalous your behavior. Then again, there were but two rules in that saloon: never bore your neighbor or impede them in their God-given right to get utterly drunk at their own pace. The only major fight I witnessed was between two women; but even that ended with both participants sharing drinks and recriminations, upon discovering that the ruffian over whom they had traded punches had slipped out the door with a third.

Writers and those attracted by them (an odd psychotic breed with all of the devotion but little of the messed-up glamour of music groupies) were drawn to the Bells by its cheerful acceptance of both literary success and failure. Advice was free and plentiful, and companionship in misery always available. Booze soothed, even if it didn't heal, all wounds. Nick Browne, a notoriously sardonic and short-tempered gentleman—known to his enemies as "Hemingway without the books" but loved by his many friends of whom I was one—cast a frigid eye on proceedings from behind the stick and did his macho best to limit the number of ladies allowed into this zoo, for fear that they would contaminate our literary intentions. It was a losing battle, for what person in his right mind would sooner write books than get laid? And yet, I remember with so much fondness those long whiskey-fueled hours when someone in a rogue's gallery that comprised, but was not limited to, Dennis Duggan, Nick Tosches, Doug Ireland, Lester Bangs, Joe Flaherty, Denis Smith, Mike McGovern, Jack Deacy, an occasional Hamill, and even Malachy himself might launch forth with the bare bones of a novel that had been festering inside his head and only needed alcohol or good company to set it free. Most of these plots are long forgotten, seeds cast on a sawdust floor, never to be written; but scraps of them still bounce around my brain whenever I pass Thirteenth Street and Sixth Avenue.

Oddly enough, the only dissenting voice to this boozy camaraderie came from the one who would become most successful. My first introduction to this remarkable gentleman happened on a warm afternoon. There was a bunch of us belly up to the bar, sharing nothing but the silence, some lager shandies, and the long lovely fleeting departure of a communal hangover aligned with the promise of yet another night ahead. The door opened, yet none could, at first, be bothered looking up from the contemplation of their drinks. A dozen or so teenaged boys filed in. They were led by a truculent-looking individual, clad in a disheveled suit and a shirt that had already seen a couple of days' wear. In a dismissive sneer, he ordered the boys to feast their eyes on us one and all. "So you wanted to be writers?" Frank McCourt then inquired of his Stuyvesant High School English class. There was no answer. He shook his head in dismay and motioned to us. "Maybe you should take a look at the end result."

That was the Bells. Despite our best efforts, Turner and Kirwan of Wexford had a couple of close shaves with fame, particularly when "Girl Next Door" became the first song about lesbianism to gain national radio play. Two yobs from Ireland were, for a brief moment, accidentally in the vanguard of women's liberation. Jesus, those were the days! We never even came within an ass's roar of fortune. Still, I wouldn't trade one hilarious memory for all the trappings of a rock star. I hope you're doing well, Pierce. When they come to noting Ireland's best songwriters, no list is credible without your name up front. Ready for a few bars of "The Boxer"? Get those Taurus bass-pedals out of the cellar, Niall Crumpet, and roll a couple of big ones. C'mon now, boys, please!

10

WHO KILLED BOBBY FULLER?

It's Saturday night on the Lower East Side
I'm sittin' here contemplatin' suicide
I just got mugged down in Tompkins Square
When a skinny-assed junky stuck a bayonet in my ear
I can't believe you gone and left me for a dentist
Whatever happened to my existentialist?
If I can't find out I never will recover
I gotta know—who killed Bobby Fuller?

I know that you think that I'm out of my head
'Cause I haven't been givin' you the love that I should
I just sit here playin' his old 45s
Wishing to Christ that Bobby was alive
He's still out there playin' "I Fought The Law"
But no one is sayin' exactly what they saw
If I can't find out I never will recover
I gotta know—who killed Bobby Fuller?

And now you've gone and found another significant other
I hope your teeth fall out whenever he kisses you
You'll come crawlin' back when you discover
I found out who killed Bobby Fuller.

I know it's an obsession but what can I do
Oh darlin' I'm still so in love with you

There's a senorita down in El Paso
I know that she's got some of the answers
She's older now, ready to speak
So tell your dentist to cap someone else's teeth
If we can't be friends, we can at least be lovers
I gotta know—who killed Bobby Fuller?

From Home of the Brave, *EMI Records 1994*
Published by Starry Plough Music/EMI Blackwell Music (BMI)

I OFTEN WONDER what Lester would make of it all? It's hard to imagine that he'd fit into today's musical-industrial complex. Mister Bangs was the real deal and everyone knew it: the best and most respected rock critic in New York City, and so much more. He lived, dreamed, sweated, drank, and shat rock 'n' roll. It was part of the very air that he breathed, and it could inflate or deflate him accordingly. Many of the stories I hear about him now, and even the characterizations, appear exaggerated at best; the myth, as usual, has taken over and the man has suffered for it. To me, once you pierced the sometimes gruff exterior, he was a very warm, even simple, individual who had a wonderful way with words and a sardonic appreciation of the world's absurdities. But more telling, he had an even keener sense of where rock music had come from, what it was all about, and where it could eventually lead us. This was all contingent on musicians staying true to a very pure artistic ideal: a shaky foundation upon which to build any dream. Yet, woe to those who deviated from this given, for Lester could be one hellacious son of a bitch if he got his teeth into you.

There were the great moments, too, when all seemed possible. One in particular springs to mind. He had gone over to the UK to cover a new band called the Clash. Lester was always suspicious of hype, but Strummer's crew reeked of authenticity and, on the strength of one diamond-hard album, many of us were already heavily invested in them. None more so than Lester. I happened to be in the Bells the night he arrived home. He came right over to me, beaming from ear to ear. This was quite uncharacteristic for he often seemed, on first glance, to be in the midst of a glowering argument with himself. Don't get me wrong. Lester had a wonderful smile, big and goofy. But he was moody and could be a difficult drunk, not so much judgmental with other people—as most drunks are—but bitterly so toward himself.

On this night, though, all was well with the world. He tossed back his first shot, grimaced from the taste, then studied me and nodded. "Everything you want to hear about them is true," he said, choosing his words carefully. "Not only are they the best, but no one's ever going to get to them." He was on a roll, and I sat there spellbound at his evangelism, marveling at the Kerouac-like picture he began to paint. Funny thing about the man: although he could feel music to its core, he didn't see or hear it like a musician. I wanted to know what they played, when they played it, how did it sound, what amps and guitars they used, was it true that Mick Jones actually used effects—heresy in the punk world? I might as well have been talking to Billy Carter about the influence of serialism on Philip Glass. For technical details were not part of Lester's frame of reference. He was patient with me, in the way that a big brother knows that the kid has to talk himself out before you can really get through to him.

Then we turned to the songs, the social significance of the band, and the effect Strummer's *cri de coeur* was having on Britain and would eventually have on the United States. I kid you not. We actually did talk about things like that back then and, even more to the point, fully believed in them. That was Lester's turf and his eyes were shining. He'd been let down before, but this time he'd caught a glimpse of something pure and formidable over in the UK, and he was determined to spread the word. Because, when you got beyond the patina of cynicism that he sometimes cultivated, rock 'n' roll was real life to Lester. It wasn't some kind of controlled soundtrack to universal commerciality that you download into your iPod and onanistically groove to in the comforting isolation of your earphones. No, it was loud, communal, tribal, squealing, squalling, and in your fucking face—360 degrees of an unmitigated sonic assault that sucked out the very air all around you. And he'd rediscovered it in the punky heart of London.

And while he waxed on about how the Clash was changing the way the UK thought about itself, he kept returning to one point—one small detail that said it all for him. They actually let fans sleep on their hotel room floors. And not just, or even, to have sex with them, but to demonstrate their solidarity and get them in out of the sleety English rain. While he glowed on, I measured myself against this revelation, in my smug self-satisfied way: hey, I had let a punter or two crash on my motel floor in my day. He caught my drift, but he was in a good mood and didn't go for the jugular, as was the case in many of our conversations. Instead, he smiled and winked. "And not just once in a blue moon. Strummer did it every night of the tour!" That gave me pause for thought. While I wouldn't have minded a nice safety-pinned, tattooed, and tartaned waif curled up next to me, I wasn't sure I was up for a room full of surly Mohawks snoring at the foot of my bed—and every night, too. We knew each other pretty well by then; words weren't necessary. Lester had me, and he knew it. Just nodded his QED—not in an unkind way, but we both knew that, even putting music aside, the Clash were the real deal and I, for one, would never be able to hang my hat quite so high.

Ah Jesus, Lester, why the hell didn't you stay alive? Black 47 is no Clash—who is? But we do give it 120 percent over 120 nights a year; we're as political and populist as they come, don't play the game, never do the same set twice, and believe that the gig's the gig, no matter how big or small. All that being said, I have to admit that we still very rarely let people sleep on our floors. So, I guess we'd always be wanting in your eyes. Such is life, but I still think you'd have liked the band. Especially in the early boozy, four-sets-a-night days when we were trying to pull it all together. That's what you liked more than anything, wasn't it? A band reaching out for the far side—never quite able to make it, but willing to implode from the effort. That was always your point: that rock 'n' roll should never be perfect—always that one heartbreaking shiny shilling short. And you were right, too. The minute rock 'n' roll becomes in any way comfortable or by rote, then you should toss a jagged joker into the mix; and if that doesn't work, then take an ax to the whole thing, and start from scratch all over again, blinded, bloody, and without the least prospect for success, but still determined to get to the other side, wherever or whatever the hell that is.

I remember the early nights in Reilly's, cursing at the audience, but more so at myself, slinging down shots, anything to stop me thinking in that linear rational manner that's anathema to rock 'n' roll. And I thought of you on those nights, Lester, and all the things you told me. I also remembered you in the hungover mornings when I knew well that the shows had been great, yet shuddered with mortification at the things I'd said and done. But I'd learned from your committed ravings all those years ago in the Bells, when you'd sneered at my pretensions and flayed me of my considerable smugness, back when your eyes would be popping near out of your skull for the love of the things that mattered to you. And I'd listened attentively in your wreck of an apartment, with the dawn throwing up over Sixth Avenue, when you played me raucous music so sublime, the tears would come to your eyes.

Lester was one of the few men I knew who would cry right in front of you, either from fury or a raging appreciation of the absurdity of life. He was also one of the few critics big enough to even consider admitting that his judgment might have been totally wrong. One of the great things about the Bells was that reputations were hung on a hook by the front door. Everyone was deemed equal and judged by their wisdom or smarts. Lester was endlessly fascinating to me, because he had such a store of knowledge about American music. Not that he didn't know the English scene as well as anyone, but he was acutely aware that he hadn't lived it, especially when talking to someone from the other side. I could tell him what we were actually doing and thinking when we heard a song for the first time. That's what he was interested in: how rock music fit into the fabric of regular life, and how it actually affected people.

That's how he came to tell me about Bob Seger. Bob had made it with the *Night Moves* album and, though this might not be part of his myth or legend, Lester was proud of his Detroit boy. We were both convinced that "Astral Weeks" by Van was one of the great pieces of music recorded, and Lester mentioned that Bob had gone through a similar introspective period, during which he'd played around Michigan with an acoustic guitar. This was news to me. Lester warmed to the subject and wondered just what type of music Bob would have turned out, had he continued in this vein. It didn't matter, however, because he reckoned that Seger had an innate truthfulness and would do his best, no matter what. It was always interesting to hear Lester rave on about artists that you wouldn't normally associate him with. For, despite his obvious integrity, he was aware of his own myth and tended in his columns to hew fairly rigidly to self-imposed strictures of taste and convention.

Some time later, Seger released another album and Lester savaged it in the *Voice* or some such periodical. It wasn't just a put-down but a real rip-the-arse-out-of-the-wanker-type review. I didn't like the album much myself, although I felt it had a couple of decent tracks. It seemed bombastic and overwrought. Yet, I didn't think for an instant that Bob was selling out; rather, merely going where he was always heading. I was having a bit of a bad time around then, and was already into the whiskey by the time Lester entered the Bells. I tore into him before he'd even had time to settle on his stool. I don't know why. Perhaps I felt that Lester was letting himself down, but the main thrust of my argument was that here was a guy like Seger who had given everything to music and finally was making a few bucks for himself, and the likes of Mister Bangs wouldn't be content without dragging him through the gutter and destroying his reputation.

Mister Bangs fought back in his characteristic, take-no-prisoners style; but he must have been going through something, too, because gradually I felt him weaken. I was now up on my own bombastic high horse: lashing into him and every other critic who had never eked out a living playing in a band, but who had the temerity to raise their pens against the noble musicians who did. Suddenly, to my amazement and then dismay, Lester was in tears at the bar, totally distraught over this perceived treachery to his fellow Motown compatriot and vowing to write a disclaimer. He didn't. But that's beside the point. I was humbled by his compassion and willingness to admit he was wrong. I'm still a bit ashamed of my own attack on him. But whiskey and failure can do that to you.

I barely recognize Lester's growing wild-man-about-town legend, though I saw that side of him occasionally at CBGB's. But everyone put on a show there. That was the nature of the place. Surrounded by fawning acolytes, Lester would oblige with his Hunter Thompson—of-the-Bowery act: becoming larger than life or surly and morose as befitted the occasion and the vibe of the band then playing. I would pretend not to see him, and he likewise. At times like that, he reminded me of Norman Mailer; and to my mind, their best writing is oddly complementary. They also shared an awareness, an acceptance even, but also a disquiet at the myth being created around them. It's the devil's own deal to know that your own personality will eventually be subsumed by the legend you've worked so hard to create.

Talk about legends. Lester and I were both enthralled by the story of Bobby Fuller and I wrote this song for him. In the original recorded version, I was so exhilarated that I slammed the mic stand to the floor at the end and shouted out, "Where are you now, Lester Bangs, still drinkin' down the Bells of Hell?" To my regret, I asked EMI to lose that last line. They were considering the recording as a single, and I felt that it might impede radio play. What an idiot! Isn't the record company supposed to practice that kind of censorship? The inspiration for the song and the truth of it would have been so much clearer. Instead, though, the track was well reviewed; some wondered why an Irish band would feel compelled to write about a Texan rock 'n' roll footnote. It was Lester who first explained to me the mysterious circumstances of Bobby's death. He questioned why a very driven character like Bobby would "swallow a gallon of gas" with so much music and life to look forward to.

I often wonder now—what killed Lester? I suppose there's some kid out there reading *Psychotic Reactions and Carburetor Dung*, who'll someday write *Who Killed Lester Bangs?* Like most, I would suspect it was an accident. We were all such a bunch of fuck-ups back then. If there was a way to do a thing arse-backward, then that's how we did it. But there's a very fine line between carelessness and couldn't care less.

All I know is that Lester wanted to be a musician above all else. He could feel, see, and hear music like few others I've known. But he couldn't play it for shit. He had a great hurt within him that drove his voice into some kind of primal scream, but his songs lacked the sublimity that he could bring to bear when dissecting the music of others. I don't know why; it always puzzled me when he would ask my opinion on a lyric, or rant a verse of some dirge into my ear at three in the morning. The songs always emerged bitter and violent but lacking the vision that obviously inspired them; it was easy tell that they didn't pass muster in his own heart of hearts. What can you say? They were average and only inspired interest, because such an icon was singing them to you. And that's what Lester had become in the end.

I didn't see him for a year or two before he died. The Bells was gone and I was living with a woman who didn't drink. Life was changing fast. Radio sucked, Emptyv was in its ascent, and both were killing the thing we loved. I had adapted or was living a lie, whichever way you want to look at it. I'm still not sure, except that very little of the music I was making back then has any appeal for me now. Little soul, little roll, just a vain attempt to fit in with the fashion of the times. I had committed the cardinal sin— learned how to compromise in order to move up the ladder. I can only shudder at what that period must have been like for Lester? Where did he fit into Reagan's plastic '80s?

The truth is, he didn't, and he'd be even more out of place today. I can't imagine him, gray streaks in his walrus moustache, popping up on CNN or VH1, a senior talking head, dispensing his wisdom for dollars a second. Still and all, I wish to Christ he was alive, to make some sense of the mess of banality we're all being sucked into. For I'm sick to death of his imitators. Many of them have his sardonic way with words, his fury, even his blighted wisdom; but they're so devoid of the passion and soul of his love for rock 'n' roll. And that, above anything else, made Mister Bangs special.

11

TRAMPS HEARTBREAK

When I was young, I knew it all
But I didn't even know the time of the day
I laughed at you and your forebodings
Made fun of all you held dear
I was ashamed of your peculiarities
So old-fashioned always out of phase
So one night I left you aching
Took the light from all your days.

Occasionally I'd write you a letter
Telling you I was doing just fine
I guess I was for a long time
Or was that fog inside my mind?
But late at night I'd think about you
'Cause I knew you'd be thinking about me as well
I was stuck on an out-of-control express train
Local stops purgatory or hell.

It's a long road with no turn in it
It's an odd love without a portion of heartbreak
If I hadn't laid all of that hurt upon you
I wouldn't be stuck out here like a fool
Cruising down along tramps heartbreak.

I played with life like old chess pieces
Discarded rooks for kings and queens
Seared the hearts of those who loved me
Ah, those faraway hills looked green
And as for you my true companion
You deserved so much better through the years
I wish I could return your wasted days
Melt the smile frozen in your tears.

I'm going back to where I come from
Though I don't fit there anymore
I've got some friends and blood relations
They won't turn me away from their front door
Find a cabin out in the country
I've had it up to here with cities and towns
With the wind as my companion
Maybe I can turn myself around.

I'm going back, beg for your forgiveness
What made me think I knew it all
Even though you're a long time gone now
Only you can cure my troubled soul
Stand in front of your marble tombstone
Feel the cold granite inside my heart
Splinter into sticks of dynamite
Each one tearing me apart.

It's a long road with no turn in it
It's an odd love without a portion of heartbreak
And if I hadn't laid all of that hurt upon you
I wouldn't be stuck out here like a fool
Cruising down along tramps heartbreak . . .

From Trouble in the Land, *Shanachie Records 2000*
Published by Starry Plough Music (BMI)

YOU GET SO tuned into the streets, it's like they're paved, pulsing, and running through your veins. New York is like that. It grips you like a mistress and won't let you think about home. The place is so all-enveloping and seductive, it's sometimes hard to remember that you had a life before you settled there. If time flows like a river through other communities, it rushes in flash flood through the concrete canyons of Manhattan. Contrary to opinion, the city does sleep, but with one eye open; and even on the doziest of nights, you can hear the crackle of dreams, for New York is the ultimate city of possibility. But there's a price to pay: the days, weeks, and seasons gallop by you in dizzy abandon, like two-bit winners out at the track. At first, it's all hunky-dory; the years and the opportunities stretch out in front of you, and you cherry-pick like a kid at Toys R Us, delighted and seemingly so in control.

But the city knows exactly what it's doing. Like a coke dealer, it feeds you just enough to keep your interest: a great concert, a wonderful exhibition, an overpowering love—they're all there for you. Then you get a bit deeper in and think that there'll always be time to pull back, but why bother now, you're having the time of your life. Until one day it dawns on you that you're so busy keeping your head above water that there's little time for the concerts and the exhibitions anymore; and as for that now less than overpowering love? You're juggling so hard you just might have to drop her from the sheer fatigue of it all.

The trick, of course, is to get out and go to the mountain while you're ahead. Come back refreshed and replenished. Or maybe, just grow up and realize that life is going on in infinite ways all over the world, with nary a thought given to the complexities and overload that you're experiencing on this small island. But that resolution quickly evaporates, when you step out on the street, and the speed hits you once more, and you're so glad to be alive and living the type of life you always wanted in this city of crackling dreams.

I was here almost three years when my mother wrote to say that my grandfather was sinking. People didn't phone much in those days. It was too expensive. Calls were for pure emergencies.

The phone ringing in the middle of the night is the emigrant's worst nightmare. That minute or so when you wipe the sleep from your eyes, clamber out of bed in the darkness with every imaginary catastrophe back home flashing like some cheap Hammer movie before you. The relief and annoyance to find it was only some friend who had scored and was looking for a bed, or a floor, or a toke, or a joke to get him through something. Still, it was always hard to get back to sleep with the cold, dread sweat still damp on your brow.

My mother's letter was tactful and caring. She knew my situation. The immigration lawyer had advised us not to leave the country until our cases were settled and green cards in hand. Still, I wanted to see Thomas Hughes one last time. She said not to make too big a deal of it, he probably wouldn't recognize me anyway. But I knew he would. There was always that link between us. And I owed it to him in so many ways—give him one last view of reality. For he had drifted back into the world of his youth around the turn of the century. He had been sinking even before I left, and I often heard him mumbling about Black '47. He uttered those simple words with such a degree of horror and awe. In his dementia, he was again listening to the stories his own father had told him of the people dying by the roadsides with grass stains on their mouth. His voice conveyed a spiked pain beyond hurt and sadness, but also a resolution that this incalculable travesty should never be allowed happen again.

I wanted to prove him wrong. On my last visit, he was sitting up on a hard-backed chair, dressed in his best suit, waiting for me. Father Jim had secured him a room in a clerical rest home nestled amid the Wicklow Mountains. I had missed the bus from Dublin and was late. He had been waiting for hours, erect as ever and poised at the edge of his chair. Everything, except his fading consciousness, was so in place—freshly ironed shirt, cuff-linked wrists, his watch chain polished and dangling across his waistcoat pocket, his white hair spiffed back, face shaved. The nuns were fond of him and tended to his every need. But he was contemptuous of his dependency on others, and his eyes flashed as he watched me cross the polished sitting-room floor. He didn't say much, but it was one of his good days and he was aware of everything.

I had my program down pat. I had grown used to his silences and could monologue as effortlessly as a Catskills comedian. I kept my parting piece until last, but my mother must have warned him for he leaned forward at my first words, head cocked like one of his old gun dogs. I lied that I was only going away for six month and that I'd see him at Christmas. I joked that I'd probably run into his childhood friend, Joe Cuddihy, who had gone to America as a boy and was never heard from again. He listened to my spiel and nodded, almost imperceptibly. He knew the game well, how incredibly difficult it is to emigrate, how harder still to get home. He'd been around it all his life. Knew that, in these matters, chance would far outweigh any human plan. He also knew me better than anyone, and was surely worried for me. He had allowed me my teenage wildness, lack of judgment, and sheer obduracy. He instructed my mother to let me be, that "no one learns from telling, only from doing."

And now the time was running out between us. The last Dublin bus would be at the gates in minutes. I had to leave and he knew it. I took both his hands, gnarled and still calloused from the years of chipping and shaping stone. I squeezed them like I had as a boy when there were only the two of us against the world. I told him I'd see him soon. His eyes smiled gamely in one last big effort, but he didn't believe me for a moment. This was good-bye, and that was all there was to it. I turned away and hurried across the room, my eyes blurred. A nun stepped from the shadows and opened the sitting-room door for me. She must have been there all the time. "Go now, we'll look after him for you," she murmured. And then I was out on the long tree-lined avenue and running blindly for the Dublin bus.

After I received my mother's letter, I grew restless and anxious at being alone with my thoughts. I headed west across St. Mark's and into Eighth Street, past Hendrix's Electric Lady Studios and into Sheridan Square, skirting south of the Bells, ignoring the Head and the come-ons from the hustlers on Christopher, down past the bars and craft shops and onto the West Side where Montgomery Clift gave it all up in Badlands. Then, as I sat on the dock jutting out into the Hudson and gazed out at the haze over the Jersey skyline, I remembered a different route in a different lifetime.

I was only a little boy then and used to accompany him on Sunday afternoon spins around the country in his blue Morris Minor. We would usually visit a graveyard where, from sheer idleness, I'd study his chiseled face while he stared for hours at the headstones in rapt silence. He knew this operation bored me to tears, so he'd often vary the excursion with side trips to a series of abandoned Cistercian monasteries; there, in the ruins of these once all powerful religious communities, he'd examine the gutted granite window frames while I'd hunt for birds' nests in the tangled ivy. Sometimes we'd cross onto a headland poking its nose out into the swell of the South Atlantic, and wince from the salt spray lashing our faces; or stroll along a deserted strand while hailstones punched tiny holes in the damp sand. From time to time, I'd seal fake SOS messages in bottles and toss them into the tide. He never chided me about this dishonesty, although I was often apprehensive, for I was never quite sure just where his moral scruples began and ended. There seemed to be some magical line in his mind between practical good and accommodating wrong. I knew that it troubled him because few shared this same demarcation, but he rarely complained. That wasn't his nature. No, better to accept life's blows and silently chew on them rather than show weakness by prattling on like everyone else. He was younger then and very strong; if I got tired he would toss me up on his shoulders and carry me back to the car. For a man used to lifting hundredweight bags of cement, a boy of fifty or sixty pounds was surely small potatoes. He enjoyed our games and physical closeness, but everyone else was kept at a strict arm's length.

He had a web of friends all over the county and was welcome in many houses for a chat and Sunday tea. I marveled at the stories these old people related to one another, not so much the events or characters that they talked about, but the way one tale would meander into another. Thus, one might begin with a hurling match that took place in the '50s, dart back to the birth of the sport in mythic Fianna times, then on up to the Gaelic Athletic Association's resurgence before the War of Independence. One person might break in excitedly to report on seeing a famous figure like Michael Collins at a game, whereupon this sighting would lead to a free-for-all that led you to believe that every major character in Irish politics might have once upon a time taken up the *camán* and *sliotar*. The exchange might end up with a long and oft-times painful analysis of Wexford's current hurling prospects. After an hour or two of this conversational ping-pong, the subject would fizzle out, and all would stare into the fire.

This silence would fascinate me no less than the actual discussions. For there was no tension in the stillness between these people. The quiet was merely a marking of time, when everyone retreated to the comfort and sustenance of their own thoughts. And then the lady of the house would stir herself and break away from this fire-gazing; usually, she'd wet another pot of tea or attend to some household task, but gently, so as not to disturb. This activity would give everyone time to gather their thoughts and perhaps reflect on the problems of the morrow. But soon a new subject would be broached, gather steam, and head off down the highways and byways of communal Irish memory and existence.

They talked of a world, too, that had almost faded—a shadowy parallel universe peopled by ghosts, spirits, and other manifestations that had been only recently banished with the introduction of electric light into these rural communities. The old people no longer believed as fiercely as their grandparents had, but they were mindful of this other world and kept a weather eye out for its intrusions into our own. Most of them knew of someone with a foot in both dimensions; occasionally one of these seers would drop by for a cup of tea. Man or woman, they were usually of a silent nature, but took all things in. Always deeply respected, they were deferred to, but never referred to. "The sight," as it was called, was a gift but burdensome; it took a sound mental as well as physical constitution to shoulder its responsibilities. As I played with my toy cars or read my comic books, I would sometimes

look up and catch a pair of deep eyes testing me, for they were
interested in children, especially those who showed any trace of
the gift. This examination was always deeply uncomfortable, and
I'd look anxiously over for my grandfather. But he would have
already noticed and would give me a reassuring wink, before
deflecting both the tester and the mood of the moment with
some observation or riposte.

Before we knew it, the night would be upon us, and we'd be at
the front door bidding our good-byes; the man of the house might
secretly pass me some sweets, or the lady hand over a dozen eggs
in a thick brown paper bag, along with the admonishment that
they be carried home on my knees and not left to crack in the
backseat. Then the clutch and accelerator would be pressed down
in tandem, the Morris Minor would roar into gear, and we'd head
off down the laneway to the byway that would eventually lead like
a tributary into the main road back to Wexford.

We traveled many routes home—not always the shortest or
most logical—as on Sundays my grandfather liked to cherish the
illusion that he was fancy-free and not responsible for family, business, or the many demands on his time and emotion. But there's
one road that will always stick in my mind. The New Line was a
military thoroughfare built by the British army between their
naval base in Duncannon and the town of Wexford. This seaside
fortress had at one time been of great importance to the empire—
James III used it to flee to France after his defeat by William of
Orange at the Battle of the Boyne; it would have been considered
one of the main bastions of defense should Bonaparte have
invaded. The empire was gone, the fortress crumbling, but the
road remained. It was an anomaly for Ireland. Straight and flat in
great stretches, as far as the eye could see. To the child it was a
wonder. To the old man it was foreign and out of sympathy with
the rambling countryside. It was something else to him, too,
darkly dangerous and symbolic, but it would take me distance and
years to understand the nature of that anxiety.

As soon as we filed onto its tar-backed straightness, he would
invariably begin the rosary. Like many republican men, he had a

devotion to the Virgin Mary and felt that she had not been compromised by the alliance of Mother Church and the repressive Irish Free State. He only ever recited the Sorrowful Mysteries. Perhaps he had forgotten the Joyful or the Glorious, or did sorrow more suit his mind-set at that time of life? He liked the calm uniformity of this most common set of Irish prayers—so did I, for that matter. The stirring Apostles' Creed began the ritual, followed by the first mystery: the Agony in the Garden; then the Our Father, chased by ten utilitarian Hail Marys counted on your fingers, and topped off with a speedy Gloria before hitting the Second Sorrowful Mystery—the Scourging at the Pillar, and so on while your mind blurred and the miles raced by. We'd glide along in the rain, hail, or snow; and if it was a clear night we'd watch the moon and the stars turn the silent countryside into an angel-pale paradise, our voices interlocked in the murmuring mantra.

One day, when I was about fourteen, to my surprise he remained silent for some minutes after we turned onto the old military road. He must have noticed my anticipation, but he allowed the quietness to dangle between us. It was his way of announcing that he had something of import to say. At such times, he could be miserly with his words and always chose them carefully.

"They call this road the tramp's heartbreak. Do you know why?"

I did not, but chose not to speak because no answer was expected. He let the question hang fire before continuing. "The tramp does not wish to know the length of his journey, nor where it will take him. On this road, all of those things and more become apparent."

I still didn't speak. I knew that my task was to listen and make sense of what he said. He just stared ahead, his hands gripped tightly around the steering wheel, as if it might jump from his grasp.

"You're at an age now where the world will demand answers of you, and you'll ask questions of it." He paused as if to savor his own words. I remained stock-still, I knew he was about to say something important. If I made a sound he might retreat into an impatient silence and deem me not grown up enough yet for adult discourse. It had happened before. I could tell he was measuring me out of the corner of his eye. He had a very penetrating way of honing in completely on whatever subject was to hand. Then we came out of a copse of trees and the moon lit up the countryside all the way down to the distant Atlantic shoreline. He turned his attention away from me and cast a glance at the magical landscape. Then he spoke very quietly and in measured tones. "The life fully lived will have its share of turmoil. It's the nature of things and I would wish you nothing less."

He sighed and put the car into third gear, for we were approaching a small incline. When we had crested and were cruising down the other side, he changed into neutral and allowed the car its head. He did this frequently, for the idea of saving even a thimbleful of petrol appealed greatly to him. Then he said with a certain bitterness, "Don't ever get stuck on a road such as this. You'll know what I mean in good time."

He didn't say the rosary that night; soon after I became too grown up for our excursions and wished to spend the time with my friends. At first I felt guilty, but he understood. He continued his Sunday rambles alone until he was too frail to drive.

We finally got our green cards in early December and took the next available plane home. It had been three years since we left. We got gloriously drunk in Tomorrow's Lounge; the party continued out at Kennedy and we had the 747 on its ear with our shenanigans. People smiled at us. Young men going home for the first time, pockets full of money to squander, lock up your daughters, line up the pints, the boys are back in town. The clouds were low to the ground but we cheered and applauded when the plane touched down at Dublin Airport. My mother took me to one side in the lobby and whispered, "Your grandfather was buried two days ago. There was no point in ringing. It would only have upset you that you couldn't come." Then she hugged me and said, "For one who was so conflicted, he passed away quietly in the end."

12

BLOOD WEDDING

Carlita is waiting down on C & 9th
In mantilla and lace
And her lover's knife
Cries out for revenge
But she is silent like a stone
And beautiful in her widow's weeds
I wait in the darkness forever now alone
Too late for any tear shedding
While his bride waits down on C & 9th
For her blood wedding.

Why did you have to go out tonight
With the full moon in scarlet
And his silver knife
Waiting for you
And the remains of your life
Ticking away like some pitiful clock
I who could not even be called your wife
Safe and warm in your bedding
And you the bridegroom off on your way
To your blood wedding.

And the Ukrainian ladies light candles in the street
Where his body lay bleeding
And the projects are silent
Bracing for the heat that must come
From his blood wedding.

Carlita, why do you hate me so much?
I long for your body
I die for your touch
On my burning skin
And the smell of your perfume
Will always remain on my bed.
But I died every time
You entered his room
I could not let him go on living
And now you wait down on C & 9th
Dying to celebrate my blood wedding.

I wait in the shadows of C & 9th
With my fingers caressing
His sacred knife
You loved my body
He loved my soul
You thought you knew me
But what do men know?
Except my lover whose shape is etched in chalk on the street
Soon to be washed away by the rain
While you wait in the darkness
Dreading the shock of my knife
At your blood wedding.

And the Ukrainian ladies light candles in the street
Where his body lay bleeding
And the projects are silent
Bracing for the heat that must come

From his blood wedding
Your blood wedding
Our blood wedding . . .

From Home of the Brave, *EMI Records 1994*
and New York Town, *Gadfly Records 2004*
Published by Starry Plough Music/EMI Blackwell Music (BMI)

IF YOU'VE EVER a mind to live at home again, don't stay away for three years. Too much water will have flowed under the bridge. Many things will have stayed the same: the wind, the rain, the mossy-backed walls, the smell of the coal fires at night; even the fish and chips will retain their indelible taste, though they were no longer wrapped in newspapers. You will have moved on, however, and so will your family, though their love may even be deeper and more meaningful than you remember it. But your friends will look at you now in a way you don't recall: checking you out for some change in your personality, an affectation of speech, perhaps, or some new Yankee mannerism. And they'll find these surface changes aplenty. What did they expect? That you lived in a vacuum, regularly took speech and slagging classes to retain your pristine accent and your acidic sense of wit?

You will become aware of these changes, too. If you're of a docile nature, and keeping the peace and fitting in are things that matter to you, you'll hasten to ameliorate and soften the new ticks and touches, whereas if you're vaguely resentful about the whole process, you'll go out of your way to heighten and sharpen the new knobs on your personality. You'll make a point of leaving your change on the pub counter New York style, no matter how many times the bartender shoves it toward you. You'll extravagantly tip the same unionized employee or, if you're really pissed, throw him a fistful of the newfangled silver change that you can't be bothered coming to terms with. And when you're really out of it, and notice people sniggering behind their hands at the new broadness in your accent, you might even stand with fist to heart and belt them out a verse or two of the "Star-Spangled Banner." Then, for good measure as you're being escorted to the door, you might for fairness' sake blast forth the Irish national anthem. If you're of a political bent, it might also behoove you to roar back, "You're nothin' but a crowd of Free State, blue-shirted bastards!" And for good measure, rip off a couple of bars of "Take It Down from the Mast, Irish Traitors . . ." when you're lying in the gutter outside.

For the most part I tried to fit in and matched my steps accordingly. I could tell that I was a bit over the top after three years on the streets of the East Village. Oddly enough, it was easiest to be yourself with the older folk. They were less judgmental. They'd seen generations of emigrants come and go to London and Liverpool, and they had an idea of what you were going through. The softness in their eyes was genuine when you came to call on them; their delight in seeing you went a long way to letting you know that you'd always have a home among them. The old houses spic and span for your visit, the nervous laughter in the hallway, how well you looked, and the style of you! The fire lit, the tea and cake laid out in the rarely used parlor; and you played your part to the letter, the well-edited and exaggerated stories of how great you were doing, what and who you'd seen, everything ticking along like clockwork, until the awful inevitable question: "When are you going back?" Or as my mother learned to phrase it over the years, "How long will you be able to stay with us?"

When the tea and the cake were all gone, the man of the house would produce a dozen warm bottles of McArdles or Guinness, and you'd finally loosen up, your stories would become the slightest bit more risqué, to the delight of the ladies, until the shadows would deepen and it was time to go home to the mammy because she hated to have the good evening fry go cold while waiting for you. And there'd be much cluck-clucking about this, and hadn't the poor woman been on tenterhooks for months now in anticipation of you coming home. Then there'd be hugs and final kisses and "You'll be sure to come back see us again next Christmas, won't you?" And you would for certain; because they'd reopened avenues to the sparkling fields of your childhood, and helped you remember all the simple obvious things that, like a fool, you'd forgotten. Then you were out in the cool night air, with the stars diamond clear beaming down on you in a way that they never did in New York, while the smell of the chimneys summoned up so many palpable memories that it seemed impossible that you'd never fit in again.

But you couldn't. Something had happened. The city had left its mark on you, and no matter how much you drank or talked or reminisced, you now knew irrevocably that this part of your life was behind you. Oh, it would always be there. You'd keep coming home, and there'd be nights when anything seemed possible—nights when the intervening years seemed flimsy and could be swept away, and you could start all over again and be the boy you used to be. But those nights got rarer, as the years tallied up and the city sunk her narcotic talons ever deeper inside you.

The deep-sea sailor could see it. Nights when we'd bring a crowd back from the pub, I would catch him observing me, noting the changes. He'd seen it all. Been away a hundred times and returned. He knew what it was like not to fit in. But his wife and family were in Wexford, and he always had that reason to return. Though I'd flirt and have vacation flings for many years, he knew I'd never end up with any of these girls—it was just a game; there were others more important waiting in my future. At times, I'd see him glance toward my mother, in seventh heaven with her two fine strapping sons home and gathered around her, and I could watch him count the cost of emigration that would eventually take its toll on her.

It wasn't just that I had changed. Ireland was on the march. The European Common Market had become a fully fledged reality. New highways were replacing the old blackberry-trellised winding roads; huge grants of money were pouring in from Brussels to modernize the infrastructure. Old crumbling weedy Wexford walls that I had loved and taken for granted were fair play now for pick and bulldozer. Edwardian, Victorian, and even Elizabethan structures were being leveled without a thought for posterity—just auld bloody things in the way, knock 'em down, make room for that new supermarket with the ten different brands of toilet paper! No doubt, some of this needed to be done, but many babies went out with the bathwater before the country woke up and cried halt.

And in the countryside, the "bungalowization" had begun in earnest: beautiful hills and riverbanks scarred by phalanxes of white stuccoed monuments to tastelessness. "But sure, don't the people need to live somewhere?" Everyone seemed oblivious to the loss. And when you mentioned it, they looked at you as if you were "one of them busybodies down from some Dublin Georgian society." Money has a way of inducing mass amnesia. A society that had been uniformly poor and barely getting by had been given its first mass taste of prosperity. The older people could put it into perspective—they remembered only too well the bad old days. But the young were in a hurry to forget and wholeheartedly embraced the new reality.

Up until then, two matters were never discussed in Irish life: religion and money. Since there were few Protestants left in the South, the first taboo was no longer relevant. But now, to my surprise, the talk was all of finance: how much each person was earning, the cost of the new car, house, television, suit of clothes, everything was on the table. The old people shook their heads at this lack of propriety, but the young rattled off figures like drunken accountants. Who could blame them? It was all so new. But one missed the old discretion.

And then, you finally stopped looking inward and realized that those who stayed behind had the right to do and be whatever they wanted, and you might as well be swimming up a millstream as wishing otherwise. It happened to me one night near the end of the trip. I had grown tired of some party and was climbing up the hill to my parents' house. I turned around and looked down on the familiar landmarks of the town: the twin churches and the Italianate Franciscan friary where I had served Mass, all potent symbols of the authority that limned my childhood. Now, though a deep ache of memory still linked me, I could finally see them as they really were: mere buildings, gloomy or joyful, depending on your mood. I took in a deep draft of the smoky air, sat down on a garden wall, and watched the brooding town doze toward the dawn.

Three girls turned the corner. They didn't notice me hedged in by lilac bushes, for I was still as the grave. They were coming from a

dance at White's Hotel and were bursting with the lilting chatter of
tipsy teenagers. Two of them had just been kissed in laneways and
were still full of the magic of it all; the third had a boyfriend off in
London. They teased her unmercifully for her fidelity. She gave
back as good as she got, saying she'd kissed better gorillas, and
wouldn't ride either of their Romeos for the exercise. They stopped
to light cigarettes and I thought of Bridie and how she and her girlfriends used to carry on after the dances: verbally lashing the various lads they had encountered, each one vying to trump the
other. But when I tried to summon up her face, it wouldn't come
into focus. Another dark-haired woman kept intruding and
melding with the soft features I could usually distinguish so clearly.
I almost forgot the girls laughing around me. Then the church
clocks chimed twice and the girls hurried on. Their chatter continued to echo even after they had turned a corner. Eventually, all
was silence again. But I knew that more than the thrill of their
voices had passed.

A couple of weeks later I saw Carlita in the Kiwi, an after-hours
saloon on Ninth Street, and remembered her face from the night
in Wexford. I had seen her around Tompkins Square previously—
she just hadn't registered in a conscious manner. This surprised
me, for she was an extremely good-looking woman and stood
out in any company. She had coarse black hair that flowed down
to her waist. It often looked unkempt, for she had a habit of
tossing her head back when she walked. She had been a dancer
and that probably accounted for her purposeful stride and defiant
bearing. Like many people who have been onstage, she had an
instinctive awareness of the possibilities of light. I can picture her
still in silhouette—poised as a cobra, head slightly thrown back,
chin thrust forward. Like many beautiful women she had a slight
defect—a small white scar just under her mouth—but this only
served to highlight the richness of her pink lips. It was her eyes,
though, that set her apart; they were a deep gray, canny, judgmental, and fierce as any osprey.

That was also the first time I heard her voice. Hard and guttural
with an edge of the streets, it had its own peculiar music. It's odd

how well I can recall the sound because she never spoke directly to me, though I must have been in her presence a hundred times. But there's little I've forgotten about Carlita, though I'm not sure she even noticed me. Puerto Rican women had little time for gringos; their men tended to encourage such dismissal. Not that Carlita ever needed the approval of a man. That was far from her style.

The Kiwi never closed, the party went on around the clock, but the mood could ebb and flow dramatically. It was always wise to ease in unobtrusively and get the lay of the land before raising your head. This was easily enough accomplished, for the standard first order was a Heinken and two joints. This purchase cost $4 and it would have been considered the height of bad manners not to leave the extra dollar for a tip. Etiquette also demanded that the first joint be passed down the bar after your initial toke. With a constant stream of new customers, one was constantly high.

The bartenders varied, but my favorite was Margarita, a very fetching Cuban transvestite, who augmented his already significant height by wearing three-inch heels. He had a dead crush on my brother Jemmy and I shamelessly angled free drinks for myself by promising to intercede for him, should Jemmy ever have the need of a "real woman," which was how Margarita described himself. Carlita didn't care for this very exotic creature and treated him/her with a frosty silence. But she had a lot of time for Jimmy Reece, a black man in his late forties who became a mentor of mine. It was Reece who noticed my head bopping to Coltrane one night and screamed down the bar, "You got it, babe. It's your first time. I can always tell." And he was right. Up until then, all jazz had seemed like so much wanking to me. The combination of Dutch lager and Columbian weed had opened some crack in the door of my perception and allowed Trane and his genius to slither in. After that Reece took pleasure in turning me on to Miles, Mingus, and Thelonious, broadening my horizons, even if my musical abilities could never keep up.

I learned a lot from Reece, not the least Carlita's story. Jimmy was a fragmentary thinker, and speaker, for that matter; one had to spend time juggling a sky full of information until a piece would drop in one's lap and complete a puzzle that he might have initiated some months previously. This probably had something to do with the fact that after he left his job at RCA on a Friday, he would make his way straight to the Kiwi where he would remain until early Sunday night. Then he would solemnly bid everyone good fortune in the coming week and take the train home to Harlem. He was beloved by all and died on a Monday morning when a doctor misdiagnosed raging pneumonia for general fatigue. Given the circumstances of Reece's weekends, I suppose that error was understandable.

Reece's method of education was not unlike that of Jesus or the Buddha. He often spoke in parables and riddles, and left you to glean your own findings and opinions from a jumble of warnings and non sequiturs. He indicated that I should keep my distance from Roman, a Ukrainian carpenter. Roman had a wife and a number of small children; I often saw them take a turn around Tompkins Square Park on a fine Sunday afternoon. It was rare for a Ukie to frequent a black/Hispanic after-hours. Rare too for an Irishman, but I lived across the street and had neighbors' rights. Roman lived over by Second Avenue and obviously came east for a reason. A hard man who rarely showed any feelings, he was good-looking, if somewhat coarse, with the build of one who had known the inside of a gym in his younger days. In my mind, he had gone a little to seed and I felt that Carlita could do a lot better. Still, she was obviously smitten, for on the rare occasion that he paid her any attention, her proud glare would dissolve into a soft, girlish smile. Late at night, when I began to obsess on this, I knew it was time to go home; Roman was not a man to mess with.

Reece used to bristle when Jesus walked in the door. He would even make a show of turning his back on this midlevel smack dealer from the projects. Reece had a thing about heroin; said it had killed Bird and the sheer musical loss was incalculable. Jesus was impossibly handsome in that *West Side Story* kind of way, and he knew it. He had a way of looking through you that was distinctly unpleasant. I can only imagine how a woman felt under the same scrutiny. His was a brittle brooding presence and he took offense easily and often. Some nights he seemed quite a bit younger than the other two, but the

streets had poured cold concrete into his eyes and I could never relax
in his presence. I had no idea that he, too, was sleeping with Carlita.

Neither had I ever seen a cop enter the Kiwi. It was generally
assumed that someone in the precinct was being paid off. It was a
real eye-opener to see the red-faced sergeant throw open the door
and let the sunlight stream in on that Sunday morning. He was
furious and cursed out Margarita for being a spic fag, and that was
only the polite beginning of his introduction. He slammed a night-
stick down on the counter; glasses, bottles, and joints jumped as he
roared, "All of you fuckin' scum out the door!" Obediently, we
trooped out bleary-eyed into the late morning. Up the street, on
the opposite footpath, some elderly Ukrainian ladies were already
on their knees in a circle mumbling their prayers. The body was
covered with a white sheet. Someone said it was Roman.

The Kiwi prudently closed for a couple of days until relations
were restored with the precinct. Reece advised me to keep away
from the funeral and the projects. He muttered something about a
"blood wedding,"—local slang for a crime of passion. He also hinted
that Roman's death was unlikely to go unrevenged. I usually took
his advice in these matters, but curiosity got the better of me.

DeLeon's funeral parlor was crowded on that sweltering day. I
hardly recognized anyone in the crush; for the most part they
were Ukrainians, the women in black, the men stocky, their faces
bloated from the long boozy wake. Reece was the only person of
color there; he seemed to be well regarded, and mixed easily with
the mourners. I tried to catch his eye but he didn't see me. His tall,
lithe frame swayed willowlike above the group of tradesmen and
janitors who gathered around him. Though the air-conditioning
was on, many people were sweating, unaccustomed to wearing
suits and formal dresses in such warm weather. The mortuary was
heavy with the sweet overpowering scent of white lilies. I felt suddenly nauseous; the murmur of the mourners seemed to drop
some decibels and my ears began to roar with the white noise of
silence. I felt sure that I was going to faint and reached out for a
large brass candlestick to steady myself. When I wiped the cold
sweat from my brow, the feeling passed and I was fine again. But I

was now in the line to view Roman's corpse. It wasn't someplace that I wanted to be, shaky as I was; however, there didn't seem to be much choice but to shuffle forward and pay my respects.

The line moved slowly. Roman's immediate family was seated next to the coffin. I nodded at a few people but his wife made a point of ignoring me. Perhaps she didn't wish to speak with anyone associated with the Kiwi. She was a heavyset blond woman, thick now about the ankles, yet you could tell that she had once been a pretty teenager. Her eyes were red and puffy from crying, but she was already, in some odd way, resigned to widowhood. Then it was my turn and I looked down at Roman. I hadn't known him well: a word or two in the bar, a nod of recognition on the street. Still, I tried to summon up some sense of sorrow at his passing. I stared at him for a couple of moments and tried to remember a suitable prayer, but I felt like a hypocrite for, if truth were to be told, I was jealous of the man. I had done my duty and was just about to leave when I felt a shudder run through the crowd. It seemed as though all conversation had been drained from the room. Instinctively, I looked around for Reece. He was standing deadly still and staring at the door, his features frozen with concern. And then Carlita approached the casket.

Roman's wife screamed with anger, or was it anguish? She brushed past me as if to block Carlita's way. But one of the old ladies grabbed her and pinned her to her widow's chair. I'm not even sure that Carlita noticed. She seemed to glide along the mourning carpet, poised but intent, a force unto herself. Her eyes were glazed but deathly focused; if I hadn't stepped aside, I think she would have knocked me over. When she reached the casket, she halted for a second and flicked back an errant strand of hair from her face. She bent over slowly and kissed Roman's porcelain forehead. I had to admire her. She kept both her cool and her mantilla intact. She whispered something in Spanish and crossed herself. Then she strode out the door into the dog day heat. I hurried after her, but Reece grabbed my shoulder and told me not to be a goddamned fool. By then, Carlita was already striding down the street toward the projects, off to settle her sacred score.

13

BANKS OF THE HUDSON

On the banks of the Hudson my love and I lay down
Just above Forty-second Street while the rain was pouring down
When I covered her with kisses, the sparks lit up her eyes
We made love like mad angels while the Jersey trucks rolled by
She said, "Don't you ever leave me, oh for God's sake don't let me down!"
So I made her all kinds of promises how I'd always be around
But the speed was ripping through my head, I'd only one thing on my mind
So good-bye, my love on Forty-second Street
If I don't get out of here I'm going to die.

On the banks of the Hudson, my love and I lay down
Just one more midnight left to kill, then I'm out of New York town.
I could feel the Ice Man closing in, I could almost smell his gun
But that twenty grand I beat him out of would help me start again back home
She said, "Don't you ever leave me, oh for God's sake don't let me down!"
Then I thought about what they'd do to her when they found out I'd left town
But the fire was racing through my brain, I'd only one thing on my mind
So good-bye my love on Forty-second Street
If I don't get out of here I'm going to die.

Don't say I should have stayed with her
You don't know the full story about the girl,
I only used her just as much as she used me
But sometimes, you just got to get out of New York City.

On the banks of the Hudson my love and I lay down
Just above Forty-second Street while the rain was pouring down
When I covered her with kisses, the sparks lit up her eyes
We made love like mad angels while the Jersey trucks rolled by.
She said, "Don't you ever leave me, oh for God's sake don't let me down!"
But how could I ever take a black girl back to Wexford town?
Just then the streets of fire turned to blood, a yellow Cadillac cruised by
And as I raced up Forty-second Street, the Ice Man shouted,
"Hey, Paddy, it's time to die."

From Black 47, *independent 1991 and* Fire of Freedom, *EMI Records 1993*
Published by Starry Plough Music/EMI Blackwell Music (BMI)

VOODOO CITY

Paddy came down to Voodoo City
Met a lady on Bourbon Street
She was dark and she was beautiful
Swept that boy right off his feet
Running from the man in New York City
Fled down south to beat the chill
But the Ice Man had me in his sights
For one too many unpaid bills.

Oh . . . Voodoo City
Oh . . . Voodoo Girl
Oh . . . Voodoo City
For God's sakes keep your hands off
My Voodoo girl

Marie Laveau was the lady in question
Fell beneath her crescent spell.
Nights spent drinking in the Quarter
Soon turned into a living hell
She said she knew how to protect me

From all the evil in my past
But New York is not scorned so easy
Ice Man tracked me down at last.

Moonlight on the misty river
Mist around the old gaslight
Heard his footsteps on Toulouse Street
Disappear into the Creole night.

Candle waver on the altar
Marie, she dance on the naked floor
Flame light up her sacred body
I hear a key turn in the door.

I scream at her, "You have betrayed me"
The hurt explode inside her eyes
She throw herself across my body
Bullet choke her voodoo cries.

A raven rises from her body
The Ice Man stare in disbelief
I crash through her garret window
Race like fire down Bourbon Street.

From Home of the Brave, *EMI Records 1994*
Published by Starry Plough Music/EMI Blackwell Music (BMI)

FALLIN' OFF THE EDGE OF AMERICA

Jackie said, "I'm dying
Take the words out of my mouth
I'm a long way from home, guy
And I wish I could hold out
'Til the sun rises in the morning
I don't want to go at night

She'll be sleeping around now
She won't see my passing light
I don't want to say its over
What's the point but then
Here I go fallin' off the edge of America again."

Jackie said, "I'm freakin'
Hold on, man, don't let go.
I'm sorry for what I done to you
Just don't leave me here all on my own.
Take that letter out of my back pocket
But don't read it, man, whatever you do
It's just a note and a lock of her hair
Send it back to her, it's okay, man, it's cool.
I don't want to talk about it
Words just cause too much pain
Here I go falling off the edge of America again.

Got my back to the Pacific
I'm a million miles from home
On a tightrope called America
With no place left to go

Jackie said, "It's over
I can see the dawn coming up
All along the Tenderloin
The Ice Man, he's shootin' up
And all the drunks are stumbling home
But, at least, they got stars in their eyes
Now you've put me so far behind you
Do you really call this a life?
Nothing to do but to go on
Turn your collar up to the rain
Here I go fallin' off the edge of America again . . .

From Trouble in the Land, *Shanachie Records 2000*
Published by Starry Plough Music (BMI)

HEROIN WAS EVERYWHERE. It snaked through the East Village like the plague. Its main shopping plazas were on B and Third, C and Ninth, in the piss-stained hallways of the Projects on D, and down at the edge of the world on Stanton Street. You could feel it rustle through the trees during murky dawns in Tompkins Square, before it spilled across A to the gentrified numbered avenues. Its fashionable side was forever splayed along St. Mark's in the shape of biker-jacketed skeletal bodies, their razor-thin faces ashen and joyless, their hollowed eyes scouting the horizon, passing the hopeless hours until the Ice Man chose to rip them off one more time. And next to them, doing the Fourteenth Street wobble, their lady friends, once wholesome beauties in small-town Jersey or on the lawns of Westchester—harridans now, holes in their tights from nights on their knees doing whatever it took to get one more fix, one more shot, and so it went. Down in my neck of the woods, junkies were like the poor of the Bible: they were always with you.

It's not that everyone did it. Far from it. But it was always there, only a nod, a phone call, or a stroll away. All you needed was a crisp Andrew Jackson between your thumb and index finger and the world was at your command—the first few times anyway. And you would be amazed at who was using. Everyone from the expected rockers to secretaries who worked uptown and never missed a day's work in their lives. A snort in the morning while applying eyeliner; a tootski at lunch in the ladies' room, and then a mad dash home on the subway, and the relief of kicking off heels and the dust of the day, before spending a languid evening on the couch with their own special friend.

Once you'd kissed it, you could spot its glassy-eyed imprint everywhere. You didn't even have to see the user, just hear the lame, enervated excuses: "Oh man, I don't know how I missed that appointment" or "I just can't believe I didn't hear the alarm this morning." Most musicians had a brush with it at one time or another. But even if you didn't, it was a part of your life. The man with the powder was king and all his lackeys bowed before him; if you happened to be involved with one of them, you were bending, too, and you mightn't even know. For his devoted subjects had to come up with cold cash, so everyone ended up paying for their habit. They'd go through friendship, health, wallets, windows, bars, locks. You could even nail them to the floor and they'd rip their hands off to score. Man, they even cut a hole in my roof one time, came down through the ceiling on ropes, and cleaned out the little they'd left on their last visit through the lock-picked door.

You couldn't trust a junky as far as you could throw him. The powder ate holes in every part of the psyche from conscience to self-respect. It took time to catch on to its ways but when you did, you were immediately the better for it, though you often felt hard-hearted and cruel. I was a huge fan of Johnny Thunders, the New York Doll, even though I never saw him at his best. He was always fried, slurred, and surly; but you just knew he still had it inside, and from time to time he'd show flashes of heaven that made all his junky braggadocio worthwhile. I loved to watch his fingers. They were long, lean, and grasping, and seemed to strangle the fret board rather than glide along it. But, sweet Jesus, could he wring chords and short bursts of stinging melodies out of that battered Strat! He was the quintessential rock 'n' roll outlaw going to hell in a hurry. He made Keith Richards look like Martha Stewart with a hangover.

Then one winter's night I found him curled up in the tiny vestibule of my building on Ninth Street. It was his fingers I recognized first. He was always careful of them. And even now in his crashed-out stupor, they were neatly draped over his knees. It was late, but I spent some time looking down at this waste of rock 'n' roll history. For a moment I wavered. Wouldn't it be the right thing to take this guy upstairs, put him on the couch, give him a bath and a good meal, and send him off renewed in the morning? But it was only a moment. I'd been robbed, cheated, and swindled by every junky I knew and Johnny, no matter how talented, would have been no exception. And so I bade him a silent, if hypocritical, Godspeed and slept in my own warm bed, while this eventual legend shivered in his sleep down below. He was there the next couple of nights, and then I saw him no more. He OD'd in New Orleans years later. Given his taste in winter lodging, I was surprised he lasted that long.

Heroin and cocaine, its icy sister, provided a frazzled backdrop to those East Village days. Being a musician and on the scene, all drugs were available, usually free. Getting musicians high was considered the thing to do. When a player had smoked your dope and fired off a great solo, then you were, by extension, playing your part in the music. For the punter, it was an ego trip. For the boys on the bandstand, it was part and parcel of life. Getting high without buying was our God-given due. Like most, I snorted smack a couple of times but, luckily, it didn't appeal to me. Even then, I considered it a dumb, hospital-smelling turnoff that made your stomach queasy, before you crawled off into your hole to indulge in a couple of hours of navel gazing. I had enough of a hermitic problem as it was, seeking solace too often in my own company. Any drug worth its salt had to get me up on my high horse and out into the world, not send me reeling back for the safety of my own four walls.

For one thing, I had an incident with opium. I got turned on to it at the Bells and took a liking to its sweet stickiness. Without really paying much attention, I began purchasing my own little stashed secret every Saturday night. I was very disciplined—as I thought—and anointed just a couple of gigless nights, when I would light up and stare at the wall for three or four hours. Unlike smack, it seemed organic and utterly manageable, while endowing a razor-sharp clarity to the brain and dispatching a surge of physical well-being throughout the entire body. The world's—along with your own—problems appeared to unknot in front of your very eyes; all things became clear and ultimately possible. Until one week, when my contact didn't show up, and I found myself frantically trying to track him down. After a nail-biting couple of days, he returned my calls and I scored a double— just to be on the safe side—and all again was well with the world. However, on the 6 Train down from Spanish Harlem, I was faced with the sudden alarming epiphany that I was hooked.

To say I was stunned would be an understatement. I hadn't, for the life of me, felt this creeping up. Opium was just something that I did on my own to make Sunday's invasive loneliness easier to bear, or midweek more interesting, and all the other things that junkies say to delude themselves. And I was a junky? The very thought made my stomach turn. This kind of thing didn't happen to a reasonably sensible guy from Wexford town. It was a special hell reserved for the cadavers on St. Mark's. All the way home, the little inner narcotic voice of reason tried to comfort me: "It'll be okay. Just this once and everything will be all right. You can quit next week." But I knew all about "next week" from the living dead I saw all around me. No, there was nothing for it; I had to face the music. But throw away a nice $40 chunk? It went against my whole upbringing. And yet, if I took it, I'd just be giving into the little voice, right? And then, there'd be next week and the one after to deal with. It was a dilemma. Eventually, I decided on a compromise. I'd smoke the whole chunk before midnight, then go cold turkey the next day—just like the John Lennon song. Seemed like a plan.

I smoked until it felt like it was coming out of my ears, two weeks' worth in a night. At one stage, I grew paranoid and felt that the neighbors were watching me, so I closed the blinds and felt more secure. In the end, I wasn't quite sure if I was high or just asphyxiating. I was a bit unsteady and decided to lie down on the bed for safety's sake. I passed out into the most vivid of pleasurable dreams until a phone rang, off in some vast aerie, and would not give up. I must have slipped out of the unconscious, for I realized I was awake, but terribly groggy. The phone was still ringing; by instinct I crawled off the bed and set off in the darkness on hands and knees to stop its bloody noise. In the sitting room, I tried to reach up to pull the string for the light, but discovered that I was unable to stand. I dropped to the safety of my knees again and knocked over the phone. I lay there on the floor and could vaguely hear a tinny voice calling my name. It took me a while to realize that this spectral summons wasn't coming from inside my head. I groped around and put the receiver to my ear. It was my mother.

Oh sweet divine Jesus! Just the person I needed to talk to at that moment. She hadn't heard from me in some time. A dalliance with Chinese opiates can lead you to neglect your obligations. I mumbled a spiteful son's word of complaint regarding her calling me in the

middle of the bloody night. There was a pause, worthy of two preg-
nancies. She seemed confused when she spoke again, "Now, is New
York five hours earlier or later?" She might as well have asked me to
recite the rosary backward. I lay there on my shaggily carpeted floor,
wishing only to be allowed to pass out, so that my mother could
return to whatever dream she had surfaced from.

She must have laid hands on *Old Moore's Almanac* or consulted
with my father, for it wasn't long before she stated with some
authority that if it was three in the afternoon in Wexford, by her
reckoning that would make it ten in the morning in New York—
barring a leap year entered into the equation. Irish mothers are
like that: always throwing curve balls to keep you off balance. I
raised myself on a quivering elbow, blinked three times, and saw a
crack of light leaking in around the corner of one of the shades.

She said I sounded strange and inquired if I was okay. I couldn't
say for definite, but I was even less certain how to go about
explaining my state of head and mind to her, sitting safe and
sound in her kitchen in Wexford with, no doubt, the sobering rain
pouring down. And so I reached for a common denominator and
managed to stutter that I had a hangover that would kill a piebald
pony. This analogy seemed to be well within the terms of her reference; still, she laughed a hair uncharitably and advised me to
remember that many on both sides of my family had alcoholic
tendencies, and she wouldn't be at all surprised if such a fate had
been visited on me. She further advised that, should such a thing
be available, I should drink a pint of goat's milk every morning;
this would be good for both bones and liver, two parts of my
anatomy that might be called upon to shoulder their share of
hardship in the years to come. She further cautioned that I should
watch out for myself and be sure to get a good night's sleep every
now and again.

I told her that the prospects of guaranteeing a regular supply of
goat's milk in the East Village were uncertain at best. But, by
Jaysus, there was little problem in securing a good night's sleep. To
the best of my knowledge, I had just notched up thirteen hours
filled with the most pleasant of dreams, and might have gone

around the clock if she hadn't called at this ungodly hour. She said wasn't that marvelous, and broke off for some moments to inform my father of my feat. His comments were apparently less than subtle and, from what I could gather, centered around the conviction that were I to put in an honest week's work a lot of my problems, sleeping and otherwise, would disappear. Accordingly, her upbeat mood had modified somewhat when she returned. She appeared to be speaking to my father, too, for there was an edge in her voice when she noted that I was probably still growing and needed every hour of sleep I could get. I must have passed out at that stage; for when I awoke at three in the afternoon, the phone was still to my ear and beeping away to its heart's content.

I was groggy for the rest of the day, and it wasn't until the evening that I remembered, with alarm, the second part of the bargain with myself. No more opium—instead an enforced diet of turkey, and of the cold variety, also. The next couple of weeks were murder. Depression mixed unmercifully with lack of self-worth; to these two was added a growing suspicion that the end of the world was nigh and that yours truly was responsible for this turn of events. Added to which, I was in the throes of an advanced constipation that was threatening to cripple me. When I consulted an encyclopedia in Tompkins Square Library, I discovered that this state was normal for one kicking "the devil's dream," as some nineteenth-century British missionary described it. Throughout a yawning third and fourth week, I could barely drag myself around. I couldn't even get drunk. Nothing seemed to work. I was so despondent that a lady friend of my acquaintance decided that if I didn't know what I wanted, she for damn certain knew what I really needed. The next morning I felt like a new man, and I hardly ever think of opium now. I must say, though, that the charitable and acrobatic exploits of the lady still jump to mind every now and again.

Whatever about my relationship with "the devil's dream," it was one colossal break that I didn't have the same fondness for heroin. Sharing needles was the way business was conducted down on Third Street; it would have been considered the height of bad form to whip out one's own spike and turn up the nose at the needle just extracted from your buddy's vein. This friendly custom was to have serious consequences in the late '70s and early '80s when the "Curse" swept through Alphabet City and wiped out a whole generation of smack-heads. This affliction was later diagnosed as AIDS. New threat—new tension! You could almost touch the paranoia and stress. Yet, no one could put a finger on it. Coke whores, dealers, drinkers, musicians, everyone was running scared. The whole scene was jittery, out of sync, and racing against time and a lethal mysterious enemy that no one had yet identified. It's not that there weren't good times. We partied away and lived for the day—and night; but there was an underlying feeling that something was coming to an end, a counting down, a ticking of the clock. I used that mood, and the backdrop of the anarchistic city in many Black 47 songs, and especially in the above triptych about Paddy, the Black Girl, and the Ice Man. There's a final fourth to come someday; hopefully, that will conclude the story.

The Black Girl's name was Cheryl, among others. She picked up an occasional shift in the Kiwi. But her sphere of operations was more the West Side Deuce from Times Square toward the river, and that string of dicey Eighth Avenue bars above the bus terminal. Was she a bartender who danced on the side or a stripper who occasionally bartended? She was evasiveness itself, and I never really got to the bottom of what she did. The truth is, I didn't want to know; and anyway, she'd always tell you what you wanted to hear. So what was the point?

She was sassy on first view, totally self-confident and together, but I never met anyone so fragile. She reminded me of a shapely willow tree that drooped toward the stream back home on my grandfather's farm. She would bend this way and that before the breeze. You'd expect her to break at any instant, and yet she never did, in my company, at least. She had a touch of a southern drawl but it was coated with a Bronx veneer; add to that the particular varnished finish that the old Forty-second Street bestowed on all its graduates, and you had a very distinctive accent. She told me she had grown up on army bases but was raised by a grandmother in Hunts Point. She just might have been telling the truth, but I never knew. I eventually stopped asking.

She was totally clean around me, but I always had the nagging suspicion that she was a user. She had that walking-with-her-God shuffle so down to a tee. The men with whom she hung out seemed to bear out my theory; and as for her girlfriends, well let's just say they weren't exactly Daughters of the American Revolution. Like many people on the Deuce she never seemed to sleep, but would on occasion disappear for days on end without any kind of notice. I presumed she was crashing. She would reappear, totally rejuvenated and talking the proverbial mile a minute. She was far from good-looking, but who cared; there was something about her presence that disguised any unevenness in her features. She had large mesmerizing brown eyes that drew you in; once there she could soothe any ache and restore the most troubled of psyches. Being a stripper she had a body to die for, but that's a whole other story. In the years that she was healthy, she gave off a kind of animal sheen and could effortlessly light up any room if the notion was on her. I don't think I ever met a man who didn't think he had a chance while in her company; and yet she was fastidious, to the best of my knowledge. But there were large chunks of time when I didn't see her . . . what can I say?

I could never figure what she saw in me, except that I demanded little from her. After coming from lily-white Wexford, in my eyes she personified exotica. I can't even imagine what I was to her. I loved taking her to those straight midtown Irish bars. She'd get done up to the nines, and always wore the Billie Holiday gardenia in her hair. Add that to her best southern belle accent and she was quite the ticket. I'd put on my tight pinstripe suit and a pair of twin-toned shoes, and we'd make the scene. Irish joints weren't used to her kind of black folk and didn't quite know how to deal with her. And so she'd sashay outrageously around the Green Derby or Flanagan's—a cross between Lawdy Miss Clawdy and a chocolate Scarlet O'Hara. Eventually, she'd go one step over the line—you could take the girl out of the Deuce but the Deuce was rarely far from Cheryl—and we'd be politely escorted to the door. Then we'd head off in tears of laughter to the nearest Blarney Stone where no one was ever asked to leave. I guess, water always finds its own level.

She would usually find some reason not to sleep with me, and I didn't make a big deal of it. I grew used to her ways and took things as they came; besides she never left me totally out in the cold. She knew just how to string someone along. I thought about taking her home, more to show the lads than anything else, but I knew it was impossible. What would she have done in Wexford when she needed to disappear? Gone to church or the county library? It wouldn't have been pretty. At the time, I wanted to go live in Tangiers, do the whole Paul Bowles trip. I asked her to come with me. Figured she'd make out all right there. I'm not even sure she knew what Tangiers was. But she agreed. She liked the idea of making a fresh start. But in the end, she couldn't come up with her end of the money. And then something happened with the band and I went away for a while. By the time I came back she had gone. No one seemed to know where. Margarita heard that she'd started a clean slate in New Orleans.

It might appear that she didn't love me, but I think she did, in her own peculiar way. And so, I've followed her in song to the two other mystical capitals of the United States—New Orleans and San Francisco. She'd fit in well in either. She was a child of her times, though. A real innocent whom the streets had made hard, on the outside anyway. She was at home on the Deuce, where the smack and the coke and the dreams and the fluidity of the scene kept everyone off balance. That suited her. She was always just teetering on the edge—of America and everything else. I hope she's still alive. I somehow doubt it.

14

FORTY SHADES OF BLUE
(For Kevin wherever you are tonight)

Ah, it's midnight on the Bowery
And your feet are soaking wet
And you drank your last brass farthing
You'd sell your soul for a cigarette.
And the sounds from CBGB's
Are comforting to you
Then you think of the green fields of Ireland
And you feel forty shades of blue.

You're back on the drink since September
And your head feels like a sieve
And you know that you're going from bad to worse
But you just don't give a shit
And the hymns from the Sally Army
Sound heavenly and true
Then you think of your friends and your family
And you feel forty shades of blue.

You got a great future behind you
But you're going nowhere fast
Just up and down the Bowery
From Canal Street to old St. Mark's.
And you wonder what she's up to now
Did she really find somebody new

How the hell could she just walk out like that
On your forty shades of blue?

And you wonder how it come to this
Was it always in the cards?
Working is for idiots
And you loved the smell of bars
And the letters that you sent back home
Were full of all the things you'd done
But they don't say you're down there on Bleecker Street
With your hand out on the bum.

Now the dawn's coming up on the Bowery
And you're heartsick and soaking wet
With your tongue hanging out for some Irish Rose
You'd sell you soul for a cigarette
And someday I'm goin' to give up this drinking
And maybe someday I'll win the lottery too
Then I'll go back home to old Wexford town
Paint her forty shades of blue.

Forty shades, forty shades of blue
Ah, Johnny Cash, where are you now
I got such a need of you
Johnny Cash, the man in black
Where are you, Johnny, where are you?
I'm down here on my knees, baby
Down here on St. Mark's waiting for you
And your forty shades of blue, blue, blue, blue. . . .

From Black 47, *independent 1991, and* Fire of Freedom, *EMI Records 1993*
Published by Starry Plough Music/EMI Blackwell Music (BMI)

TELEVISION WAS THE best band on the Lower East Side and everyone knew it. True, the Ramones and Talking Heads became a lot bigger, but there was nothing quite like the icy blue of our Bowery boys.

Tom Verlaine was the far side of cool, while Richard Lloyd's guitar was like a sonic chain saw obliterating all before it. When those two locked horns in CB's, it was as if the shattered glass on the streets outside was sucked back whole into its original panes, before smashing once again into even more infinitesimal smithereens. "Venus De Milo" was a twisted revelation, an anguished, anxious eye opener that for ten revelatory minutes made sense of the chaos we inhabited. Tom and Richard rarely even acknowledged each other onstage, but their guitar lines snaked symbiotically around CB's cobwebbed walls before disintegrating in squalls of controlled feedback. I never caught a hint of reverb or delay effecting their amps, just pure clawing chords, dry and sharp as the January wind that flayed the homeless bums on Houston Street. I liked Billy Ficca on drums and Fred Smith on bass, yet always wondered how the songs would have sounded with a hint of funk or blackness added. But that's a musician's fantasy. On Television's fieriest of nights, even Hendrix might have headed for the hills.

Talking Heads were amazing, too, and they got better every night I saw them, right until the end. I once took a piss next to David Byrne in CB's subterranean men's room. It was at one of their earliest gigs and it was rumored that he was off the boat from Scotland. Just to make him feel at home, I gave him a Glasgow Celtic wink before inquiring how they came up with their sound. Perhaps he felt I was coming on to him for he looked away nervously before stuttering that they were doing their best to be like everyone else—just weren't very good yet. He did not have a Scottish accent. The Heads had a quirkiness that was compelling, and they did eventually add the funk; but they were too self-consciously arty and structured to be capable of really summing up the psycho city in the way Television did. The fans recognized that, even if the reviewers and tastemakers didn't. When the Heads opened, the crowd would often shout, "Turn off the radio, turn on the TV."

The mean streets around the Bowery sizzled with electricity when Television played CB's—no more so than the night Mister Hot Shot Record Company Guy, Clive Davis, arrived in his fur coat to check out the buzz. His entourage swept through the crowd like a panzer division. The band, however, was distinctly unimpressed. It was great to see Tom look right through Clive like he was some Uptown hustler come down to peddle his wares. Not that Clive seemed like a bad type. The two cultures just didn't jell. Television didn't end up on Columbia or Arista and become the household names they should have been. But they did make two albums of jagged magic, and their sound hasn't aged or become background for toilet paper ads.

I was proud of all the bands that played CB's. The Ramones exploded right out of a souped-up comic book and Joey was a gentle gangly giant with a kind word for everyone. A glazed Debbie Harry mistook me for someone else one night, kissed me sweetly on the cheek, and told me how much she'd enjoyed my performance. I presumed she was talking about the stage. The Dead Boys were very underrated but put on some of the best shows, while Suicide's intensity and couldn't-give-a-damn cheesy synth chops never failed to blow me away. So why do people say nothing much happened in the '70s? They obviously didn't visit the Bowery. Or hear the Clash, the Pistols, or Rockpile; and they sure as hell didn't witness Mister Marley's mesmerizing shamanism. Yet, anytime you see the decade portrayed, it's always a crowd of clowns in bell-bottoms swaying to "Rock the Boat Baby," or a gaggle of coked-up wannabe Tony Maneros trooping into that overpriced tourist trap, Studio 54. But you'll never, in a month of Sundays, see Tom Verlaine in black jeans, shredded T-shirt, and chalky face blazing out a string of emaciated chords that could make your hair curl. That might show what the wicked, frantic streets of New York were really all about. And we couldn't have that on TV now, could we? It wouldn't really sell those rolls of toilet paper. So rock the boat, baby, and tell us how much the whole decade was traumatized by Watergate and Mister Nixon, as if anybody on Avenue B gave a rat's ass about what a bunch of dick-heads down in D.C. were up to.

I would sincerely doubt that Kevin ever heard Television, though he lived the nails-scraping-across-metal life that their songs evoked. His musical taste, however, ran more toward Rod

Stewart and Johnny Cash. He was from Corish Park, the same
housing estate that my parents used to live in, and I had watched
him grow up, an appealing but unpredictable boy. He was a twin
and that would prove pivotal in his life. I lost track of him when I
went to the States, but heard that he and his brother went off to
London together. They lived rough like many young emigrants,
squatting in abandoned buildings and living the cider high life, one
foot back in Ireland, the other on the platform of Paddington Station. The details got sketchy, but there was a tragedy and his twin
didn't make it. Then followed the inevitable spaced out-years
coming to some kind of terms with the loss, before Kevin hooked
up with a young American student. They married. And I can see
them now: Kevin and his young bride, radiant after the registry
office ceremony, hair down to their shoulders, in suit and dress—
as formal as they'd ever be—the latent devilment in Kevin's eyes,
the love that loves to love in his love's.

He surfaced in Brooklyn and my brother, Jemmy, who had
risen up the ladder in the construction world, took him under
wing. But Kevin was a dreamer and there was always a new racket,
some new start, accompanied by that eternal twinkle in his eye
that veiled the latent hurt. One day he'd be a super with a plan to
buy a building, another a swimming-pool salesman up in Connecticut. He was devoted to his wife, but you could feel the wildness inside of him, just bursting to get out. He was careful with the
drink back then—holding it at arm's length; but you knew that
some crisis or other would eventually come roaring down the pike
and send him reeling off the deep end. I think he knew it, too. But
he was brave and tried everything for diversion, including his
wife's taste in music. I once attended an Iggy Pop show with the
two of them. I was with Sheila, who was happy to be out on a con-
ventional date with another nice couple—or so she thought. The
place was packed but Kevin shouldered his way through the
crowd until all four of us were jammed up against the stage.

The Ig was in one of his dramatic humors and teased us unmercifully by refusing to come out onstage. His excellent band played
intro after intro; most of us cheered this pantomime, but the less

patient grew tired of the routine. And then he appeared, shoeless, his shirt already off, his muscles gleaming in the strobe lights. He surveyed the hall, a master viewing his minions. Suddenly, he did a perfect back flip and landed on the balls of his toes—still defiantly staring out at us. Apparently, our appreciation for this feat didn't come up to snuff. For he wheeled around and headed back to the dressing room. We howled in dismay and he stopped dead. When he turned back, his penis was out. Pandemonium broke loose. He stood there—a ravaged Adonis—the lines of hard living and experience dug bone-deep into his face. Then he stepped onto the lip of the semicircular stage and slowly padded along it with all the deliberation of a panther, halting occasionally as if about to relieve himself.

I caught a glimpse of Kevin's face. He'd seen God—or the part of Him that resided inside his own wild soul. Another couple of threatening steps and Iggy was towering above us, and there he halted. Now I always loved the guy and had a thing for his outthere behavior; but I had little desire to be pissed on by the man from Michigan. I appeared to be the only one in my immediate circle who felt that way; Kevin was leading the crowd and—to my amazement—Scientology Sheila in a chant of "Do it, Iggy, do it now!" Kevin's eyes were blazing. God in a urinal, and right over our heads, too! I raised my arm to shield my face from the coming flood, but just then the band segued into "China Girl" and Iggy began singing.

Descents can be fast or slow in the city, but they're always relentless. I don't know what happened to his marriage, but I saw Kevin on the street soon after that. He was selling ties on St. Mark's at ten in the morning, singing a convoluted medley of Johnny Cash and Rodney, his whiskey-breath wildness frightening away any potential clients. He didn't give a goddamn. Another afternoon, I saw him heading uptown. I had some money problems at the time, and Kev was always good for a laugh, so I hailed him. He was friendly as ever and delighted to see me, but confessed he was a bit strapped for time as he was on his way to San Diego. When I inquired what flight, he doubled up from the laughter: "I'm hitching, man!" The son of a bitch was in a hurry to beat the rush-hour traffic through the Lincoln Tunnel—not a bother on him, not a penny either. He gave me a hug and hurried off to the far side of America, full of hope or illusion, a man on a mission. I watched him go: the mucky kid with the twinkle in his eye who used to ride tinkers' donkeys around the fields of Corish Park. The whole thing was absurd. I ran after him and took him to the nearest Citibank machine and added another $50 to my burgeoning overdraft. He promised he'd send a card when he arrived. And he did, about a month later. I had it on my wall for years—a symbol of hope. If Kevin could make San Diego on $50, then why couldn't I conquer the world with my Citibank Checking Plus?

He should have stayed there. Hadn't he learned any lessons from Ratso Rizzo? I'm sure love had something to do with his eventual return; but it's a lot easier be a bum in languid sunshine than freeze your butt off in a screeching Manhattan winter. His wife took him back a number of times, and then one day he became a fixture around St. Mark's and the Bowery. At first, he was pretty together, found a doss house for himself every night. For Kevin was resourceful and, when the mood was on him, he could draw dollar bills out of thin air. He was also a shark of a darts player and had graduated with honors from Tommy Roche's Pub in Wexford, no place for the shaky of hand or the faint of heart.

What he used to do for love, he now did for money. His main fleecing spot was a joint on St. Mark's. He had his own set of custom-designed feathery darts; they were too light and sensitive for me, but Kevin could toss them through the eye of a needle. He would spend hours polishing his moves until he spotted a sucker. This would usually be a wannabe Paddy in from the 'burbs, or some idiot who'd spent a month in London and now fancied himself the Chancellor of the Exchequer. Kevin could smell their illusions a mile away. As soon as he had their attention, he would aim for a triple or double 19 and bounce the darts off the wire onto the floor; this setup would be accompanied by much lamenting at his fading skills.

Eventually, the sucker would propose a game, usually for a couple of bucks and drinks. Kevin would continue his wild throwing until the last minute, then come from way behind and just manage to pip his prey at the post. He would then drop to his knees and praise the good Lord in Heaven for his luck. The sucker would let the money and drinks ride and go double or nothing for the next game, and the one after that as Kevin's method acting reached heights never even conceived at HB Studios. The anointed would always think they were in with a chance until they reached the magic $64 loss. Occasionally, one might be drunk enough to cough up $128, or on one memorable occasion, even $256.

Those were the good nights. But there were others, like when he got a tooth knocked out by a bartender, sick of his customers being bilked; and the worst, when a cab sideswiped him on the Bowery. He found a new home, too: on the platform of the downtown Spring Street train station. It was a rough winter and one day I saw him limping around Cooper Union. He hadn't seen me, nor had time to put on his devil-may-care face. I knew he wasn't going to make it. I gave him whatever money I had and headed home. I was walking down Broadway when the Phil Ochs's song, "There But for Fortune," came to mind. I banished it as best I could. I had my own life to lead, later for Kevin! But I'd seen the great Ochs down and out at the bar in Folk City, arguing with himself and the world, and the image of him swinging in his sister's house out in Far Rockaway wouldn't go away.

When I got home, I picked up the phone, called Dominic Kiernan, the mayor of Wexford, and told him what I'd seen. About a week later, I got a call from Kevin's sister in London. If I could find Kevin and persuade him to go, there would be a ticket waiting for him the next day with Virgin Airlines out at Kennedy Airport. I couldn't believe it. There were so many times that I hadn't picked up the phone in other circumstances. Was it that simple? I called Jemmy, who was well able for Kevin's wildness. He promised to take him in, lock him up for the night, and put him on the plane the following day—if I could find him.

Have you ever tried to track down an alcoholic in New York City? Well, I had a couple of things to go on: it was unlikely he'd be drinking up at the Plaza or the "21" Club. I started with the darts bars. Oh, they remembered him well, but he was banned from all of them now. Someone said that a sailor had stomped his sacred darts into pieces and that Kevin had flipped. I tried the wino joints down below Houston and got some leads that he was last seen drinking up at the Jefferson on Fourteenth—not a good sign. But no sight of him there or anywhere else. I gave up.

I actually felt better about myself. I'd given it a good shot. To hell with the whole thing! I figured I'd head down to McSorley's and have a couple as a reward for my good intentions. On a frigid day, there's nothing quite like Mattie Maher's blazing potbelly stove to chase the tremors away. I was rounding the corner on Seventh when I almost tripped over Kevin's long legs. There he was, sitting on some steps, drinking a 40 and in the height of good humor. He obviously had come into some money and a change in fortune, for he was freshly shaved, showered, and newly outfitted. He was delighted to see me and wanted to pay me back the $50 from the San Diego trip. Told me he had a new girlfriend, was out doing job interviews, and life couldn't be better.

All this in the course of a week? He caught my confusion and wondered what was the matter. We looked straight at each other, and he held my gaze for a couple of moments, then backed off; but not before I saw the old hurt lurking around in there. I couldn't tell if it had to do with his brother or his wife, but it was back and it was real and it would be the death of him in New York City. With that, a truck pulled off, and an icy blast of wind surged across Cooper Square and hit us both head on. I didn't know about a new girlfriend, clothes, or job interviews, but I knew that one more slip and this Wexford cowboy wouldn't be riding off into the sunset. I rattled off his sister's offer. He took it totally in stride and said: Sure, nothing wrong with a little visit to London and he'd be delighted to hook up with Jemmy and spend the night out in Brooklyn reminiscing; and that just by chance he happened to have his passport with him and that he could ring the new girl who was very family-oriented anyway, and would totally understand him rushing off to London and out of her life for a couple of weeks. Just like that—just like Kevin.

There was many the slip twixt the cup and the lip, and much adventure before Jemmy poured him safely on the Virgin airliner. Kevin has had his ups and downs since then. Dominic, the angel of light in this story, failed to get reelected. I can't speak for Wexford town, but I know its many emigrants are the poorer without his selfless concern for us all. And Kevin? Well, there's no happy ending to this story. But he's alive, and I'm told he can still shake a Rod Stewart leg when the humor is on him. He's heard of "Forty Shades of Blue," but never actually heard it. Dominic, who is still his long-suffering sponsor, told me that he'll play it for him sometime—when the moment is right. I have something else for Kevin. It, too, awaits the proper moment.

A couple of years back, I was standing in line in a coffee shop down in Tribeca. The woman behind me tapped my shoulder. She was dressed formally and tastefully, late thirties I would imagine, self-confident, and successful, but with a hint of doubt and even hurt in her eyes. I had been dreaming, as one does in those situations, and figured she knew me from the band; yet there was something familiar about her that I couldn't quite place. She wasn't surprised that I didn't recognize her. We hadn't met since the Iggy Pop gig. Jesus, how many lifetimes ago was that? Though, when I looked at her closely, it wasn't hard to see the girl behind the woman. She was now a lawyer in a firm devoted to family affairs—in particular, battered women. We talked for a minute and I told her about Kevin and how he'd ended up back in Wexford. She seemed relieved that he was safe and sound, but didn't want to hear any more. It wasn't that she was being unkind, but she'd obviously been through a lot and had come to terms with the past. She saw no profit in revisiting it. This put a bit of a pall on the conversation, for we had little other points of reference. I was about to turn back to the counter when she asked me if I would do her a huge favor. I was reluctant. To be honest, I was a bit miffed at her refusal to hear about Kevin—no matter what she'd been through, it seemed cruel to me. She caught the tone of my voice and said I'd understand in due course. She asked me to meet her there at the same time the next day.

I almost forgot and was late arriving. She was still waiting but impatient to be gone—some appointment or other, or more likely she just wanted to get this episode behind her. She handed me a package, wrapped up and addressed to Kevin. She said it was all that remained from their life together. She was remarrying in a couple of months and wished to make a new start, all connections broken with the past. She couldn't bear to burn the package or throw it out; and then, by chance, she'd run into me. Would I take it, look after it, and, if I judged the circumstances right, give it to Kevin?

I didn't want to get involved. I don't know why. It wasn't that big a deal. There was real pain in her eyes; it was obvious she couldn't wait to get away from me. She took my silence for affirmation and stood up to go. The package remained on the table between us. She said thank you, though I still hadn't agreed to anything. She turned and tried to keep it all together while walking out. I could tell she was fearful that I might call her back. And then she was out the door. I watched her through the window. She barely smiled and then walked off down Church Street in her well-cut suit.

I sat there drinking a coffee and tried to ignore it. But I couldn't take my eyes off that bloody package. Eventually, I ripped it open. Easier said than done, for she had wrapped it as if it was going around the world in eighty days. It gradually emerged from its mass of thick brown paper and scotch tape—their wedding album. And there they were, Kevin and his young love, radiant after the registry office ceremony, hair down to their shoulders, suit and dress, as formal as he'd ever be, the latent devilment in his eyes, the love that loves to love in his love's.

It's buried in my drawer now under a mass of Black 47 memorabilia. Occasionally, when I'm searching for something, I come across it. The next time I talk to Dominic, I'll ask him if the time is right yet.

15

CZECHOSLOVAKIA

One bright and sunny morning, down by Avenue B
As I was returning home from a night of debauchery
I met me landlord, Boris, "Yoh," says he,
"Would you ever go over to Czechoslovakia
And marry me daughter for me?"

He waved a pistol and five thousand dollars in me face
"She better be a virgin when she hits the States!"
I told him I had some business with the Pope in Rome
So he threw in a ticket to Italy on me way back home.

Would you ever go over to Czechoslovakia
Marry me daughter for me?
She's the finest girl in Prague that you'll ever see
Her name is Citizen Gerty, a Communist is she
She wants to come to America, be a capitalist just like me.

When I landed in 'Slovakia I drank a dozen pints
But when I caught a glimpse of Gerty I nearly died of fright
She was six feet in her stockings, she viewed me with dismay,
"Is this the best they can do for me in the dear old USA?"

But despite me splitting headache, I wooed her like a man
Very soon thereafter, we were married in Prague
I remember Boris's pistol, me vow of chastity
But when she pinned me to the bed that night, I gave up instantly.

Bright and early next morning,
I went to see the Pope in Rome
Gerty left for America
To make New York her home
She landed down on Avenue B looking for a mansion grand
But Boris was drunk, the building stunk, the city was mad
She'd been had
This was the height of depravity
Not what she'd seen on MTV.

I wasn't faring much better with the Holy Father in Rome
Some Turkish wise guy had whacked him and he wasn't even at home.
So I landed back in New York, oh so sad,
Stared down the barrel of Boris's gun, Jeez was he ever mad.

He accused me of buggering his daughter, to make matters worse
She'd spent over twenty grand in Macy's and in Saks
She sat there in her underwear, gave me a dirty wink
But when I thought about the credit cards
Me love began to shrink.

So we drove her out to Kennedy, fourteen trunks and all
We said a prayer for the dear old Holy Father back in Rome.
As her plane rose over Rockaway, Boris, he said to me,
"Would you ever go over to Czechoslovakia,
Marry me daughter for me?"

From Green Suede Shoes, *Mercury Records 1996*
Published by Starry Plough Music (BMI)

KEVIN WASN'T THE only one suffering from heartsickness. I was
going through hell with Sheila. As they would say back in Wexford:
What ailed me to fall in love with a Scientologist? We had been
living together on First Avenue for some years; and in typical L.
Ron Hubbard fashion, she had sorted out various problems in my
life. I had come to some kind of terms with heavy drinking, and my

financial affairs were in order—in fact, we were running a successful typing business, and when I wasn't out with the band, I could be found hammering away at an IBM Selectric for a buck fifty a page. Still, it was a tempestuous relationship. Apart from the clash between the rock 'n' roll lifestyle and the squeaky clean demands of her religion, Sheila was attractive and men tended to get smitten with little difficulty. It wasn't exactly that she led them on; more like, she never dispatched them with the speed that I considered appropriate. Trying to balance my innate jealousy with a belief in Aleister Crowley's admonition to "do what thou wilt shall be the whole of the Law" caused me all sorts of turmoil.

Still we were happy in our own way until the Major Thinkers began to "make it." This was the band that Pierce and I had put together after the demise of Turner and Kirwan of Wexford. Jesus, talk about jumping out of the frying pan and into the fire. What an opening line this new name gave to critics! I remember Geoffrey Stokes, a future friend, writing in the *Village Voice* about a show we did with Moving Hearts. "Moving Hearts are major thinkers, the Major Thinkers, alas, are not!" And yet, we were popular around the Lower East Side. I'm not sure how you'd describe the music for it mutated through the early '80s: punky new wave spiced by a dash of Irish and a little attitude, with the obligatory cool haircuts and some good melodic songs.

In what now seems like a constant search for an identity, we were always trying something different to attract attention. We once toured the Midwest with UB40 in the midst of a heat wave, dressed in tweed jackets, shirts, plaid ties, and cavalry twill trousers. One night in Detroit, we had to use a razor blade to cut Hammy, our drummer, out of his sweat-soaked pants. The UBs were at first amused, but then impressed that we stayed the course despite the meltdown heat. You can't say that we didn't have commitment. It's pretty hilarious, but we were considered so hip that CBS Records actually paid us a weekly fee to hang out with Cyndi Lauper and help her transition from the rockabilly look of Blue Angel to what she eventually became. What a joke! We were just a crowd of bozos who dressed up for the gig and returned to black jeans and T-shirts as soon as we'd scored at the party. Meanwhile, Cyndi instantly sussed out the plastic nature of the scene and, with one stroll through the thrift shops of the East Village, reinvented her whole look and career. We continued to send our invoices to CBS with the message that Cyndi was starting to shape up, and managed to stay on the payroll for a couple of extra months. Such was the scene.

Ironically, this small boost in my income—not to mention self-esteem—signaled the end of my domestic bliss with Sheila. I became too big for my boots to be bothered with such mundane matters as a flourishing typing business. I wanted to hit the nightlife and get an even hipper haircut. This latter I achieved by having a green lightning streak burned into my orange hair. I think I still have a groove in my scalp from the treatment. To add insult to injury, around this time our song "Avenue B Is the Place to Be" received major airplay. We were suddenly the toast of First Avenue, the local boys who had made it: out all night and full to the gills and nostrils with the requisite perks of the day. This did not sit well with Sheila. She did what any self-respecting follower of L. Ron Hubbard would do—threw me out.

I can't even remember what the last actual argument was about, except that it continued all night, as these things do; and after the door slammed I found myself walking up Avenue B in a drizzly early-morning rain. Talk about Gordon Lightfoot! I had nothing with me but a change of clothes, my guitar, and a fractured heart; nor did I have any idea where I was heading or what my next move would be. The East Village was deserted except for a posse of punks departing the Robots, an after-hours on the avenue. One of these was a bleary-eyed stringer for *Rolling Stone*. He had been a little contemptuous of my newfound fame but, upon hearing my story, advised me to call everyone I knew and tell them of my plight.

It was as good advice as any. I had at one time rented some rooms, a mere ten yards away, from Boris, a crazy Czechoslovakian ex–border guard. It was worth a shot. There were no bells on the cast-iron door; but when I shouted up his name, Boris looked out the window unshaven and clothed only in his wife-beater undershirt and a droopy pair of off-white drawers. He must have bolted down the stairs for he had the front door opened within seconds and was greeting me like the returning prodigal. As it turned out, one of his tenants had OD'd the day before and an apartment was available on the spot. Within thirty minutes of leaving Sheila—her bitter denunciations still ringing in my ears—I had in my possession the keys of my new home. I was later to find out that this had little to do with my delightful personality. Boris had initiated a form of racial cleansing in his building and would have taken in Jack the Ripper, as long as he was white.

My new landlord was a recovering alcoholic and in his drinking days had found great friendship and comfort in Irish saloons. He could hum a passable version of "Danny Boy" in a broad Czech accent, and was quite impressed that I was a musician, especially one who made a bit of money from the game and could even be heard on the radio from time to time. One had to tread carefully with Boris, however, as he saw life very literally. He had a glowing letter of thanks from Ronald Reagan on his wall. This was for a hefty donation he had sent the Gipper. When I told him he was probably the only Republican on East Third Street, he looked at me with scorn. "I come America be rich, so join rich people's party. Make sense, no?" It didn't then, but it does now.

And yet he presided, with much understanding for the frailties of human nature, over his erratic empire. My neighbor, Maria, a buxom, foulmouthed Puerto Rican, did a brisk business in trading her favors behind the hallway stairwell. She would stride past you, nose in the air, her customers pulling up their trousers in her wake, as if this was the most natural situation imaginable. And in a way she was right, for one eventually got used to this sight and the operatic haggling that preceded it. On the second floor lived a man who kept a roomful of chirping yellow canaries, while his neighbor's pride and joy was a fearsome fighting cock that aggressively greeted the dawn from his windowsill come hell or high water. On the floor above them, an old Polish couple occupied an apartment whose floor was raised over two feet with a bed of garbage; they slept upon this among a dozen or more wild cats. They had no truck with electricity, and the rest of us lived in fear of a fire from the candles that they kept lit at all hours. A one-legged, but remarkably agile, heroin dealer lived across the hallway from me. The remaining apartments were occupied by a shifting selection of junkies, whores, transients, and welfare recipients. These latter were aristocrats in Boris's eyes, as the government remitted their rent checks as regular as rain. He could often be found in the hallways haranguing his other tenants in a plaintive mixture of Spanish, Czech, and English. Not surprisingly, the main subject of these encounters appeared to be the many and fantastic reasons why people would not pay their rent.

Smack ruled Third Street. It was a homegrown industry and provided employment for many locals, as well as a never-ending store of unmitigated heartbreak. You went to bed with the cries of the dealers outside your window, and you awoke to the singsong tones of "357—357," the name of most popular brand of the day. There was an ever-changing hierarchy of dealers, abettors, and users on the street. The Iceman, as he was called, rarely came around, and when he did it was usually in a large yellow Cadillac. Beneath him a group of lieutenants oversaw the action. They tended to rank in importance from their chief who occupied the choicest spot on the corner of B and Third. I'm not sure whether this was because the crossroads made flight more possible in case of a raid, or that those closer to Avenue A had to endure the wrath of the Parish Priest of the Holy Redeemer Church who led sporadic processions of protest up the block. Business would then grind to a halt and the dealers would gravely and, without any trace of irony, cross themselves and murmur an Ave Maria, until the good father and his few followers retreated back into the church, his point made, if not taken.

The papermen were next down the ladder. They were so called because they rolled up their *El Diario* or *Daily News* and beat the junkies into obedient lines before doling out their daily fixes. This had a twofold function: to maintain order and humiliate the users, thus keeping them in psychological as well as physical debasement.

These papermen, on the whole, tended to be very courteous to the apartment dwellers and would, at your approach, beat an opening in the line to allow you unimpeded entry to your doorway. Next came the watchers on the street and the rooftops, their function being to signal the approach of a cop car or undercover narcotics men. This occupation was usually doled out to kids and the semi-handicapped, as it was a rarity to see a cop on Third, although the precinct was almost within hailing distance.

The toilet workers, as they were called, were lowest on the totem pole. This vermin guarded the doors of abandoned build-ings and charged a dollar entry to the junkies, who could then shoot up in peace within the cool, filthy interiors. Plunging a spike in one's arm on the street was frowned upon for reasons of public relations. It was not uncommon, however, for junkies to forego the dollar admission and seek out the nice dark spot under our stairwell. Most, however, did not consider this worth the stress, as they would have to deal with the shrieks of Maria when she arrived to conduct her own business.

The whole regime might sound formidable, as well as oppres-sive, and it was, but it's amazing how one can get used to the direst and most threatening of circumstances. And, to be fair to them, the hierarchy did its best to ensure that those who lived on the block not be discombobulated by this round-the-clock bazaar. Jesus Ortiz, who ran the show outside our building, could be downright charming and was willing at the drop of a hat to pass the time of day discussing the merits of both the Yankees and Mets, depending on your preference. In his leisure hours, he drank in the Kiwi and always sent me over a Heineken accompanied by a very formal nod of appreciation. Although, I didn't care for his pro-fession, I always accepted this token of regard. For I too was desirous of maintaining good community relations and, besides, was in no great rush to commit suicide.

Boris had no such compunctions. Obviously, something unto-ward had gone down between him and Jesus before my arrival, for their relationship was frigid to the extreme. One night I received a phone call from Boris. This was how he conducted business with me. Social niceties were handled on the stairway, but business was always conducted by phone, even though we lived only two floors apart and I could hear his actual voice through my window. Not on the night in question: in a harsh whisper, he instructed me to turn out my lights and keep an eye on the street, but, under no circumstances, show my head. From what I could gather, he was about to shoot Jesus. Before I could protest, he hung up.

This scenario presented a number of problems: I had no wish to witness a homicide, even on a scumbag like Jesus. On the other hand, I was some months behind on my rent and my compliance with the task at hand seemed to mean a great deal to Boris. I crawled over to the window and raised an eyelid above its lip. The Iceman was on one of his infrequent visits, and Jesus was introducing him to some new employees, with all the deference one might afford a visiting CEO. There was a sudden explosion that ricocheted around the narrow street and I hit the deck with alacrity. When curiosity got the better of me, and I managed to surface, the Cadillac had already burned rubber around the corner and the previously bustling street was deserted except for Jesus who was imploring the mother of God to intercede for him, as he crawled off toward Avenue B. I, too, crawled across the floor, but into bed and stayed there until the following afternoon when I judged it safe to venture out again.

Boris barely commented on his marksmanship except to lament that "Jesus son of bitch! No stand still!" Ronald Reagan would have been proud of this newly minted American vigilante. Jesus resumed his duties some weeks later, limping along on a gold-topped cane. He now studied everyone with a gimlet eye, and I shuddered at the very sight of him, for fear my guilt by association would be obvious. Nonetheless, this shared secret between Boris and me served to deepen the bonds of friendship, and he often thereafter invited me to his apartment for a belt of various potent European liquors. Even though he himself no longer drank, he still liked to be around drinking. He also proudly showed me his private arsenal of weapons; this ran from Saturday-night specials to an Uzi automatic that scared me shitless. I didn't realize it at the time, but he was obviously checking out my moral fiber and prepping me for the great adventure that would soon be at hand.

Though we now slept in different apartments, Sheila and I decided to see each other again on a trial basis. Love dies hard, I suppose. Boris was lost in admiration for her Scientology work ethic and advised me to marry her, proclaiming that that there was nothing so great in American democracy as a woman who might be willing to provide for her man. At any rate, he was very interested in our relationship, not only our degree of devotion to each other, but how this played out in any financial dealings we might have. Thus one evening, after a long interview on the stairs concerning this very subject, he summoned me by phone to attend him at his apartment. He was very nervous and paced the floor, insisting that I knock back a couple of hefty dollops of some foul-smelling Czechoslovakian hooch. He took my hand in both of his, looked deeply into my eyes, and offered, what I considered, a very attractive business proposition. For $5,000 and two years' free rent, I was to write to his only daughter, Gerty, fake a postal romance, go to Czechoslovakia, marry the lady in question, bring her back legally to the United States, and then, without any fuss or bitterness, divorce her and return her to the bosom of her father. There was only one snag: I would have to reside behind the Iron Curtain until I could persuade the Czech comrades that I was, indeed, bona fide in my intentions. Boris assured me that I was well up to the task. Oh, and one extra condition: Gerty must remain a virgin. He stroked the Uzi for emphasis and cast a very hooded but threatening glance my way. When I blanched, he hastened to reassure me that since I was in love myself with a woman who one day might provide for me, such temptation should not be hard to overcome. He then showed me the picture of a healthy pigtailed maiden dressed in native peasant outfit who reminded me of a less than svelte Eva Braun.

I was somewhat taken aback at Sheila's lack of enthusiasm for the project. In fact, she was downright hostile about me tying matrimonial knots with any woman, let alone someone connected with Boris, a man she deemed to be of a lowly moral character. She then gave me an ultimatum. Forget Boris's scheme or forget her! Try as I might, I could not get her to grasp the complexity of the situation. I didn't want to lose her affection, or a return to her very comfortable apartment on First Avenue; still, I had given my word to Boris and I had seen what happened to Jesus when relations had deteriorated with my trigger-happy landlord.

I had to come up with a substitute, but my friends either thought I was joking or else didn't want anything to do with an Uzi-toting, unhinged, Central European ex–border guard. There was only one man up to the task: Jim No-Coats. (A semi-legendary figure around the Village, he had gained this name for his refusal to wear more than a skimpy silk shirt on the bitterest of winter days.) James was well beyond weather, and many the other thing, too. Neither did he foresee any problem with the proposition, even down to the fact that I should get a $1,000 brokerage fee and the two years free rent, on its successful completion. He did, however, have one extra condition. Boris would have to throw in a ticket to Rome on Jim's way back from Czechoslovakia, for he had business of an important nature to discuss with the pope. This nugget of information didn't phase me in the least. Jim had often intimated that he had close, if not familial, relations with Jesus Christ Himself in Heaven, or wherever He happened to reside in those crazy days.

It was quite the meeting between these prospective in-laws. I did my best to smooth things over. Jim, to give him his due, did his part, too. He tied up his gorgeous waist-length golden hair in a ponytail and wore one of his more conservative outfits for this summit, although his scarlet silk shirt with the gold trimmings still managed to take the sight out of Boris's eye. However, couture aside, the sticking point in the deal, as I feared, was this infernal ticket to Rome. Boris smelled a rat and demanded to know Jim's business with "El Papa." No-Coats declined to answer, circumspectly stating only that this was a matter between him and the representative of Christ on Earth, and was thus entirely private, confidential, and beyond any bargain. From my neutral, if invested, perspective, it seemed as if we were going around in circles, for neither of the principals was in a mood to compromise. In the end, I proposed that the extra flight to the Eternal City would have to come from the $5,000. Both declined to comment. Then, in an exercise in brinkmanship, Jim stood up as though to leave—though he later told me he was looking for the bathroom. Boris rose, too, but said that this compromise seemed eminently fair, whereupon a deal was struck.

Jim entered into the postal courtship with his accustomed passion and dispatched biweekly ten-page missives declaring his undying love and affection for Gerty; these tended to be a little florid for my taste, but were based on her beauty in the pigtailed photo, not to mention the testimonials he had received from her father as to her general comeliness and unquestionable virtue. Gerty replied with rather terse notes in Czech—that Boris labored over in translation—to say that the feeling was reciprocated; in various addenda, she did appear curious about the length of Jim's hair, along with questions on what shampoo and conditioner he tended to use. And so it went, until a month had passed, when Jim wrote that he might possibly die of a broken heart unless Gerty promised to be his bride. Gerty hastily replied that she could not stand by and be responsible for such a tragedy and so would accept.

The die was cast, the ticket bought, and after a meal of rice and beans on Avenue B, Boris and I bade farewell to Jim who, ever parsimonious, took the bus out to Kennedy and headed for Prague. He did not write for some weeks, much to the anger of Boris. In fairness to him, he had to overcome a number of difficulties. Neither Gerty nor anyone in her village spoke English. This collection of shacks was in the deep sticks over a hundred kilometers from Prague. Gerty, too, was not quite what she had seemed in the photo. Gone was the pigtailed comely maiden. She now favored miniskirts and had come into her own as it were, standing five feet ten inches in her nyloned feet to Jim's five feet six inches in his Docs. Not surprisingly, she also outweighed him by nearly thirty pounds. Because of these circumstances and certain of Jim's statements—ever principled, he refused to tell a lie—the comrades were suspicious of his intentions and, given the paranoia of the times, feared that he might be on the personal payroll of Ronald Reagan because of some statement Boris had made on the visa application. They insisted that he stay at least another three months to prove the depth of his ardor. Boris, to his dismay, was forced to telegraph even more money to preserve Jim's façade as a smitten wealthy American.

In these months, there were many gaps in communication and on Third Street, Boris and I could do little but speculate. The strain was getting to him and he disappeared for long periods, returning with a troubling bouquet of alcohol and mints on his breath. Then one day, he accosted me on the stairs. He was smiling like a lunatic and showed me a letter from Jim, along with a picture of the wedding. Relief! The hooks were well and truly attached. All that needed to be done was to pull these two fish home. Still, I was a little apprehensive when I saw the fervor of the wedding kiss, for I well remembered the stipulation regarding virginity. But who was I to darken such a promising moment? Jim was already bound for Rome and Gerty would be in New York within the week. I was off to the Midwest with the band; Sheila had signed up for a new Scientology course—my gift to her for her love and ongoing devotion—the cost of which was to be paid from my share of Jim's dowry. All was well with the world.

I was in Cleveland when the news broke that the pope had been whacked. Details were sketchy, but it seemed that the gun had been fired by a foreigner. Jesus Christ on a bike, No-Coats had taken out John Paul and assured his place in history! I must confess that there was a little selfish apprehension involved. Could the deed be traced back to an Irish rock singer and his Czechoslovakian landlord on the Lower East Side? Had No-Coats snagged one of Boris's guns during our meeting in the apartment? In the end, I was greatly relieved to discover that a right-wing Turk with Bulgarian left-wing connections had instead plugged El Papa. However, security had been upped all over the continent, flights bumped, and a general blacking out of communications prevailed.

Boris waited a lonely day and night at the airport for Gerty's plane; when it finally arrived, though her name was on the passenger list, his daughter was not to be found. He thereupon took a cab back into the city and went on a monumental bender. As luck would have it, Gerty arrived on the very next flight from Prague with no loving father to greet her. With nothing but a scrap of paper and a scribbled address, she managed to take a cab and arrive at the family hacienda on Third, in an understandably stressed-out state. From Boris's flowery letters she appears to have been expecting a beachfront in Malibu or a chalet in Aspen at the worst; instead she had to park ass, bags, and expectations on the sidewalk and wait through the humid night in the midst of the heroin bazaar for her father's return.

After years with barely a tipple, Boris's hangover was ferocious and when he eventually staggered down Third, he could scarcely see his daughter, let alone give her the welcome she expected. If Gerty had been merely cold and unresponsive, who could have blamed her? But instead, she flew into a rage that brought Jesus and other members of the hierarchy running to mediate, for fear that the cops might be called and a good day's capitalism ruined for all. Despite everyone's best intentions, the longed-for reunion was not off to a good start.

Things were somewhat smoothed the next day when Gerty discovered that Boris's credit cards could open the door to a consumerism that heretofore she had only dreamed of. This spree, or more likely assault, that centered on Macy's and Saks, continued for some days while Boris worried that Gerty's profligacy might single-handedly swamp Mr. Reagan's growing deficit. In a couple of furtive phone calls, he disavowed his plastic, causing a tremendous rupture in relations with his Marxist daughter.

Meanwhile, the man who could have greased the wheels of the reunion was in a bit of a spot in Rome. Informing the authorities that he had information that could lead to the spiritual uplifting of the fallen John Paul was probably not the wisest move, given the circumstances. The end result was that Jim No-Coats never got to see the pope, and despite his protests was sent packing back to the States. Being possessed of a serene and accepting nature, he considered this to be God's will and decided, from then on, to confine his evangelical mission to America. All very well for an unattached prophet, but he was now a married man. Within hours of his arrival, he was informed by his wife of the singular cruelty of her father and that he, No-Coats, must step up to the plate and provide for her in the manner to which she had grown accustomed. This could be arranged, declared Jim who did not take his marital duties lightly; Gerty was more than welcome to take up residence in his single room of a midtown SRO hotel. Boris, who had now seriously taken to the bottle, returned home to find a note initiating him into his worst nightmare: that Jim and Gerty's relationship had progressed beyond the platonic.

I arrived back from the Midwest into this maelstrom, dizzy, disoriented, and many pounds lighter—this was the infamous UB40 tour where we wore the tweed jackets et al. My answering machine was reeling from Boris's livid messages, many promising dire recrimination. Added to this onslaught were some increasingly frantic ones from Sheila requesting that I pony up the money I had promised to fund her Scientology pursuits, for it was a firm tenet of L. Ron's philosophy: no muddy—no study! I began to wonder if a little trip home to visit my mother might not be in order and made some hasty inquiries from Aer Lingus about the availability of emergency seats to Dublin. I was to find out that, while the national airline put great emphasis in faith and hope, charity was not one of their strongest suits.

Events were moving fast. Gerty was hardly enamored by the luxury afforded in Jim's spartan room; she fled the coop as soon as her husband went back to work. I heard through the grapevine that father and daughter had reconciled, but there was no sign of them on Third Street. Perhaps, they had taken a trip: a little sightseeing in D.C., perhaps, or an excursion to the Catskills or the Shore. The silence was reassuring. Maybe all was turning out well: Jim and I would be paid, while Boris and Gerty would live happily ever after. For a few days, all was quiet on my answering machine except for Sheila's accusatory diatribes. These did not overduly concern me. While L. Ron's followers might have been formidable money collectors, still, to the best of my knowledge, they did not wield Uzis. In fact, I was beginning to wonder if our relationship was destined to be star-crossed. It was one thing being involved with an intense woman, another dealing with the demands of her money-craving, very dead guru.

Then, out of left field, No-Coats arrived at my door. Gerty had called furtively from an apartment in the depths of the Bronx. Unbeknownst to us, Boris had some months earlier leased rooms up there with the intention of setting up house on her arrival. It appeared that things were not working out as planned in this happy household—the shit had hit the fan over her deflowering, an event that Gerty slyly refused to confirm, and Jim considered unlikely. Boris would hear none of it: he was now holding her hostage. Jim, being her legal husband, must rescue her from this alcoholic madman. Upon successful completion of this maneuver, she had assured him with some loving blandishments that they would live happily ever after.

From my own point of view, I felt that we had gone well beyond the bounds of duty. It flashed through my mind that flights to London were much cheaper and more available than those to Dublin. Jim appeared to read my thoughts and shook hands gravely with me. He absolved me from any guilt, but was determined to gird his loins, go to the Bronx, and rescue his lawful wife, no matter how unworthy she might be. Unworthy was rather a genteel way of describing the lady, I groused silently; from my perspective she was nothing but a big, selfish, hysterical, overwrought, and overweight bitch on wheels! But what could I do? I had no choice but to accompany my comrade. Jim would have been a happy evangelical camper plotting a trip to Rome if I hadn't dispatched him on a matrimonial mission to Prague. For all I knew, we had upset the psychic heavens and, but for my intervention, the Holy Father might now be skiing in the Alps instead of lying flat on his arse in the Vatican, plugged like the Thanksgiving turkey.

We were a silent duo on the subway up to Fordham Road. The thought of Uzis, Saturday-night specials, and .357s were never far from our thoughts. It was overcast, stiflingly humid, and the Bronx did not look its best. I had rarely seen it in midday before—almost always in the pulsing nights when the bars were jammed and the laughter uncanned, or even at dawn when the hopes of night still fill your head. Now it seemed gray and morose with its head down against grim reality. It took some time, but we identified the building and found the ground-floor apartment at the end of a long, dimly lit corridor. Then we shook hands and hugged each other, before No-Coats put his best foot forward and rapped on the door. I stepped judiciously to his right, whispering that I would cover that angle in case there was a side door through which Boris would emerge. Coincidentally, this took me out of the line of fire of the Uzi that I was sure the ex–border guard was even now aiming at the door.

We could hear some muffled voices and shuffling footsteps, and then someone looked out the peephole. I had to hand it to No-Coats. He stood there steadfast as a Christian confronting a gladiator. Could I have imagined it, or did a divine glow emanate from his very being? I had no such eternal fire burning within, instead I was shivering to the very soles of my heretical shoes. A number of locks were drawn back and then the door opened slowly. A haggard Boris in his standard droopy off-white drawers wavered unsteadily in the hallway. He totally ignored No-Coats but motioned me inside.

"Take her. She bitch! He her husband." With that he motioned to the four rooms overflowing with a jumble of new furniture, appliances, clothes, knickknacks—some half-opened, but most still packaged. The scene was like unto a Daliesque vision of a consumer society gone apeshit. In the middle of all this stood Gerty in very tasty lingerie, languidly applying mascara while slipping in and out of a number of designer outfits. This activity did not prevent her from hurling a torrent of Czechoslovakian invective at Boris or leaning over and crying on No-Coats's lightly clad shoulder. Boris, for his part, cast himself down on a new couch, still wrapped in store plastic. He was a bitter man, broke, too, by the look of things. For a moment, I considered asking him for an advance on the $5,000 owed for a daughter safely delivered from Soviet hegemony, but on second thought I didn't think the time or the setting appropriate.

I'm not sure if Gerty even said good-bye to her old man, although there was one final furious exchange as she closed the door. By then she was already preoccupied with directing No-Coats, me, and six large suitcases on a safari-like expedition back to the subway. She didn't even acknowledge my presence, except for an occasional bark when she felt that I was lagging in their wake. In any case, I had enough of her and her lip by the time we'd dropped off her baggage at Jim's hotel.

I slept deeply that night but was awakened at dawn by No-Coats on the phone. In the background I could hear anguished screams, while Jim wearily explained that perhaps it would be best for all concerned if Gerty returned to her native land. They had already been in contact with Boris, it seemed, but he had steadfastly refused to fork out the airfare. Jim was the soul of tact and reason but, seeing that I had introduced him to this disastrous affair, could I now do some major thinking and get his lawful spouse off his hands without the cost and bitterness of a protracted divorce case?

I was baffled. But as was my habit in times of stress, I took a walk down the banks of the East River. There, looking out over the dirty water at the Domino Building, the germ of a solution began to crystallize. I called No-Coats from a pay phone, told him to have his wife showered, shaved, and whatever else Central European ladies did to make themselves presentable; but above all she should be packed and ready, for we had a full morning ahead. It took a bit of doing, but in the end all three of us arrived at the door of the Czech Consulate where a well-coached Gerty berated all émigrés, America and Ronald Reagan in particular. She thereupon begged to be repatriated. The comrades were overjoyed at this publicity coup and we skedaddled—with nary a tear or word of good-bye from Jim's wife—right before the media arrived to bear witness to this triumph of Marxism over heartless capitalism. Jim went back to work, I returned to bed, and some days later

Gerty flew home to Prague, a hero to the masses, the six cases full
of the fruits of Macy's and Saks accompanying her.

Boris did not pay us, nor did either of us have the cojones to ask
him. In fact, he never mentioned the incident, until some years
later when he prevailed on me to swear in court that he was crazy.
This did not require perjury for he had taken to addressing
Jesus—the divine, not Ortiz—while prowling around the
building. I even once heard him under the stairwell trying to persuade Monica that her Redeemer was less than happy with her las-
civious conduct. Despite all my efforts, he lost the case and
eventually the building, and returned to his homeland. Soon
after, Sheila and I called it quits. She lives in Clearwater now, close
to the heart of Scientology. Jim fell into some property out in
Montauk and has the best job in the world. He runs a dance studio
and dispenses advice to beautiful young ladies new to the city. He
still does not wear a coat in the dead of winter, but he does show
up at Black 47 gigs every now and again, when we make a point of
playing "Czechoslovakia" for him and the other happily divorced
men present.

16

BOBBY SANDS MP

My name is Bobby Sands MP
Born in the city of Belfast
Divided by religion
I grew up fast
I was stabbed and I was spat upon
Family run out of its home
Only one solution
Turn the whole system upside down
But the system had other ideas
I got lifted for carrying a gun
In a trial without a jury
I got fourteen years from the judge.

Screws beat me up regularly
They couldn't break me because
I had the love of my comrades
And a burning faith in my cause.
Still I left a girl outside pregnant
Married her while on remand
Now I got a son and a pain in my heart
When he doesn't recognize his old man.

Your soul's on ice
But they can't stop the desire
To break on out
When your heart is on fire.

We wouldn't wear their convict clothes
So they stripped us to the bone
Threw in some threadbare blankets . . .
And when they jeered us about our nakedness
As we slopped out down the halls
We wouldn't come out of our prison cells
We smeared shit on their prison walls.

Stuck in an eight-foot concrete box
With a bible, a mattress,
And the threat of violence every day . . .
Can I make it through these fourteen years
Will my son remember my face?
I don't blame her for the separation
But for Christ's sake let him keep his name.

Five simple things we ask of them
Five simple things denied
But Thatcher will not compromise . . .
I ask my mother's permission
To finally break her heart
We have come to a decision
Hunger strike.

Three comrades starve behind me,
I pray to God that my
Death will lead to compromise . . .
I can no longer see your face
My bones break through my skin
I'm going back to Belfast City
You can't cage my spirit in.

From Green Suede Shoes, *Mercury Records, 1996*
Published by Starry Plough Music (BMI)

THEY CAME FROM all over the city, down by subway from Inwood, and the Bronx, over the bridges and through the tunnels from Queens and Brooklyn, or by ferry in from Staten Island. They drove or took buses from Jersey, Connecticut, Upstate, Pennsylvania. They came from far and wide to make their views known and their voices heard outside the British consulate on Third Avenue. They were far from chic, but they wouldn't even have been able to pronounce the word, for what's fashion when stacked up against conviction. They stood out like sore thumbs from stressed-out, emaciated Manhattanites; they were rarely slim and most had never seen the inside of a health club. They had little need for tanning salons either, for their faces were windswept and sunburned, with worry and age lines etched deep from long days on factory floors or in delivery trucks. Many wore spectacles, their eyes clouded from the glare of the cheap overhead lights they worked beneath in offices and storage rooms. But whatever they looked like, there was always a quorum of them tramping up and down the avenue, often silent, but determinedly bearing witness.

They were mostly in their forties and up. Few of the young stepped out with them at first, for it takes years and hard-won experience to have memory of memories. These protesters were mostly second-, third-, and fourth-generation Irish-Americans; although many were descended from the survivors of 1847 who had never left the East Coast—never forgotten either, nor forgiven. More were the sons and daughters of republicans who left in disgust after the Civil War defeat of 1923. They were joined by those who had fled the poverty of both body and spirit in the Ireland of the 1950s. Regardless, they were all part of the tribe, come to protest the imminent death, through voluntary starvation, of a young chieftain.

And make no mistake, Bobby Sands was a leader to these people, with more moral authority than any trumped-up *Taoiseach* back in Dublin. But these craggy souls were hardly the types found schmoozing with Ted Kennedy or Hugh Carey at some Irish consulate soiree. Not a lace curtain to hang between them, they were the faithful who kept the flame of Irish republicanism alive in the back rooms of smoky pubs at Sunday evening socials throbbing with the music of accordions, fiddles, and banjos. These were the ones addressed and solicited by shadowy men from Belfast and Tyrone over on visitors' visas—the hard core who gladly forked out crumpled twenty-dollar bills in the hope that one day a united Ireland might become a reality, and not just another pipe dream fueled by chasers of cheap beer and shots of Power's Whiskey.

Many recognized one another from conventions and other protests; some had even danced together in halcyon days out on the Irish Mile in Rockaway or at the Jaeger House Ballroom up on Lexington Avenue. For the circle was small, if committed and devout. An occasional well-known figure would stand out: an O'Dwyer, or a McCourt, perhaps, or some visiting musician, or up-for-election politician; but for the most part these activists were content with their anonymity. A couple of anarchists made the trek up from the Lower East Side, a few stragglers from Spartacus and other Trotskyite groups added muscle; and when the word spread, there were Tyrone boys aplenty and serious young women from Derry and West Belfast come to keep the faith. But it was the tribe that kept the flag flying in the early days.

They were an odd bunch: serious and cerebral by times, chatty and cliquish at others; but I liked them and admired both their integrity and their single-minded devotion to Irish unity. They had little use for pragmatism, and put even less value on the opinion of the media's scribes and talking heads; I suppose they reminded me of my grandfather. One in particular even looked like him: white haired, squat, and muscular with a face set in granite, conviction cased in steel, all his instincts tuned to the force of his own moral compass. They could be difficult, too, and were often hard to play for at their socials and fund-raisers. The flame of republicanism was all-important to them. If they heard or caught that in one of your songs, then they might turn briefly and acknowledge that you were indeed on the right path; but music was mere background to them. Always, eyes on the prize! And now they had a new focus. Bobby Sands was the man of the moment, and his clock was relentlessly ticking away.

It was as if they knew Bobby from birth, though few had ever met him. But they recognized his type: young Northern revolutionaries, up for the drink and a bit of *craic,* but deadly serious about the new world they would create when the Brits were finally sent packing. The tribe had met them at the Sunday evening socials, put them up at their houses, and kept their pictures on mantelpieces long after they'd gone home. And when these young men were interned, they wrote to them and sent Christmas cards and food parcels to the Kesh and other camps. They stayed in the homes of the young men, too, when they visited the North, and counted down the years until release with their wives, mothers, and girlfriends. Bobby wasn't just a symbol to them: he was a symptom of sixty years of state-approved discrimination and sectarianism. They felt a fierce pride and protectiveness toward him. He was one of their own. That was the difference between them and their native-born Irish detractors. They still had the links with Armagh and Fermanagh, had kept the faith down through the black years of partition, unlike many of us in the South who had become apathetic from British and Free State conditioning.

One of the nasty little secrets of the Diaspora is that most native-born Irish do not care for Irish-Americans. They find their new hosts slow, literal, brash, and unfashionable, rather like country cousins with broad accents and even broader tastes. They call them plastic paddies and find their political beliefs naïve and hopelessly out-of-date. They particularly abhor it when someone from New York or, the Lord forbid, California says, "I'm from Mayo," or "Donegal is my home." The Irish-Americans—taking pride in their heritage—simply mean that their ancestors came from these counties, and by extension so do they. How many times have I winced at the raised eyebrows and sneers of some gobshite just off the boat unwilling to concede, or even welcome, this stretching of a point.

But I'm hardly a one to talk. I came over here as snooty-nosed, narrow-minded, and biased as the worst of them. How could I have been any different? Despite my grandfather's best efforts, I had been subjected all my life to the constant barrage of the British media machine. You can't live on the doorstep of an empire and not be, at least, subconsciously influenced by it. I watched their soccer games, laughed at their comedians, copied their fashions, listened to their music, and absorbed the subtle slant of their newscasts all through my youth. Is it any wonder that it took me years and a continent's distance before I began to break through the lacquer of my conditioning and think for myself?

As it was, I was traveling the country playing for Irish-Americans and thus got a crash course in their hospitality, honesty, and sense of themselves. I had no choice but to enter into discourse with them, learn of their beliefs, aye and of their prejudices, too. In the end, I grew to admire many of them—a tough resourceful people who had fought their way out of the slums of the East Coast, despite the bigotry visited on them. I was incessantly curious about their ancestors, how they got here, what they went through, what kept them going? Many had taken the time and energy to find out, had listened to stories at a parent's or grandparent's knee; others were ashamed that they knew so little, and more didn't give a goddamn one way or the other. Of course, there are morons among them to rival any race. That's a given and there's sweet damn all you can do about it. Still, I grew fond of many Irish-Americans and, as far as I was concerned, they could say they were from whatever back-of-beyond county or one-horse town they cared to. What was it to me?

Back during the Hunger Strikes, the British press sneered at them unmercifully. What else was new? *Punch* magazine had depicted their ancestors as a bunch of thuggish simians. Old habits die hard—old prejudices take even longer. Elements of the Irish press had also mislabeled them as naïve and easily led by Belfast gangsters. They all miss the point and the truth. What I saw on that green line outside the British consulate was a folk memory and even a hatred brought roaring back to life. These people weren't misled. Far from it! Many of them were reliving the fears, anxieties, and loathing of those who had been thrown off the land, discriminated against, or denied a proper education, and who had eventually scraped up the fares to escape from a country that had abandoned them. These activists refused to forget; they were merely keeping the faith with their forebears who had sweated and saved their stray dollars to make better lives for the coming generations. They were the tribe and it was now their turn to give back.

And give back they did. There was a majesty to these people that was humbling. Day after day, they surmounted their own small identities by declaring that this travesty of justice, unfolding three thousand miles away, should not be allowed to happen— just as there was a majesty in Sands: a talented, but little known revolutionary who paid the ultimate sacrifice for a point of principle. And it was all so Irish, too, no matter what the media, British or Irish, pronounced. Sands had invoked an ancient tribal right: when wronged by your more powerful enemy, go sit on his doorstep and starve yourself until the shame causes him to relent.

Margaret Thatcher did not have the sense or the good grace to attempt a meaningful compromise with Sands and his comrades. No matter what one thought of the conflict in the North of Ireland, who could have denied that those prisoners had a political point of view and were pursuing it for political ends? That's what the hunger strike was all about; that's what the ultimate points of principle hinged on. And that's why the protestors lined Third Avenue every minute of the day for months on end, until ten young men starved to death. And when it was over, Irish America was not the same. A new generation had been politicized and would hand down a new folk memory to their children and the generations following.

Eventually, the protest became a cause célèbre. The cameras showed up and so, too, did actors, politicians, and all manner of celebrities; there they remained as the days counted down and Bobby, from his prison cell, won a great parliamentary victory. At first, we thought this might spare him: that the Iron Lady would surely see some sense, or offer a measure of compassion. It was not to be. The heartsickness grew worse, the appeals continued, but, finally, after sixty-six days of torment, Bobby Sands MP slipped into legend. The tragedy was only beginning. The comas, blindness, and bone-sharp bodies of the nine others kept apace with a regularity that never became numbing, only horribly inevitable. And still, Mrs. Thatcher would not bend; indeed, she counts this travesty one of her finest moments. The poor woman. Her own party has already disowned her. History will judge her even more harshly.

In the end, the sacrifice became so horrible and otherworldly that many found it too difficult to keep on protesting at the consulate. But the tribe never faltered or lost faith. Right to the bitter end, they came in by subway from Inwood, and the Bronx, over the bridges and through the tunnels from Queens and Brooklyn, or by ferry from Staten Island. They drove, or took buses, from Jersey, Connecticut, Upstate, Pennsylvania, and I will never forget them.

17

BLACK ROSE

Mister Frankie Diamond was my best friend
We were partners in a business down on C & Seventh
Nothing ever got this good brother down
He was a real live wire in an electric town.
Frankie started hangin' with an uptown girl
A Harlem lady in the social whirl
Saturday night he'd put on his best clothes
Go out steppin' with his Black Rose.

Now Frankie went upstate for a couple of years
A guest of the nation, he was in tears
Called me up, he said, "Hey, friend of mine,
I got one favor to ask you while I'm doin' my time.

She's the Queen of New York City
She bewitch all men's soul
She the blood that flow right through me
Don't be messin' with my Black Rose
Keep your hands off my black, my Black Rosie."

While Frankie was upstate his Harlem girl
Continued to spiral in her social whirl
So I paged her from my gig on East Seventh
I said, "Hey, babe, doin' anythin' round about eleven?"
She said, "Uh-huh" in her uptown voice

So we met at Beirut for cocktails and ice
When she crossed that room in her tight red dress
I wasn't thinkin' of Frankie, I have to confess.

She said, "Hey, best friend, let's go back to my place
I need to fix my mascara and remodel my face."
But it rained on the way back to her house
And when she closed the door she took off her blouse.

She's the Queen of New York City
She bewitch all men's soul
Next thing I know I'm whispering sweet nothings
Lying in bed with my Black Rose
Making love to my black, my Black Rosie
He don't own you
So stay with me tonight . . .

At nights I'd lie there and listen to her breathe
With the sweat on my brow how could she sleep
So deep, so sweet as calm as a rock
While I pushed back the seconds oozing from the clock?
Now the letters I wrote Frankie returned unread
The word leaked out I'd be better off dead
But in the crimson dawn Black Rose would unfold
Drain all the poison from my soul.
Drain me, Rosie, drain me girl

Now I'm standing up here on Forty Deuce
Another terminal man waiting for his bus.
Here come Frankie with his head all shaved
Is that a piece in his pocket or is it a blade?
Now I'm lying face down in the terminal dirt
With a hole in my chest, I don't feel no hurt
I don't want to go to heaven, I've been there before
Just spent two years in paradise with my Black Rose.

She's the Queen of New York City
She bewitch all men's soul
When you go and find her body
Bury me next to my Black Rose
Still in love with my Black Rose
She's up in heaven now my Black Rose
You won't be makin' love to my black
My Black Rosie, he don't own you
So stay with me tonight for the rest of your life . . .

From New York Town, *Gadfly Records 2004*
and Home of the Brave, *EMI Records 1994*
Published by Starry Plough Music/EMI Blackwell (BMI)

FORTY DEUCE

As I roved out one May morning on down by old Times Square
I met a sporting lady, Sweet Nancy was her name,
She said, "Me dearest darling, oh you're so young and you smell so sweet
But you'll age ten years in forty days, down on Forty-second Street."

She took me upstairs to a room with cobwebs on the wall
Said, "Lay down there, me darling, you and I are going to have a ball."
As she kissed me virgin tears away, she sang in her sweet voice,
"Fare thee well, my Forty-second Street, good-bye my Forty Deuce."

In the years to come I had occasion to remember Sweet Nancy's song
For I fell in with bad company and lived my life all wrong.
I did everything forbidden by bible, book, and creed
'Til I'd no more virgin tears to shed down on Forty-second Street.

I fell in with two blackguards, Spider Murphy and Jem Black
We terrorized Hell's Kitchen, we robbed both white and black.
And we never gave a damn about the narcos or the vice
For the days were short but the nights were long down on dear old Forty Deuce.

One night on Seventh Avenue I was accosted by the law
They said, "We've got your number lad, your time is getting short
Take our advice, me bucko, kick the dust up with your heels
And leave your false companions down on Forty-second Street."

But I was young and stupid and loyal to a fault
I had a package in me shirt to deliver to Jem Black
When I handed him his contraband I was pounced on by two narcs
Spider Murphy had betrayed me, farewell my Forty Deuce.

I spent ten years in Sing-Sing going slowly up the walls
With revenge the only motive that kept me alive at all
I came out of there a different man, cruel, vicious but discreet
I bought a gun and I went back home down to Forty-second Street.

I followed Spider Murphy into a church down by Times Square
I blew him to sweet Jesus while he was kneeling at his prayers.
If you're ever looking for Jem Black, don't bother trying home
For he's forty feet down under the Hudson's raging foam.

So fare thee well, Sweet Nancy, give back me virgin tears
I'm going back to Sing-Sing for five and fifty years
Please hold me like the first time and sing in your sweet voice,
"Fare thee well my Forty-second Street, good-bye my Forty Deuce."

Fare thee well, Sweet Nancy, I'll never kiss your lovely mouth no more . . .
Fare thee well, Sweet Nancy, I'll never kiss your lovely breast no more . . .
Fare thee well, Forty-second Street, good-bye my Forty Deuce.

From Green Suede Shoes, *Mercury Records 1996,*
Published by Starry Plough Music (BMI)

BEFORE RENTS GOT out of hand in the mid-'80s, New York City was full of small bars with character and a story. Though they were often dives, each had a life of its own that did not wholly depend on clientele, staff, or owner. One such place was Del Monte's. It was located on the ground floor of Boris's apartment building on East Third Street. A couple had been murdered there in the late '60s and many locals crossed themselves when passing for fear of the evil eye. They weren't kidding. The whole building was jinxed, but I believed it was only superstition. I would discover otherwise later on.

Another such saloon was Downtown Beirut on First Avenue. It was dark and sweaty—even in winter—played the Dead Kennedys and the Clash at ear-crushing volumes and was designed to look like a war zone. Though it gave off a feeling of "anything goes," it was actually run with an iron fist by an elderly Polish lady whom we called Granny, albeit never to her face. I never saw her in action in Beirut, perhaps because the mainly punk clientele only looked fierce and had little stomach for real violence. But she also ran a joint on the corner of First and Houston: a lively establishment with a less fashionable set, it sported a far broader demographic. At nights, a drunken accordion player alternated between polkas and dirgelike improvisations on Chopin's melodies for an audience of Poles, Solidarity groupies, morose Ukrainians, cabbies in need of a shot and a restroom, those in want of relative quiet and cheap vodka, and the detritus that tends to congregate at all great crossroads. I once saw the diminutive, bespectacled Granny leap from behind the bar and pummel a huge psychotic black vagrant with a rusty cast-iron frying pan. The battle was brief, loud, and excruciatingly brutal, and when it was over Granny returned to her perch behind the bar without so much as a comment. Lost in thought, she resumed her usual staring off into the night, while the accordion player continued his gloomy excursions through the Nocturnes, never having opened his eyes or missed a beat.

This would have been a couple of years into Ronald Reagan's presidency when many people, sensing that the jig was up, had become tense and anxious. Reagan, at first, seemed like a joke; but this joke had become sour and was turning on many of us. The man might be looked on with regard in many areas now; but in the East Village he was considered at best a dope and at worst a duplicitous oaf whose support of any gangster to the right of

Attila the Hun led to the rape and murder of nuns down in Central America. History will make that judgment, I suppose. But say what you like about him, the fortieth president and the America he wrought ended the extended '60s, and changed the life we lived down on the Lower East Side.

Maybe it was time anyway. Things were getting a bit stale. I first noticed the change round 1983: people actually boasting about the amount of hours they worked! This was the height of anomaly, as heretofore we only crowed about the hours racked up partying or hanging out. One might stay up all night writing a thesis, making costumes for a performance piece, or finishing a recording, but that would be done under the influence of speed, booze, or some other enhancement, and the brand and amount ingested would be a declared addendum to the achievement. To work on something for the sake of *just* making money would have been considered quite gauche and, when occasionally necessary, would have been whispered discreetly, not crowed to high heaven for the world and your fellow drinkers to hear.

But things were coming to a head throughout the whole community. Yuppies were unaccountably on the march; even Pierce and I were not unaffected by the changing times. Alphabet City, which was basically a dump with cheap rents, had been profiled in magazines all over the world as a happening scene. The trendy poured in wishing to become a part of this illusion. Landlords pricked up their ears; these new arrivals held jobs and could actually pay on a monthly basis. The welfare recipient was no longer the most desired of tenants. That was the beginning of the end. Maybe Boris had a point. Send in a big check to the Gipper and join the party of the rich people!

The music business was in flux, too. Free-form radio had all but disappeared. Even college stations were beginning to flirt with play lists. MTV, which up until then had seemed harmless, was now extending its banal tentacles, and the innocuous pop video, which could have had the makings of a new art form, had already become just another marketing tool. Musicians, as usual too dumb, blind, tired, or acquiescent, didn't realize that our world had been co-opted and that the ground had already shifted beneath our feet.

Oddly enough, the Major Thinkers were at their apotheosis. This is somewhat of a grand word for a new-wave pop band, but apropos the times, since the air was full of such pomposity. Through dint of radio play and live appearances, we had been plucked from the struggling masses and signed to a deal by Portrait Records, a division of the almighty CBS/Epic label. This was your standard unconscionable record contract that every musician would give his left ball to sign. But what the hell, most people had one to spare. Sign anything, our lawyer said, and the earlier and more often the better. He was just as keen to play the great game; and besides, we could pay him back the money we owed for all that free, but disastrous, advice.

Now the haircuts were really coming fast and furious. We were even encouraged to charge them to CBS. It was also pointed out that we should become more high-profile and, to that end, tables, drinks, backstage passes, and other perks were provided us at the Ritz, Irving Plaza, and wherever else apprentice rock stars made the scene in those days. I must have met a million other poseurs, many of whom like myself didn't have a clue what game they were playing or who they were playing it for. I regularly had a pain in my hand, head, and arse, along with a pocketful of business cards, to show for my troubles the following morning.

We were signed to the same management team as Cyndi Lauper. This was a huge advantage because we were able to open for Cyndi on her rise from clubs to sheds and beyond. It was a dizzy effervescent period and it gave me a troubling, if insightful, look at what stardom is all about; but it also served to camouflage the fact that I was finding the whole scene increasingly unsatisfactory. All I knew for certain was that if I drank enough I could bullshit along with the best of them; still, there were the sober moments in the morning when you wondered what you were doing and where this was all leading. But hey, who cared when you had audiences of ten thousand grooving to your songs and you could steal the Dom Perignon from Cyndi's dressing room as soon as she hit the stage.

Cyndi was an amazing performer. I swear she could take the telephone book and turn it into a credible song. Her vocal chops and pop instincts were astounding, and she could alternately shake an audience to within an inch of their lives or transfix them with sheer emotion. She was also driven to succeed like no one I'd ever known, and she had all the talent and mental toughness needed in the dog-eat-dog music business world. But the pressures, some of which she undoubtedly brought on herself, were at a constant white heat. It would have been fascinating to watch, except that it was all happening to a person I cared for. Some accused her of being a control freak, and her conduct at times was outrageous; but, in essence, she wanted things to be right. That was considered a utopian notion in the music business, which, for the most part, was not used to, or prepared for, the success she engendered. Einsteins were few and far between in our world— sound businessmen with vision almost nonexistent. Maybe that's what made the environment so enticing to the many clowns who couldn't wait to become part of the scene. Cyndi had no tolerance for them, and eventually they drove her crazy. I'm so glad to see that she's regained equilibrium as well as respect. For she has few equals when it comes to putting across a song.

Unwittingly, she did something really important for me. She made me question if this was the kind of life I wanted and, more important, if I had the drive to succeed at it. I had the tools. After all, songwriting, despite all the mumbo-jumbo, is a craft and I had put in the years. Inspiration, of course, is needed and God knows where it comes from, but I had more than enough of that, too. The simple fact is: if a song can appeal to an audience of a hundred or a thousand, then that same song, when broadcast on mass radio or television, will appeal to a hundred thousand or a million. But that's only the beginning. Are you then prepared to work twenty-four hours of the day, give up all private life, not to mention sanity, and blithely walk through walls to not only get to the top, but stay there? Cyndi was. Around the same time I saw U2 make a good, if less than overwhelming, debut at the Ritz. But that lead singer, Bono! Not only would he walk through walls; he'd actually go out and build the bloody things barehanded, before demolishing them. I wasn't sure I could say the same for myself.

I don't think Pierce and I ever knew what hit us. We were suddenly hurled topsy-turvy into the slipstream of a rising international diva. It was thrilling at first, but harder as time went on to keep one's head above the waves churning in her wake. There was a general air of unreality afoot. I think her handlers actually liked it when she regularly lost her head over some dumb detail. That way, it was easier to control the big picture, which, of course, concerned money. Money changes everything, she sang every night, and the sentiment couldn't have been truer. Money, too, or rather the lure of it, was ever present and fueled the coke-driven fantasies of our major record company. No one at CBS seemed to know what they were doing; no one was in control or willing to take responsibility. Michael Jackson was making money hand over fist and now Cyndi was adding to the pile. No worries! More where that came from. And we, the Major Thinkers, with our songs on the radio and remixes roiling the dance clubs, were like mice nibbling around the corners of a gigantic slice of golden powdered cheese.

We were given an expense account and dispatched to a recording studio in Connecticut, there to remain until we had finished our "pop masterpiece," *Terrible Beauty*. The demos for this album had been completed in one long terrific session. Portrait Records was thrilled. They loved the songs, we had the haircuts and the Cyndi connection, and with a video and a bit of that old luck of the Irish, there was no saying where we would end up. But first, we had to rerecord everything. No one, including ourselves, insisted on the obvious: release the songs as they were. Instead we labored over new tracks: analyzing and deconstructing every note of the demo, trying to recapture by craft what we'd accomplished through spontaneity. I don't know how long it all took. Much of it is a mind-numbing blur, because we'd quit for weeks and head out on the road to entertain Cyndi's ever-growing audience of prepubescent she-boppers. Then we'd return and reimmerse ourselves, Sergeant Pepperlike, into our masterpiece.

I think we finished it, but I'm not sure. In any event, we stopped recording. But what was to be the first single? Five tracks were selected and bandied about the company for months, opinions solicited off everyone from the president on down to the pizza delivery boy; each one unwilling to step out from the pack and stamp their name on a track, for fear that if it failed, they'd be identified as the prime mover. Cyndi, in a true mark of friendship, came in and sang a duet on one of the songs to give us some added marketability.

Finally, "Love Like Lava Flowing" surfaced as the front-runner, having reached some kind of a company consensus. We were, however, smack dab in the middle of the remix era, giving the head honchos another cause for prevarication. Pierce and I mixed the goddamn thing three times, while a number of "hot" producers of the day gave it their best shot. Eventually, we were once more back to five choices of the single, with a camp rallying stolidly around each. While tracking down a Black 47 song some years back, I found an unmarked dusty cassette and gave it a spin. Lo and behold! The five sacred mixes popped out, replete with memories of haircuts and she-boppers. For the life of me, I couldn't tell the difference between any of them. But, back in the '80s, I would have fought and died for my favorite, whichever it was.

I suppose one of the mixes was finally chosen, because a tentative date was set for the release of album and single, and the holy grail of an MTV video was dangled before us. In our own minds, it would not be long until we, too, would be hanging our beer bellies out of a yacht full of models, à la Duran Duran. Then, one day out of nowhere, the phone rang and our manager casually mentioned that the project had become "old." Portrait Records was dropping the band. Just like that.

Bad news travels fast. People who had been calling every day attesting to my genius had now apparently developed second thoughts and would not take my calls. Down at Mudd Club and up at Max's, I had to line up and pay for my drinks like every other peon. Ladies who used to delight in arriving at clubs on my arm now hid in the ladies' when they saw me coming. Your sex appeal does an amazing about-turn when you're no longer the next big

thing. All of this might have been bearable, but then our publishing company, on finding that there was no record deal, with-
drew its promised advance, and the band grinded to a screeching
halt. We were broke, disgusted, and, to add insult to injury,
slapped with an audit by the IRS. Sheila sent me a cheer-up note
from Clearwater and wondered if perhaps the time wasn't right
for some Scientology counseling. Even Boris commiserated with
me and offered to put in a word with Ronald Reagan.

The sad part, though, was that the creative steam had run out
of the Major Thinkers. It just wasn't fun anymore and when
music stops being fun, it turns in on itself and loses purpose. Pierce
and I had been through hell and high water together and always
managed to laugh in the face of disaster. For the first time, neither
of us had that urge to pick up the pieces and start at the bottom of
the ladder again. Pierce wanted to record a solo record. And me?
Well, I really didn't know what I wanted to do except write, not
just four-minute pop songs, but plays, stories, novels, whatever.
But most of all I wanted to become myself again. The problem
was, I couldn't even remember what myself was anymore. In the
words of Copernicus, I needed to go to the mountain.

We had met this very large, outrageous Polish-American when
the Bells of Hell was temporarily relocated to the legendary Five
Spot on St. Mark's. One night toward closing time, in keeping
with the Five Spot's reputation for jazz improvisation, someone
suggested that we allow a poet to perform a piece with us. We'd
have been happy to have a one-legged orangutan with a stutter
strut his stuff, for the place was almost empty and we had another
thirty minutes to kill. The gentleman in question—resplendent in
a dazzling silver kaftan that could have taken the eye out of a
Forty-seventh Street jeweler—instructed us to introduce him as
"Copernicus—the Poet of Nevermore" and then begin playing
whatever was dear to our hearts. He would take a measure of our
music and join in with some suitable theme, when the notion
struck him. No problem, Pierce and I hastened to inform him,
after draining our pint glasses of Southern Comfort. We could
almost read each other's minds back then, and launched into the

intro of "Whiter Shade of Pale." The Poet of Nevermore was not endowed with any knowledge of rock or classical history and was astounded by this seemingly inspired improvisation. The notion struck him instantly and big time. He bawled, yelled, threatened, crooned, and delivered thirty minutes of his "none of us exists" philosophy while we tore through crescendo after improvised crescendo on the beautiful Bach rip-off.

I seem to remember that we cleared the room of the few remaining stragglers, but all three of us were mightily impressed by our efforts. Over the years, Copernicus would often show up at the end of the night and we'd take the improvisations even further. It was liberating to get up onstage and not have a clue what you were going to play, just catch the flow of the others, let your feelings and impulses take over, and go wherever the piece took you. This called for a certain amount of bravado if not bravery, curried with a pinch of studied nonchalance; but flying by the seat of your pants opened worlds that we had never suspected even existed. A blend of Southern Comfort and Colombian Red did nothing to hinder these ethereal explorations. What nights! And they weren't confined to music. When the gear was packed and the money pocketed, we'd hit the town with a vengeance.

I had always been interested in the netherworlds of New York City. I knew the cracked streets of the East Village like the back of my hand. I loved to wander through the seediness of Forty Deuce and be an observer, and sometimes a bit player in some of its dramas. But now I had a partner, and a giant of a one at that. Harlem was his playground. He had an amazing facility for languages and could mix easily with anyone, from the pope to a one-legged prostitute. Money was no object; Copernicus was generous to an extreme and thought nothing of supporting a mushrooming entourage on his periodic starbursts through night town. If I had known Sweet Nancy by sight before, now we were way beyond a first-name basis. She was always happy to see us for we were like Christmas arriving, bedecked in mistletoe and tinsel, and would light up the Deuce with our shenanigans. No woman was too beautiful to talk to, no character too outrageous or dangerous to approach. Theater people perennially lament the lack of serious plays on Broadway and with good cause. But if they had only taken a few strides over to Seventh Avenue, the pre-Disney Deuce was throbbing with drama so intense that O'Neill or Tennessee would have burned out just watching. Life was a perpetual red alert, and death only a simple mistake or a crude gaffe away.

And when the Deuce rolled up its sidewalks and Sweet Nancy went home to bed, as she sometimes did, we would head up to Black Rose's after-hours in Harlem. That's where I met her and Frankie Diamond and a cast of hundreds, denizens of the white powdered night and the dark eyes and the slender thighs, Sing-Sing graduates, and the like. Back then, the days were short and the nights were long and sleeping was something you did when the sun was long up and you could no longer keep your eyes open. It was a different world and I often wonder what happened to you all. Back in the day, I was full of the moment and couldn't believe that our sporting life would not last forever. How wrong I was, Rosie.

18

INTO THE WEST

When I was a boy I traveled the roads
Nothing but the wild west wind ahead of me
Then I moved to the city, put on a suit
Like a straitjacket it nearly choked me
I listened to all of their corporate lies
But they never really fooled me
'Cause that song in my heart was beating right through my chest
And I knew that the fire would drive me out of my skull
If I didn't get back to the West.

Ah, the old days are gone and your freedom's gone with them
But the memory remains, it's always there tormentin'
Just when you think you've found some peace
A pair of black eyes sends you reelin'
The road rears up her head, and you know you've got that feelin'
For the rain in your face, the sun in your hair
The fire in your blood roarin' again
The earth beneath your feet—not like these streets
Chains around your chest—
And you've got to get back to the West.

You've worked like a dog, but you've nothin' to show for it
Just some lines around your face and a pocket full of bubbles
She's laughed at all your jokes, and she's sick of all your dealin's
'Cause you're not the man she loved back when you had the feelin'

For the rain in your face, the sun in your hair, the fire in your blood roarin' again
The earth beneath your feet—not like these streets
Chains around your chest—and you've got to get back to

John Wayne, Gary Cooper, Alan Ladd, Audie Murphy,
All out there ridin' the range on their eternal journey.
You used to look up to them from the front row
At the Saturday afternoon pictures in the Abbey
Reach out to them now, they won't let you down
They'll take you ridin' off into the sunset with
Ava Gardner, Bogie, and oh my dearest Marilyn
Are you still hauntin' the laneways of Wexford in your eternal glory
With the rain in your face, the sun in your hair, the fire in your blood roarin'
again . . .

From Jim Sheridan's Into the West, *EMI Records Soundtrack 1994*
From Elvis Murphy's Green Suede Shoes, *Gadfly Records, 2005*
Published by Starry Plough Music (BMI)

THE MAJOR THINKERS went out with a bang at Irving Plaza on St. Patrick's Day, 1985. I had no idea it was to be our last gig. We were on a double bill with Stockton's Wing, a visiting Irish band. I have become friends with their players since, but on that night there was a feeling of rivalry between the crews. Although we usually headlined at Irving, we went on first; now that we had lost the record deal, some of the starch had been knocked out of our ambitions—more time for partying after the gig was the general consensus. To the best of my memory we put on a really good show, but as we received the post-gig liggers in our dressing room, our soundman bustled in and told me that he was leaving in a hurry. I think, in retrospect, that there was a message embedded in our brief exchange. However, someone had just slipped the band some ecstasy, and my mind was already in the throes of a certain delightful confusion.

If it was my last date with the Thinkers, it was my first with a beautiful green-eyed choreographer for whom I had been composing music. I had invited her along to impress her with my popularity and man-about-the-East-Village insouciance. She didn't appear particularly bowled over by the music or my strutting but was mildly amused by the post-gig rock 'n' roll nonsense. She definitely stood out in the seedy dressing room in a simple black dress, red Parisian heels, and matching lipstick. Dancers always know how to hold themselves—the least movement, the most attention. I was impressed by the way the action surged around her but never seemed to touch or affect her. Still, when Stockton's Wing came on, we stepped outside onto the dance floor; I enjoyed their music but it also cut down on the competition from the male liggers within. It was very odd out there. The whole sound was drenched in reverb, out of kilter and coming at me from odd directions. I wasn't at all sure that the band might not have been listening to Sonic Youth, and were giving the more spaced-out, feedback-oriented side of their repertoire a bit of an airing. She merely thought it strange and otherworldly, adjectives I would never have used to depict the Wing. However, she was an admirer of Yeats, and dancers often inhabit a different plane from the rest of us; she also seemed to be taking a shine to their fiddler. I hastened to assure her that he was a solid Clare man and wasn't from anywhere remotely near Dooney. She looked at me oddly. Not for the last time either.

When we ran into an anxious Pierce back in the dressing room, he quickly disabused me of Sonic Youth's latent influence on the proceedings. Our soundman, in a fit of pique after being insulted by his Irish counterpart, had stripped the board of its house EQ settings, and for good measure swapped a number of inputs—including reverb and delay—into less than correct channels. This piece of mischief was the root and reason for Stockton's Wing's foray into the realm of the avant-garde. To compound matters, Pierce had just run into their road manager who demanded that he come to their dressing room later, duly abase himself, and apologize for the Major Thinkers' foul behavior. Unlike Falstaff, I have never been certain that discretion is indeed the better part of valor; still, I have to admit that on that holy St. Patrick's Night, I deserted my hometown mate. After hailing a cab for my date—dancers, alas, must be at the barre rested and limber at nine every morning—I hurried across the street to Tramps saloon and watering hole. There, with Buster Poindexter in full throttle on "Danny Boy" and "How Are Things in Gloccomara?" I experienced vistas and visions of plastic shamrocks and green leprechauns leaping to life. In fact, I seem to remember a number of them accompanying me home to Third Street, where they had reverted to their dormant phase by the time I regained consciousness the following evening.

Reality kicked in over the next few days, though it was of an odd sort. Hollow, delayed, and reverberating, much like the sound of Stockton's Wing at Irving. This was not helped by Portrait Records, in their wisdom, deciding that even though they themselves would never release *Terrible Beauty*, they would need a fee in the ballpark of $100,000 before they would even dream of parting with this "masterpiece" to us or another record company. I personally didn't have a hundred bucks at the time, so that put me out of the running. Pierce was similarly down on his druthers.

This new reality or malaise went way beyond money, however. I had grown sick of the rock life and, not by coincidence, sick of myself, too. I had been on a nonstop roller-coaster ride for over ten years and I couldn't even recall the original reason for stepping aboard. I had come to America for what? Some vague notion of "making it?" But making what? I wasn't even sure what the concept meant anymore. I had no interest in a big house in Malibu. Nor was I desirous of owning fast cars or even faster women. But what the hell did I want? I had to confess that I didn't have a bull's notion. I did want to create. But what did that mean? Write songs? Form a band? None of it appealed to me anymore.

It was all such an eye-opener. What was I doing? Where did I want to go? I had put all these existential questions on some kind of back burner where they had simmered for over ten years. Now they were stewed to the roots—so much so that I could barely articulate the questions, let alone come up with any kind of meaningful answers. But I did know that I didn't have the least desire to be Larry Kirwan of the Major Thinkers again. That life was over. I'd had great moments with Turner and Kirwan of Wexford and the Thinkers, but it was all past tense. So, after settling my case with the IRS, borrowing the money to pay my penalties, I hopped on a plane to Luxembourg with my now choreographer girlfriend and ended up living in France and Ireland for the summer.

What a break to be free of "making it." I didn't give a damn if the whole music industry blew itself to bejaysus back in New York. It had nothing to do with me anymore. I stopped listening to the radio, turned off the television, and began tuning in to myself for the first time in years. That was a revelation, but not a particularly pretty one. I discovered that I had become nothing less than a stressed-out series of knots and anxieties. If Dylan was tangled up in blue, then I had been trussed head to toe in violet polka dots. But that summer, in Angers, Paris, Wexford, and Galway I allowed the strands to unravel in their own way.

If you ever have need for a boost to the soul, go west; leave Galway City behind and head deep into Connemara. There's a connection in that wild land between the rocks and the water, the sun and the heather, the rain on your face and the moonlight on the mountains. It's a timeless place of turf and sky and space and rain seeping up from the boggy ground, where mad donkeys gaze back at you while solemnly chewing the cud. There's an oldness that has no time for rush, reason, religion, or any of man's follies and egotistical notions. And if that doesn't quite fix you and you have a need for extreme unction, then take the boat to Inishmaan, the middle Aran Island. It's the quietest place on Earth. Out there, the veil often parts and the ghosts of Synge, Pegeen Mike, and the Playboy watch you from behind tall windswept walls of gathered stone; if you can just let go for a moment and leave yourself open to their charms, they'll ease the most troubled of souls and soothe the worst case of heartscald.

There's but one pub, An Córa (the bottom drawer in which young women store linen and lace for their wedding night and married life). One evening in that establishment, we watched *Dr. Strangelove* on television and listened to a young bartender try to translate and explain the action and irony to a dozen or so ancient toothless Gaelic speakers while they sucked on their pints. The task was monumental, and eventually the young man threw up his hands in exasperation and declaimed, "Ah, would yez ever go figure out the fuckin' thing for yourselves!" With that admonition,

I realized that my own rock 'n' roll life had been culture-crossed and just as convoluted, but that I'd already made some of the necessary internal changes. I was just about ready for the fray again. By the time I arrived back in New York in the fall, I felt moderately sane; I had also drifted to the conclusion that I would now devote myself to the craft of playwriting.

I had been dabbling at plays for some years. But a craft needs patience and devotion, and I'd always put playwriting on the long finger. Like anything worth doing, you need time to make all the mistakes and a few more into the bargain. I signed up with Script Development Workshop and was assigned a director and a troupe of actors. Every Monday night we rehearsed and knocked into shape a musical called *Requiem for a Rocker*. After eight weeks, we staged it in front of our peers and an invited audience; this showing caused no end of controversy. It was well acted, directed, and rehearsed and not badly written as these things go; but its scarcely veiled autobiographical content—the coming apart at the seams of a rock 'n' roller—elicited bitter debate. There was a school of thought that felt that this subject had about as much chance of hitting Broadway as a musical about East Village junkies, cross-dressers, and AIDS victims; my supporters felt that one never knew what way tastes would turn in the seasons to come. For myself, I felt rather like the Irish playwright Brendan Behan, thrilled to pieces that anyone would even bother arguing about something that I had written in the first place.

I began to see a future for myself as a budding O'Neill, although the stars were soon swept from my eyes by the sheer amount of work and perseverance needed to turn out even a mediocre play. In no time at all, I realized why so many playwrights, and writers in general, become alcoholics. It's a bitch of a game with long hours, much loneliness, and little, if any, financial reward, not to mention that the perfect play has never been written. Still, I had plenty of time on my hands and nothing else on my plate. I did make one very vital pact with myself: that any play I completed would receive a production, no matter how minimal. I would be responsible for no more *Terrible Beautys*.

19

LIVERPOOL FANTASY

I walk down the lane with me head in the clouds
Me brains may be scrambled, but I don't heed the crowds
With their football and pools, their weddings and wakes
Their political goals and their kids' birthday cakes
And I shout at the chimneys and scream at the breeze
Hey, you out there, can you hear me Liverpool fantasy?

I look at the dawn through the Everton rain
The whole city is sleeping, just the milk bottles wait
To be taken and washed and filled up and then
I wish they'd take me and remake me again
So I shout at the milkman and I scream at the priest
Hey you out there, can you hear me Liverpool fantasy?

I'm sick of the dole and I'm sick of me life
I'm sick of your politics and I'm sick of me wife
I'm sick of your pity and I'm sick of being fired
And I'm sick and tired of being sick and tired . . .

And I walk down the lane with me head in the clouds
Me brains may be scrambled but I don't heed the crowds
With their football and pools, their weddings and wakes
Their political goals and their kids' birthday cakes
And I shout at the rooftops and I scream at the trees
Hey you out there, can you hear me Liverpool fantasy?

From Elvis Murphy's Green Suede Shoes, *Gadfly Records 2005*
Published by Starry Plough Music (BMI)

I HAD BEEN sketching out an idea for some time about what would
have happened if the Beatles hadn't made it. I suppose I was still
wrestling with the "making it" syndrome. Liverpool Fantasy sprang
from two separate but linked thoughts. I had once heard someone
argue that John Lennon would have been successful no matter
what field he had chosen. At the time, I was inclined to agree. But
after experiencing many of the pitfalls of the rock 'n' roll life myself,
I concluded that the opposite might be more likely. Lennon, to me,
was never the cuddly idealist that he was later perceived as in the
United States. Indeed, he was much more recognizable: a chip off a
working-class block with all the good and bad qualities that entails.
He was not unlike a Wexford teddy boy who had learned to harness
his anger. Added to this, he put me in mind of a number of musicians back home—more talented, undoubtedly—but definitely cut
from the same cloth, and with the same inherent character traits
and flaws. Arrogance, paranoia, or just plain bad luck had caused
them to blow their shot; they now bitterly walked the streets of
Wexford and Dublin, their great futures well behind them. It wasn't
a far stretch, at least in my imagination, to see old Johnnie still stuck
in Liverpool, especially if he had been deprived of Paul's pragmatism
to soften his rough edges.

I also wondered just what effect the Beatles and the new youth
culture had on UK politics. Back in 1968, Enoch Powell made his
infamous Rivers of Blood speech, predicting that there would be
great turmoil if the immigration laws were not changed. Powell
was a riveting orator, one of the few intellectuals in the Conservative Party and a possible future prime minister. He was also fiercely
honest and articulated what many were thinking, even if it made
for uncomfortable listening. He delivered this speech in the era of
Swinging London and it was, for the most part, greeted with disdain, especially by the young. The Beatles had changed the country
and the way the UK perceived itself. But would Powell's
"prophecy" have been received differently if Britain had been more
depressed, repressed and xenophobic—as it was in the pre-Beatle,
post-war years?

I based the play on these two thoughts, mixing the dynamics of
working-class musicians' lives with the threat of a right-wing

paramilitary takeover in Liverpool. If *Requiem for a Rocker* had caused a bit of a stir, *Liverpool Fantasy* almost shut down the house during the post-performance discussion. What in the name of God was I thinking, and how dare I desecrate the memory of the warm and fuzzy Saint John? That seemed to be the majority opinion; while again, I had a sizeable body of supporters who thought I was only half-mad and deserved, at the bare minimum, the right of free speech.

I decided that I'd put all my eggs in one basket and go for a production of *Liverpool Fantasy.* To say that I couldn't even get arrested with this play might be stretching a point, but it was certainly declined by the many theaters and producers to whom I submitted it. I talked this over with an actress friend, Monica Gross, who decided that not only would she would direct the play, but that we two would raise the money and produce it.

"Raise money?" My stomach did a flip. I had never asked for a penny in my life. Even back in Wexford as a boy, I had worked summers, bought my own clothes, and paid my own school fees. She caught my reaction and reassured me that it was no big deal: just get a letter together stating what you need, and send it to everyone you know. Simple as that! Monica was a dynamo with a will of pure steel. She opened her calendar, marked a date for a spring production, and then set about moving mountains to achieve that goal. And just as she had promised, friends came out of the woodwork with their twenties and fifties. It was an education on the fly, for we never knew where the next dollar was coming from, except that come it did. We found El Bohio, a community space in an abandoned school off Tompkins Square, run by a group of aging but still committed Young Lords—wonderful people with open hearts of gold. Under their approving and enthusiastic eyes, we converted the theater into the back streets of politically charged Liverpool. Next, we hired an assistant director, Kate Baggott, who would go on to direct a number of my plays. We then auditioned, cast, and rehearsed a bunch of experienced and beginning actors. And, oh by the way, through all this Monica and I fought like dogs about the meaning, content, and thrust of the play.

I received an amazing eye-opener into the convoluted theatrical world of New York City, its many delights and pitfalls. Coming from the cutthroat world of rock music with its much higher budgets and expectations, theater was at once archaic, far more principled, intellectual though often harebrained, and worlds away more bitchy. It also had a great fondness for calling a spade a shovel, then taking all of a tearful night to figure out that it might actually be a spade after all. But theater is always invigorating and no matter what anyone says, the playwright is still at the center of the circle, and always the cyclone. One learned to be careful and keep a buttoned lip, even when sure of an answer, because words, once uttered, could always be used to nail you to the cross of your own script. Actors were ready to drop anything and flee from the bosom of their director for the stray chance of hearing some pearl of wisdom drop from your lips. This was exhilarating, at first, but fraught with peril. Nothing you ever said, no matter how casual, was forgotten. No wonder thumb sketches of Arthur Miller portray him as cerebral with lips pursed tightly together as though he were suffering from constipation. The poor man is probably scared shitless of asking the way to the bathroom, for fear the question may be referenced back to one of his plays.

Directors amazed me from the get-go. They would take your hand, gaze into your bloodshot eyes, and spout on like a broken tap about protecting the "purity and integrity of the work," then, in the next breath, decree that you should change tone, length, character, and even the title of the bloody play. Monica was no exception and she did this in the most reasonable and logical manner. Nowadays, I'm much more aware of writer/director boundaries and ethics, but we were partners in this venture so, as far as I was concerned, anything—no matter how sacred—could at least be discussed. That didn't, of course, mean that I would agree, and I was the veteran of many the argument with Pierce and other musicians in my previous incarnation. Hence, the title was not changed to the somewhat enigmatic, if unoriginal, *Parallel Lives.* But Monica came up with an even more startling suggestion: that each of the original characters in the play should have a reflected Julian (Julian being the disaffected semifascist son of John Lennon). This was nothing short of mind-boggling, as along with the four Beatles, their wives, girlfriends, and Pete Best, there should now be added to the cast a duplicate cadre of young actors.

I fought this tooth and nail but Monica was adamant: the play needed "expanding." In the end, for a bit of peace of mind, if nothing else, I went along with her suggestion. It may have been one of the great moments in New York's theatrical history when she explained this concept to the experienced and already somewhat bilious lead actors. I was only sorry that I didn't take down the many salty comments and astounded reactions, for I had been provided with the genesis of a tremendous play within a play. But Monica had nerves, if not balls, of steel; she persevered, and with the full support of the playwright, won the day. However, I demurred from writing any extra lines for these shadowy doppelgängers, and eventually they were perceived as Julian's gang and did serve to "expand" the play considerably, if not in the manner intended. In such a fashion does theater work—or rather, adapt. I became friends with many of Julian's gang, and all received their equity cards. Monica's imagination had served to enrich each of us in a number of ways.

Liverpool Fantasy has been produced many times over the years and never fails to provide the stormiest of a rehearsal process for it deals ultimately with the perceived failure of the four main characters, even while they try to remain truthful to, or come to terms with, their dreams. Allow eight actors on the cusp of middle age to chew on that concept for four or five weeks and see what happens. It takes the firmest, most confident, and conciliatory of directors to navigate the shoals of testosterone, raging hormones, and downright errant behavior that this play seems to engender. Suffice it to say that the original rehearsals were lively to the extreme. Many tears were spilled but, amazingly, no blood. And, in the end, the play opened and became a much-talked-about success. People flocked down to Avenue B to take a look at these Beatles who never made it. We extended the show a number of times and moved to a larger theater in El Bohio. It could have run indefinitely but, toward the end, we needed an extra infusion of money and both Monica and I were worn out from the process. The play has a life of its own now and resurfaces frequently. I always try to see it. But I doubt if I'll ever learn as much about life and theater as I did in those turbulent months down in El Bohio with that great woman of the stage, Monica Gross.

The following year, *Liverpool Fantasy* was invited to the Dublin Theater Festival. This move had been initiated by a group of the actors with connections in Ireland. They preferred a more experienced director and went with Geoffrey Sherman of the Hudson Guild Theater. I was by then immersed in a new play, *Mister Parnell,* and had little to do with the production, until Geoffrey pulled out right before departure for health considerations. The play had reverted more to its original format, losing Julian's gang, and matters seemed somewhat under control. I was to discover otherwise, when I joined the cast in Ireland the day before final dress rehearsal. To add to the normal stress that the play lays on actors' fragile psyches, some of them would be performing in front of home audiences for the first time in years. I was sympathetic to this pressure, having been through it myself with bands. Still, I was unprepared for what I found.

You could almost touch the anxiety level inside the theater. The first run-through was dreadful. Lines not known and blown, exits and entrances all over the place, hostility seeping outward from the stage. I wasn't even sure where to begin. I cleaned up what I could, but instinctively knew that the overall pessimistic mood was the main problem. I've since come to understand that while the writer may be responsible for the actual lines the actors speak, a production depends on the director finding that particular psychological fulcrum on which the play can balance. It had proven way beyond me, for the next day's dress rehearsal swung up and down like an unhinged seesaw. I was aghast; it was obvious that the advice I'd given was now proving more hindrance than help. I was about ready to hit the pub and then the airport, for hell hath no fury like the Dublin critic. The green-eyed choreographer, who had recently become my wife, watched, too, and quietly noted that I had but one option. Get them on- and offstage speedily and in one piece, and let the gods do what they would with the play. And so we worked through the night on the entrances and exits, until the whole cast was moving around like they were on a newly waxed dance floor.

Quite fittingly, the Eblana Theater was in the basement of Dublin's bus station. Not quite the Deuce but with the occasional transient echo. It was packed with critics, punters, and those Dubliners whose sixth sense had informed them that they might be about to witness a spectacular failure. Charlie Roberts (father of my buddy Keith from the Young Dubliners) was the stage manager. He was standing in the wings before opening curtain and caught my eye in the audience. He grimaced, drew a finger across his throat, and simultaneously blessed himself in one fluid motion: theatrical shorthand for "we may be shagged but we'll live to fight another day." And then the lights went down. The opening scene was a speech by the leader of the fascist National Front, followed by a semi-riot. All well and good, until the script called for the cast to be chased from the stage and reappear within seconds in the next scene as the younger Beatles. Dennis O'Neill, playing Father George Harrison, however, tripped during his exit and brought down a couple more with him. I was horrified but the audience figured this to be the height of realism. Dennis never missed a beat, but crawled off manfully as though he had just been wounded on the Somme.

It's strange how something extraneous can turn things around onstage, but that moment broke the ice. Then again, maybe the fear of failure kicked in. Whatever, the cast came out swinging in the next scene. The play took off like a rocket, actors almost skidding on- and offstage. I wasn't sure the audience could tell what was transpiring, such was the pace; but the sourness of mood had evaporated, leaving in its place a touching play with some very appealing and sympathetic characters. At the end, there was a silence: no one was quite sure if the show was over. Then prolonged applause and many curtain calls. We were all heroes and, with lightbulbs flashing, obliged our newfound fans by getting gloriously drunk with them.

The next morning, the reviews were uniformly positive and the party photos suitably beaming. *Fluid* was a word used to describe the production. More like greased bloody lightning, I thought. We had shaved almost fifteen minutes off the usual time of the play. Then I made the first-time director's classic mistake. Nobody had warned me to beware of the second-night blahs. I don't know whether it was because of hangovers, lack of adrenaline, or the receding fear of failure, but this was the most dismal performance I've ever witnessed of any of my plays, and I've suffered through some doozies. The actors barely crawled onstage before meandering their way through lines that seemed devoid of any humor, let alone any spark of an uplifting nature. It was as if they'd all been thrown into some Liverpudlian cesspit and didn't have the energy or commitment to crawl out. Luckily, the only critics were from the evening papers. Though they duly butchered the show, to my mind we were let off lightly. But who reads evening papers anyway? The word had already spread around Dublin through the early reviews and the fervor of the first night's audience. We were a hit, try as we might to mess it up.

I love actors. I love their generosity, their support for one another and for playwrights in general. But they are, indeed, an odd bunch. I suppose it's the constant rejection. It's hard enough getting up in the morning, without knowing that at practically every audition you'll be subtly, or otherwise, informed that you're not quite up to snuff. Your general musician would turn to jelly, or junk, after the first couple of put-downs. I've always wondered why actors don't just form their own companies; that way they'd be able to get up onstage two or three times a year in work that they love. Noel Faulkner, the original Ringo, put it to me that the acting profession never dealt with the '60s. I don't know about that. But I would make a case that there is little of the spirit of '76 knocking around Broadway. The punk movement liberated so many musicians from the thrall of record companies, music promoters, and the biz in general, while most actors will still trot out in any piece of tripe just for the privilege of getting onstage. Bring on the day when a couple of Mohawked Strummer-like visionaries strut their way through Sardi's or Joe Allen's on their way toward turning the whole theatrical world on its ear.

New York actors, in particular, have another huge drawback. They have to deal with the insidious Method and the legion of quacks who foist it upon them. I passed through a wall of fire in my own dealings with Mr. Strasberg's legacy. Not that there is anything wrong with the Method of itself. Whatever gets you up and running is fine with me. I even went to the source, made my pilgrimage to Moscow, and eventually studied Stanislavsky, such was the amount of theoretical bullshit I had to endure from people who had barely ever cracked a book of the master's, let alone been up onstage. On one divine occasion, an actress who was meant to be merely observing the action in a pivotal scene burst out crying and diverted attention from the leading man. When she came offstage, I asked her what in the name of Christ could she possibly have been thinking of? To which she replied, "My character felt like it." I was lost for words at this lack of common sense; the aggrieved leading man, however, happened to be passing by and snarled, "Well, just let your character know the next time she's so moved, she'll feel the toe of my fucking character's boot halfway up her arse!"

Ah well, theater is unpredictable, if nothing else. Toward the end of the Dublin run, there was some resentment between the actors playing Pete Best and John Lennon. The one playing Best was a Method freak, perennially pushing the envelope on his few but vital lines. This, not unremarkably, drove Colin Lane, the actor playing Lennon, around the bend. As the run progressed, Best from Liverpool had become a dead ringer for Jimmy Dean in Rebel Without a Cause, replete with Indiana mumbling and a slouch that would have done Brando proud. Lennon always had his back to Best when the fired drummer made his entrance onstage. Hence, one evening, he was the only one in the theater who did not realize that his antagonist was dressed in full biker leather and motorcycle helmet. He did notice, though, that Best's usual opening lines were muffled and distant, and that the audience was in stitches of laughter. I wish I could have bottled the look on Colin's face when he spun around, ready to icily deliver his normal put-down. Instead, there was an amazed standoff of some seconds before he shot back in perfect Liverpool accent, "Would you ever take that fuckin' thing off so I can hear what the hell you're sayin'!" Ah well, those moments are, I suppose, what makes theater "theatah" and keeps us all involved with this impecunious, but vital, old lady.

20

DESPERATE

Go to the church but the preacher he just preach at me
Go to the club, but the women all ignore me
Want a relationship, I want to have a family
I'm schizophrenic, paranoid, tell me what is wrong with me?

Desperate, I'm desperate why won't you hold me
Desperate, I'm desperate for the next moment
Desperate, I'm desperate I feel so lonely
Desperate, I'm desperate for the next moment.

Go for a job, but they don't like the look of me
Say "grow some hair, this is not 1970"
I want a Donna Reed but she think I'm too kinky
She don't like perverts, why ain't I a yuppie?

Desperate, I'm desperate why won't you hold me
Desperate, I'm desperate for the next moment
Desperate, I'm desperate I feel so lonely
Desperate, I'm desperate for the next moment.

From Black 47, *independent 1991*
Published by Starry Plough Music (BMI)

WE WERE LOST. No two ways about it. Gloriously, desperately lost. Our driver up on tiptoes striking matches in the pitch darkness, trying to make sense of an old wooden sign that was pointing any which way but the direction of the twin forks up the road. A couple of the guys had awoken but, seeing no city lights, had just given up and gone back to sleep. The last night in Berlin had been a humdinger and there were hangovers to be dealt with. The big man was studying a map by candlelight and muttering his now standard response to everything: "Motherfucker." We had already dubbed this the Motherfucker Tour since we were all using the word with abandon. Where did he get a candle from anyway? In the same place he got every other goddamn thing? One of his twelve cases. From a needle to an anchor they were stored within, along with an abundance of paranoia. We'd even found him boiling pots of rice on twin Bunsen burners in his Berlin hotel room, for Christ's sake, while the rest of us were digging into a spread in an Italian restaurant that would have trumped Mama Leone's.

The twelve bloody suitcases had been a bone of contention right from the first donnybrook at Kennedy Airport. Mike Fazio had shown up with an extra bag, throwing the minutely fine-tuned luggage limit for a loop. There followed a scene of chaotic consolidation at check-in, as underwear, sacks of rice, eating condiments, stage costumes, and God knows what else were refolded, repackaged, and then sat upon to make them fit within bags already bursting at the seams. This activity was accompanied by much roared use of that unfortunate word. Parents made vain attempts to shield inquisitive toddlers from the sight, sound, and fury of a large hirsute man finally cracking after much provocation, both real and imagined. To top it all, we were then summarily informed that part of our duty was to lug along his suitcases on this nutty safari through the far depths of Eastern Europe and into the punch-drunk, but still standing, Union of Soviet Socialist Republics. Imagine the furor that news caused among a gang of drunken, stoned New York musicians, who were then ordered to hand over their passports for safekeeping.

He didn't get the passports. Nor had he brought along a compass. We could have done with a generator, too—throw some light on the country. I hoped that George Herbert and his generals

n and Ita Kirwan.

a and Larry Kirwan.

(Above left) Johnny Byrne showing me the shirt his mother sent as '93–'94's Christmas present. He said it made him look like a muscle man. This is the goofy Johnny I'll always remember. The photo makes you smile and that is exactly what he wants you to do.

(Above right) Black 47. Photo by Chris Cuffaro.

(Below). Joe Strummer, Geoff Blythe, and Larry Kirwan after opening f the Pogues at the Brixton Academy, London. Christmas 1990.

Kirwan, San Francisco 1993. "40 Shades of Blue."

(Above) Geoff Blythe, Jeff Lad, Fred Parcells, Chris Bryne, and Larry Kirwan at Reilly's, 1990.

(Below) Neil Young and Larry Kirwan at Farm Aid. Ames, Iowa, 1990.

Kristofferson and Larry Kirwan at Farm Aid. Ames, Iowa, 1994.

(Above) Fred Parcells, Geoff Blythe, Larry Kirwan, and Chris Bryne in the front window of Reilly's, 1990.

(Below) Thomas Hamlin and Larry Kirwan at Reilly's, 1990.

s Byrne, Fred Parcells, and Larry Kirwan in Black 47's first publicity photo. Soho, 1990. Photo by Mark Blandori.

Larry Kirwan publicity photo. Photo by Tricia Karsay.

back in D.C. were taking note: if you're going to invade Czecho-slovakia, better bring along your own bloody electricity, otherwise the tanks are going to be backed up like the BQE on a wet Friday. Then Hammy spotted it: a dim light about twenty yards down one of the forks in the road. He called for silence, and we all heard the thin reed of a melodeon, hemmed in by a murmur of voices raised in mournful song. Could it be? Out in the middle of nowhere—a pub, a saloon, some oasis where a thirsty wayfarer might snag a drink. After all, it was almost midnight and not a drop had been lowered since Berlin's bawdy bacchanal.

"Get back in that motherfuckin' van!" Copernicus snarled, but the two of us were already scampering toward the promised land.

By this point of the tour, we had found it easier just to ignore his demands. It cut down on endless arguments. Much better to act deaf, dumb, and blind—live up to your reputation as an irrespon-sible musician—just follow your will and face the consequences later. But by Christ on a tricycle, if it was a pub, it was an odd one! For one thing, it lacked a shingle hanging in the limp night air to welcome the lonesome traveler. On the plus side, the door was slightly ajar with a flicker of light glancing out across the rutted yard. Lucky it hadn't been raining. Another note for the generals: bring along plenty of tarmac if you don't want your whole thirsty army disappearing down into one of these Czech potholes. The Cross Bronx Expressway was small potatoes when lined up against the main roads of this ramshackle country.

I had my hand on the vestibule door, yet hesitated. Suppose this was a private house? There could be a nutcase inside, his Uzi lev-eled at me even now. I was, after all, an expert on Czechs, their doings and motivations. The not-so-distant scene of No-Coats and myself outside Boris's Bronx door flashed before me in agonizing detail. But the thirst had taken over, putting the run on all pru-dence. Besides, at the very worst, there appeared to be a party of sorts going on within. The voices rose and dipped in stolid, if unre-markable, support of the melodeon or whatever class of a box it was. And so, I pushed in the door.

The scene, while strange, was oddly familiar. Around a half dozen wooden tables was seated the most decrepit-looking bunch of drunks that I'd ever had the good fortune to witness. In the corner of the room, a log fire was burning, though it was nearing midsummer. A number of strategically placed guttering candles illuminated the customers. They were all decked out in some shade of utilitarian brown that matched their thick russet faces. Some had stopped singing to cast a wary peasant eye at our entrance, while the rest continued their dreary hum; I got the distinct impression that not even an appearance of the Archangel Gabriel in full feather would have caused much of a stir to this bunch of rummies. When the bandonéon, for such it was, creaked to a halt, I remembered that the scene reminded me of the *Potato Pickers,* though Van Gogh's crew looked a lot more spiffy and a damn sight more appealing. Now that we were over their doorstep, most gazed at us in bleary-eyed wonder; the rest were too far gone to bother their humpy asses.

Over in one corner of the room stood a small rough wooden bar of sorts, with some bottles stored behind it on a couple of drooping shelves. Employing the universal etiquette of bar patrons, Hammy and I bellied up and examined the fare. None of the hooch seemed even vaguely familiar, nor did anyone volunteer to serve us, or even bid us the time of the day. We stood there on the earthen floor, not sure of our next move. By this time, most of the singers had resumed their droning chant, and I could only imagine the language of Copernicus, impatiently awaiting our return. Finally, I turned to the congregation and inquired as politely and nonchalantly as possible, "What's the chances of a man getting a drink around here?"

A couple of heads jutted forward but still no reply; my inquiry, however, sparked some kind of grunted discourse between a hag and two of her acquaintances who, on their best hair day, might have given Charles Laughton's Quasimodo a run for his money in the looks department. Nothing, however, appeared to get resolved and the two hunchbacks soon resumed humming along with the choir.

Then Hammy put his best Queens foot forward and had a go for the good old Stars and Stripes. "Beer?" he requested amiably. This caught their attention.

"Bier!" A couple of them nodded and murmured their agreement. One even took a long swig out of some kind of rough tankard, the likes of which might have been used by the villagers in the original *Nosferatu*.

"Motherfuckers!" The distant roar of Copernicus cut across the bittersweet high notes of the bandonéon. The potato pickers—for I had come to view them as such—halted in midnote and looked at one another in alarm. I couldn't be certain if the term had some kind of universal coinage, or if the enraged ferocity of the Brooklyn accent had roused the fear of Jesus in their Communist souls. Whatever the reason, I knew this was do or die. It would not be long until he'd come bursting through that door to drag the two of us out. I reached into my pocket and produced a crisp twenty-dollar bill. This I waved in a small counterclockwise circle in front of my face. Andrew Jackson in real life never produced the gasp of wonder that his picture elicited in this hovel in the back of Central Europe's beyond. The hag shot up from her broad posterior as though a red-hot poker had been inserted. The two Quasimodos kept pace on her either side. All three scurried across the floor and leaned expectantly over the rough bar counter, their pocked potato faces pasted with obsequious smiles.

"Beer," Hammy repeated as I continued to twirl the magic twenty.

"Bier!" The two Quasimodos echoed and dropped down beneath the counter. The hag was now beside herself with joy and smiled so broadly we got a full view inside her toothless mouth. She exhaled at the same time and the smell of her breath reminded me of a hot day outside the police stables in Tribeca. Just in time, her helpers dragged forth a cobwebbed wooden case stuffed to the rims with dark unlabeled bottles. There was something about their slit-eyed smiles that caused me to question the nature and taste of this concoction. "Good stuff?" I inquired, a shade too harshly.

Their faces creased in hurt alarm; they jumped back under the counter and dragged forth another similar box. There was a standoff for a moment. I wasn't sure that these jokers might not be about to poison us; but the first case was lead heavy and I was afraid of risking any more conversation for fear they might produce a third. The hag was outraged that I felt called upon to lift for myself. After much screaming, she drew out and put the toe of her boot somewhere in the upper regions of the nearest Quasi's arse. With a howl probably heard in the Kremlin, the affronted hunchback hoisted a case up on his shoulder and yelled at his partner to do likewise, whereupon they both lurched out the door in front of us. I was already expecting trouble from Copernicus and figured I'd better return with something more to his liking than mere alcohol. "Prague?" I inquired, pointing this way and that in the hope of illumination.

The whole room stared back at me blankly. "Prague?" I repeated to more dropped jaws. Then Hammy, who had been devouring guidebooks since lifting off from Kennedy, pulled off a coup. "Praha?" He enunciated expertly, and the room lit up. The whole saloon sprang into action, escorted us eagerly out on the roadway, and, to a man and a hag, pointed down one of the forks in the road. Then with the two Quasis staggering in front, they escorted us back to the van. They could now smell the dollars and were attempting to sell us more than the beer. A number of them pointed at the hag, but we found it hard to believe that they were being so literal. Even though we were a bunch of jaded New York rock musicians who had seen and done most things under God's heaven, we did have some standards. Copernicus, an accomplished linguist, loftily declined to mediate; and some moments later, we took off down the road to waves from the assembled crew, still uncertain as to the nature of their proposed barter.

There was a glacial silence in the van; our leader was obviously still smarting at our lack of discipline. This did not cause us much stress as we'd all had difficult girlfriends at one time or another and silence, frigid or otherwise, was something we were well able for. The beer tasted cobwebby, but after forcing down the first, the second and third went down smoothly enough and hit the desired spot. The road, too, had improved. An occasional light now illuminated signs pointing toward Praha and all, once more, appeared well with the world. Slouched over in the backseat, I fell to thinking about how in the name of God I had ended up behind the Iron Curtain with this bunch of lunatics.

Thomas Hamlin had been instrumental in that, too. Some six months after the demise of the Major Thinkers, he told me that, he and Mike Fazio were getting together on Monday evenings in Donny Fury's rehearsal studio down on Spring Street. Would I care to come along for a blow? I had no desire to play pop music anymore, but with the Faze involved I knew we would be many times removed from the Top Forty. Mister Fazio was a self-taught guitarist and a painter of the sonic. He could, if called upon, make his guitar resemble the London Philharmonic fed through a distortion pedal, and that even before his first drink or toke. Hammy also mentioned that Dave Conrad would be attending. Dave was that unlikely mixture of a top-of-the-line funk bassist fascinated by melody. It promised to be a pretty lethal foursome. I suggested that we invite Fred Parcells, the über-trombonist. Fred had shown up onstage at Copernicus gigs and, for about six months, hadn't even bothered to introduce himself. With sometimes up to fifteen musicians wailing away, it was often hard to distinguish just where the sounds were coming from, let alone the musicians. Fred, a man of few words, never bothered to enlighten us that he was electronically feeding his horn through an array of effects. Sometimes, instead of playing, he would sing into the bowl of the bone. This practice produced eerie spectral melodies that would not have been out of place in a psychotic funeral undertaker's home. He was also a graduate of the New England Conservatory of Music and did Latin jazz gigs up in Spanish Harlem. It was rumored around the Village that, in his off time, he had transcribed all the recorded solos of Charlie Parker.

Donny had a humdinger of a studio, though it was moderately priced. He was a bit of a recording whiz and knew his basement room inside out. Amps, mics, and drumkit were placed in odd corners for optimum effect. He would do a rough sound check, then retire upstairs where he was raising his two children. Chill Faction, for that's the name we decided upon, would then solemnly drink and smoke for the first half hour, unwinding, as it

were. We would then turn out the lights, except for one that illuminated a rickety music stand on which I would place some sheets
of lyrics. In honor of Monty Python, we dubbed the Faze and Fred,
the Ministry of Funny Sounds. It's hard to even describe the ethereal oddness of the noises and melodies they could coax from their
combined instruments. To my own untutored ear, they often
sounded like symphonic music for psychosomatic Martians
giving head; while a dancer of my acquaintance once described
them as addled Abyssinians having a successful, if bizarre, run at
Gregorian chant.

Hammy and Dave, meanwhile, were known to kick out the
jams in James Brown-influenced grooves. Each seemed to have an
innate understanding of what the other might be thinking, for
they could spin on a dime into a Sly and Robbie situation before
breaking down into an anarchistic romp and then veering off into
a perfect South Bronx hip-hop groove. I usually bided my time
and listened to the four of them before adding an Arto Lindsay
DNA-type skittering guitar somewhere above the Faze's more
melodic lines. When the groove and melody had settled into
something that I could, more or less, get my head around and
identify keywise, I would dive in from the high board and begin
singing whatever lyrics happened to be placed in front of me. This
could often be an awkward entry, but as the melodies and
phrasing settled into my head, I would gradually construct a song
on top of the musical and rhythmic rumblings emanating from
beneath. The lyrics usually concerned some manner of reflection
on various twisted and masochistic romantic relationships that
were all the go in the East Village of the day. They rarely favored
happy endings, not surprisingly, seeing that none of us had ever
experienced such a thing.

These were some of the happiest nights of my creative life. The
sheer joy of putting a song together where there had been none
five minutes before! Gone was any idea of manufacturing four-
minute "jewels" to entice the pop world. These songs were more
like carved howls at the Almighty that we could accept or reject
depending on our fancy. Sometimes the song was captured there

and then, for we taped everything; on other occasions we would listen to our efforts and, after a couple of slugs, redo the piece. But only once, and that was that. Chill Faction's songs had need of strong legs and quickly.

The beauty of all this was that we weren't trying to be anything, just five musicians going for it and not giving tuppence if we fell on our combined faces. We met for a year or two—who was counting? It was as much a social club as a band. We probably only played out about six times: explosive gigs, mostly at Tramps; nor did we care who liked us or who didn't. We never tried to pick up a following, although we gained a small one. It was all about the music and the self-expression, and when Chill Faction's day was up, we just didn't schedule the next Monday and that was that. No tears, no regrets, just the experience and a surfeit of memories. Later on, all five of us would play varying roles in the formation, philosophy, and recordings of Black 47, but that would be a different kettle of fish and somewhere down the line.

When Copernicus approached me about putting a band together to take to Eastern Europe, I didn't look any further than Chill Faction. He had been in touch with various political and dissident groups in Germany, Poland, Czechoslovakia, Lithuania, and Russia and proposed a run from Hamburg to Moscow. What a trip! And at what a time, June 1989, with the Iron Curtain rolling back, even if Reagan's incompetent CIA couldn't see what was obvious to anyone with half a brain. We had already witnessed the rumblings in East Germany. We had no idea that we were about to be a part of the process in Czechoslovakia.

The organizers of our gig in Prague were beside themselves with worry when we lumbered down the main drag in the early morning. They were dissidents straight out of central casting: intellectuals with berets, chiseled beards, penciled moustaches, ubiquitous cigarettes, and cappuccino enthusiasm. Much of their English was broken, but there was a familiar ring to it, both in cadence and vocabulary. Everyone seemed to be taking a walk on the wild side, waiting for my man, standin' on a corner with a suitcase in their hand, before it dawned on us that many

Czechoslovakians had learned their English from Lou Reed and Velvet Underground records. As we poured out of the van—almost legless after the long miles from Berlin and the cobwebby beer—they embraced us like long-lost brothers.

But there was another angle to their relieved enthusiasm. As they checked us into our hotel rooms, they informed us that our show was being moved from a local boys' club to the ice hockey stadium. We were to be one of the headliners for the first major unauthorized rock festival in Czechoslovakia. From what I could gather, they needed the reputation of major foreign "superstars" such as the Copernicus Traveling Circus to book the ice hockey stadium. I refrained from telling them that, on our best night, we might have pulled a hundred people at Max's. But they were on fire with enthusiasm, and I'm not sure that this small detail would have made any difference. Their main goal was to throw down the gauntlet to the Communist authorities. Who or what helped them didn't seem to matter. We had just happened to stumble in at the right moment in history. They had, they assured us, the blessing of Václav Havel, one of my playwright heroes, so who were we to argue? Over many shots of Armenian brandy, we stumbled even more, but managed to rise to the occasion and toast the coming revolution; and long live rock 'n' roll and Franz Kafka, William S. Burroughs, Charles Bukowski, not forgetting Zeus himself, Mister Lou Reed.

It sounded like a plan on the night. In the morning, it had a good ring to it. And at the sound check it was still plausible. The backdrop of the huge stage was a Day-Glo futuristic canvas that looked as though it had been assaulted by a Czech disciple of Jackson Pollock on acid. Looking out at the massive empty auditorium, though, I wondered if we would even put a dent in the floorboards, considering the size of our usual audiences. The attitude of the organizers was the universally worrying catchall: "No problem." Some of the best bands in the country, they assured us, would also be playing, and the call was out far and near. They were as good as their word. We had to fight our way into the stadium—packed with twelve thousand people, while outside another eight thousand milled about seeking tickets.

Copernicus nervously strutted around backstage, his chest
thrown out like a cock-sparrow: all these people here and to see
him! The rest of us, less enthralled with ourselves, caught the
opening bands. There was a fervor to the crowd that I had never
before witnessed. This was much more than just getting high and
catching some music. It was rock 'n' roll actually doing what it
was supposed to: uplifting minds and hearts and leading the attack
against monolithic statist thuggery. I had been inclined toward
socialism for most of my life, but the scum ruling in the Eastern
Bloc had nothing in common with any of the ideas that I held
dear. They believed in central government all right, but they used
it to dominate and control and, above all, to hold on to power.
And now, their militia was ensconced in the top tier of the balcony, with guns pointing at the stage and the huge audience. I
turned to the nearest dissident leader. He was dressed all in black,
cigarette drooping from his mouth. With as much requisite coolness as I could muster, I inquired what he thought of the situation.
He took a long pull on his Gauloise and grinned as the smoke
poured from his nostrils. "Hey, babe," he began and I half-expected
him to exhort me to take a walk on the wild side. Instead, he
waved his cigarette at the crowd. "They cannot all of us kill."

It was not exactly what I wanted to hear. In fact, it was hard to
take one's eyes from the top tiers, especially with the gunmetal
glinting in the psychedelic lights. But the music was spectacular.
I stood at side stage entranced by Pulnoc. A number of the players
had been involved with the infamous Plastic People of the Universe. Though apolitical, these musicians had actually gone to jail
for playing their music—a far cry from New York where the
worst you might expect was a kick in the butt from a cop for
smoking a joint. Although Pulnoc played regular rock beats, a
deep Central European drone drove the songs and informed the
Czech lyrics. The darkness of midcontinent spilled out from the
stage and was returned with vehemence by the audience. The music
rose and subsided in waves and encircled us all. Milan Hlavsa, lost
in his darkness, pounded out a bass that shook the walls of the
arena and Tony Duchacek, guesting from the band Garaz, an

everything-that-Elvis-should-have-been rocker, took off his shirt
to reveal the perfect torso and nailed us all with his ripping bari-
tone. I had no clue what they were saying. It didn't matter. I
understood every word. rock 'n' roll was made for the dark flow
of the Czech language. This was music that had been contained
and constrained for years and, on this day, it was bursting forth at
the seams, spurred on by the fire of freedom.

And then we were onstage ourselves. We knew a thing or two
about drones and pulsing overtones from nights in Max's and
CB's. I had found the perfect throbbing setting on our synthesizer
and the Faze added to it a Janáček-type figure that sent murmurs
through the audience. Then Hammy and Dave kicked in a Lower
East Side funk rumble and we were away in a canter, gradually
building the tension until the eyes of the front rows popped and
the crowd surged forward to the stage. When we had it at fever
pitch, Copernicus strode on. He had in his hand a huge Bible. We
dropped the volume but kept the intensity pumping; he opened
the tome and showed it to the crowd. They hooted back their
recognition. When he had them in his fist, he slammed the Word
of God to the stage. Then he pointed up at the militia in the balcony, lest there be any misunderstanding, before roaring out, "I
have always been in trouble with the Authorities!"

The English speakers in the crowd understood and cheered
madly. Gradually his words were translated and passed on to the
others; wave after wave of applause broke out across the floor and
swelled toward the balconies, until it felt like the roof was going
to lift off and take with it the guns of the oppressors. It was one of
those rare gigs in a musician's life where Murphy's Law is totally
suspended, transcended, and everything goes right. Perhaps on
that occasion, it would have been hard to go wrong anyway. But
Copernicus won the day with that perfect nine-word challenge.
The audience was there to demonstrate that they would no
longer be slaves, no longer be taken for granted in their own
country. We simply showed up and acted as catalysts. Still, it's an
amazing feeling when the times and your own small destiny inter-
sect. We should have broken up on the spot for everything after

was anticlimactic. We had great gigs ahead, particularly in Lithuania where people brought out their children just to hear the forbidden American sounds, and then stood in line for hours to shake our hands. Somehow or other we got to play in a huge Communist Party theater in Moscow for thousands of dissidents, and strode down the Arabat after the gig, heroes to the crowd. But that night in Prague was one-hundred-proof magic. It changed a lot of lives, and the dissidents who organized the event showed the youth of Czechoslovakia that they could successfully challenge a corrupt and rotten government.

It changed me, too. I had left New York for Eastern Europe still disgusted with rock music and what it had become. But I had seen firsthand that the old girl still had claws and, when put in the right situation, she could go after the eyes and jugular of all the mediocrity arrayed against her. She had given me new life. I didn't know how I was going to do it or in what way, shape, or manner; but I was determined to start a new band and have one last blast at creating something new and vibrant and, above all, political.

21

PADDY'S GOT A BRAND NEW REEL

So Papa's got a brand new bag
What's the big deal?
Up in the Bronx
Mary's gettin' drunk
Paddy's got a brand new reel.

Workin' like a dog out in Queens
Seven or eight days a week
Goin' to confession
Is your granny's obsession
Paddy's got a brand new reel.

I don't give a damn about you
'Cause you don't care about me
Hey, Charlie Haughey,
I'm sick of your party
Paddy's got a brand new reel.

And when I go back home
As I eventually will
Hey politician
Better get a mortician
Paddy's got a brand new
Paddy's got a brand new
Paddy's got a brand new reel.

From the original Home of the Brave *cassette,*
and Black 47, *independent 1991*
Published by Starry Plough Music (BMI)

IT'S FUNNY HOW all the influences from your past can combine and send your life hurtling off in a different direction. At the time you have no idea that this is happening. But as they say in the theater: everything begins with a thought. Forming Black 47 began that night onstage in Prague; yet some of the ideas that would guide the band had already been in play for years. Oddly enough, the theater brought me back to music, though one could even say that my grandfather played a part in the genesis of the band.

I had been wrestling with a play called *Mister Parnell* ever since finishing *Liverpool Fantasy*. Charles Stewart Parnell led the Irish Parliamentary Party through the 1880s and came very close to gaining home rule for Ireland. He was called the Uncrowned King and was worshipped by the mass of the people. Yet, many deserted him when he was cited in a divorce case as the lover of Catherine O'Shea, the wife of a renegade member of his party. He later married her, but not before gaining the opprobrium of the Catholic Church. He lost a series of by-elections in Ireland and died in 1891. With his death went the last chance for a peaceful transition to a united and free Ireland, albeit one that, like in Canada and Australia, would have maintained a special relationship with Britain.

One of these by-elections was held in Carlow when my grandfather was ten years of age. His immediate family split over Parnell. Some followed the man and others the Church; they did not speak until many decades later. He often spoke to me about the bitterness engendered by the "split." The story was full of drama and ultimate heartbreak; it involved all of the great staples of Irish life: the church, politics, sexuality, ambition, inheritance of a large sum of money, betrayal, and eventual guilt. Because of the strictures of Victorian life, few knew that Parnell had lived with Catherine for many years as man and wife, and that they had two girls who were the hidden pawns in the case. I was determined to get to the bottom of the whole miasma and show, through a musical play, what exactly had transpired. And so I set off with great zeal to uncover the songs that would have been on the lips of the people around 1890. To my surprise, I already knew them all, for they had still been current in the Wexford of my boyhood

where they were rendered in the same stilted Victorian style of
Parnell's day.

This exercise sparked off a whole new train of thought. On the
way from my mind to the cassette recorder, the old melodies cast off
much of the Victorian calcification and revealed their beauty. One
that springs to mind is "The Sally Gardens." That melody, though
exquisite, can seem very hackneyed in its original treatment; yet,
cut away all of the extraneous vibrato and showboating, and it rings
as clearly as a mountain spring. What, then, if the tune found its
own backbeat? You can't walk around New York with a melody in
your head and not find a rhythm propelling it. At the time, I was
experimenting with drum machines and could, in minutes, knock
out whatever beat came to mind. It wasn't long until "The Sally
Gardens" shook off the dust of a century and morphed into something more dynamic and driven. I heretically scrapped Yeats's beautiful, though perhaps oversentimental, lyrics and set the story in
modern-day Manhattan. But the song still lacked contrast and tension, so I added an instrumental theme and a bridge. The trick was
to write them in such a way that they would perfectly complement
the original melody and seem as though they sprang from it. Thus
was "Forty Shades of Blue" born.

One of the ways I supported myself in the period between the
Thinkers and Black 47 was by writing music for modern dance. In
the East Village of the '80s there was great interaction between
musicians, choreographers, and dancers on both a professional
and social level. In fact, it was in this milieu that I met my own
choreographer and began composing pieces of music for her company. Most of the modern dance music of the time was very min-
imalist and Philip Glass-influenced. I'm a great appreciator of
Phil's music; in fact, Pierce and I heard him work out a number of
his signature pieces when he lived upstairs from us on First
Avenue. There was a cold mechanical feel to much of the offerings
of his imitators, however, and music to me has always been about
passion and humanity. In reaction, I began to experiment with the
warmest and most live instrument: the human voice. But I found
that choreographers did not wish to set dances to English lyrics,

for fear of being mistaken for MTV skits, a kiss of death in the then rather purer artistic world.

I started to use Gaelic. Back in Ireland, we had all gained a rudimentary knowledge of the language in school, but because it was compulsory and the teachers had not been native speakers, most of us had dropped *an Gaeilge* immediately after graduation. Yet, many of the words were still knocking around in my brain. I would record pieces of music on synthesizer or guitar and drum machine, then run the tape and sing in Irish off the top of my head. This use of our native language had a powerful effect; it was as if something almost feral brushed by me, bringing me back in touch with the most distant of my forebears. For the first time, I really saw that many things had been taken away from us, while often ill-fitting replacements had been roughly superimposed over both our culture and perception. There is a saying in Gaelic—*Tír gan teanga, tír gan ainm*—a people without a language is a people without a soul. There had to be a foundation, and it struck me that I had been building my own career and life on a heap of sand. I loved rock music but, at the heart of many of my songs, there was an emptiness because I wasn't black and hadn't come from R & B; neither was I southern with roots in rockabilly; nor inner city and sprung from hip-hop, or Jamaican with reggae as my inheritance. I could and would definitely use all of those influences, but I needed to finally come to terms with my own background.

Speaking of things roughly superimposed, I had to make peace or, at least accommodation, with religion. There is something exuberant and full of life about the Irish temperament that is not suited to the two strains of Christianity that have dominated the country for the past two centuries. Catholic Jansenism and doom-laden Presbyterianism often bring out the worst in Irish people and both have left a profound stamp on our artistic sensibility. (This is not to confuse these two bodies with the earlier native Celtic Catholic Church or the first Irish Presbyterians who refused fealty to king and country if it meant honoring bishops.) You had only to look at our history to see the sad, often sectarian, effect these two foreign influences have had on the affairs of the country; I only had to look inside my own heart and mind to witness firsthand the repression that dogmatic Catholicism fosters. As a boy, I had revolted against it because Catholicism failed to take account of our natural sexuality. I had also bucked against its Northern counterpart because it had allowed the good side of its message—the unhindered communion of the devotee with God—to become distorted into a discriminatory hatred of Catholics and Catholicism.

By using raw pieces of the Irish language I caught some glimpses into what the Irish nature could have been without the introduction of these two prudish and intolerant forces. I wanted to get back to the earthier, more joyful roots of the Irish character. Right from the start there has been a Dionysian element in rock 'n' roll, probably because of the black R & B influences; but I could see traces of the same, if more subdued, strains in Irish folk music and poetry. My choreographer and I had already brought the primal and achingly sensual Gaelic poem, "Lament for Art O'Leary," alive on the stage. A theater piece, unfortunately, is seen by few, and once its run is over, it replays only in the memory of those who attended. I knew there had to be a way of mixing modern popular music and Gaelic sensibility to allow for the free-flowing expression of the old, uninhibited Irish soul.

These realizations didn't spring from some kind of sudden epiphany: there was no road to Damascus for me. I didn't either, to my shame, go out and relearn Gaelic, but I did allow all of my Irish influences to come to the fore on long nights of thinking and writing; and I nurtured them carefully so that they would eventually become part of a foundation on which to build Black 47.

Playwriting, for the most part, is solitary work. You spend long hours wrestling with characters and scenes, for every word and action must be true to some spine or original idea. Make one slip in the plot, have one actor say something out of character, and you snap the theatergoer out of the fantasy you've been spinning. The play is essentially over at that moment. You've failed. In fact, you can fail in so many myriad ways with a play, I sometimes wonder why any of us put ourselves through the years of thought that often go into the making of one. And that's without even dealing with the key ingredient: drama. Damn those Greeks! It would be so much simpler if we could all agree to just write slice-of-life vignettes such as is shown every night on television. But no, the greats from Sophocles through Shakespeare to Shepard have all succeeded in bringing the human condition to the stage in dramatic form, and if you want to even kiss the dust that arises from their feet, you better figure out how you're going to inject some tension into your own poor flaccid offering. In other words, playwriting's a bitch! It takes time and it changes you—not always for the better.

I'd always had a bit of a solitary, closed-off streak. Music had been my savior—"my special friend," as Jim Morrison pronounced; it had got me out in the world, joining bands and performing in front of people, as opposed to throwing shapes at the bedroom mirror. It's not that I was particularly shy, although there was an element of that too, but I never had a problem spending long periods alone. Playwriting was a perfect excuse for that kind of antisocial behavior. To write plays, you need time on your own. Chill Faction was kaput and Copernicus played infrequently; I had no outlet for performance anymore and I didn't care. But I could feel myself changing, becoming quieter, often lost in thought, an observer rather than a doer.

One night I was home alone in New York, as usual writing away. I got stuck on some phrase or other. A vague feeling of discontent began to rise in me. No matter what field of writing, you get that from time to time and usually manage to shrug it off. But this was different. The discomfort surged, until I was almost paralyzed with doubt and depression; the more I tried to focus on the phrase, the more the very notion of writing and indeed everything I was doing with my life appeared nonsensical. I had a sudden uncontrollable urge to get out of the chair, the room, the building as fast as I could—get outside—just walk, take in a couple of mighty lungfuls of air, and go anywhere, do anything but what I was doing. I almost took the door off its hinges on the way out, and headed over to the East Village. I hoped I might run into some old friends, but instead I felt like an exile arriving home after years overseas. Everywhere seemed the same: the smells, sights, and sounds, but I didn't recognize anyone and was further alienated by an overall self-conscious attempt at coolness that I hadn't remembered, or perhaps recognized, back when I used to live in the area myself.

I was already on my way up Second Avenue when I had an overwhelming desire to hear an Irish accent. This was a new one on me. But as I thought about it, I realized that, what with living down in Soho and not playing the Bronx anymore, I no longer ran into Irish people, except for the occasional nanny in the park. I was full of a raw nervy energy. I figured I'd walk up to the strip of East Side Irish bars in the Fifties, have a couple of pints, listen to some Paddies and banish whatever was ailing me from my system.

I was cruising past Twenty-eighth Street when I noticed Paddy Reilly's Bar. I could hear the strains of music and figured I'd stop in for a quick one before pressing on. The joint was brightly lit and about half full; I was just about to turn and go, for I felt strange and out of place. Just then the barmaid caught my eye and smiled. I doubt that most barmaids ever realize the power they have to make a man feel at home and welcome in those first few wavering seconds. This one had been a nurse, and would ultimately become in-house psychiatrist and big sister for a generation of Irish bands; so perhaps she could sense my unease. I ordered a pint and when she brought it over she asked if I'd care to risk a shot. It was by far the most sensible suggestion I'd heard in months. I told her I'd have a Jameson's, but not to contaminate it with even a suggestion of ice or water. She watched me toss it down and nodded her approval; she then informed me that whiskey often put a better spin on things. No truer words had ever been uttered.

She told me she hailed from Monaghan. With the whiskey flowing, I remarked that she couldn't be held responsible for such misfortune and wasn't that "Big Tom" country? She said she knew the man personally, gave me a playful slap on the back of the head, and told me to behave myself—there were gentlemen present who would not stand idly by and see a lady insulted. After the second pint, I went over to a table to watch the band. I didn't like to leave the barmaid whose name was Dympna, for she was cheering me up greatly and could give as good as she got; but I've always felt a bit weird talking while musicians are performing, perhaps because I've endured so much of it myself.

The band was called Beyond the Pale. They were very pleasant and easy on the ear, but had a slight edge that kept your attention. There were four of them: a brawny and handsome lead singer who played guitar and had a very melodious voice; an intense uilleann piper who also played various whistles and a bodhrán while singing along in unison on most choruses; and two good fiddle players—a man and a woman. They would play a set of three or four jigs and reels, and then the singer would deliver a couple of songs. Although I became familiar with most of the tunes in the years to come, at the time I couldn't tell a jig from a reel to save my life. The choice of songs was interesting. I remember "Wish You Were Here," a lament for Pink Floyd's first guitarist, the schizophrenic Syd Barrett, as well as pieces by Neil Young, Christy Moore, and Dylan. The band had a sloppy, easygoing feel that suited the mood of the place. No great attention was being paid to the music, a fact that didn't seem to bother them. From time to time, though, much like at a Grateful Dead concert, the audience would totally tune into the vibe and sing along with fervor; then, just as suddenly, they'd return to wholesale drinking, obviously the main reason for most people's presence.

I was glad to be there, too. There was a warmth and conviviality to the room, and to the performance, that set my mind drifting back to the early days of Turner and Kirwan, when we weren't as consumed with originality, and would play whatever we wanted, when we wanted to. I realized with a pang that those had been happy times: I hadn't been worried about sets or encores or what the business thought about me or the band; it was all about the music and that indescribable moment when it connected with and then captured the audience. That brought to mind also the burnout pressure-filled last years with the Major Thinkers when we'd play the same set every night, until you were like an eternal traveler who knew every bend on the road and could remember exactly how you'd felt the last time you passed that spot. Success in the music business, I thought, was all about that: corralling a feeling or a moment, coming up with a suitable marketing plan, and then pounding it into the ground until the whole world identified you with your song or sound. But that dull concept was so far from the reasons that had originally propelled me into music. No wonder I had quit.

I was lost in thought and didn't hear the first time my name was announced. I even looked over my own shoulder to see why everyone had turned round. To my horror, the piper was informing the crowd that I had been a member of the late great Major Thinkers, and if they clapped loudly enough, I might favor them with a song. That was the last thing on my mind. I was enjoying just sitting there in the warmth of the bar with the even warmer glow of the booze coursing through me. And then Dympna was at my side with a full glass of whiskey and a smile to beat the band, and I took a sip, and then a slug, and then another, until singing seemed like the most obvious thing in the world.

The guitarist, Patrick McGuire, seemed relieved to hand over the guitar; no surprise, after three sets onstage. Chris Byrne, the piper, told me he had seen a number of Thinkers' shows and asked me what I wanted to play. I told him I hadn't a clue. It felt strange to have an acoustic in my hands again. One desolate night some years previously, I'd smashed my own when I felt I didn't have anything more to say or sing about. The crowd was waiting—and so was I—for some kind of inspiration. When it didn't come, I took another slug of John Jameson's best, and told the players to hang on, I'd just play whatever came to mind. I can't recall what I sang. I do remember ending up a long time later with Dylan's "Like a Rolling Stone." I'd had the time of my life, but been in a daze that I only came out of when sitting at the bar.

Soon after, Chris joined me. I was surprised that the other three had left so soon. He shrugged: it was their last night and the band was breaking up. I remembered the hint of tension earlier, and things fell into place. I'd been through it myself and sympathized. With that, we took to drinking, aided and abetted by Dympna. I was surprised that Chris had seen the Thinkers; we were more of an East Village-oriented band. He said he always kept an eye on things Irish. It was my turn to shrug.

We talked about Bobby Sands and the effect the hunger strikes had on both of us. It was odd speaking with a committed Irish republican after so long. Even during the Sands protests outside the British consulate, I had been as much observer as participant, and now I was listening to many of my grandfather's political stances from the mouth of a younger man. We talked about the demise of the Clash, the death of Bob Marley, and the dearth of any kind of meaningful political music. One thing we were both agreed on: music could have a positive and challenging effect on society. We also focused on Ireland and America and the differences between each country's perceptions of the other. He was sizing me up on this because he had, in the past, keenly felt the snubs of native Irish toward Irish-Americans.

I was much taken with his many humorous edgy retorts that had me almost falling off my stool with laughter. On a serious note, I told him that I felt that there would be no change in the Northern situation until the United States got involved. Parnell believed that, as did Collins. He thought there was little chance of such a thing happening while the Republican Party governed the White House. I didn't think the emasculated Democratic Party would be a whole lot better, but he didn't see that there was much choice. We both felt that Irish America needed a radical boot up the behind and that it was more likely to come from the grass roots up rather than from the current sterile leadership.

We drank on until the dawn and it was great to be with someone who knew exactly what you were talking about, even if he didn't agree with everything you said. I realized just how isolated I'd become from music, politics, and Irish life in general. In the end, Reilly's was closing and even Dympna was going home; I helped him load the PA into his Ford Escort, and even that felt good; it had been a long time since I'd humped gear. We moved downtown to the Emerald on Spring Street for more drinks and talked right through the sunrise. In the end he grew silent and I asked him the problem. He said that, with Beyond the Pale breaking up, he was in trouble. There were gigs to be fulfilled and he didn't have a band. It seemed so simple.

"I'll do it," I said. Maybe he'd been working toward that all along, or perhaps my offer came out of the blue. Whatever! We shook hands on the matter. In the end, I remember standing on the corner of West Broadway and Grand Street around seven in the morning and nodding to one of my neighbors on his way to work, while bidding Chris good-bye. I had a feeling that my life was about to change. I had no idea how much.

22

ROCKIN' THE BRONX

Got a job in a band called Black 47
I was doin' nothin' special after eleven
We learned some tunes wrote some songs
Bought ourselves a drum machine to keep the beat strong.

We bought the *Irish People,* the *Echo,* and the *Voice*
Rang a few bars said, "We got a new noise
And it would please us greatly to come on uptown
Show you Paddies how we get on down."

One o'clock, two o'clock give us a chance
All we want to do is be rockin' the Bronx
Three o'clock, four o'clock what do we want?
All we want to do is be rockin' the
Rockin' the Bronx!

Well, we got a gig in the Village Pub
But the regulars there all said that we sucked
Then Big John Flynn said "Oh no, no
You'll be causin' a riot if I don't let you go."

Then a Flintstone from the Phoenix gave us a call
But when he heard the beat he was quite appalled
"D'yez not know nothin' by Christy Moore?"
The next thing you'll be wantin' is "Danny Boy."

Chris is chillin' on the uilleann but he isn't alone
Here comes Freddy on the slide trombone.
Add a little guitar, Geoff Blythe on the sax
Gonna shoot you full of our New York fix!

Then we went into the studio made a tape
Frank Murray from the Pogues said, "I think that it's great."
Galigula said, "It could be a hit
And if it falls on its face who gives a shit?"

Now everywhere we go we cause a fuss
'Cause we play what we like, our sound is us
Got a whole lot of hell, a little bit of heaven
That's the story so far of Black 47.

From Black 47, *independent 1991 and* Fire of Freedom, *EMI Records 1993*
Published by Starry Plough Music/EMI Blackwell Music (BMI)

CHRIS SHOWED UP at my place straight from work. He carried with
him his pipes, whistles, bodhrán, and a gun. He was a cop. I had just
been running through a new song called "Too Late to Turn Back" on
electric guitar and drum machine. I wasn't exactly sure just what I
was going to play on the gigs, but I no longer owned an acoustic, the
natural accompaniment for the pipes. "Too Late" was turning out
well and Chris liked the feel of it. I had the drum machine programmed to a tense pulsing beat. I taught Chris the instrumental
line that I had written for the synthesizer and we played the song. It
sounded great; so within minutes, and purely by chance, the original
bare-bones Black 47 sound was created. There were some other originals that we also rehearsed including "Desperate"—which we
linked with Bob Marley's "Three Little Birds"; "Land of DeValera"
and "Elvis Murphy" also come to mind. I wrote down too a list of
about fifteen covers that ran a gamut from Dylan, Van Morrison, and
Marley to traditionalists like Ewan MacColl and Dominic Behan.
Chris gave me a tape of jigs, reels, slides, hornpipes, and slow airs and
I set to work trying to figure out what in the name of God I was going

to play with them. The idea was that the covers be replaced by originals as quickly as possible. From such small beginnings, we headed off to conquer the world by way of the Bronx.

On the way up in Chris's car, we hammered out three sets and decided that from then on we would repeat the first for a fourth, on the assumption that few people were likely to stay and listen to us over the course of the five or so hours involved; and if they were so fanatical, they would scarcely be sober enough to remember just what we'd played in the first set anyway. We needn't have troubled ourselves, for the reality was that those who were there for the first set were invariably history by the second. The first gig, at any rate, was likely to be a piece of cake, or so Chris predicted. It was a political benefit featuring Bernadette Devlin McAliskey; we were to warm up her audience, then keep them entertained after she had finished. It would be a hometown crowd, as it were, and who gave a damn at benefits anyway, Chris also reasoned. I was thrilled at the very thought of sharing a stage with Bernadette. She had been one of my childhood heroes and I had vivid memories of her manning the barricades in the Battle of the Bogside.

The gig was in the back room of a pub in the North Bronx. This establishment, appropriately enough, got dynamited some years later and I can't say that I shed many tears. The place was deserted and the bartenders ignored our arrival; little had apparently changed in my years away from the only borough on the mainland. But things began to look up in the bare-as-bones back room, for we found Dympna stocking a makeshift bar. We set up our equipment carefully, like two infantrymen thoroughly preparing for a baptism of fire. Vocals, drum machine, and Chris's pipes went through the PA; but after knocking cobwebs off the walls with my first few distorted chords, I figured my electric guitar would do well enough through its Fender Vibrolux amp. We had no monitors and so I ran the drum machine through the guitar amp, an unusual move, but I figured if we couldn't hear the beats all was lost. Because of the loudness of the guitar, we had to jack the volume on the pipes, thereby inclining us to feedback. But what did we know? We were starting from scratch and entering virgin territory.

I think there were five or six people in the room at the beginning of the first set, including Tom Gartland, a soundman I knew from the Major Thinkers. He helped tame some of the initial feedback by moving the PA speakers further in front of us. This move, however, did little to entice the main body of the crowd who chose to wait for Bernadette out in the front bar. The five or six who grew to a dozen midway through the set had no problem talking over us, and yet they would lapse into a stony silence after each song. I would mumble something about the origins of the next piece, although this did not seem to be required and caused our audience to look up in surprise. With all the audio problems and the fact that we had never played the songs through a PA or in front of people, I suppose we didn't do too badly, but I felt somewhat deflated and even a bit humiliated leaving the stage. It was a new situation for me. Whatever band I'd ever been in before, audiences may not have liked us, but they sure as hell never ignored us.

In the break, Chris seemed a bit dispirited and kept to himself. He had never before played with an electric guitar, not to mention a pounding drum machine. It was all a learning experience for him. I, on the other hand, had played with damn near every manner of instrument known to man, and the going was hard enough for me. Besides, he had a certain stature in this community, with many friends in attendance who were taking a dim view of this new musical experiment. The uilleann pipes are somewhat sacrosanct with Irish people; many feel that they should be unaccompanied or whispered behind on an acoustic guitar. One can only speculate what they thought of a fully effected electric bleeding all over the situation. I talked to Gartland, who had experience in these matters, and asked him how it sounded. "A bit quiet," he replied, somewhat enigmatically. In retrospect, he was probably talking about the crowd, but in my nervousness, I took him to mean the volume. Dympna, once again sensing my unease, gave me my pint but placed a glass of whiskey next to it. I drained the whiskey and it gave me the usual Dutch courage. "Tally-ho," I murmured to myself, for no one else present seemed to give a hoot one way or the other. "I might as well be hung for a sheep as a lamb!"

The crowd was beginning to ooze in, more likely because there was now so little room out front than from any desire to hear us. As we took to the stage, a number of them were quizzing Chris about Patrick's absence. I jacked the master volume of the PA up a couple of notches and likewise my amp and distortion pedal. We began the second set with "Too Late to Turn Back." It seemed only appropriate. The pulsing programmed kick drum immediately got the audience's attention, but when I threw in the first distorted vibrato chord, I could barely hang on to the feedback. My amp was leaking into the vocal and pipes microphones, not only creating new guitar overtones—the likes of which I had never heard before—but adding reverb and delay to the already effected drum machine. It was a maelstrom of sound that Thurston Moore of Sonic Youth would have been proud of and infinitely more capable of handling. But the title of the song said it all. I was still wrestling with the words, not to mention the overdriven guitar, and couldn't spare the couple of hands needed to lower the various volumes. The room was beginning to swell and shake from this apocalyptic roar; the punters had for the first time stopped talking and now had their eyes fixed firmly on the stage. Trying to feign indifference, Chris and I remained stone-faced, though I, for one, was praying like a martyr for the song to end.

Everyone appeared stunned and relieved, but there was still an eerie silence when the closing chord finally died out. I managed to turn the volume controls down and we continued with "Three Little Birds." With this choice, we were back on safe ground, for who on this planet does not like Bob Marley? Straight away a couple of people got up to dance and those hanging around the walls resumed talking; we were, I felt, home and dry. With a bit of coaxing, I even managed to entice some of the very drunk to sing along with the chorus. All was well and good until we segued somewhat unsteadily into "Desperate." The dancers, though flagging a bit in energy, continued to do their best Bronx Rasta imitation, as the beat was the same and, like many in the years to come, they thought that this original was also a work of Marley's.

But life is never simple in the Bronx. A couple of rough-looking

customers, hair greased, chins shaved, and dressed to the nines in
their Sunday best suits, shirts, and ties, now swaggered up to the
front of the stage and began to give us the hairy eyeball. This is
always a bit discomfiting, but I had endured many such punky
confrontations in CB's and the Mudd Club; and Chris was a cop,
so even on our first outing we were far from pushovers. One of
these gobshites gestured imperiously to let me know that he
wished to speak, and would I ever have the decency to stop singing
and entertaining the rest of the crowd, so that he could take a
moment of his precious time to confide a message of great import
to me. He might as well have been talking to the Great Wall of
China for I totally ignored him, though I did concentrate my best
beady-eyed glare at the red rims of his jaundiced eyes. Further-
more, I repeated the final chorus of "Desperate" so many times
that I was heartily sick of it myself. But he had stamina, I'll grant
the bastard that, and held his spot in front of the stage until the
bitter end. May the fires of hell be still burning a new arsehole in
him, the ignorant son of a bitch!

When I could take no more of the song, we finished with a long,
drawn-out, loud, and tasteless crescendo that would have done
credit to Grand Funk Railroad on an off night. Through all this I still
managed to continue boring holes in the off-whites of my antagonist's eyes. But he only halted one beat before delivering the message
that was dearest his heart. "Play an Irish song, will you, for the love of
Jaysus!" He bellowed in frothing, gravely affronted anguish.

His request was ignorant to the extreme, though not nearly as
bad as I had expected. I kept glaring at him for so long, and in a
manner devoid of all emotion, that if he'd even possessed a
glimmer of intelligence, he might have concluded that I was a perfectly working robot. Little did he know that I was waging an inner
battle to calm myself, with a view to summoning up an appropriately scintillating repartee. When it emerged, however, my reply
was far from perfect, although it's been much quoted in sanitized
form. Instead of the measured sneering cadences I visualized, it was
delivered in a somewhat strangled, persecuted whine: "I'm Irish! I
wrote the fucking thing. What does that make it, Swahili?"

I had meant to deliver this sotto voce and only to the cretin himself, but forgot that I was standing in front of the microphone. It resounded throughout the room, especially the F-word, which though used prodigiously by most Irish people, is by common concordat never uttered from the stage. The room stopped in midmotion, as though struck lifeless by this foulest of blasphemies. I was a bit shocked myself, for I hadn't meant to say it. The collected bunch of suited oafs in front of me shook their heads in such a mixture of chagrin and sorrow that I feared they might fall to their knees and beseech Jesus and a full complement of saints and martyrs to publicly castrate me for this affront to Irish propriety. The chief cretin, his brow now furrowed in concentration, appeared to be still wrestling with some deeper meaning to my reply, the African reference in particular having thrown him for a loop.

I waited no more but got stuck right into Van Morrison's "Wild Night," the opening chords of which could get a one-legged jennet dancing. But the damage was done; the floor was swept free of dancers, most of whom had retired to the four walls in some haste for fear they, too, might get struck down by God's almighty thunderbolt of revenge, which was undoubtedly even now on the way. We soldiered on for another half hour or more. Though there was still a core of bilious indignation, the room gradually filled with political activists who couldn't give a damn what language I'd used or if we'd played "In-A-Gadda-Da-Vida" backward, as long as there was a good turnout for the speaker.

And then there was tumult by the door, with bodies being pushed aside for Bernadette who was escorted through the room by a burly entourage and onto the stage. Even my antagonist and his crew put aside their resentment, for this was not an insignificant moment to any of us. She was still small and contained, but you could sense the restive energy percolating just below the surface. The tomboy prettiness that we'd all fallen for as teenagers was long gone. And why wouldn't it with all the store of disappointments she'd had to endure? Not to mention that she still had shards of Loyalist bullets lodged inside her. But Bernadette always had greater issues on her mind than mere looks. It made little difference anyway, for the inspired are always beautiful, and she radiated that same suppressed calmness, kindness, and fierce commitment in her forties that she had as a spitfire twenty-year-old on the battle-scarred streets of Derry. Except that now it was all mellowed by a hint of sadness, even a deep understanding of the iniquities of the world—but never an acceptance of them.

If Bobby Sands was the lost young chieftain that the tribe desired and mourned, Bernadette was the living moral force of her people. There was pride in that room and almost a wonder; for everyone knew that, though diminutive in physical size, we had a giant in our presence. There was concern, too, for her and an urge to pro-tect. She might have escaped the Loyalist death squad who had been allowed to breach the supposed security around her house, but we all feared that an RUC bullet still had her name on it.

I winced as she climbed onto the stage. A Vietnam vet had once told me that, with VC shrapnel still rattling around inside him, there were as many bad days as good. This was not one of Bernadette's better ones. But she quickly gathered herself and impatiently shook off whatever physical ailment had just troubled her. She smiled in comradely fashion, murmured some words of encouragement, and shook hands with us, then drew herself up and looked out across the room. The doors to the outside bar had been thrown back and the crowd was jammed to the four walls. The jukebox was still playing some dumb song and across the expectant murmur of the crowd someone shouted out, "Will someone turn that feckin' thing off!" And when it was finally unplugged, a silence descended on us all, drunk or sober.

She took a measure of the room and summoned up her energy. Her head nodded slightly as she drank in the quiet. Then she smiled, at first almost ruefully but then openheartedly; the warmth radi-ated from her, and each of us knew exactly why we loved her: because no matter what—through thick or thin—Bernie would always tell us the truth as she saw it. It didn't matter if she was screaming at a British prime minister, consoling some poor bat-tered protester, or haranguing a bigoted auxiliary, you got the same deal from her. Many now saw her as a gadfly extremist; and she had been banished to the sidelines, as much by the leaders of the Nationalist community as any Free State government or Tory dictatorship. For she was an absolutist who believed only in the truth, no matter how impolitic or intractable that might be. Tact was never her strongest suit, and you could not depend on her to be politically correct or take advantage of the moment. That was beyond her. But what made her difficult to deal with on the slippery corridors of power in Dublin, London, or D.C. endeared her to the dispossessed dreamers in that bare Sheetrocked backroom in the Bronx. Along with Gerry Adams, she embodied the hopes and aspirations of those nationalists who would never bow down to bigotry or a jackbooted British presence in their country. And of the two, Bernadette often burned brightest, for she was bound by no party or movement and could say what, when, and to whom she liked without fault or fear of a quote that might come back to haunt her.

Her message that night was simple. Young men and women were being picked up by the British army on the streets, in back alleys, and on country roads of Northern Ireland simply for being Irish and wishing to live under an Irish government. The much-boasted-about British birthright of habeas corpus had long been suspended and these young people were being held in custody and interrogated without benefit of a lawyer or any other form of due process. They were then being sentenced to prison for lengthy terms by bigoted judges in juryless courts, often only on the word of some paid informer. This was British justice and she had no time for it. Things had to change now, and things must change before there could be any talk of peace. And you understood in a flash why this woman was considered by her people to be a Joan of Arc of the laneways of East Tyrone and the rainy streets of Derry and Belfast. For when she spoke, everything became crystal clear, and hope was rekindled that the truth would win in the end, no matter how hopeless matters seemed now. That had been Bernie's message when I first saw her and, despite all the years and the heartbreaks and lives sacrificed, it hadn't changed an iota. She believed it, and no matter how much we might have despaired and given up the faith, when she spoke to us, so did we.

In the midst of her oration, a very drunken woman, who looked forty but may have been in her late twenties, burst out crying and mawkishly declared, "Bernie, you're the only one who understands. I've suffered too and so has my family, you're the only one. . . ." And so on and so forth until we were all embarrassed, and some rough men told her to hush up, be quiet, drink some coffee, and don't be making a drunken *óinseach* of yourself. But Bernie held up her hand to silence them and listened to the woman for what seemed like an eternity. In the end, she bade the sobbing drunk approach the stage, leaned down, put her arms around her, and whispered something in her ear. The woman spoke some more, but now quietly and more sensibly, and Bernie listened to her, until she felt listened to, whereupon she strode off through the crowd, her face glowing, well satisfied with herself.

After a deep sigh, for the encounter had siphoned off a lot of her energy, Bernie continued. And I was impressed beyond words, and so was everyone else in that room; not one of us would have given that drunken woman a passing thought, let alone five or ten minutes of our precious time. But that was the difference between Bernie and us. And that's why we love her and always listen to whatever she has to say, no matter how absolute or extreme she may appear in the eyes of others.

23

LIVIN' IN AMERICA

Oh, it's six o'clock and it's time to rock
And me head is beatin' like a drum
In the cold daylight, I feel like shite
And I can't remember last night's fun.
Then the foreman says, "C'mon now, boys,
Stick your fingers down your throats and get to work"
And I wish to Christ, I'd stayed home last night
'Stead of drinkin' in America.

Oh, I knock down walls with big iron balls
I mix cement by the ton
With me tongue hangin' out for a bottle of stout
Sweatin' bullets in the Brooklyn sun
Then I think of her up on Kingsbridge Road
Did she mean what she said last night?
Oh Mammy dear we're all mad over here
Livin' in America.

On me way downtown I think of that clown
And the things that he said last night.
Did he mean them at all, or was it just drink talk
Oh, I must look a terrible sight.
Put me makeup on as I watch the sun
Rise high over Fordham Road

Oh Mammy dear, we're all mad over here
Livin' in America.

Oh the kids aren't dressed and the house is a mess
The Yuppies are networking again
Kiss their darlings good-bye, "Oh, we'll be late tonight
But we should be home by eleven."
Oh me little dears, dry up your tears
Your parents are too busy makin' money
Oh Mammy dear, we're all mad over here
Livin' in America.

Workin' with the black man, Dominican, and Greek
In the snows of January or the drenching August heat
No sick days or benefits, for Christ's sake don't get hurt
The quacks over here won't patch you up unless they see the bucks
up front.

Lookin' after babbies from crack of dawn 'til dusk
Changing dirty nappies and cleanin' up the house
Is this what I've been educated for
To wipe the arse of every baby in America?

Now the day is done, take the subway home
Squashed up like some sardine in a can.
In the Blarney Stone I drink a gallon of foam
Till I'm feeling half meself again.
If she comes tonight, I'll ask her outright
What the hell, nothing ventured—nothing gained
And if she takes a chance, she might find romance
Now she's livin' in America.

See him standing there with the ring in his ear
And the grin on the side of his face
With the fag in his mouth, oh I should watch out
For they say that he's a real hard case.
Should I take me chance or say no thanks

What the hell, nothing ventured—nothing gained?
Oh Mammy dear, we're all mad over here
Livin' in America.

From Black 47, *independent 1991,*
and Fire Freedom, *EMI Records 1993*
Published by Starry Plough Music/EMI Blackwell Music (BMI)

ALTHOUGH WE PLAYED Brooklyn, Queens, and Manhattan in the early months, the Bronx was the main game. It's hard to imagine its vitality now, but back in the mid-'80s and on through the early '90s you could stand on the corner of Bainbridge Avenue and 204th Street, throw a stone in any direction, and you were likely to hit an Irish bar, or at least a crowd of punters shifting from one to another such establishment. The strip was pulsing with life seven nights of the week. People came from all over the Bronx, Upstate, and even from the other boroughs, to drink, dance, and hopefully hook up or engage in some sort of romantic endeavor.

What was it about the Bronx? I can't say I ever had a totally easy time up there, but I loved it nonetheless. There was something about turning off the Thruway at the Fordham Road exit that set my spirits soaring. I suppose it was the passion. They didn't like Black 47, in the early days; in fact, for the most part, they positively despised us, but at least they let you know. It all changed once we got on the radio. By then we could have played Ulan Bator, let alone the Bronx, and had people hopping. But they did care about their music up there. Unfortunately, their taste was quite specific; we were not, to put it mildly, a part of it. And oh the battles!

While waiting for Chris in the lobby of my building on those brutal winter nights of '89–'90, I would check, oil, clean, and tighten each nut and bolt of my mental armor, for I knew every molecule of my psyche would be assaulted in the hours ahead. We were lucky, though—without realizing it at the time—for Black 47 formed at the tail end of an important cycle in Irish immigration. There had been a boom in construction in the mid-'80s. At the same time, the Irish economy was sinking through the floorboards. Thousands of young people emigrated and flooded into the Bronx. These new arrivals, mostly illegal, took jobs off the books in construction, or as nannies for the growing cadre of yuppies making their fortunes on Wall Street. It was a cash-rich economy and lots of it poured back into Bainbridge.

I've often heard it said that Irishmen have two dreams: to own their own pub and a share in a racehorse. I don't know how many ended up with a piece of a pony, but lots who made money in that boom invested in bars, especially up the Bronx. And since the strip already had music seven nights a week, it behooved all of these new owners to employ more musicians. Oddly enough, there were never enough bands to go round, probably because the players could make more money knocking down walls with sledgehammers than knocking out punters with guitars. This was all well and good until the bottom fell out of the economy sometime around the end of '88. Now the pinch was in. Construction was way down, cash was tight, and the only ones still making money were the nannies; yuppies, after all, still had a need of lily-white hands to wipe their little darlings' arses. There was a lot of pain rippling up and down the avenue when we hit the scene in November '89, but there wasn't the least problem in getting the "shtart," as the lads off the boat called it. Bars were in need of punters, music was a draw, and most owners were delighted to give us a chance, for one night anyway.

My initial reaction to the hostility toward Black 47 was bafflement. It was only music after all. What was the big problem? On top of that, I'd been hearing all this talk about the "new Irish" and their broad taste in music: U2, Christy Moore, the Pogues, the Saw Doctors, the Waterboys, Sinead O'Connor! Jesus, I thought they'd greet us with open arms. We were playing original music, as fast as I could write it, and many of the songs were about the immigrant experience. I was convinced we'd be hoisted up on shoulders and carried triumphantly around the bars—two prophets come to bear witness to the joys and heartbreak of life on Bainbridge. Well, it turned out that they did love their music all right, and that's exactly what they wanted to hear: "Dirty Old Town," "The Cliffs of Dooneen," and "Fisherman's Blues," a carbon copy of the jukebox, and nice and quietly in the background, too, thank you very much!

One of the problems was that I had been out of touch with popular music since the breakup of the Thinkers. I had no idea what people liked anymore, nor did I particularly care. What I did know was that I had no intention of being part of any band that had its head skewered backward looking toward Ireland. This was going to be an Irish band for sure, but a New York one—not Dublin, London, or Bally-de-back-of-fucking-beyond. I could appreciate the talent of these new Irish acts, but Black 47 would have its own songs, dealing with its own experience, and later for the consequences!

Those consequences were not long in coming, and pretty dire. Within a month the word had spread up and down the avenue about this new combo, and it wasn't exactly glowing. Our attitude and expectations were as big a problem as the music. For one thing, I refused to stand on a stage with a television playing in front of me. Perhaps it's because I don't watch the box on a regular basis, but I find that my eyes are constantly drawn to it. And, if I'm going to be singing my guts out, the last thing I want to look at are bar stools full of backsides staring back at me while their owners' heads are tilted toward the idiot machine. So, not to make too fine a point of it, I insisted that all television sets be turned off before we played a note. This simple request appeared to be akin to demanding that the bartenders get down on their bended papist knees and foreswear the one true faith of their martyred ancestors. Most of them couldn't even fathom that I might be asking such a thing, but when they saw that I was serious, the standard response was, "Ah Jaysus, sure aren't the lads watchin' the match!"

"Fuck the match and the lads and the horse they all rode in on," was my mental response, but this sentiment rarely needed translation to words. Usually, they turned it off for fear that I might be so totally out of my skull, I could be carrying a gun, and the tips just weren't worth dying for.

Next I would set up two cheap floodlights on the stage: an intense red and a deep blue, as that's what I'd seen Pink Floyd and the Dead use to cast their spell; I figured we'd need every help we could get to set the mood for the stimulating experience that was about to unfold. Then, I'd amble back up to the bar once more and suggest that all the house lights be switched off or turned down sympathetically low. "How, in the name of Christ, are the lads supposed to read?" would be the next explosion from behind the stick.

"Send them to the fucking library, they're here to see Black 47!" was a reply I remember giving on one abominable night.

"They are in my fucking arse!" The barman countered and he motioned down the bar to a crowd of slobbering eejits, the likes of which had probably never even heard of the Beatles, let alone Black 47. But I held my ground and eventually my reluctant adversary did kill a bit of wattage, although he made a dismal attempt at preserving face by muttering that he was only doing it to save on electricity.

By this time most of the patrons would have become aware of our presence and were probably even mildly amused by the carry-on. Breaking balls was the biggest pursuit in the Bronx, and seeing the usually imperturbable bartender losing a bit of cool was something to be treasured. In those days we always kicked off the show with "Home of the Brave." This began with a thunderous semi–hip-hop drum-machine loop. Because we didn't have a bass player, I always programmed in a very deep and heavy bass drum, as well as adding a hint of reverb and a very short delay to thicken the overall sound. This particular strident beat would rattle any loose dentures in the house. I would then rip off a couple of screeching high vibrato chords just to make sure we had their undivided attention. Chris would come in blasting at full volume, playing the shit out of the reel to make sure that he could be heard above the preceding din. When the empty glasses were hopping in unison off the bar, I would snarl the first four lines:

> Just got over from the Emerald Isle
> And I'm glad to see you're all doin' so fine
> It feels so good to be finally
> In the home of the brave and the land of the free!

As the months and the firings and the frustration mounted, the snarl became coated with a dollop of bitter sarcasm, and these lines morphed from a statement to a challenge. This throwing down of the gauntlet was usually answered by a mass eruption of butts from chairs, dollars angrily yanked from the counter, and an exodus to the door, accompanied by a raising of the middle finger of the right hand as they passed us by. At first, I tried to adlib a "fuck you too" into the lyrics for every finger pointed heavenward, but this proved beyond my considerable improvisatory powers, so we took to staring straight ahead and pretending we couldn't even see, let alone care, that our audience was hemorrhaging. By the time the song was over, the bar would be near deserted, except for those alcoholics too far out of it to even hear us; the bartender's head would be buried deep in his hands, his regulars gone, his hope of having a decent tip night departed with them. To add insult to injury, he would now have to suffer through four sets of mounting stridency practically alone, with nary a begrudging soul to share his complaints. This was not a happy time for anyone.

Lest it seem like I was impervious to the reception we were receiving, nothing could be further from the truth. I would arrive home sober from the stress, and totally drained. Usually, I would sit and stare out the window at the blinking red light atop of the World Trade Center while the dawn came up; and I would recount the night, wonder what I could have done better. I regretted the tone and substance of many things I said both onstage and off, but I never doubted that we were on the right track. In those first months there were few, if any, glimmers of light at the end of the tunnel, but it never occurred to me to give up. I was at a point in life where there was no choice but to go on.

Sometimes I'd be beside myself with pent-up fury. If Shane, Christy, and Mike Scott could write and perform what they liked, then why couldn't I? What was so threatening about being original? And why were we provoking all this hostility anyway? The music was raw, to the point, and somewhat ironic, but so was life in the Bronx. The songs were a reflection of everything I was seeing around me. Obviously, my sensibility was at fault and, probably, my talent. But there was nothing I could do about that. This was how I saw it, and I knew no better way of calling it. I would console myself by paraphrasing the Dorian Gray introduction: if you're not encountering a negative reaction with new work, then it's not new. All very well, Oscar my dear, but what if you're getting nothing but a negative reaction, where does that leave you? Or does it leave you anywhere at all?

After a couple of months, things began to look up. Three or four hardy souls would be waiting to see us as we humped in the gear, and in the course of a night those who might be on their way downtown, or the purely curious, were dropping by for a drink and sometimes even staying. We were also picking up a political crowd and, slowly but surely, getting a reputation. In my own head, I had drawn a line with Black 47. No more holding back. I would put everything into it and see how the dice dropped. Too often in the past, I had only given 100 percent. I knew, from watching Cyndi, that wasn't near enough. The question was, how far above par could you stretch yourself? There had to be total commitment, and if that took overloading at 110 or even 120 percent, then so be it. Pedal to the metal, kick ass, and take names! I didn't care if every begrudger in the Bronx got in our way, we'd either deal with them or go right through them. Chris was behind this, although it was a lot harder for him. He was well known on the strip and was losing friends by the minute. But when you're at white heat, that's a small consideration. And besides, were they really friends in the first place?

Through all of this, the band was getting better. I was the one in most need of improvement. I had the attitude down pat from the first; but my guitar chops, such as they were, needed bolstering after so many years away from music. Playing four and five hours a night and matching a drum machine's precision was just what I needed. With no bass to swing off, I was forced to come up with a new style, heavy on the bottom strings. Though they were tougher on the fingers, I began using a heavier gauge for my E, A, and Ds. Even if I wasn't playing a figure, I would make sure to always first strike one of the bottom two strings of the chord and let it ring before choking, even while hitting the upper strings.

This would cause either a drone or overtone that, if in tune, would combine with the kick of the drum machine to simulate the effect of a bass guitar. I also began to work melodic bass lines into the chords of songs; you can still hear that influence when we play "Fanatic Heart" live. I programmed my digital delay to thicken the sound of the guitar, as well as fill the air with both overt and subliminal waves that made everything seem fuller. I hadn't been a fan of Sonic Youth for nothing. The Edge from U2 is a master of that tactic, although his programming is beautifully planned and executed, while mine tended more toward a random, improvised shot in the dark.

But it was the songs that were really adding substance to the sets. Within a couple of months, Van's "Wild Night" and "Into the Mystic," and Dylan's "Just Like a Woman" and "Positively Fourth Street" were history and replaced by "Rockin' the Bronx," "Banks of the Hudson," "Her Dear Old Donegal," and the above, "Livin' in America." Oftentimes, I'd write one of those in the afternoon; we'd quickly run through it at my place, talk it through in the car, and then belt it out during the opening and last sets in the Bronx. At first, these new songs would be all over the place and rarely received recognition save for a turned-up nose or a what-the-hell-is-that-piece-of-shite? But performing them twice a night, four or five times a week, soon put a shine on them. My strategy was: if a cover song is going well, drop it; that way you'll be forced to replace it with an original that should do the same job. It was a brutal scorched-earth policy that caused no end of distress; but it was also the quickest and most effective way of becoming an all-original band. There was just one drawback: you had to suffer in silence onstage until the new song took root and could hold its own.

Then, there were the firings and the arguments with owners almost every night. The modus operandi in the Bronx was that once you were hired for a Monday, you ran that night into the ground until you either quit from shame and lack of people, or the owner let you go. That's how the scene got stale: bands getting complacent, playing the same songs in the same set, week after week, until people ran by the bar for fear of being called in and withering away from the boredom. This rarely happened to Black 47 because we were usually out of there after the first night. Occasionally, we'd make it through a second or third week, but only because the owner hadn't noticed the drop in his takings or had been on vacation and hadn't heard the complaints of his regulars.

Oh those regulars! They broke my heart, and when they didn't succeed in doing that, they definitely broke my balls. But the saving grace of the Bronx was that there were way too many bars and far too few musicians. So, get fired from one and you'd just work your way down the strip to the next and so on, until sometimes you could even go back to the first, because the owner who hated your guts had managed to sell out to some new stars-in-his-eyes sucker who hadn't yet heard that your band sent every punter heading for the hills or, even worse, the pub next door.

Around this time, we got a new weapon. Fabulous Freddy Parcells! Fred had been on the road with Pierce during Black 47's first gigs. When he got back, he heard through the grapevine that I was in a new band. He had only ever played with me in improvisational situations, so he assumed that 47 was of that ilk. He showed up one night, bone in hand, and plopped down next to Chris, with as usual barely a word of salutation, and just began blowing along under the pipe lines. It was a wake-up call for me. The sound of the bone and the pipes together was both magical and mournful. It reminded me of a New Orleans Gaelic marching band. I'd never even considered that particular combination of instruments before. But Fred is a consummate musician. He would tape all of our gigs, study the tunes at home, and add harmonies and counterpoint to the lines the next night. The band instantly became richer and more accomplished.

Besides that, Fred was going through a breakup in a relationship and fit right into the Bronx heavy drinking stay-out-all-night ethos. Many of the punters who would run a mile at the sight of Chris and me arriving, took a second look now that this Guinness-swilling, virtuoso bone player was blowing holes in the Sheetrock while turning the tunes more toward the melodic and away from the confrontational. Fred came and went a number of times over the first couple of years, but whenever I heard that pipes-bone combination, I knew we were onto something, though I wasn't quite sure what. Come to think of it, we never asked him to officially join. I suppose it's a bit too late now; we're stuck with Fab Freddy.

One of my bitterest regrets from the days with Turner and Kirwan and the Thinkers was that we had done so little recording. We were always waiting to be "discovered" by some record company and propelled to the top. Over the years, we were discovered on a number of occasions, but the top remained elusive. So much smoke on the water, I suppose, but I had personally left a number of very good songs unrecorded or languishing on dusty cassettes under someone's bed. I vowed that this wouldn't happen with Black 47 and so, within months of our first gig, we were in the studio recording our first EP. We called this *Home of the Brave;* it was only ever released on cassette. It contained the eponymous track, along with "Paddy's Got a Brand New Reel," "Too Late to Turn Back," and a cover of Dominic Behan's "Patriot Game." This recording was to provide us with two breaks.

Janet Noble, the playwright, was an old friend of mine. Her latest play, *Away Alone,* had for its subject young Irish immigrants in the Bronx, and was just about to open at the Irish Arts Center. She had been to a couple of our gigs and liked the rawness and spontaneity. She suggested to the director, Terry Lamude, that he include our music to give the play authenticity. I gave Terry the mixes of "Home of the Brave" and "Paddy"; he used extracts from each as bridges between the many scenes. The "new Irish" flocked to the play and it became somewhat of a phenomenon. Oddly enough, though they were unwilling to listen to the same songs in the bars, they were thrilled with their use in the play. Then again, Terry had done a masterful job of editing. When the play got uniformly good reviews, the music also received favorable mentions. We had taken our first faltering step toward legitimacy.

Frank Gallagher (Galigula from "Rockin' the Bronx") was a feisty little opinionated Scot who had originally done sound for Talking Heads. He then did a stint with the Major Thinkers before returning to London. In December 1989 he was working for the Pogues and their manager, the infamous Frank Murray. He and Hammy were partners in crime and, when in New York on New Year's Eve, they hooked up. While out for a stroll in Soho, they dropped by my place where I was dubbing cassettes of *Home of the Brave*. Galigula had hardly heard the first verse when he exploded, "I can get that released for you, Paddy!" (That's what he called everyone born within spitting distance of Ireland.) "Murray's started a new label and he's looking for shite just as bad as that." I tossed him a couple of copies when they were heading out the door and forgot all about it.

Chris and I headed to Bay Ridge that night. We were playing in a dive on Fourth Avenue. I remember the gig well because my brother, Jemmy, and many old friends from the days in Tomorrow's Lounge showed up. We had a blast, although the other customers were all ossified and didn't think too much of us. The owner must have been of the same mind, for he left before the end of the night. That wasn't unusual. But when we went to collect the "envelope" from the bartender, he shrugged and said he knew nothing about it. It was now four in the morning. Everyone had gone except for a couple of drunks snoring at the bar. "What can you do, lads?" The bartender shrugged as he prepared to close up.

What, indeed? We loaded out the gear into Chris's little Ford Escort. Up the block a Korean deli had been held up and a man shot. The sirens of the cop cars and ambulances were still screaming, their red and amber lights flashing. We stood on the cold flagstones of Fourth Avenue, reluctant to go home penniless. "Welcome to the bloody nineties," I muttered to myself.

24

HER DEAR OLD DONEGAL
(SLEEP TIGHT IN NEW YORK CITY)

Now that she's so far away, so far away
From her dear old hills of Donegal
I wonder does she ever
Think of me at all?
On that wet Monday I drove her down to Shannon
We drank brandy and kissed in the airport hall
She said she'd be definitely home by Christmas
But since then, not even a word, not even a phone call.

Now some of the boys said she'd gone a little bit crazy
Said they seen her running round the Bronx hanging out with a rough crowd
I wonder does she ever
Think of me at all?
'Cause I've got no intention of hanging around this dump forever
Wondering if she's going to love me or leave me
Or is just about to deceive me
So if you see her, you tell her
You better, you better, you better just

Sleep tight in New York City
Now you've got a different angel watching over you
And you know I've tried to ring you
Your phone is always busy
And I don't think I'm ever going to get through again to you.

So in the meantime
Dream on in New York City . . .

She'll be stepping out down Bainbridge Avenue right now
Going down to the Village Pub on her nightly crawl
I wonder does she ever
Think of me at all?
Just one more Amaretto for fortification
Then it's "good night you good people one and all
I got a girlfriend, I got to go see her over on Broadway."
Who does she think she's fooling at all?

'Cause her dark angel waits on the corner
With his silver pills and his Spanish charms
Just one more moment's hesitation
Before she falls into his arms
Now anyone else, they'd go over there and rescue her
Drag her back to her dear old Donegal
But she left all that so far behind her
So if you see her you tell her from me
You better, you better, you better just

Sleep tight in New York City
Now you've got a different angel watching over you
And you know I've tried to ring you
But your phone is always busy
And I don't think I'm ever going to get through again to you . . .

From Black 47, *independent 1991, and* Fire of Freedom, *EMI Records 1993*
Published by Starry Plough Music/EMI Blackwell Music (BMI)

THE VILLAGE PUB was by far my favorite place to play in the
Bronx. It teetered up around the top end of 204th Street, looking
down its crooked nose at Bainbridge and the rest of the strip
below. It was part of the scene, but quite apart, too: not quite a
stop on the rounds, more like an all-night destination. It had a

dark, comfortable, vaguely sinister character, whereas many of the other joints were more like well-lit sheds, charmless as the reception rooms of Irish hotels, on which many were modeled. Most of the spirit of the Village sprung from its owner, John Flynn, who was an extremely warm, effervescent, but somewhat complicated, man—aren't we all? He was an anomaly up on the strip: an owner who actually liked music and the company of musicians. John had grown up on the rugged streets of the South Bronx when it still had a sizeable Irish-American community. He told me once, with more than a hint of pride, that his was the last Irish family to vacate their block; he emphasized that they were not run out; they chose to leave of their own volition. I never questioned this. It would have been hard to imagine getting John to do anything that he wasn't totally down with. He was tough as nails, but had an openness about him that was foreign to other owners and indeed to many punters up around Bainbridge. His pub became home to anyone possessed of a certain wildness, beyond just getting smashed, although, God knows, there was enough of that in the Village, too.

Musicians especially liked the place, for they were welcome and there was always a slate available in down times. Women who liked musicians tended to hang out there, too—also those women with an independent streak who didn't totally fit into the scene. Women like Mary in the above song who stood by the jukebox and stared at you through wild country eyes, especially when she thought you weren't looking. Women who had suffered some kind of disappointment, but, above all, women who weren't going home. The Village was a haven for the Marys of the Bronx, for although sex was always an option there, it wasn't a pickup kind of place; a woman could enter alone and not be hit upon, unless she wore that notion on her sleeve.

It was somewhat the same for men: the kind of joint you could go of a night and emerge a day later pale, thin, beyond interesting, lost behind shades and just dying to get home to the familiarity and solitude of your own apartment. No judgmental stares were directed at you in John's pub. Most people who frequented the bar had, on occasion, taken a dive themselves; the lights were low and you could disappear into one of its darkened banqueted corners and have no one be the wiser for it. Very nice girls didn't go there, except maybe on a dare. It wasn't that type of place. It wasn't worth the loss of reputation. There was talk of drugs. The uptight didn't venture in either, for the atmosphere could be unsettling, hard to define, not quite threatening but . . .

Neither was it a bar to throw your weight around. Hard-as-nails Tyrone boys, many of whom the British army would have liked a little word with, tended to gather there and would have had little patience for drunken wankers. Add to those a lot of strays, professional drinkers, and others of the walking wounded and you had a volatile cocktail just waiting to be stirred. And yet, overall, to those of a certain disposition, there was a rare easiness about the place, especially for the Bronx. You just had to watch your p's and q's, keep out of people's faces and off their toes; if you followed those few ground rules, as the poet Marley proclaimed, every little thing would be all right.

I don't know when I first met John Flynn. Probably up in Leeds or East Durham in the Catskills. One hundred miles above the city, you had an Irish summer scene unto itself up there; most of Bainbridge spent at least Memorial Day Weekend bouncing around its bare-boned resorts and watering holes. John had a great fondness for Turner and Kirwan; we played for him often. Later, whenever I'd get down on my luck, I'd give him a shout and he'd invariably throw me a couple of nights until I'd get back on my feet. The Village was a natural setting for Black 47—full of drama, instability, and girls like Mary who recognized themselves in our songs. We had great nights there and tough ones, too, until John had to regretfully fire us over an economic issue. Had I been in his shoes, I would have done the same. But I said something carelessly that was taken out of context. It caused a great rift between us that shouldn't have happened to old friends. But the times were tense and we were both running on adrenaline; things like that can and do happen. Still, the Village Pub was always like a beacon of craziness and warmth to me and some of our best early songs like "Her

Dear Old Donegal" and "Livin' in America" were written specifically about the place. Many others were worked out on its tiny
stage, and I still miss it. Why is it that all the good pubs go under
before their time?

Paddy Reilly's, too, was in rough shape due to the economic
downturn. That was the only reason we got hired. But it was
exactly what we were looking for: a base in Manhattan. Chris and
I were great believers in residencies. You didn't have to advertise,
word of mouth had a chance to spread, and if people knew you
would definitely be in a pub on a certain night, they could set their
clocks and ramblings around that. The problem with the other
boroughs was that, in general, a guy from Queens wouldn't travel
up to the Bronx to catch a band, barring Hendrix hopped out of
the grave, Strat in hand. Likewise, a girl from Bay Ridge wouldn't
have a bull's notion how to get to Sunnyside or Astoria. But
everyone could find their way into Manhattan, and no matter
what their reason for coming, they would have need of a couple of
cocktails to grease the wheels of the subway ride home. So, when
the word spread that Dympna had hired us in Reilly's, the dozen
people from each borough who had followed us faithfully in their
neck of the woods, all converged on Manhattan to see us. Add to
that mix various friends, relatives and interested creditors, and we
had a pretty full room on the first night of our residency.

Reilly's was across the street from the projects on Twenty-
eighth and was basically a hole in the wall that boasted a crack
darts team. It wasn't at all suitable for a music venue, but what pub
is? We began playing under the dartboard in the corner, where I
had jammed with Beyond the Pale about five months earlier. This
area was boarded in by a small wooden partition, atop of which
was a brass railing; this reminded me of a high-class sheep run
back home on my grandmother's farm. It was about ten feet in
length, nine inches off the floor, and so narrow that Chris had to
sit behind me while I stood up front with the guitar and manipu-
lated the PA head as best I could. We had no monitors, but would
place one of the speakers just in front of my ear. Talk about being
on the verge of feedback! And yet we had a tremendously punchy

sound that enveloped the room and bounced all which ways off
the paved floors. It was a real soundman's nightmare. But I was far
from a soundman, and doing everything for effect.

It was a great room for guitar, though, with diamond-clear but
bassy tones. I really learned how to manipulate and mess with digital delay, reverb, and feedback there. Fred stood out on the floor
to our right, directly in the way of any poor unfortunate with
need of the bathroom. Thus, when we would get in an extended
jam, there was tremendous need of strong kidneys, because Fab
Freddy rarely gave way, and one could get a head or other accou-
trement knocked off, what with his bone sliding in and out with
all the power and grace of a maniacal piston.

Around this time, I ran into Sharon Blythe, an old friend from
the downtown music scene. She had recently married Geoff who
was the sax player for Dexy's Midnight Runners, the Bureau, and
Elvis Costello, among others. Mister Blythe had moved over full-
time to the United States and was, she confessed, going up the
walls sitting at home. I told her to send him on up to us at Reilly's
so he could get out of the house, have a blow, and meet some
people. Ever the perfectionist, Geoff called and asked for charts,
tapes, or whatever a band of our dubious acclaim might have to
hand. I told him to just show up, have a couple of pints, and play
whatever came into his head. He seemed a bit mystified by that
manner of response, but arrived anyway and stood shoulder to
shoulder with Fred.

Now the need for a solid pair of kidneys was even more acute,
for it was impossible to get through to the bathroom with both of
them playing. Geoff was amazed at the scene and the oddness of
the lineup, but he had obviously seen a lot in his day and jumped
right in, ripping out stream-of-consciousness solos on both tenor
and soprano saxes. And right from the first notes, he was amazing
and stopped the show with his passion, finesse and very working
class British what-the-bloody-hell-mate attitude. The Irish republican politics didn't bother him in the least; although English as
Andy Capp, he was cut from the same broad-minded populist
cloth as John Lennon, and had long ago declared his independence

of any country or creed, bar taste, good whiskey, a well-turned ankle and original music. He was a walking, talking, empathetic solo and instantly carved out his spot with the band.

And so, we were four: pipes, sax, and trombone, with me holding down the rhythm section on guitar and drum machine. It was as some drunk observed, one god-awful strange lineup. But it was original and it worked; and right from the start we didn't have to doff our caps to anyone because we didn't sound like anyone else, still don't for that matter. There was also a magic in the air that only happens when a new band is forming, the members are listening and reacting to one another, firing riffs off the walls, and hearing them ricochet back in strains of harmony, counterpoint, and those indescribable overtones. The new songs kept coming and the crowds continued to build. Steve Duggan, manager and eventual owner of Reilly's, was now showing up and weaving his magic. Greeting the customers like the pope in the Vatican, he gained the nickname Monsignor. He also began spreading the word back to Ireland through his web of old showband contacts.

The times were bad and the price of admission was right on the ball: sweet damn all to enter and little need for a minimum, because everyone was out of their heads on pints of stout and shots of Jameson's for Fenians, Bushmills for Huns, and Power's for atheists and all others able to bend an elbow. You had to be there early and love your neighbors madly because you were going to be shoveled in right against them. That prospect seemed to turn off very few, for in the heat of the moment and the music, many a liaison ensued. The word spread around Manhattan—to hell with scummy rock clubs and their rip-off attitude! Here within spitting distance of Bellevue Hospital and the awaiting drunk tank was a scene all about music. And leave your attitude at the door, the band had more than enough for everyone.

Then out of nowhere, Galigula rang me. Frank Murray apparently did think *Home of the Brave*—shite though it might be—was a fitting first release for his new record company. Would we be interested in coming over to London, doing a few club dates, and opening some gigs for the Pogues to get our name out? Would we what? The Pogues were already legendary, although I had missed much of their ascent during my sabbatical from the scene. Still, I was familiar with a couple of their songs and was more than aware that Shane MacGowan was a major songwriting talent. I was particularly attached to "A Pair of Brown Eyes" and "Rainy Night in Soho." Both of those gems spoke to the Wexford teenager who had visited London—they summed up a particular time and era for me, much as I was attempting to do in my own adopted city.

This must have been around December 1990, for our first gig was the Pogues' Christmas Show at Brixton Academy. Oddly enough, this would mark another anniversary, for it was to be the last time that I smoked an illegal substance. On the night we arrived, I'd had a few tokes of hash and promptly lost my voice. I spent the day of the gig in Hyde Park humming warm-up exercises to the pigeons while vowing to various saints and sheep shaggers that if my voice returned, I'd never smoke again.

I daresay I was the only straight and sober person in Brixton that night. Probably just as well. The big hall was about half full when we took to the stage, but right up against the crowd-control barriers about four hundred Pogues fanatics greeted us, middle fingers aloft, chanting, "We want Shane!" This was before we'd even played a note. It had all the makings of a dismal evening. We were using the Pogues' amplifiers and by the time I had mine sorted out, the chant had built to a roar. I was already furious with myself over the strained vocal chords. I felt I'd let the band down and was in little mood for the ignorance confronting us. There didn't appear to be much point in appealing to their better natures: "Ah, come on now, lads, give us a break, will you? You might even like it."

Instead, I had a flashback to our first night in the Bronx. I jacked up Phil Chevron's Roland 120 to the far side of 10, likewise overloaded my distortion pedal, then struck an open E-major chord. A monstrous banshee screech of volume, feedback, and distortion fed into every mic onstage and roared like the Concord out of the PA. I felt like a quivering Moses on Mount Sinai with the power of the Lord surging through me as I hung on to the guitar for dear life. The chanting and booing was a thing of the past as our detractors stuck fingers and indeed fists in their ears in an effort to save some small part of their hearing. Then without further ado or even a mention of what had just transpired, we kicked off with our usual opening lines: "Just got over from the Emerald Isle and I'm glad to see you're all doin' so fine. . . ."

It would be nice to say that we finished our set to tumultuous applause; it was actually more like the end of a sullen, rain-soaked Third Division English soccer game with no one having managed to put the ball in the net. In essence, we swayed but few minds; but there are probably a couple of deaf Shane devotees who'll never forget us. And just as had happened with UB40 and the Major Thinkers, the Pogues came right out swinging and wiped the floor with us. They were probably just a hair beyond the top of their game at the time, but were still one of the best live bands in the world. There's nothing quite like getting your ass kicked by a great band to improve you. If you're not going anywhere anyway, a blow like that can run you out of the business; but if you're a professional, then you mentally and spiritually toughen up and raise your ante, just so the next night you can hold your own onstage and not be disgraced again. There's also something about being in the presence of greatness that allows you to dream and makes you better, if only by osmosis.

The Pogues were a marvel on those gigs. It wasn't that any of them was a virtuoso but, as a band, they jelled into a rabid, riotous, gloriously well-oiled music machine. And Shane had it all: the songs, the presence, and that particular zeitgeist with his audience that only comes around a couple of times in a generation. He is also exasperating to many people. They feel that if he was a bottle or two soberer, or looked after his voice and soul, he'd be that much better. They want the gleaming forest, but without the inevitable dead or poisoned wood that goes into the making of it. Just give me his talent, they reason, and I could use it to better advantage. But it doesn't work like that. You get the whole package or nothing.

If I have any issue, it's with his audience. Many come only to take a gawk at Shane the drinker. On some nights, the loudest applause is when he hoists a glass to his lips. I had seen the same story play out with Johnny Thunders and it wasn't pretty. Shane has written over thirty classics that will be sung and listened to wherever Irish gather. He deserves better. No one knows what goes on in the heart of a drinker. If I were forced to speculate, I would imagine that the Pogues were worked into the ground all through the '80s. Shane probably developed an aversion to touring aimlessly and needlessly. But that's his affair and his only.

I took four years off the road myself and I was lucky; I gained a fresh perspective that enabled me to come to some kind of terms with the consumptive nature of the music business. By good fortune, I was also out of the scene at a time when I might easily have become influenced by Mr. MacGowan. For watching him that night in Brixton, I recognized all of his influences and knew that I shared so many of them: Ewan MacColl, Luke Kelly, Dominic and Brendan Behan, Irish showbands down to the gray suits, and all manner of Irish pub music and behavior. He had synthesized these into a beautiful and individual whole that sometimes took my breath away and made me proud to be in the presence of this seanchai or wise man. Long may you live, Shane, your songs will last forever.

While we were carousing across North London, David Herndon, the music editor of *Newsday,* received an unsolicited article about the band that he tossed in the garbage. He didn't care for the writing style and promptly forgot about it. Some months later, he was walking down Second Avenue and had to step off the sidewalk to get by the crowds outside Reilly's. He managed to get inside the door, took in a set, and asked if he could assign John Anderson, the music critic, to do a piece on us. John, sensing a good street story, followed the band around for a liquid week, spending most of it in the Bronx and Reilly's. The ensuing article was long and comprehensive, and was as much about the social significance of the band as the music. Why were we, unheralded, filling rooms around the city? What was the band saying that should cause such word of mouth? He had a great eye for detail and how we fit into both the

Irish and American scenes. Nor did he stint on the vernacular and street quality of the lyrics or our uncouth between-song patter.

One night in the Bronx, I dedicated a song to "every asshole owner who has ever fired us." Nothing out of the ordinary. Life was full of sturm und drang und melodrama at the time: all grist for my onstage mill. When the article came out it caused a minor sensation and alerted the city to what we were doing and the uniqueness of the scene we were creating. Unfortunately, next to my quote about asshole owners John Anderson inadvertently, and without malice, mentioned John Flynn, the one person who had fought to keep original music alive up in the Bronx. Chris and I were both awakened by a livid Mr. Flynn who had been laughed and sneered at by the actual assholes who had fired us. It was an awful situation for, apart from hurting a friend, John was not a man to be taken lightly. It took many years, degrees of freeze, and a lot of pain to redress the situation. It's funny how you often end up hurting the ones you love the most. It was loners and righteous individuals such as John who went out on a limb for Black 47 in the early days, and who were the backbone of any success we had. We're all friends again now, but I wish I could take back the years and rearrange that one hurtful paragraph in the first great city-wide write-up the band received.

But that would be just as hard as it was to ignore Mary, with the wild country eyes, staring up at the band in the Village Pub all those nights ago. Sleep tight in New York City, girl, we never spoke, but there'll always be a song just about you.

25

THE HISTORY OF IRELAND—PART ONE

Let me tell you the story of a girl called Eva
Married this Norman dude, a.k.a. Strongbow
On their bloody honeymoon they reached the conclusion
The Gaelic Nation is just an illusion
Just a bunch of sacrilegious sheep-shaggin' minions
At least that was the English Pope's opinion
"Go forth, Strongbow, reform the Irish Church
And if you conquer the country, well such is life."

The Irish bogtrotters didn't like this idea
They had an arcane notion about the benefits of freedom
Resisted fiercely with cudgel and spade
'Til they were run off the land by the Papal jihad
Those who came to terms with foreign domination
Learned to speak English, it beat starvation
The rest humped turf out in the country
Dreamed of Riverdance and coming prosperity.

Sit you down, sit you down
Let's talk about battles lost but never won,
That's the history of Ireland, part one . . .

The years passed by, kings and auld pontiffs too
'Til up in the North arose two men called Hugh
O'Donnell and O'Neill from Donegal and Tyrone

Asked the King of Spain to kick the English home
But they got psyched out at the Battle of Kinsale
The Spanish Armada took a dive in the rain
O'Neill found Jesus with the Pope in Rome
And the Brits poisoned Red Hugh's sangria in Spain.

A lot of things happened, I'll skip over them fast
A lot of little battles, guess what? We lost.
Let England fight its own wars, if you please,
'Cause getting Ollie Cromwell pissed off was not a good idea
He scorched our arses with his burning cross
Introduced us to sectarianism
Banished our youth to the Jamaican fields
That's why Bob Marley sings those Gaelic melodies.

But we don't give up easy, less sense than courage
We backed Jimmy Stewart instead of Willie from Orange.
Oh man, that was our biggest mistake
Just think what we could be doing today
Every twelfth of July we'd beat the lambeg drum
Marching up the Falls to a tum-tum-tum
While over in the Shankhill, they'd be saying the rosary
And listening to us sing the Sash Me Father Wore before we

Heard all about the French Revolution
Yippee, no kings no future!
Cut our hair like the citizens in Paree
The Wexford croppy was like the accessory
But the traitor's kiss was our best fashion
Lord Eddie Fitzgerald got the English hatchet,
We followed Father Murphy through hell and high water
Into excommunication on a hill in Ennisorthy.

Oh, then they stuck us with the Penal Laws
What a break, they hung all of our lawyers
And doctors and teachers and fathers of the church

And if they caught you riding, they'd even steal your auld horse
'Til randy Dan O'Connell emancipated us
But we didn't have no time to celebrate because
Black '47 killed off half the country
So we split for Liverpool, Australia and America.

Those of us left were a sad old bunch
Beaten down by the state and the church
Afraid of our lives of divine intervention
The bishops didn't want any more of that auld revolution.
When Charlie Parnell got the drop on Gladstone
We had Home Rule for the taking,
But we stabbed him in the back over Catherine O'Shea
And we're still feeling the pain to this very day.

Oh, nineteen sixteen, nineteen twenty-one
You all know the story and I'm sick of going on.
This Irish history's just a pain in the arse
Poor old James Connolly wouldn't know what to make of us.
'Cause now we're Europeans, we take our orders from Brussels
Don't need no more of that Irish republican muscle
The ghosts of Pearse, Tone, Emmet and McDermott
All waltzing off into a Celtic Tiger sunset.

From Kilroy Was Here, *Gadfly Records 2001*
Published by Starry Plough Music (BMI)

BLACK 47 WAS always more than just a band. There was a political dimension, too. To us on the inside, this made perfect sense: both music and politics merged seamlessly. To others on the periphery, however, the two elements must have often appeared dichotomous. Politics scared some people, while others felt that there was a time and place for such matters, and a rowdy bar was not a proper forum. Chris and I both felt that since politics was part of our lives, it was entirely appropriate to introduce this subject in any setting. From the start, we were perceived as Irish republican and we were, although to different degrees. Yet both of us were careful not to be seen as promoting any kind of violence through our songs; and in truth, the only lyrics that could be construed in that context was the line that I included in "James Connolly": "Hold on to your rifles, boys, don't give up your dreams of a republic for the working class, economic liberty." And that was a statement supposedly uttered by the man himself as an exhortation to his left-wing followers to beware of the aspirations of right-wing republicans when freedom was finally achieved. We were a lot more interested in getting people to think and question the status quo, rather than to send them out rushing for their balaclavas and armalites.

It was an odd situation because many bands on the circuit would mouth off all manner of militant republican anthems such as "Come Out Ye Black and Tans" or "Boys of the Old Brigade" and be ignored for their troubles. But everyone knew Black 47 was subversive, had a left-of-center agenda, and meant business. There was no question in either of our minds that British policy in the North of Ireland was pigheaded, morally wrong, and demeaning to the Nationalist population. Neither of us ever recognized the validity of the Northern statelet, and it was a rare occasion when we'd even dignify it by its official title—Northern Ireland. To me, it was a gerrymandered, bigoted, and failed entity, artificially created to ensure a Unionist majority; it amazed me that British people, many of whom I liked and admired, had sat idly by for fifty years and allowed a sectarian clique in Stormont Castle rule the roost in a jackbooted fashion. It did not surprise me, however, that their collective chickens were finally coming home to roost with a vengeance.

I wasn't in favor of the violence that was going on in the North; in fact, I felt that with each massacre perpetrated on behalf of the nationalist community, we lost the moral high ground. Yet I opposed the suspension of habeas corpus, the use of emergency powers, and juryless courts. Who could not have been appalled by the systematic abuse of the rights of the nationalist people by the British Army and the sectarian police force? I also felt that the

British government must not only stand up to the Orange thugs who were laying waste to Catholic neighborhoods, but must also be seen to do so. I never hid the fact that I supported the inalienable aspiration of Irish people for unification of the country. Still, I knew that the Protestant people would never feel at home in the all-pervasive Catholic atmosphere down South, nor should they be expected to. My solution was for a phased British withdrawal, with a time set for eventual unification within a European context. This would call for a European peace force to police the flashpoints and to prevent the long-prophesied bloodbath. I recognized that the situation in the North was enormously complex, and that my views on the problems were far from simplistic and not readily rattled off in a couple of extremist slogans. Despite this, sometimes to my amusement, but often to my horror, I was tarred with an extremist brush. For it was accepted in many quarters that if you stood against British policy in the North, it logically followed that you were for violence.

Within months of forming the band I was warned that we were painting ourselves into a corner and that Black 47 would never realize its full potential in the music business because of how we were perceived politically. But what would Black 47 have been without the politics? A bad-looking Corrs with some good songs? We were attempting to fill a void: to become a "voice for the voiceless," as Paul Hill described us. That aspiration meant a lot more to me than any amount of presence in the Top Forty, and still does. Anyway, to look on the bright side of things, if nothing else, politics introduced us to a wide array of fascinating and principled people who would provide us with inspiration, friendship, and a great deal of comic relief through good and bad times.

Paul Hill, Gerry Conlon, and Paddy Armstrong came into our lives out in the Tower Ballroom in Queens sometime in 1990. Along with Carole Richardson, they were known as the Guilford Four. They had all served fifteen years in British prisons for the bombing of two pubs outside London. Evidence had been tampered with and it was obvious that they had been framed, but the British authorities had refused to release them for fear of losing

face. They became regulars in Reilly's, and though it was obvious
that each had deep issues yet to confront, I was always amazed at
how little bitterness they had retained from their years of incar-
ceration. Rather, they were full of fire for righting various wrongs
not only in the North of Ireland, but in other repressive trouble
spots around the world. They were a beacon to many Americans,
Irish and otherwise; the young especially could relate to them, for
their belief in human rights, and even revolution, was always tem-
pered with glasses to the brim full of rock 'n' roll, Guinness, and
good times. Their one failing was that they never wanted to call it
a night. But back in those days, who did?

We had now moved from under the dartboard to a stage by the
window and the people who couldn't gain entry would stand outside,
and stare at our quivering butts while grooving to the sounds leaking
out. Hammy arrived one night with his djembe and a beggar's ban-
quet of percussive instruments, including a Foster's can half full of
rice grains that he shook around like some maniac from Melbourne.
All of a sudden we were five and growing, with the personality of the
band expanding in time with the songs. One of the most requested
was Chris's defiant "Free Joe Now." This became one of our signature
songs, and will always summon up the memory of the last great
unified Irish-American struggle for justice.

Joe Doherty was a member of the Irish republican movement
who escaped from prison in the North of Ireland and made his way
to New York City. Somewhat ingeniously, he took a job as a bartender within a stone's throw of the British consulate. He was
picked up and held in the Tombs, counting among his jail mates
the Teflon Don, John Gotti. Claiming political asylum on the
grounds that he would surely face a threat to his life should he be
returned to the British penal system, Doherty challenged extradi-
tion in a number of courts. His case engendered much interest,
not only in Irish circles but across a broad spectrum of American
politics; at issue was not so much the man, but whether the British
government should have the power to influence the Bush admin-
istration and through them the U.S. judiciary. The tribe took Joe
to heart and fought tooth and nail to keep him in the country.

The battle went on for years and we finally lost. Joe was extradited and sent back to prison in the North. This loss caused great bitterness and was followed by a resolve on the part of many Irish-Americans to quit their dalliance with the Republican Party and seek to elect a Democratic president. After some licking of wounds and reorganization, the Doherty movement became the foundation for the final, and perhaps most important, Irish peace and justice initiative: bringing Sinn Fein in out of the political wilderness. But that would be well in the future.

Back in the early '90s, Reilly's was electric with political fervor. It was a real thrill to go to the pub every Wednesday and Saturday. There was always a new song to try out, a new audience to win over, and you just never knew who might show up. One night I literally had to blink my eyes. He was slouching by the corner of the bar, one leg crossed over another teddy boy style, short back-and-sides haircut with a brushed up oily quiff, deep red bowling shirt, black pants, high soles on his twin-tones, sucking a bottle of beer and digging the music with an intensity foreign to most punters. We were getting used to celebrities by this time, but how do you keep your eyes off Joe Strummer? He left before the set ended, but the next night he was up in the front row bopping like a teenager. He followed every chord I played on the guitar and would nod in appreciation or understanding at a particular voicing, but it was the interplay between the horns and the pipes that nailed him, for if anyone could hear that New Orleans Gaelic marching band connection, it was Joe.

He was cool to talk to, too, offhanded about everything, interested in influences, and cross-referencing the lyrics with songs both popular and arcane. He never mentioned the Clash, nor did I. It was his night out, as it was to be on many other occasions. One evening, when dancing next to him, Vin Scelsa, the DJ from WNEW, had the courage to say what we all felt: "The Clash are the only band that matters." Joe looked him in the eye and, without missing a beat, pointed at us and said, "No, they're the only band that matters now." For obvious reasons, I've never mentioned this before, although Vin has often told the story on the air. But, as you might imagine, to a musician it means more than any award. It doesn't matter that it was a universe more than we deserved, and it's all water under the bridge now; for the grass is green above our hero, and mere words won't make him stir. But for what it's worth, you were far too generous and polite, Joe. Vin was on the money, there was only one band that mattered, and you were its young chieftain. Wherever you are tonight, mate, you've more than earned your place with the angels.

26

DADDY IS A ROCK 'N' ROLLER

Daddy is a rock and roller,
He plays in a rock 'n' roll band
Dresses in black leather
And travels all over the land.
He's always out there playin' gigs
He's hardly ever home
But I know he misses my brother and me
When he's out there on the road.

When we get up in the morning
Mommy says, "Be quiet
'Cause Daddy came home just an hour ago
And he's gigging again tonight.
Don't knock down his guitar case
Leaning against the wall
And don't trip over his amplifier
Out there in the hall."

May all your dreams come true, Dad
May all your dreams come true
When all your rock 'n' roll is done
We'll still be there for you.

May all your dreams come true, Dad
May all your dreams come true

When all your rockin' days are gone
May all of your dreams come true.

When he takes us to the playground
With his coffee in his hand
He watches us play with the other kids
But he's thinking about his band.
He's differenter than the other dads
Doesn't join our games
Always writing those songs inside his head
But I love him just the same.

And when I'm a teenager
I'm gonna join a rock 'n' roll band
With my brother playin' lead guitar
I'll be the drummer man.
And maybe Dad could jam with us
Oh man, wouldn't that be cool
And we could hit the road with him
And never go to school.

May all your dreams come true, Dad
May all your dreams come true
When all your rock 'n' roll is done
We'll still be there for you.

May all your dreams come true, Dad
May all your dreams come true
When all your rockin' days are gone
May all of your dreams come true.

From Keltic Kids, *Pirate Moon Records 1996*
Published by Starry Plough Music (BMI)

I NOW HAD two very young children and could often be seen navigating a double stroller, full to the brim with two beaming—or scowling—redheads, around the streets of Lower Manhattan. My wife was back at grad school and teaching dance, with the result that I was on early call most mornings, no matter what time I had arrived home. This put a certain crimp in my style, but I adapted heroically: much like a horse I could sleep standing up, or in any other position for that matter. I had discovered a locked playground in the vicinity of NYU. Getting a key to this ploughed up Garden of Eden was harder than gaining membership to the College of Cardinals, but through a little old-fashioned chicanery, I eventually prevailed. Soon after I had laid on a four-course breakfast of milk and cereal, followed by cereal and milk, all three of us would repair to this inner sanctum, which in those days more resembled the exercise yard of Mountjoy Prison in Dublin than a modern recreational area. It mattered little, for I neither heard nor brooked any complaints. There the kids could be set free to run around and frolic to their little hearts' content, with no hope of escape.

The adults present were mostly Irish and Jamaican nannies and they congregated by nationality on separate benches. I was the lone male; the fathers of the other little darlings were either masters of the universe who toiled down on Wall Street, or professors imparting knowledge in the nearby leafy halls of academe. I was adopted by the Irish nannies, and fussed over by the Jamaicans who were bemused that a "white mon" might not only have heard of Gregory Isaacs or Bunny Wailer but could hum a passable, if hoarse, tune of either. At first, I divided my time between the two benches, but gradually came to sit more with my compatriots, since they were some degrees more tolerant of a man who had need of an occasional snooze. We shared coffee, doughnuts, and confidences, and they loved to hear the gossip and goings-on in the various pubs that I had been carousing in only hours previously. For my part, I drowsily, but earnestly, listened to and empathized with their hopes and dreams and histories; I was also steeped enough in immigrant etiquette to discreetly turn away when their eyes would soften at the mention of some small townsland in Mayo or Donegal. All of them wished to go home someday, Vera most of all, apparently, for there was an empty space on the bench one day, and

I was told, in almost shameful whispers, that the loneliness of Astoria had finally broken her, and that she had departed on a day's notice. But most were resigned to staying and putting a brave face on things. Until one day, Una, who rarely spoke, put a spike through many a heart when she bitterly sighed: "Three years and you're still coasting, five and your tottering on the brink, seven, and the only time they'll ever see you again is for weddings and funerals."

There was a deep silence, while each of us grappled with this looming truth. That was the first time it hit me head-on that my parents were not young anymore, neither could I think of what weddings I'd be attending in the near future. Just then, someone's child fell and scratched his knee. Though there was no need for it, we all ran over to check out the disaster, eager to break the gloom that Una's words had cast on us. The Jamaican ladies joined us, cluck-clucking with sympathy. I'm not sure they even heard, but those words reverberated on many levels through the Key Park that day.

Chris and Geoff were also raising young families, so I suppose you could say that as a band we were somewhat family-oriented, although there was little discussion of family values in the van. Still, I suppose we were breaking the stereotype of the single, narcissistic rocker. There was always this or that teacher's conference, doctor's appointment, or birthday to be attended and stayed awake at. There was also the issue of making enough money to support children. You can, as they say, make a killing in rock music but rarely a living. We had, of necessity, to prove this canard wrong.

Right from the start, Chris felt that the idea of playing music and not getting paid for it was the height of stupidity. This might seem obvious, but the rock business is sustained by the practice of doing gigs for peanuts, with the hope that someday, if you're one of the infinitesimally few, you and your guitars will end up in a mansion with a model for company; or, as my father used to put it: "Live horse until you get grass." Chris had come from a no-nonsense world where playing in a band was a second job you worked at to make some extra money—end of story. The Irish bar scene, luckily for us, operated on the same principle. In 90 percent of cases, though, when all the costs are taken into account, bands actually pay for the privilege of strutting around the stage of a rock club for forty glorious minutes. I know. I did it often with the Major Thinkers and we were well up the ladder of popularity, with songs on the radio and a record deal.

But I'd had more than enough of that bullshit. Black 47 was founded on the somewhat revolutionary concept that band members would actually get paid every time they played. Our innovation was to work the well-remunerated cover band circuit, but instead perform all original songs. The success of this strategy demanded that our songs be strong enough to replace the perennial U2, Pogues, Waterboys repertoire. It called for an almost blind adherence to a drastic Darwinian survival of the fittest: if a song didn't break through almost instantly with the audience, then it would be summarily dropped and replaced. On occasion, though, there was still need for fortitude and blind faith, mixed with a degree of cussedness, because not every song takes off on first playing. One of our most popular, "Maria's Wedding," struggled for almost six months before it finally held its ground. This seemingly simple ditty proved almost beyond our capabilities to perform and put over; it has any number of illogical chords, changes of key, oddly placed solos, combined with tricky stops and starts. When we played it with the Letterman Band, Paul Schaeffer, an adroit musician/arranger, even commented on the weirdness of the structure. I had been just about to ditch the piece when it was rescued and resuscitated by a group of NYU students who came specially every Wednesday to hear about the trials of loving Bensonhurst Maria.

That being said, you could have all the good songs in the world, but if you didn't have a band with the muscle and flair to bring them to life, then you were in for some long stormy evenings on the Irish bar circuit. In short order, you had to mesmerize and turn a pub on its ear, so that the punters would forget that they had actually dropped by for a couple of quiet drinks with, perhaps, a couple of staves of easily ignored muzak sighing in the background. It was imperative that you be firing on all fours from the minute you took that stage, not just aurally but visually, too. Each member of the band had to be a star in his own right and build up his own group of admirers. And you'd better have real attitude—not your standardized rock-video peacock posing that might cost you a couple of teeth if some Connemara man took exception to your strutting—but a leave-me-the-fuck-alone-I'm-a-whole-lot-crazier-than-you-are sense of yourself that really sprang from your music. Thus, although Black 47 was song driven, because of our roots, we would never be your patented singer/songwriter band. The strongest would lead on the night, and we would all fall in behind him; and were he to flag, then someone else would bounce off his last relevant notes and ping-pong right on up to the front.

I was heartily sick of the slavish Irish attitude of merely embracing the music most popular at home. We were living in New York City, for Christ's sake—home of greats ranging from Miles Davis to Joseph Heaney, David Bowie to Tito Puente, KRS-One to Tony DiMarco; we had reggae, funk, rap, noise, Sligo fiddling, Kerry shlides, salsa, Santeria, and every other manner of music imaginable at our fingertips. Why couldn't Black 47 take these influences, wrap them around thirty originals, and become one of the best bands in the world? As far as I was concerned, the only thing that could conceivably hold us back was fear of failure and, in my own case, the ubiquitous crippling Irish inferiority complex. With two kids at home to be raised, I no longer had the luxury to wallow in either. I took my full inheritance of loser's attitude, drop-kicked it over the Brooklyn Bridge, and I've had better days ever since.

I felt that we should not play outside the Irish scene; instead we should let the word spread and have the world come hear us on our own turf. This strategy was working wonders. With the release of the *Black 47* independent CD in early '91, we now had an actual product. Because it was self-financed, it had taken some time to record: a hundred bucks here, two hundred there, for blocks of inexpensive studio time. This was when Johnny Byrne first became involved with the band as our studio engineer and sometimes soundman. Vin Scelsa, who had introduced the independent

single of "Funky Céilí" to major radio, now took to playing long
sets of our music on his show. He also had a music column in *Penthouse* and wrote about what, to his mind, the band stood for. *Rolling
Stone* did a glowing review of the CD and things really began to
take off. We now even began to charge a cover for live shows.
Record companies sent people down to Reilly's to see us.
Although this was validation for the band, whether through cock-
iness or bitterness at the way the Thinkers had been treated, I was
less than impressed. We left word at the door that there be no
comps, no guest lists, especially for industry people. That's always
been one of my pet peeves. There is no record company in the
world that won't reimburse their scouts the price of admission to
see a band; and yet, these half-baked arbiters of taste always insist
on being "on the list," denying the band their one source of
income. Fuck you and your list! We even considered charging
them double; we were doing quite nicely without them. And if
they asked for a copy of the CD to take back to their bosses, I'd
send them over to Steve Duggan behind the bar, but warn them
in advance that they better have $15 in their fists. Never was a
Cavan man better suited for such a task.

Joe Strummer messed up this strategy. Now that the word was
out, I had been receiving calls from various rock clubs. Since I
well knew the fiscal policies of these establishments, it was easy
enough to shake them off—just ask for what you were worth
and they'd soon hang up. But I kept receiving persistent calls
from Walter Durkacz at Wetlands. After beating around the bush
for a time, I named a price that I felt would be out of his bracket
and left it at that. Finally, I got a wearily submissive call back from
Walter, who later became a friend and confidant, saying, "All
right already! Just take the bloody gig so I can get Strummer off
my back." Joe had been tormenting him to give us a booking, and
felt that we should be expanding our horizons. We did play for
Walter, and Wetlands became an important stop on our circuit.
The club is closed now, the building converted into high-priced
lofts, and the city is the poorer for it. One night some power
broker will have his slumbers interrupted by the ghost of James

Connolly awakening the masses at the foot of his bed, so many times was the great man's memory invoked under that roof.

But I was wary of all gigs in new places, especially those charging admission. Each one had to be weighed on its merits. Part of the difficulty was identifying the strength of our fan base, although we now had the stalwart Tom Schneider sending out monthly cards to our ever growing mailing list. We were getting a lot of publicity and may have had lines outside Reilly's two nights a week, but I was never certain just how firm this base was and if they would travel and pay a higher ticket price than they were accustomed to. I was still consumed with building our following from the ground up and moving the band steadily forward. Have people come see you in a club that you couldn't fill and you exposed this strategy in a needless way. Reilly's was safe, as was the Bronx at this stage; all we had to do was play a couple of blinding sets and we could impress anyone with our constantly rotating audience and the depth of their appreciation.

In the end, even with Walter offering a headline spot, I would only agree to do a guest set or coheadline. One of the great gigs from that period was a double bill with John Trudell, the Native-American poet and performer. We dedicated our set to the Cherokee Nation who even on the Trail of Tears managed to collect money for the victims of the Famine of 1847. John had no need to dedicate anything. He was a towering presence and the embodiment of his people; his dignity and brooding intensity onstage in Wetlands and later at Farm Aid—where he was the only performer booed—still gives me chills.

Vin Scelsa's championing of the band broadened our base immeasurably. His was the last uncensored voice on major rock radio. He played only what inspired him, and his audience loved him for it. Radio had, for some years, been co-opted by big business. This change had happened because of the introduction of the play list by "consultants" such as Lee Abrams who, perhaps more than any person, is responsible for the sad state of rock radio today. His brilliant idea was that stations should streamline the number of songs played in a week to a chosen few, thus giving that spot on the dial a more recognizable and more easily marketed identity. The end result was that most stations lost their individuality and you can now travel this country from coast to coast and hear nothing but the same ultimately deadening thirty songs on your car radio. This "innovation" exponentially increased the power of the major record companies, for what independent company or artist could compete with their marketing dollars? Of course, you can pay a monthly fee for satellite radio and expand your fare, but it will hardly be long until "consultants" begin to fine-tune the nature of that medium too. But the change went even deeper. Radio was our voice. We listened to our favorite disc jockeys for flair and distinctiveness, but most of all for an expression of humanity. Now it's difficult to tell them apart from the ads they're so busy cuing, and often even harder to differentiate the ads from the music they play. Take a bow, Lee. I hope you made plenty of money for your troubles, for you well and truly pissed all over the dreams of so many musicians and listeners who lived for and depended on an independent radio forum.

By 1991, it was getting hard to remember a time when DJs actually chose their own music and made an art form of the way they showcased their unique tastes. Then you heard Vin, and the power and glory of radio would come flooding back. It was a bitter pill for many of us to realize that rock music as a vehicle for change had had its day. But for six hours on a Sunday night, Vin turned the tables, literally and figuratively; he showed the world just what a force music could be, if left to the taste of the DJ rather than the corporate music director far more concerned with satisfying his advertising overlords, his Nielsen ratings, and the inevitable financial bottom line.

Vin went against the grain and played Black 47, an unsigned band. We came up to the station to perform and he interviewed us live. Not only were we getting our own music and message across, we were helping this FM Che Guevara keep a dream alive. He spoke for the dispossessed of the airwaves: those who grew up with freeform radio and listened to it as a soundtrack to their lives. I had been one of them. Judy Greenberg and Murad Heerjee were two others. Judy heard this broadcast while driving on the Long Island Expressway. She later told me that it was the first music that spoke to her in years. She pulled off the expressway and called her brother, Elliot Roberts, in L.A. Elliot was manager to Neil Young, Tracy Chapman, and Ric Ocasek. The next Wednesday he flew in and caught the band in Reilly's. He was funny, irreverent, and on the ball. We had the songs, he said, and, with those in hand, he could land a three-legged giraffe a record deal. He was pretty tied up with Neil Young and was in the midst of divorce from both his wife and Bob Dylan. He could oversee our career from L.A., but suggested that Judy and her partner Murad could run things in New York on a day-to-day basis.

There are three types of people who become rock managers. Those such as Elliot who could successfully manage the CIA; those who unearth one good prospect, get lucky, and stay in business for a number of years; and those very nice people with stars in their eyes who have no business being within spitting distance of the other two types, or the various leeches and scumbags—including musicians—who inhabit the rock music world. Judy and Murad were the latter. To say that they gave Black 47 their all would be an understatement. It would also be fair to say that they hadn't a clue how the business works or what it takes to keep a band functioning, moving forward, and on the road. My first instinct was to tell them to go back to appreciating music and not get involved with this most unforgiving of games. But I figured that since Judy was Elliot's sister, he'd look out for her, and maybe I could show them some of the ropes myself. Still, there's a ruthless and cunning quality needed to make the least inroads in the music world; I was to find out that no one can teach you how to acquire it.

We were suddenly accelerating into hyperactivity but, as yet, I could see the forest for the trees. Elliot felt that, although I had done a good job up until now, I should quit micromanaging the band, leave that to professionals, and concentrate fully on the creative and performing sides. His partner in Lookout Management, Frank Gironda, would supervise Murad and Judy, giving us as many managers as the gospels had writers. This sounded like a good plan, at least on paper, since I was definitely getting frayed around the edges from the nonstop work. The reality, however, was to prove different. We now also had two agents, Marsha Vlasic who handled the rock bookings and Steve Duggan working the Irish side. Dealing with these two very headstrong characters would have taken the judgment, not to mention the balls, of Solomon. Either could, and did have, Murad and Judy for breakfast any old day of the week. The crux of the issue was that Marsha thought we were overexposing ourselves in New York by playing in Reilly's and that we should instead be working the prestigious rock clubs around the country. Steve, along with the band who liked the steady money, wished us to continue playing his place. He was also receiving good financial offers from Irish pubs and festivals in the same cities that Marsha wished us to play for peanuts.

Up until the changeover, I had been able to mediate and call the shots on a gig-to-gig basis. But with me out of the picture, even with all the goodwill in the world, matters got out of hand. I was still only a phone call away and was constantly being solicited to mediate some squabble or other. As happens in these situations, when you're rising quickly, everything can be worked out, though it all takes time and energy. But when you hit some bumps in the road, seeds have already been sown that can lead to bitter fruit.

But for now all was wine and roses. One night, after we had finished our set, a very tall and attractive couple swept into Reilly's and was ushered to a hastily vacated table. I recognized Ric Ocasek instantly. He was tall, spectral, all in black, and sporting a wry smile indicating that not only had he seen everything, but that he could also predict any pileup rumbling down the pike in our direction. Yet, no one was paying the least attention to this guy who had sold over thirty million albums with the Cars. Instead, both men and women were falling over backward to ogle his wife, Paulina Porizkova. I must have been the only one in the room who'd never heard of her.

It turned out that Elliot had given Ric a copy of the Black 47 independent, and Ric, in his quietly deliberate manner, had listened to and analyzed the CD down to the last overtone. I liked him from the instant I joined them at their table. He was quite happy for Paulina to be the center of attention. We sat on one side of the table, while the whole room almost toppled over on her side, such was the crush of people trying to secure autographs or just see if she was as beautiful in real life as on paper. That was fine by me, for Ric was an intriguing person. He spoke to me in detail about the songs. They had obviously touched him, and he was interested in both their origins and their structure.

I told him how much I had been moved by his song "Drive." He had no problem in accepting praise, which is such a relief, as it cuts out a lot of unnecessary beating around the bush. He added that the song had become a bit uncomfortable for him since many women identified with it, and wondered how he knew the details of their particular nervous breakdown. At the end of a long, intense conversation that coincided with Paulina signing the last autograph, he said, "I know exactly how to take what you've done with your CD and make it better." He hit a nerve, for I had been unsure what our next recording move should be. I had written a number of promising new songs, but I felt that those on the independent CD deserved a much wider audience.

"Fine," he said. "Let's work on the best songs from the independent, then remix them. We'll record the new ones from scratch, put them all together, and end up with a wonderful album."

It all seemed so obvious. As he stood up and helped Paulina into her coat, he added: "Only one problem, we're leaving for the islands in three weeks. But we can easily finish by then." And with that, they and their glamour swept out the door, as quickly as they'd come in.

27

AMERICAN WAKE

Open up the door, she's standing there
With the smile in her eyes, but the gray in her hair
Betrays the fact you strayed far from home
With your drinkin', your smokin', your whorin' around.
Sit down by the fire, put your feet on the grate
Spend the night reminiscing till the hour grows late
Always remember at the end of the day
You can always go home, you just can't stay.

Then it's off to the pub to see your old mates
They all look older but nothing has changed
And you drink 'til you're nearly out of your head
"Hey what are yez all doin' snakin' off to bed?"
Then you're outside her flat but she's no longer there
The tears scald your eyes as you think of her hair
In the photo they sent you of her wedding day
You can always go home, you just can't stay.

Then you see her at Mass with the kids at her side
And it all comes back in the blink of an eye
The tears and the laughter, the love and the lies
And that dress she wore the night you said good-bye.
Then her husband says, "It's good to have you back."
She smiles for a moment and squeezes your hand
But you know what she's thinking, she doesn't have to say
You can always go home, you just can't stay.

And you swear to yourself time and time again
It was all in the past, she don't mean anything
Now your life is full of laughter and bars
What did you leave behind?
Just the sun the moon and the stars.

Then it's up in the morning at the crack of dawn
With your stomach churning, she says, "C'mon now, Sean
You'll be late for the plane," but that crack in her voice
Betrays the fact that you made your choice
A long time ago, now there's no turning back
'Cause last night you had your American Wake
And the bells are still ringing, can't you hear what they say
You can always go home, you just can't stay.

Say good-bye in the wind and the pouring rain
One last drink at Shannon Airport then we're out of here.
Catch you again next year
Landing at Kennedy, all you feel is the pain
But it's too late
'Cause last night you had your American Wake

From Home of the Brave, *EMI Records 1994*
Published by EMI Blackwell/Starry Plough Music (BMI)

HAVE YOU EVER stood at the bar in Shannon Airport, hungover and heartbroken, the very stomach falling out of you, trying so hard to keep it together? You trade stupid jokes with the bartender or anyone else who happens by, taking care only to glance sideways at your mother, for fear you might lose yourself in the soft, still sadness of her eyes. You murder a couple of pints of Guinness to give you enough ballast and courage to get through the next half hour. Then you either hear the final announcement for your flight or you just can't take anymore, and blurt out, "Well that's that, I'll see you next Christmas," or "Maybe you'll come out yourselves in the summer." Any bloody words that bring it all to a closure, before you break down and blow the whole façade you've been carefully constructing since the morning you arrived.

In the old days, they always insisted on walking to the very last barricade. There the deep-sea sailor would shake hands and slip me the dollars he'd been saving especially for this moment. I could never pull the wool over his eyes; he knew that I was heading back totally skint, and might have trouble getting into Manhattan from the airport. Besides, my mother needed the last hug, when she could hold on for that extra allowed second, while the passport-checker averted his eyes. They were older now and, by common silent consent, we agreed to finish things up in the bar; it was easier that way, they could fuss over the two grandchildren, making sure they had sufficient crayons and Cadburys for the long trip. They looked smaller and older, and all three of us were consumed with the idea that this might be the last time we'd say good-bye. Even the deep-sea sailor looked frailer. He had long since quit the ships and even the oil rigs up in the North Sea. His face was lined with understanding and concern, though he masked it with his usual fatalistic humor. He was finally landlocked and missed his own comings and goings; he now relived them vicariously through my brother and me—this gave him some kind of escape hatch. But he knew how hard this was on my mother, so he was a full party to any kind of distraction we could throw in her way at these awful partings.

I wonder did they think me unfeeling because I could never look back and wave the way others did. Instead, I'd make a big show of ushering the two children on down the corridor, repeating questions that I'd already posed a number of times, until they'd look at me through their little boy eyes, wondering if Daddy was okay, and maybe he shouldn't have stayed out so late last night. Eventually we'd be on the plane and lifting up over the Shannon Estuary while my parents would be taking the long drive back to Wexford, my father for once allowing my mother the comfort of Gay Byrne's radio show in peace, instead of making his usual mockery of the man. And within half a day, we'd be back in New York, opening bills and junk mail, and listening to distraught messages on the answering machine; before I knew it, the city would already have its claws in me. The pain would still be there, though no longer quite so sharp, and even the vivid details of one more American wake would be blurring into all the others and tumbling head-over-heels into the past.

I'd be unsettled for those first days, skittish as any junky. For the city is an addiction, and I was hooked. But my mind would keep straying back to Wexford and a more simple way of living, where I was accepted for just being a part of my family. There seemed to be so much less striving and mental turmoil there; you were what you were and that was all there was to it. Then I'd remember I had come here for independence: to find both myself and my own niche in life. With Black 47, I appeared to have achieved some of that: we were already being referred to as "the house band of New York." Yet, I wondered just where one thing began and another ended. New York was so consuming, I could no longer tell if I was living my life as planned, or if I had just become another well-oiled cog in the city's machine. But those thoughts would barely make it through the first jet-lagged week, before I'd be totally immersed once more in the band's dramas, triumphs, and inevitable setbacks, and the city would have her way with me again.

It was a thrill to work with Ric. He is such an underestimated person. People tend to think of him as a caricature of sorts: someone who wrote a lot of very successful pop songs for the Cars, as if that in itself was chump change. Ever try writing a great pop song? Having been unsuccessful myself for many years, I had a real respect for anyone who could get people to not only sing along with your songs, but actually fork out the cash to buy them. And I've never listened to "Drive" without marveling how such a simple song can summon up raw vistas of loss and loneliness inside me. But Ric is also a great producer. He dived right into the creative process of Black 47. He lived those songs, got inside them, and found out how to broaden them, both sonically and aesthetically. Having spent long months in the studio with Mutt Lange sweating every minuscule detail, he was now more concerned with the overall sound of the recording rather than if an individual instrument was coated by the latest technological gloss. I'm very proud of my production of the independent *Black 47* CD. There's an honesty to the arrangements, combined with a certain dry sparkle to the sound. It also captures a time and place, even an era, very well. But Ric questioned many of the production conclusions I had arrived at. He opened my eyes to new possibilities and, in the end, we were able to deepen and expand the mood and make the songs more palatable to a wider swathe of people.

Our modus operandi was to first discuss various options for a song; then he would set me to work, either using guitars, synthesizers, percussion, or vocals. As long as matters were moving along to his liking, he would sit there on his studio couch, sketching in a pad, while listening intently. He's a keen illustrator and I loved to check out his very detailed line drawings. Whenever I hit a glitch or a point of confusion, he would suggest an option that was invariably the quite obvious solution. It was as if he could inhabit your mind and foresee the answer to the problem you were about to confront. Eventually I would lose effectiveness, collapse on the couch, and he would take over. I might nap or go home. He would continue through the night and when I arrived early the next afternoon, he would have some mixes or guitar lines set up for me to listen to.

While he had a late breakfast with Paulina I would give him my opinions. He was totally open and would, in an instant, scrap something he might have worked on for hours if he felt I couldn't live with it. He was a whiz with drum machines and worked to update or simplify what I had already laid down. Likewise with the newly popular guitar synthesizers. Listen to the gauzy beauty of the intro to "Fanatic Heart" on *Fire of Freedom*—that was Ric's innovation. While he was always cognizant of the fact that Black 47's sound was very much our own, still he was fearless in raising or lowering the volume of any instrument during a mix and didn't give a damn what a player might think. He could be cool to the other instrumentalists—not in a cruel way—but the song was his focus, as it was mine, although being a player in the band, I was much more aware of the feelings of the other members. His idea, though, was that we already had good mixes with the Independent CD, now we should improve on these for *Fire of Freedom,* despite any hurt or personal cost.

In the end, we began to run out of time and moved to separate studios where each took charge of separate mixes. I'll always remember hearing what he did with "Funky Céilí." I think he only added a couple of big guitar chords, but he changed the dynamic of the mix by bringing up and adding a warm reverb on Geoff's soprano sax while tucking the pipes in right under it, thereby giving an almost Disney-like jauntiness to the track. This version was a bit jarring to me at first, but radio loved it, as he predicted they would. He never had any doubt but that "Funky" would be the first single, while I felt that "Maria's Wedding" was much more commercial. He was right. I had been around studios for years and was an old hand at the game, but I learned an amazing amount in those three weeks that Ric and I worked together.

And one day it was finished and I've hardly seen Ric since, although I often think about him. Life was roaring by. Record companies were coming down every night to see us. They were almost a fixed presence in Reilly's now, and for the most part we didn't put a lot of pass on them. Some, however, left their mark. Seymour Stein from Sire arrived one night in a limo. He was a legend in the business and I had a lot of respect for him, having signed Talking Heads and the Ramones. We got him the best table in the house. There he remained as if nailed to his seat, his head down, his brow furrowed in concentration, while people danced and cavorted around him. He seemed to be listening with his whole body, his concentration so intense it was intimidating. It was hard not to stare at this titan evaluating us. After ninety minutes of music, he was still bent over. I hardly dared approach him. When I touched him on the shoulder he started to attention, very alarmed and disoriented. He cast a great sigh of relief when he recognized me and shook my hand gratefully. He had just got off a plane from Europe, rushed in from Kennedy, and slept through the whole blistering set.

The constant scrutiny was beginning to wear on the band.

Would we never get signed? I was of two minds about the whole process. Perhaps we should go our own way and set up an independent record company. For, through experience, I was mindful of the fact that the day you sign a recording contract is the countdown to a band breaking up. On the other hand, that meant losing Elliot and his infrastructure, and would I be able to run the whole rigmarole myself while out on the road? Would the band go along with such a radical idea? It was all a bit too much. So, after being vetted, prodded, dissected, and bored by every idiot who had even done an internship in a record company, it was all down to two people with integrity who actually knew the ropes of their business: Danny Goldberg from Atlantic and Pete Ganbarg from EMI.

Danny loved and respected the band for its political stands, as would become evident later, but he was hesitant about the actual signing. This may have had as much to do with his own job security, as any doubts about our commerciality. And so we went with Mr. Ganbarg who was living, eating, drinking, but not sleeping with Black 47. Pete was relentless and detail oriented. He related to the band on a lot of levels and totally believed in us. The A & R (artist and repertoire) man's traditional job is to first sign a band, provide suitable songs, and then ensure that a commercial record is delivered in a timely manner. We circumvented much of this procedure since Ric and I had already recorded *Fire of Freedom*. Everyone agreed that the album sounded not only great, but original and fresh, too. Black 47 was red-hot both on the street and with the media; with Pete rallying EMI behind us, it appeared that we were all set for a blast at the stars or, at least, a respectable jaunt around some decent nearby planets.

Even now with the benefit of hindsight, it's a little hard to put the whole thing in perspective. EMI was both growing quickly and consolidating its position in the United States. But there were forces within forces within that company. Many departments seemed to be vying for power, each with their own opinions on how success could be guaranteed. Elliot would only deal with presidents and the like, leaving poor Judy and Murad to deal with all lesser company mortals. I saw the inner dealings mainly through Pete's eyes and it was a fascinating, though oft-times dis-concerting, education. This three-way split of information, how-ever, was to lead to the inevitable communication problems; but at first, there was a wonderfully benevolent feeling abroad: "We have this great streetwise band. Now let's not blow their street-cred, just move these boys forward."

During our relationship with CBS, the Thinkers were ever-present in the Black Rock offices. We were even dropping by for coffee, not so much to see anyone, but to raid their new-releases closet and sell the records at Bleecker Bob's. This time, I resolved to keep a distance and channel any concerns and ideas through Pete. That worked really well, for the most part; but a decision had been made early on within the company that was to have major repercussions. Instead of releasing *Fire of Freedom,* we would instead send out an EP of songs to radio in the form of a CD. The first single or "emphasis track" would be either "Funky Céilí" or "Maria's Wedding." Two more songs would be added to round off a "perfect" EP. I was a little apprehensive, as I've always felt it's better to go with your best first shot—there may not be another. But I was assured that *Fire of Freedom* would be ready and available in stores very quickly, should we get any significant airplay. Elliot signed off on it and it seemed like a good plan. It was, too, at first.

But now, the infighting began in earnest. What other songs should be added to the EP? Should these then be included on *Fire of Freedom*? Everyone in the company had their favorites. It seemed for a while that the EP would end containing up to fifteen songs. We had to show our political side, so "James Connolly" was included; we had to show our roots, so "Black '47" gained a spot. But I insisted that "Connolly" and "Black '47" had to be on *Fire of Freedom,* as they were the heart and soul of the band. I did feel that "Our Lady of the Bronx" could be on the EP and left off *Fire.* In the end, five songs were slated for the EP: "Funky Céilí," "Maria's Wedding," "James Connolly," "Black '47," and "Our Lady of the Bronx." It was decided that a limited number of this CD be manufactured and put in the marketplace as a collector's item and a taste of what was to come. With the help of their art department, we constructed a pastiche of photos that both summed up the songs and the band. The EP was dispatched for mastering and production.

About a month later, the proposed cover for *Fire of Freedom* was presented to me and I promptly threw a fit. It was a picture of a cottage on the side of a mountain in the West of Ireland, with little relevance that I could see to New York's Black 47. But the marketing department loved it, I was assured. Well, the marketing department could stuff it! But despite my escalating tantrums, the head of product management held firm. They had spent a lot of time and energy in their search for the proper cover and we'd just have to like it or lump it.

Finally, Elliot was called in to mediate with the heads of departments. I couldn't believe it. What was their investment in this very nice picture but totally wrong image? After breakfast, lunches, and every other imaginable on-their-dime meeting, various one-on-ones, and a final threat on my part to scrap the whole album, it was decided that the company would pass on the cottage cover. Instead of having me sit down with a visual artist—which is how all the other Black 47 covers have since been done—they insisted on doing the work in the sanctity of their own privacy and then present me with an alternative. But all of this was taking time. In the meantime, the EP went out to radio. Two weeks later, "Funky Céilí" was ripping across college radio. The EP was rushed into stores and sold out promptly, often taking weeks to get manufactured and restocked. No matter how many were pressed, they were swept off the shelves. We were all caught like rabbits in the headlights: not only did we not have *Fire of Freedom* ready to go—we didn't even have a cover yet.

Now the hammering really started at the doors. "Funky Céilí" was soon the most requested song on alternative radio nationwide. It became so popular that radio stations were even playing a hastily put together parody, replete with a caricature of my accent. We were suddenly hit for countless interviews and more photos sessions than any Ford model. With such a deluge of publicity, Reilly's had to hire new security to keep the crowds out. And still no cover for *Fire of Freedom*. Finally, they took me to one more lunch; I'm surprised I didn't already have an ulcer. They showed me a rough version of the eventual *Fire of Freedom* cover. I thought it a bit dark, but after a bit of lightening up and a few changes, I signed off on it. This was around Christmas 1992. It would take over another two months to get in stores. We settled on a St. Patrick's Day release.

This is when we needed cohesive management—some kind of overall strategy. But everything was reaction rather than action. *Time* magazine wants to do a piece, so everything is dropped. MTV wants you up there. Can you do *Conan* tonight? We were being hit from all sides. It was exciting and we were living on adrenaline. But the clock was ticking down. My belief, after all this, is that you have a two-month window in which to maximize your opportunities. And it wasn't for want of money or good intentions from EMI, or the talent or energy of the band. But the lack of a firm hand at the helm to navigate the shoals out of the harbor and get the offshore wind in our sails hurt us immeasurably. Instead of standing back from the fray for a few days and coming up with a plan, we were being run from pillar to post, squandering our shot, getting played off the air, selling the stand-in EP by the bucketful, but still no *Fire of Freedom* in the stores.

But we did have a video and it was causing waves at MTV. In its black and white rawness, it stuck out like a sore thumb, and there was a joy to it that people responded to. Added to which, we had EMI Records totally enthused and fired up over the band. From President Daniel Glass down to the lowliest intern, it was a given that we were the next big thing. We finished off 1992 as conquering heroes in New York, playing at the Ritz in the old Studio 54. All was well with our world—or was it?

28

LOSIN' IT

Chuckie said I don't know what's going on
I'm down on my knees
I'm ah uh oh losin' it
Been up and down this New York town
Lookin' for a break
Just a fair shake of it
But the people all got concrete in their eyes
And their points of view
The taxis and the mailboxes
All want to make love to me
Exactly like you used to do

And oh . . . I'm ah uh oh losin' it
Oh, I'm down on my knees . . . losin' it

Here come a cop, "I heard she left you, son,
It's time that you
Picked up the pieces
The whole town is talkin' about you
Ever since your waitress
Gave you the deep freeze."
Now she's runnin' with a cab driver
Who swears he's the crucified King of Siam
But Jesus is comin'
So hold on, he's just stalled up around the bend.

You say, why don't I go see a shrink?
But I don't need to spend a grand a month
To know that I'm out of my head
'Cause you said
You'd be better off dead than livin' with me.

My boss said, "What the hell's goin' on?
The whole firm knows
That you're losin' it."
I just jumped up on his desk
Did a Celtic war dance
Teach that fool a lesson
Then I burned all your lingerie
Tried stitching it back together again
Then this clock started tickin' in my head
And oh oh oh, here I go again

And oh . . . I'm ah uh oh losin' it
Oh, I'm down on my knees . . . losin' it

From Home of the Brave, *EMI Records 1994*
Published by Starry Plough Music/EMI Blackwell Music (EMI)

SUCCESS IS SUCH a marvelous thing. You suddenly realize that you really are the wonderful person you always suspected. Lest you think this is mere egotism, rest assured that hundreds of people will be on hand to buy you drinks, slap you on the back, share in any financial gain that might accrue to you, but most of all to bask in the glow emanating from the sheer majesty of your personality. And if, from time to time, you hear a little voice in the back of your head dissenting with this overwhelming majority view, it takes little effort to tune this lone protester out or even squash it forever. The truth is, though, if you're at all on top of things, you don't have the bloody time to even think about it. There's always one more interview to be done, one more photo taken, one more radio station visited, or should one descend to gutter language, one more ass to be kissed.

I knew something about it already. I'd had little tastes of success with Turner and Kirwan, the Thinkers, and *Liverpool Fantasy*. Even so, I just wasn't prepared for the full razzmatazz of the modern publicity machine. All of a sudden, you're in the spotlight. It's your turn, baby, step right on up! Everything you say and do is treasured and becomes fodder for even more publicity. The buzz is you and you are the buzz. It may have been even more extreme and self-propagating for Black 47 because we lived in New York; we still played Reilly's on a regular basis and thus were perennially available. If some other "star" got a sick stomach, OD'd, or had a bad hair day, just run a camera up to the pub. There was always bound to be a celebrity of some sort getting locked; if not, I was woozily available with some quirky opinion, occasionally mistaken for wisdom, at the tips of my fingers. Of course that was the whole reason for doing a residency: you were in the same place at the same time every week, willing and able to put out exactly whatever was needed to keep you in the public eye.

Talk about celebrities. Second Avenue, opposite the projects, became Hollywood Boulevard East. I half expected Bette Davis and Clark Gable to come swanning through the door. Matt Dillon was a regular along with his rat pack. We even did a cameo in *The Saint of Fort Washington* with him and Danny Glover. Neil Young dropped by to talk about amplifiers. Liam Neeson showed up on a date with Brooke Shields. Sean Penn managed to breeze through anonymously, as is Sean's wont. Many returned because they could be themselves; we never made a big deal out of it: the show went on, with or without them. The important thing for us was the music and how to break through every night. We were the center of attention. Why cede that mythic spot in the lights to anyone else?

In fact, the celebrity parade made playing Reilly's harder. It was now more difficult for regular punters to get through the door because the star-fuckers and celebrity sleuths would get there early—their necks swiveling like swans—searching for someone, anyone who might grace Page 6, to arrive and make their evening. Lots of times, we'd have to insult them into silence, or even run them out by blowing great waves of volume and outrageousness over them. The limos would double-park outside and some new airhead model or grade B star would breeze up to the door to be met by Larry Watson and Colm Meehan, our somewhat nonchalant security detail, who wouldn't have batted an eyelid had Helen of Troy come galloping down Second Avenue and stepped naked out of her chariot. One great moment occurred when a Hollywood starlet brandishing more silicone than sense asked Larry if her table was ready. After giving her the Dublin once-over, he laconically pronounced: "No tables in there, luv. Fuck all chairs either. You'll be lucky to find a face to sit on."

It was a lot of fun to be at the center of the cyclone, especially the very benevolent one that swept around Black 47 in '93–'94. We had proved that we could do it our own way by simply letting the music do the talking and not bending to any commercial pressure. But I was never less than aware that, for once, luck was on our side and could just as quickly turn against us. Despite any claim to uniqueness, we were no better than hundreds of other equally deserving musicians in New York. This was a once-in-a-lifetime opportunity that we had literally stumbled into, and I was determined to make the most of it, to enjoy it and savor the moment. Yet it was hard to relax for I had a sense that, at best, we were hurtling through the dark with no sense of where we were going and, at worst, that everything was lurching crazily out of control. There was no overall strategy anymore. Gigs were being taken that didn't make any sense, usually because the money was good and helped balance out our expenses and some of the peanuts "career" rock gigs. But that left us zipping up and down the East Coast, then rushing back to Reilly's for our obligatory Wednesdays and Saturdays. On the surface, everything was going admirably, but I could sense that was only part of the picture. There were too many surprises, and there shouldn't be—even the good ones should have some sense of logic. We never knew what was going on, just that we were on an endless round of miles and gigs.

One night at the Chestnut Cabaret in Philadelphia, we arrived, did our sound check, then headed off for some food. On our return, the place was so packed we couldn't get through the door. I waved to the promoter. I could see he was freaking out. He was over to me like a shot and I asked him which of the other two bands was drawing all the people? He looked at me as if I was the one who was losin' it and said, "Are you kiddin' me? There's going to be a riot, they've already drank me out of Guinness!" We were the only ones who didn't know that "Funky Céilí" was the most popular song on radio in Philadelphia. Likewise in Chicago: we arrived in a blizzard dead late, the huge disco jammed and slow-handclapping for us. The Edge from U2 was even in the crowd. The last time we'd played to our base on the South Side, we only drew a hundred people. Now we were in a barn of a joint on the North Side, and they were turning away people in a snowstorm.

The gigs were great, the audiences enthusiastic and full of love for us, but it was worrisome nonetheless. There had to be a way of predicting just how many people we could draw. And, of course, there was: Nielsen SoundScan had recently initiated their computerized method of tallying the number of CDs sold in each area the previous week. EMI had been sending copies of this vital information to our office where they were gathering dust in a neatly stacked pile. I almost cried six months later when I finally discovered them and realized that the tool I'd been crying out for had always been at hand. One quick glance and I could tell where we were selling CDs, and consequently where we should be playing and when. We had audiences all over the country in cities and towns that I never imagined. It was a crime that we hadn't toured those markets and, in the process, glad-handed promoters, radio stations, newspapers, and local magazines. Instead we were hammering away at the same clubs, preaching to the converted. EMI was pouring money into us to subsidize tours that we had little need of. We had limited ourselves to a small picture at a time when we could have been furthering our career on a far larger canvas. I began to bitterly regret abdicating my role as micromanager at a point in our career when one was needed most.

Buzz is ephemeral. It's constituted of radio, TV, press, touring, meaningful songs, strong performances, word of mouth, and street credibility. When all, or most, of those aspects come together, a dynamic is created around a band: a vague, if compelling, aura that people want to go and see, touch, feel, listen to and, most significantly, become a part of. It can last a long time, or a little, depending on the ratio and amount of the above components. In the midst of our greatest buzz, the person who was working hardest for us inadvertently made a crucial mistake. Pete Ganbarg advised against "Funky Céilí" being pushed at Top Forty radio when it would have almost certainly have broken the Top Ten. Pete valued our street credibility and was fearful that such a move would cost us this ineffable quality. He reckoned that it would be wiser to wait for another song that might be more representative of our deeper political side. He did this for all the right reasons and felt, like me, that with the depth of Black 47's songs, there would be many other chances. Besides, *Fire of Freedom* hadn't actually come out yet and the CD wouldn't have been available in stores. Pete loved the band and made some other great decisions that paid off. This was just one of those things that happens in the course of a campaign; it goes without saying that it has affected our career ever since.

Of course, the lack of a cogent management structure was the real problem. Our team should have been in daily touch with the record company and a party to all such important decisions. But Elliot and Frank, not surprisingly, were tied up with Neil and Tracy, and not always in sync with the situation on the East Coast; they conferred far too much responsibility on two lovely, but inexperienced, surrogates in Manhattan. A great opportunity was lost. I could sense some of these things happening. But I had taken myself out of the total loop and only tended to jump back in to solve problems. Perhaps it's all wishful thinking, as I had a full-time job on the road with the band and the inevitable personal issues to take care of, too. I don't blame anyone else, nor should I. We all thought we were doing the right thing at the time.

Fire of Freedom came out to great acclaim in March, right in time for the St. Patrick's Day season. We didn't sleep for weeks, running this way and that around the country, soaking up the adulation. On the floor at the crack of dawn for early-morning television, live shows at radio stations, more TV on the *Live at Fives*, sound checks, gigs, ligs (parties), back in the van, on the road, into the next town, and more of the same. Coffee, booze, and Advil for your aching bones, pass out anytime you could find a seat or space on the dressing room floor. Then an agitated, excited conference call from EMI: "Guess what, guys! We're going to shoot a video for Maria's Wedding and have we got the right director? She so hot, she got them turnin' on the air-conditioners up at MTV!"

"Hey, but listen," I tell them, "I have that whole story already scripted. It's real-life Brooklyn." And it would have been great—shot right in the heart of Black 47 country—Bay Ridge noir and Benson-hurst cinema verité wrapped up in one.

"But this director's got a simply fabulous script of her own and they kiss the ground beneath her feet up at MTV." There were so many voices blurting out enthusiasm for this L.A. Godard that I couldn't even tell who was talking anymore.

"Yeah, but we like to keep a handle on things like that. We're kind of sensitive about how we're presented."

"Hey, they don't play it, what do you got? Forty thousand bucks of celluloid you play to your grandchildren?"

I should have stood firm. George Seminara knew the Black 47 vibe; he could get it down on camera with his eyes closed. He'd directed the video of "Funky Céilí," and he'd have fit into the Brooklyn scenario like a fist in a glove. But EMI didn't like George. He hadn't kissed the right ass, I suppose. He wasn't "hot," and the babe was. But I wanted him and felt badly. When a person does his best by Black 47, he stays with Black 47. That was always our way of doing things. Now we'd let George go—who was next? But, right there ahead of us, hovering in the air, was the golden grail of MTV and what that exposure could do for us at the gigs. Besides, record companies were notoriously fickle. They could just scrap the whole idea of a video in a second, and how bad could this director be?

She wasn't just bad. She was atrocious and she'd never even seen the band live or met us. Not that she was a bad person, just a young woman trying to keep her foot in the door of a rough business, and way in over her head. I sent her along our Brooklyn script and didn't hear anything back, except that she was flying in from L.A. The studio had already been booked. Not to worry, we were assured, Black 47 wouldn't have to do any acting or the like, just show up in our best threads and act like the rock stars we undoubtedly were. The Brooklyn scenario was out. She had the meister-script. It would be acted by children, and we would do cameos as some form of revved-up wedding band. Was she joking? Hadn't she ever heard of W.C. Fields? How about throwing in a couple of dancing bears, too? Hey, maybe we could bugger the bears? That way we might, at least, get the song onto some porn channels. But it was too late. The down payment had already been cashed. And so the fiasco began.

We wouldn't need to be there until 10 A.M. They would build the set the night before, and the child actors would do their parts early. Or that was the plan. The reality was different: pure chaos. This amiable L.A. director had never dealt with your regular New York City, ball-breaking screen mama before—and not just one, but eight of them with their little darlings, siblings, managers, agents, and a couple of pediatric shrinks thrown in for good measure. The two little leading assholes were already throwing major tantrums, egged on by the greatest collection of psychotic New York bitches that I've ever come across. Added to that, the air-conditioning was on the blink and the crew was up in arms. Prepubescent revolution ruled. The producer of this masterpiece told me that our director worked best under pressure, so have no fear, all would be well—just hang in there, drink some coffee, have some food, babe; stay calm and out of the way, they'd shoot our part in a couple of hours.

Though I'd put up with quite a bit of lip and backchat from my own kids, I was unprepared for the level of precocious peevishness and insolence that these untalented midgets and their bitch-on-wheels mothers threw in the course of the day. I might even have felt some sympathy for the beleaguered director if she hadn't got us all into this mess with her dumb script. The EMI representative kept reassuring me that with this female Orson Welles aboard, nothing really mattered: the fix was in and we were a sure thing for heavy rotation at the only channel that counted.

It was a long day and a worse night. The band did two quick takes of the song around midnight as the crew swept up the rented loft. How nice that we were included. We were pasty, exhausted, listless, caffeinated, or drunk, and as they say, the camera never lies. I watched the rough cut a couple of times, trying to see if there was any of it that could be reedited into something representative of the band. Well, we could have ditched all the kids' parts and showed a band that was pasty, exhausted, listless, caffeinated, or drunk, but not anything that even vaguely resembled Black 47 firing on all cylinders.

MTV was no cinch either. Our director, in the course of the day spent shooting the disaster, had apparently dropped some degrees in both Fahrenheit and Celsius. The video got a couple of spins at two in the morning before disappearing off into video limbo or wherever unmitigated trash like that eventually ends up.

Oh yeah, it was life in the fast lane all right. But now I really felt that there was something amiss. I asked for a meeting with Pete and John Cohen, head of alternative radio promotion at EMI. They were both friends and I could tell that there was a problem just by the looks of concern on their faces. I was rail thin at the time. Down to 127 pounds. Perhaps, I figured, they were worried about my health. But nothing so prosaic. They regretted to tell me that the EP idea had backfired. *Fire of Freedom* was selling well, but radio was not warming to "Maria's Wedding" as a single. Much as they liked it, the track was deemed old from being on the EP, and many of the stations had already given it some play. We'd have to provide a new single to send out and pronto! Any ideas? Could I edit "Fanatic Heart" down to three and a half minutes? Was there a way of taking the "black girl" out of "Banks of the Hudson"? We went through all of the songs with a fine-tooth comb and in the end decided to go with "Rockin' the Bronx." I headed back into the studio and got an edited version together.

We were just about to send that out to radio when I was summoned back to EMI. Plans had changed. How was I feeling? I was looking a bit on the thin side. How long would it take me to come up with another album? Why was I looking so pale? Maybe a good old slap-up steak dinner at Peter Luger's would beef me up? Did I ever think of taking a couple of days off? Who would I like to produce the next CD? *Fire of Freedom* was over. It would sell forever, but it was dead in the water as far as radio was concerned. Get some rest, lad, and get writing. I stumbled out of EMI feeling like I'd been hit over the head with a velvet sledgehammer.

29

DANNY BOY

Danny came over to old New York
From Bandon town in the county Cork
Got a room on the Avenue in Woodside Queens
And a job off the books doing demolition
He was kind of different from anyone else
Liked to hang out all by himself
Didn't hit those bars in Sunnyside, Queens
Went straight into the Village to check out the scene.

One day on the job the foreman said,
"Hey Danny Boy we think you're a fag
With your ponytail, ring in your ear,
Hey, we don't need no homos foulin' up the air."
Danny just smiled, picked up a two by four
He split that jerk from his jaw to his ear
Said, "You can stick your job where the sun don't shine
You're never goin' to stop me bein' what I am—boy!"

Then he met a man down in Sheridan Square
They moved in together for a couple of years
Said it was the happiest he'd ever been
Doin' what he wanted, livin' his dream.
We used to drink together down on Avenue B
One gray dawn he confessed to me
"Love's the only thing that makes the world go 'round
And I'm never goin' to see another sunset over sweet Bandon town."

Last time I saw Dan he was in a hospital bed
Two tubes hanging out of the nose of his head
He smiled at me with those stone blue eyes
Said, "Hey, how you doin', guy?
I'm history 'round here in a couple of weeks
But I did what I wanted, I got no regrets
So when you think of me crack a beer and smile,
Hey, life's a bitch and then you die."

Oh Danny boy, the pipes, the pipes are calling
From glen to glen and down the mountain side.
The summer's gone and all the flowers are dying
'Tis you, 'tis you, must go and I must bide
But come you back when summer's in the meadow
Or when the valley's hushed and white with snow
'Tis I'll be there in sunshine or in shadow
Oh Danny boy, Oh Danny boy, I love you so
I love you so Danny boy. . . .

From Home of the Brave*, EMI Records 1994*
Published by Starry Plough Music/EMI Blackwell Music (BMI)

IF THINGS WERE buzzing in the record world, they were positively on fire out in Irish America. Steve Duggan now had us playing in every pub that Paddy Reilly had even had a drink in, and we were becoming a rage on the festival scene. The festivals were my favorites because we could play to all ages, from two to ninety-two. Due to our appearances on Leno, Letterman, and O'Brien, we were now *the* Irish-American band and people wanted to see us in person. Some of them just weren't prepared for the real thing. They had been used to showbands playing the standards and traditional music groups content to sit on stools in the background. Now for the first time, they were introduced to full-frontal in-your-face musicians who were not only singing about Connolly and Michael Collins in very frank terms, but were also introducing them to "that great Irish revolutionary, Paul Robeson," as a number of critics referred to the African-American civil rights leader. It was one thing to sing about uncomplicated martyrs such as Kevin Barry and Roddy McCorley, but we were summoning Countess Markievicz and Bobby Sands back to life in all of their complexities, thus bringing people face-to-face with the actual political situation in the North of Ireland. This was not always comforting. Some festivals didn't even like the idea of Irish rebel music at all and would have preferred that we leave Connolly's Starry Plough banner and our clenched-fist salutes at home.

Unsettling as the politics might have been, the thought that an Irish construction worker might actually be gay really set teeth achattering. The Irish Lesbian and Gay Organization (ILGO) had placed the issue of Irish sexuality right on the front burner. And with the song, "Danny Boy," we kept the heat turned up. We would get requests not to play this perversion; but that made us only more determined. It was a time of change and we were pushing the envelope; but Irish America was past ready for a shaking up and, in our own crazy way, we were the boys to do it. For we were riding on top of the world, and we could take the heat, even if there was a price to be paid down the line. I don't regret a moment of it. Many friends had died of AIDS—staying silent would have been an insult to them. Besides, for the first time gay Irish-Americans were able to come out to a show and hold their heads up high. As far as I was concerned, it was hypocrisy to be for civil rights in Belfast and Derry and be against gay rights in New York and Boston. We were in the business of kicking sacred cows as well as sacred ass, and overnight we burst right through taboos that had been accepted for centuries. Irish America is a lot better and a more open place because of it. We had no notion of sitting on the fence—we neither had the balance nor the desire to do so. There was no middle ground for Black 47. You either liked or hated us. And to me, that's what rock 'n' roll is all about.

Nor was Irish America the only arena in which we were causing a stir. I was aroused from my slumbers one morning by an absolutely plummy British female voice inquiring if I was aware of the bad press Black 47 had been garnering in the Queen's own dominions. EMI, in their zeal to spread the word, had seen fit to invite members of the British press on a junket to see the band perform in New York; these merry gentlemen included a number from the more right-wing side of tabloid opinion. One of them had characterized us as "the musical wing of the IRA"—a rather damning and dangerous description given that the so-called pan-nationalist front had been deemed fair game for Loyalist whacking in those days. The plummy voice from EMI went on to inform me that "your people are at this very moment blowing up London." This definitely gave me pause for thought. I could not imagine my father at such a task; however, my mother was descended from solid republican stock stretching way back to General Cloney in the 1798 Rebellion. Could this Wexford grandmother be now running amok through Trafalgar Square, petrol bomb in one hand, a fistful of semtex in the other?

No, I was assured, this was not the case; but Black 47, with its "rabble rousing anthems," was apparently responsible for even parking tickets garnered in London by the IRA, the INLA, and any other lettered abbreviation beginning with an "I." It was further-more pointed out to me that songs such as "James Connolly" were, in the present circumstances, hardly likely to set the British charts on fire, nor was there a lot of point in restating the faults of both sides that led to the Irish Famine of 1847. When I inquired if she meant that the Serbs had finally owned up to coresponsibility with the British for one of the great disasters of the nineteenth century, she claimed I was being obtuse. I quoted her some Yeats, asking her to understand that since Black 47 was intrinsically political, was there another Troy for us to burn? The only Yeats she appeared to have heard of was Paula—Bob Geldof's wife. Of course she may have thought I said Croydon rather than Troy for, before hanging up, she testily noted that I was missing the point, but would soon understand. She was so right. EMI did release *Fire of Freedom,* as they were contracted to do in the UK; but when it sold out, they printed no more copies. They were equally unhelpful in aiding us attain European releases for the CD, thus cutting off lucrative continental bookings. There's more than one way to skin a cat, as they say.

Elliot was quite sanguine about the shelving of *Fire of Freedom* in the United States. It was over, we'd survived, and we were getting another shot: a new album and a recording budget of $250,000. Right there and then, we should have siphoned off $100,000 and divided it among the band. Once the word got out that a quarter of a mil was available, we were like a bull's-eye waiting to be hit. But the money came with strings attached—EMI would dole it out and there would be no payments to band members, beyond a token pittance, until the album was delivered. I thought it only fair that Ric should produce. He had come through for us with *Fire of Freedom,* and brought it in at a very reasonable cost. But EMI wanted no part of him. He wasn't "hot." Neither did the band care to work with him again. I had enjoyed the collaboration, but the musicians had felt sidelined. And, to be fair, Ric's emphasis would always be on the songs and the person who wrote them.

I was well used to being the focus by this time. It just went with the territory of being lead singer. Frankly, I didn't care who did the talking, but I was obsessed with the notion that every interview be done, every lead followed, no matter how inconsequential it might seem. You just never knew where your break was coming from. The egalitarian ethic of the band was that the junior reporter from the community college paper was as important as the senior writer from *Time.* This was a fair but exhausting principle to live up to. I tried to persuade EMI to have other members pick up the slack with the interviews, but after some initial attempts, they were reluctant. There had been a couple of missed phone calls, a few mis-understandings, and an attitude from some writers that "mere musicians" were being foisted on them rather than the almighty "singer-songwriter-front man." And that was that. EMI wanted *una voce,* and I was to be it—even if that voice was sometimes hoarse and raspy from the road and the rhetoric. The music industry was focused around songs and those writing them; musicians were con-sidered interchangeable. That was the not so unsubtle hint always abroad in those salad days. But I had been a bandsman going right back to Wexford with Elvis. I had no desire to be some precious singer-songwriter. We'd started as a band and we'd stay one.

I had no problem coming up with material for the new CD. I'd been writing all along and was happy with the breadth and direction of the songs. But with Ric out of the question, I wasn't quite sure where to turn. EMI promptly gave me a boxful of producers' reels. They all sounded polished, from a production side anyway. My question was: How would they fare working with me? I'm not the kind of person who just hands songs over to a producer and gives him carte blanche to weave his magic. I can usually visualize how the song should sound as I'm writing it, and am insistent that the spirit and spine of the inspiration be respected. I must have listened to twenty reels and talked to as many disembodied voices on the phone. In the end, I was dazed from the whole process. Pete came to the rescue and said, "Why not get a couple of these guys into a rehearsal studio, and see what ideas they come up with?"

That worked with me because many of the new songs needed a trap drummer instead of a drum machine. That was Hammy's background, but it had been some time since he'd played a full kit. I sincerely hoped he would work out, as I didn't want to go through any kind of Ringo-Pete Best scenario with one of my dearest and oldest friends. I told him the situation and we agreed that he and I would go in and work out the new arrangements with various producers. Our old mate, Dave Conrad, had grown tired of the long smoke-filled nights on the road and decided to leave the band for a writing career. We were both keen to work in a new bassist, so the mighty dreadlocked Kevin Jenkins joined us in the studio.

First up was Jerry Harrison, late of Talking Heads. Jerry was a veritable font of confidence. He breezed into that studio over on Lafayette Street, put Hammy through his paces, and worked out some great bass lines with Kev. As he was leaving, Hammy gave me a thumbs-up, and that was enough for me. There would be no Pete Bests in Black 47, and Jerry obviously knew his way around a board. Just like that, he was anointed producer.

The CD would be called *Home of the Brave*. Everything seemed to fall into place, and using trap drums again really inspired both

Hammy and me. Also, Jenkins was one serious bass player. He had begun his career as an adolescent playing with Motown reviews and had absorbed many of James Jamerson's groundbreaking licks. On his night, which was often, Kevin could nail the Heavenly Host to the floor. He put oomph in our sound, weaved magic around Hammy's kick drum, and added real soul and stage presence into the bargain. There was a sonic boom beneath us now and, as someone broadly remarked, he finally put the Black in 47. With Nico Wormworth, our road manager, doing the stage setup and Jenkins eyeing the ladies, we began to look a little like a Gaelic Soul review, which caused not a few eyebrows to be raised in the various Southies of Boston, Chicago, and Buffalo.

Jerry was very unlike Ric. He was more the collegiate type and still wore his Harvard background on his sleeve. He hit the band at a troublesome time. We had been playing for four years nonstop through all manner of controversy and acclaim. It wasn't that we paused, far from it, we were still out playing, and the publicity continued unabated; but the first flush of the affair was definitely over. The band was behind the new album, but there was also a keen disappointment that the potential of *Fire of Freedom* had not been realized.

I'm convinced now that everything would have passed off smoothly if we had recorded the band live in the studio; we had performed most of the songs on Vin Scelsa's show the week before and the ensuing tape had sounded inspired. Instead we adopted the modern and more sterile method of working from the bass and drums up, layering instrument by instrument, until the song is ready for mixing. This stripped us of our live magic and exposed every player to the magnifying glass, which had never been an issue to any of us before; intonation, of all things, became a problem. Tuning is like sex. Until it's questioned, you never think about it, you just do it and tallyho! But once called into account, all sorts of problems are unearthed. It seemed like everything that we took for granted now took forever to complete in various studios that developed all kinds of technical problems of their own. Matters went from bad to worse and the recording confidence of the band was shaken. I might add that onstage we were still blazing away and getting a further lease of life from the introduction of so many new, crowd-pleasing songs.

Jerry was a great guy with a wry sense of humor and a lot of talent. He did his best and stuck manfully to the task, but there was a lack of chemistry with some members. He was simply the right person for the wrong time; every personal issue that had been buried within the band on our ascent was now surfacing and needed to be dealt with. But who had the inclination or the energy to come up with solutions? Each of us had our own personal problems to deal with. To compound matters, the very time we were spending in the studio was costing money that could have been split among the band. This led to an added tension and a sense that the clock was ticking away, and more than metaphorically speaking. There didn't seem to be a second to stand still and do the necessary reflection; instead, it was get your butt down to a studio at the mouth of the Holland Tunnel where everyone was assaulted by allergies. There, we inched forward day by day. What should have been a joyful romp became a long hard slog.

The situation would have broken up a lesser band. I felt caught in the middle with many forces pulling us asunder. Some members were wondering just how we had gotten ourselves in this situation in the first place. I had always controlled the recording process, and now we were musically reeling and apparently going around in circles. To anyone's way of thinking, a large part of the responsibility for this situation lay on my shoulders. I know I certainly felt that way. But the old days were over. Money and expectations were now involved. I had to answer to many people, but no longer had the power to decisively call the shots. I needed to assure EMI that everything was under control, when it was anything but. Since I had been working closely with Jerry, and in a very friendly and cooperative manner, too, I had to respect his leadership; for his part, he was totally supportive of any artistic decisions I felt called upon to make. From personal experience with Talking Heads, among others, he understood the delicate dynamics between band and record company and was mindful that EMI were not only controlling the purse strings, but needed to feel good about the album for the upcoming marketing campaign. All these issues aside, from an artistic viewpoint, I was the guardian of sixteen very disparate songs that each needed individual attention and crafting. I knew within myself that the songs were strong, but as with all new songs, there were so many ways that each could be fashioned within the studio. In the end, how would they all shape up and come together to form the whole of an album? And how would this new album hold up against *Fire of Freedom,* which everyone was still raving about? All great questions for five in the morning, tossing and turning, staring at the ceiling, while worrying through each and every point.

This was, by far, my most difficult period with Black 47. Had I not been inflicted with the tuning bug myself—and allergies for the first time in my life—I might have been of more help to the band. But, as it was, one morning Jerry asked me to listen to some guitar tracks that I'd laid down. I was frazzled and out of sorts, my throat and ears on fire and itching, and I couldn't tell if the tracks were in tune or not—this despite the fact that I was tuning methodically before every take. In fact, nothing seemed right to me any more. I remember listening to the great opening chords of "Should I Stay or Should I Go?" by the Clash and thinking that even they were hopelessly out of tune; and perhaps they were, for who said that great rock 'n' roll should be nailed to A440. I promptly scrapped thirty-six tracks of guitar that I had laboriously laid down and began again from scratch. I was exhausted and depressed with the whole process. But what was there to do? I couldn't call up EMI and say that, for one reason or another, we were simply unable to bring home a finished CD. It would have been the end of us. We just had to soldier on and pray that the light at the end of the tunnel would keep getting closer.

Months later and deep into the budget, the whole kit and caboodle was handed over to Tom Lord-Alge, the master mixer. As a co-producer, this sounded almost like cheating to me. Where I came from producers recorded and mixed the songs. But that was somewhat old-fashioned, I was informed. Tom was "hot" and

RELATED TO CHRIS? ALSO A MIXER?

had worked on heaps of hit albums in the previous years, including a number with Jerry who trusted him implicitly. Fair enough. But I insisted that I be allowed to babysit the mixing sessions, for although we had recorded more tracks on each song than I thought possible, we were not using an automated board and hadn't had time to do any rough mixes. Black 47, as I knew well, had always been a difficult animal to define and was far from your basic guitar, bass, and drums type band.

Tom's mixing day began with a couple of pints of strong coffee and a plate full of very sugary doughnuts. Suitably fortified, he would then literally attack the board. He was amazing to watch. He resembled nothing less than a large schizoid two-legged panther stalking the control room, jazzing up and adding to our sound by the minute; and, boy, did this band suddenly sound good. He whipped all of those dry tracks into place. I listened in wonder as he deconstructed the first song, "Too Late to Turn Back," before putting it back together again with effected bells on. He was all a flurry of action, turning sporadically to glower at me in a somewhat intimidating manner. I had a feeling that he wasn't used to sharing a control room with the band he was mixing; or perhaps he felt that I didn't trust him. But I didn't give a goddamn. I hadn't put in the worst four months of my life to just hand over control of my songs to anyone—no matter how talented or menacing. Furthermore, I figured that just watching this madman at work would be a valuable education in and of itself.

After a full day's sonic assault, the speakers went suddenly dead, leaving my thoughts stranded in the ensuing silence. Mr. Lord-Alge was apparently finished with the mix. He slowly turned around toward me, much like Clint Eastwood in *A Fistful of Dollars.* He was a bit of a showman and I almost felt like applauding; however, though the overall sound was spectacular, the song sounded odd to me. His eyebrows almost touched the ceiling when I informed him that I'd like to live with the mix and would let him know how I felt on the morrow. Back home, on my own speakers, it still sounded great, but it was obviously quite a different song: counterpoint and harmony had replaced melody, while the verse now seemed to be doing what the chorus should have done. If that description sounds a tad oblique, then that's how Tom's mix sounded to me.

The next day, I screwed my courage to the sticking place, as the Bard advised, and informed him of my views. He stared at me as if I had totally taken leave of my senses, and when he played back the mix, I was inclined to agree with him; still, I held to my guns. He was a huge man, his eyes were blazing with indignation, and I felt there was a fair chance he might beat me up. But after a full-blown, take-no-prisoners argument and another quart of coffee, we went back into the control room. He disdainfully made the couple of moves that I suggested to restore the song to my way of thinking. Then he stood back and listened, and in all fairness to him, he immediately caught what I was after. He pounced on the control board and thoroughly ravaged it for another twenty minutes, before spinning around again and daring me to disagree that what he had done was nothing short of pure genius. This time I did applaud. The song and the mix sounded not only like what I had in mind, but even better. In fact, I felt that he had captured exactly what the band had gone through recording that album. "Too Late to Turn Back" positively drips with edginess, paranoia, and determination. This mix appeared to create a template for Tom, for from then on, I barely had to say another word; track after track ripped out of those speakers like magic and made the four months of frustration seem almost worthwhile.

Home of the Brave was the best thing we had done. Pete and EMI concurred. There is an old adage in the music business that the second album is invariably a letdown, but this one literally hopped off the turntable. It sounded different from *Fire of Freedom:* tougher and more confident. It would need all of that, for it had a hard act to follow and the times were changing fast. "Funky Céilí" had been named the second most popular recording on alternative radio in 1993 to Pearl Jam's "Jeremy." Grunge was sweeping the nation.

Now the question was, What was to be the emphasis track delivered to radio—particularly our base at college and alternative, which had both been swamped by the Seattle sound? John Cohen, who had to sell *Home of the Brave* to music directors, came right out for the intense, grungy guitar sound of "Big Fellah," the song about Michael Collins. I felt the same, eager now to get the more political stance of the band across. I particularly thought that the choice shouldn't be "Different Drummer," which was going down really well at gigs, because it was a shade too close in structure and sentiment to "Funky Céilí" and might stereotype the band as Irish only. Elliot agreed, seeking to enlarge our appeal. "Road to Ruin," "Oh Maureen," "Who Killed Bobby Fuller?," and "Losin' It" were the other favorites. Like Yogi Berra, I felt déjà vu all over again. Hadn't I been through this before with CBS?

Finally, the very affable and smart Daniel Glass, president of the company, came up with a compromise. Let's go with the safe, more poppy "Losin' It." We'll release it simultaneously to all formats: college, alternative, and Top Forty and push the hell out of it. This would be the shot. Cohen, Chris, and I were unsure, but when the president is behind it and willing to commit all the resources of the company, what do you do?

The single duly went out to college and alternative radio with a shipping date to Top Forty for two weeks later. We all waited nervously for the reaction. And then the bombshell. Daniel Glass had been fired. Everything was on hold at EMI. Or rather, as far as Black 47 was concerned, everything was up in the air.

30

TOO LATE TO TURN BACK

Wait until dawn
The streets will be cool and clean again
Then it's time to go downstairs, meet the man
He'll be sitting in a limo with a gun in his hand.
You've been waiting like this for years
Through all the laughter and the cloudy tears
Always standing on a tightrope
Through a million little bands
Always waiting for redemption
Now it's right at hand.

You'll hear me ticking like a time bomb
Ready, ready to explode
Too late to turn back now
I've gone beyond overload.
You'll hear me ticking like a time bomb
Ready, ready to ignite
It's now or never, my darling,
It's too late to turn back tonight.

Nothing left to gain
Just more of the same old thing again
Always running round in circles
Always working for the man
But tonight I'm breaking out of here

Tonight I'm going to make a stand.
I've never felt so alive
My soul is on fire and so is my mind
Now it's time to go downstairs
Meet the man
Catch his look of confusion
When I take him by the hand.

He'll hear me ticking like a time bomb
Ready, ready to explode
Too late to turn back now
I've gone beyond overload
You'll hear me ticking like a time bomb
Ready, ready to ignite
It's now or never, my darling,
It's too late to turn back tonight . . .

From Home of the Brave, *EMI Records 1994*
Published by Starry Plough Music/EMI Blackwell Music (BMI)

EMI WAS LIKE a great love gone wrong. Much of the feeling and affection remained and no one wished to say it, but it was obviously over and life had to go on. Daniel had signed us, and now Daniel was no more. The king is dead, long live the king! Would the new man have any interest in promoting his predecessor's choices? That was the question around the halls of EMI. Or would he want to make his own mark? It made little difference: the company staggered, then lurched into paralysis. All promotion ceased and "Losin' It" did not go to Top Forty radio—the whole reason behind choosing that track as the first single. The album was well received and "Losin' It" even got some airplay, especially in Boston where it is still a favorite; but all of EMI's then current releases received the kiss of death. It was a pity because I still feel that, song for song, *Home of the Brave* was one of the best CDs of 1994. I'm still very proud of it, and the songs have stood the test of time, which I suppose is proof of the pudding.

But what could you do? This was not something new for the record business. We went out on the road and pushed the hell out of the CD. For a short while it even seemed as if we might pull the fat from the fire. An appearance on the *Conan O'Brien Show* performing "Losin' It" almost turned things around. But without EMI's promotional muscle, it was like pushing a stone up a hill, Sisyphus style. Now I really regretted my insistence that "Different Drummer" not be the first track released. For it would have been instantly recognizable after "Funky Céilí," and sounded more like what programmers had come to expect from us. But the die was already cast and in this, of all businesses, there's no point in second-guessing yourself.

Then, to cap things, while on the West Coast I got very ill. I'd had a touch of bronchitis for some time, and with the constant traveling was never able to shake it. After a gig at Slim's in San Francisco that, ironically, many thought was one of our best, I had a near collapse. I barely made it back to the Phoenix Motel. The band had to leave right after the gig to get to Cincinnati where "Oh Maureen" was making a last stand on alternative radio. I felt like I was going to die, and might have, but for the night clerk—a gay young angel—who brought me soup and looked in every couple of hours until I could get to a doctor. I've always felt bad about the band driving across the country in two and a half days— and by the longer southern route as the Rockies were snow-bound—because, unknown to us, the radio station had already taken "Oh Maureen" out of heavy rotation. As usual, we were the last to know. I flew in to Cincinnati three days later, and we played the gig at Bogarts. Then we crawled back to New York, *Home of the Brave* well and truly bollocksed.

And as in certain love affairs, the parting seemed endless. Our first meeting with the new head honcho was not auspicious. When Chris and I entered his office, he barely nodded, but continued to stare at a pad on his desk. Perhaps, we figured, he was shy, had some social problem or other? He still didn't look up at us as he murmured: "I don't have the least problem dropping bands." For all we knew, he could have been talking to the cleaning lady, or was this a mantra that he intoned a couple of times a day for reassurance amid his many travails? However, after much beating about the bush regarding the awful state of the record industry—from my conversations with executives, the biz never appears to have had a decent month—he did give us a budget to record some demos and, decently enough, agreed that if he chose not to use them, we could take them to hell in a breadbasket as far as he was concerned. This was definitely an upgrade on my treatment at CBS back with the Thinkers. But the general steam had gone out of EMI in the United States, and there was definitely no future for us with the company.

Demos are for rock stars, those with time on their hands, and others who neither have the ears nor conviction to recognize a good song. Later for that, I thought, let's make a new album. We wouldn't be able to afford a hotshot producer, but what need anyway? I knew the ropes and I'd picked up a lot from observing Ric, Jerry, and the manic Lord-Alge. We worked with Ian Bryan, an outstanding, no-nonsense engineer who had put in time with U2 back in Dublin. The tracks were recorded live and emphasized our edgier, more gutlike street chops. The band played with all the old fire and passion, eager to prove themselves after *Home of the Brave.* I veered the album toward the political with songs about, or inspired by, Bobby Sands, Bernadette McAliskey, Father John Murphy, and the original Irish gangs of New York. Chris contributed "Walk All the Days," probably the most insightful glimpse into life as a cop, as opposed to the usual Hollywood spin put on that complicated profession. I wasn't looking for any frills production-wise, just a hard-edged sheen. We emerged from the studio with *Green Suede Shoes* in hand and no looking over our shoulder for approval; it had come in at less than one-tenth the cost of *Home of the Brave.*

There was no time for any licking of wounds. It was straight back to playing and proving that you can make a living, to hell with the killing. We still had children to provide for. Chris had already chucked in his pensioned job with the NYPD, while everyone else had the usual money problems and needs. Our financial affairs were a mess. Not only was the quarter of a million dollars used up in making *Home of the Brave,* we had also advanced some money for recording costs that EMI would not reimburse. We had to take some kind of stock. Judy and Murad were the first to go. I felt bad about it, but we couldn't go on as we were. It broke both their hearts for they truly did their best. This is not the easiest business to be in at times.

We replaced them with Tom Schneider who came aboard as business manager. Tom was a rock in those troubling days. He held things together and often kicked in his own money when there was any kind of a shortage. He is one of those unsung heroes of rock 'n' roll—those who work behind the scenes, and glue back together what we out front have smashed apart. Elliot and Frank stood by us, too, but we were entering a different phase: guerrilla warfare rather than an all-out frontal assault, which is their métier. We shook hands and said good-bye.

This split caused a lot of soul-searching and made me sit down for the first time and really figure out the economics of the music business. The fundamentals are no different than any other: maximize income while keeping costs down to a minimum. As in most occupations, there is a huge difference between gross and net income; the problem is that outside commissions are always based on the gross, while the band principals deal exclusively with the net. On paper, a successful musician—a breed almost as rare as the dodo bird—can take in a nice piece of change. But, before you can even think about expenses, there are some very hefty deductions to be dealt with. Managers take anything from 15 to 25 percent of the gross right from the top. Let's say 20, for argument's sake. Oddly enough, in the United States—whether by law or custom—personal managers do not deal with the day-to-day finances of the artist. That sphere is reserved for the business manager who takes another 5 percent, but will look after your banking and personal expenses, thereby turning you into even more of a lazy, irresponsible idiot than you already are—quite a task sometimes with musicians.

You're now up to 25 percent lopped off before you can even

think of heading off for a gig. But the bookings are obtained and secured by an agent who always takes 10 percent. So, in an average case, 35 percent is removed from all performance fees before the artist gets down to paying for transport, hotels, publicity, instruments, insurance, band wages, workman's comp, per diems, paternity payments, parking tickets, taxes, bail money, recreational habits, and all the unexpected costly catastrophes just waiting out there to nail you under Murphy's ubiquitous and savage law. Those figures just do not add up. Something has to give. And in our case, I had to assume the manager's job, or else the band could not have stayed together.

Managing a rock 'n' roll band is not brain surgery, although there are times when you might feel a need of it. In fact, I knew a lot more about the actual mechanics of the business than most managers, which is not much to boast about. Managing does, however, take time and energy, not to mention a lot of patience and persistence. In other words, it's not something you always feel like doing. On the other hand, now you have no one to blame but yourself. Having experienced everything that could possibly happen on the road, you know exactly when you're being lied to, although lying is not the main problem in our business. It's the glossing over of impending difficulties that leads to most disasters, for, as ever, the devil is in the details, and what manager wants to be bothered with such boring trivia when the glamour, the booze, and the bullshit are all awaiting your glorified presence at the bar. Yet, if you don't deal with these niggling doubts and feelings, they will always be sure to pop up and nail you to a cross when you least expect them. So, it was good-bye big-time management, tour buses, per diems, and all kinds of rock 'n' roll's comforting womblike waste, and hello to bottom lines, Motel 6, and arriving home with a couple of bucks in your pocket instead of more debt.

Tomes have been written about record companies and their practices. Suffice it to say that contracts are rigged in such a manner that it's nigh impossible to recoup the initial advance and recording costs. I've known people who've sold millions of CDs who are still up to their necks in debt; then there's the friend who's released eighteen albums, including one that featured a Top Ten single, but never received a dime in royalties, and other horrendous "success" stories. I won't even dwell on the legion of "failures," for most recording careers barely break from the gate—not that those lessons aren't as true and painful, but they are mercifully brief, thus rarely as tragic. There is money to be made in publishing but, even there, the record companies, by common consent of everyone in the music business, make sure you sign away a legal right to a certain percentage of CD sales for a significantly lesser share. Why do musicians put up with this, you might ask? Well, apart from most of us being pretty dumb, the answer is usually lack of good advice, a great need to be finally accepted, and a certain penchant for casting our fate to the winds.

But let me quote an example from my own experience. When negotiating with EMI, Elliot put me in touch with one of the premier lawyers in the music business. Lee Phillips is an erudite and affable man, someone who you feel is on your side and, indeed, he is. I have never met or seen the man, but, from our brief dealings, I visualize him as a silver-haired patrician—rather like one of those overlords of the Democratic Party. I had read a year's mercantile law in Dublin so I could, after repeated study, navigate and somewhat understand the incredibly lopsided, Byzantine, and unconscionable contract offered us by EMI. I carefully noted fifty or so areas of contention in this needlessly complicated document. Lee graciously offered to discuss them with me by phone. We had broached three or four points, all of which he promised that he would look into for me. However, when I rattled off a number of more major concerns I was hastily reined in. Lee's words were to the effect that, while I was undoubtedly a bright chap, did I believe for one minute that EMI thought so much of Black 47 that they would be willing to concede any major advantages set in stone within their contract?

I replied that these points were at least worth fighting for, that if we didn't then no one would. You've hit the nail on the head exactly, said he, for if they concede these points to you, then they must do so to everyone else and the whole façade will come crumbling down.

He continued: Now I understand that your band doesn't have a lot of money to be wasting on lawyers—this is not, after all, a gargantuan record deal—so you must make the decision if you want to proceed with this contract, or begin your own private crusade. I can and will win a couple of these aforementioned minor points for you—none of which will make a jot of difference in the broad scope of things— but no company is going to substantially change their record contract. It's much easier for them to walk away from any band, no matter how talented.

As I say, all of this was put to me in the nicest possible manner and I have no doubt that Lee had the best interests of Black 47 in mind. The ball, of course, was back in my court, and the clock was ticking again. We'd had record companies down to see us for a year. EMI's was the one really concrete offer on the table. The band was fraying around the edges from the constant inspection; and everyone was worn from hearing the big question over and over again from wives, girlfriends, and every flack in the business: When are you going to actually sign a deal and get the ball rolling? The moment could pass for us and would I, Hamletlike, dither away and be responsible for the inevitable decline in our fortunes if we didn't take the big plunge. Pete Ganbarg and EMI were at our sides swearing eternal devotion. What does one do? We jumped and I don't regret it. Under the circumstances, I doubt if there was an alternative.

However, in retrospect, there is a clause that every artist should fight for: the right to fair use of their CDs when the record company, in its wisdom, decides to delete them from their catalogues. Take our case again. Black 47 has been lucky. All three of our CDs with the majors have, until recently, been on sale in record stores and other outlets. Now, however, it appears that two of three have been deleted, and with the current across-the-board cutbacks in catalogue, I don't hold out much hope for the third. These CDs are our tools of trade in the music profession, and if the record company doesn't wish to make them available commercially, then there should be an escape clause that enables the band to either buy the masters back from the company at a fair price, or have the company sell us whatever number of the CDs we need to go on about our business. This has been a huge problem for working musicians down the years.

There are two ways around it. Lawyers should advise their clients about this potential time bomb—never once in negotiation has it ever been mentioned to me or any other musician of my acquaintance. Or musicians should just print up their own copies of these CDs and sell them, thus publicly challenging the record companies until this grievance is redressed. How about it Lee, Richard Grabel, Fred Davis, Bob Donnelly, and all the decent music biz lawyers out there? Can you at least mention this to the next bunch of stars-in-their-eyes musicians who stroll vestal-virgin-like into your offices? You know that 95 percent of them will be grappling with this nightmare within a couple of years. Isn't this very practical and righteous matter worth fighting for? Or do we musicians have to go out on a limb and break the law for the simple right to use our own music to make a living? Record companies won't like such a class action and, in some cases, there will be loss of the lucrative independent counsel work that helps keep your profession muzzled. But you would be on the side of the angels, and that's no small matter. You would be doing something really concrete for musicians and would help mitigate the inevitable losses, both financial and emotional, that accrue to those who have the good fortune to deal with the musical industrial murder machine.

31

GREEN SUEDE SHOES

Six months out on the road
Don't know if I'm ever goin' home
Out there in the middle of America
Out of my head, feelin' hysterical
Wishin' I was back in New York
Playin' Reilly's on a Saturday night
Man on the phone says, "I ain't jokin'
Would yez ever come and play for us out in Hoboken?"

So we hop in the van and we drive overnight
Goin' to sweet New Jersey, startin' to feel all right
But the word is out—the boys are back in town
Thirty thousand Paddies start gettin' on down.
When we hit the stage, police chief goes nuts
"What the hell am I goin' to do with thirty thousand drunks?"
He says "stop the music, I'm in charge!"
Then he goes and he shuts down all of the bars.

I don't care if you got the blues
Just kept the hell off my green suede shoes
You can do anything you choose
But don't go messin' up my green suede, green suede shoes.

Then we're comin' from Providence late one night
Three hours from home, hey life is all right

We're discussing the demise of T. Rex
Next thing we know the van is up on its ass
The window are smashed, we're bouncing off the turnpike
Troopers come and haul us off of the black ice
One says, "Hi, my name is Kevin
It's a pleasure to meet you—Black 47!"

So, we're doing Letterman, Leno, and O'Brien
Two hundred gigs a year, I'm out of my mind.
We got our picture in *Time* magazine
Hey babe, I'm livin' the American dream
Then a lawyer call up about Bridie and the baby
Want to sue my ass for doin' the Funky Céilí
I just got a message from a brother of Maria
"C'mon out to Bensonhurst, we all want a piece of you!"

But the more I play the deeper I'm in debt
If we ever get a hit, I'll be out on the street.
I never knew I had so many friends
I'm gonna run against Rudy when this whole thing ends.
I got lawyers and accountants up the kazoo
Managers and agents tellin' me what to do
With the money I'm eventually going to make
But can you lend me a token, get me to the next gig?

I don't care if you got the blues
Just kept the hell off my green suede shoes.
You can do anything you choose
But don't go messin' up my green suede, green suede shoes.

From Green Suede Shoes, *Mercury Records 1996*
Published by Starry Plough Music (BMI)

WE MIGHT HAVE lost a few of the trappings of success but controversy stuck right by us. Part of this has to do with the fact that when you're in a rock 'n' roll band, you're moving from place to place in a tizzy, as it were—a day late, a dollar short. You've no sooner put the drama of the last gig and town behind you than you're headfirst into another, often very unaware of the different conditions you're entering, or of the waters your very presence is about to roil. Word of mouth will have preceded you—if it were only concerned with the music, everything would be fine. But it's often an exaggerated account of something I might have said off the top of my head onstage, for little in Black 47 is scripted. It can also have to do with how your audience is perceived. Ours are invariably boisterous and passionate, but well behaved. They tend not to be thrice-removed cappuccino drinkers; invariably, they're into and sometimes living the characters and events in the songs. Then, too, occasionally a confluence of forces and expectations collides and causes real havoc. Such was the case when a performance by the band caused the town of Hoboken to be closed down.

Black 47 is like a perennial presidential candidate: we always seem to be working Ohio. We had just completed a week there and drove back overnight to perform at the Hoboken spring festival. We had thus missed some of the buildup to this gig, traditionally a somewhat sleepy affair. While we were away, the promoter, Chris O'Neill, had managed to secure sponsorship and advertising on a major New York radio station that widely publicized the event. But trouble was also brewing. The town had, over the years, become a mecca for weekend partying, with many residents tired of the late-night hassle. The chief of police, Carmen LaBruno, was no less incensed and had, apparently, decided to make a stand at the festival.

Hoboken is just across the river from New York and easily accessed by the PATH train. It was a beautiful day, fiesta time, and the word was out—the boys were back in town. When we arrived, the square was packed to the hilt, many people carrying their own coolers of beer and ready to get on down. As usual in such events, bands were running a little behind. That's always a problem for us. With saxes, pipes, whistles, bodhrán, trombone, drum machine, and the usual three-piece rhythm section, our changeover takes more time than is usually allotted, putting us even further behind. A 5 P.M. curfew had been called by the chief of police, so right from the start we were working against the clock. But I'm always insistent that when people come to see Black 47, they get a full show. This can often lead to frayed nerves and tempers. In this case with such a huge audience in a somewhat enclosed situation, to my mind, it was imperative that everyone leave happy. Our normal set is ninety minutes to two hours. Going on after 4 P.M. was not a recipe for a laid-back show.

The air was electric with expectation. Our friend, the then unknown Joan Osborne, had already revved up the crowd when we hit the stage. There was a heavy police presence, but that was not unusual either, on account of Chris Byrne's background. And, for what it's worth, the Hoboken cops seemed to be enjoying the scene, which though exuberant was very well behaved. The set was a blinder and the huge audience totally with us. The worst incident I recall was a lady on her escort's shoulders flashing us some beautifully formed breasts—hardly a federal offense, this side of Tiananmen Square. This is part and parcel of a Black 47 gig: people tend to let their hair down in unusual, if harmless, ways. The mood swayed depending on the subject of the song and, during our second last, the whole square stood to attention, clenched fists in the air, for a very militant "James Connolly." To my mind, everything was under control even though we were approaching 5 P.M. But when you arouse emotions like that, you can't stop suddenly, as the Connolly song does, say good night, and walk off. The tension has to be dissipated. I was now getting frantic signals to quit from various people at the side of the stage, but there are times when you have to make a judgment call, as you're the one who can gauge the mood of the crowd and are ultimately responsible for much that happens. I felt that there might have been a riot if we hadn't performed "Funky Céilí" and finished on an up note. And so we did. There were repeated calls for an encore, but no need for one; expectations had been met and people would now disperse in a happy mood. I think we had run some minutes over the curfew. No big deal in the scheme of things.

There was utter bedlam backstage. Some people were angry and screaming, others confused. After the long journey and such a knife-edge gig, I wasn't in a mood for any of it. As far as I was concerned, it had been a dangerous situation out there, we'd all come through it, and what was a few minutes over anyway? With the tension deflated, I decided to call it a day, take the PATH train back to New York, and get home early for once. But even that was a problem; the streets were jammed, with large groups of people milling about aimlessly. Someone said that the cops had ordered all the bars closed, which seemed incredible. Others said they had been advised to get out of town pronto and don't come back. That, too, sounded like an exaggeration because the Hoboken police department had been very courteous and caring toward Black 47 backstage and had treated the crowd with kid gloves during the show. But the trains were stuffed and people were buzzing from both the show and the expulsion. I was lucky to squeeze on.

The gig was done and I pretty much forgot about the whole affair but the word had spread throughout the city that Black 47 had closed down Hoboken. Eventually, I received a call from the *Daily News* inquiring what had happened. To my mind, it was history; but I gave my side of the story: everyone had a good time except for the bar owners, everyone got out alive, and hopefully the check wouldn't bounce. When pressed, I stated that the crowd was large and that fifteen thousand may have shown up—the organizers had been expecting in the region of five thousand. It seemed like a good round figure, but these things are very hard to call, as I only see what's in front of me. Linda Stasi printed this, and then called me in great anxiety the next day to say that the chief of police was not only outraged with my estimate, but had complained to her editor about the reporting. Oh Jesus, I thought, I'm going to seem like a real idiot now. I've overestimated the figure. But no, in his rebuttal the next day, the chief rather indelicately suggested that I must have had my head up my posterior, for there had been thirty-five thousand people present. This tabloid battle might have continued indefinitely, but I had no stomach for a conflagration with any police department, especially one containing so many Black 47 fans. I guess the chief was not among them. Still isn't, I gather, for last year an invitation to return to

Hoboken was hastily rescinded. C'mon, Chief, isn't it about time we buried the hatchet? Hoboken is a great town and if you have us back, I promise to keep my head out of my ass.

We were reeling in more ways than one back then. One night after playing the Strand in Providence, on our way home down 95, we got hit with a light dusting of snow. George Kornienko, our driver, decided to press on in an effort to beat what promised to be a blizzard. I was still suffering from bronchitis and trying to get some rest in the backseat, but it had been a good gig and after a pit stop somewhere around New London, I went up front for a nightcap. The promoters had given us a couple of cases of Guinness for the road and most of us, except for George and Kevin, were having a few quiet, but I suppose unlawful, sips.

The talk in band vans can vary widely from the price of turnips to Einstein's search for a unified theory, but that night it had strayed to the great T. Rex. Someone asked whatever happened to Marc Bolan? Hammy and I had just begun to explain that he had been killed in a car accident, when we went into a violent skid. Chris shouted out "Get down!" and dived back from the front seat, and suddenly we were airborne. Talk about life flashing before your eyes. We were all hurtling through the van in a death dance as we and everything inside turned over once, then righted ourselves, before hitting the concrete divider and turning over one more time, then coming to a halt right side up. It was a sickening, painful, and extremely scary experience. There was plenty of time to contemplate extinction while we tumbled on top of one another with the windows crashing in around us. At times, the road would screech by on one side, only for the van to come straight back up; then we'd all go over the other way trying to avoid the gravel, tar, and concrete flying up from beneath.

An eerie silence wrapped around us when the van finally cut out. It was punctuated only by an occasional shudder from the engine mixed with individual moans and curses. My head was jammed into the floor between two seats, while my upended torso supported Kevin Jenkins's none-too-slender two hundred or so muscular pounds. I couldn't move and, for a couple of moments we all lay still, anticipating the next move. My neck felt like it was broken, and even after Kevin disentangled himself I was still stuck. Finally, someone got the doors open and we helped one another crawl out. Just at that moment a car came swerving around the corner and hit the back of the van, sending us all spinning around once more. The time for crawling was over. We scampered out on all fours through the broken glass, each one dragging the one behind him. My neck was throbbing and felt out of whack, but then a truck came careening around the corner and all pains were forgotten as we headed for the hills. Fred Parcells was in front of me—in shock but, practical as ever, carrying a case of Guinness. Out on the road, gunshots appeared to be going off; we bolted into the trees while vehicles applied screeching brakes to miss the pileup.

Fred hid his Guinness and we watched the carnage through the falling snowflakes. Jenkins in his dusted dreadlocks looked like an Old Testament prophet on the road below. And then the troopers were there. We couldn't figure out how they had arrived so quickly, until we saw lights through the trees. Another fifty or more feet, and we'd have crashed through their front door. They were the soul of solicitation, got the man and woman in the second car out of the wreckage, and called immediately for ambulances. They also identified the gunshots as the well-shook cans of Guinness exploding on the roadway. There we stood, feeling for broken bones, each one aware of the minor miracle that had transpired: none of us had been killed. Hammy and I crawled back in the van to search for our spectacles. Amazingly, apart from a few scratches, mine were okay. But I shuddered when I looked at my usual spot in the backseat. My traveling bag, which had been back there, had gone straight through the shattered window. I later found it, ripped and broken, twenty yards back up the road.

When the ambulances arrived I mentioned my sore neck to the head medic. He immediately strapped me into a stretcher and whisked me off to the nearest hospital. Whatever about surviving the accident, I was now in real trouble. My neck was tied back so severely, I could hardly breathe. I tried to get the orderlies to loosen the stays, but I was informed that it was for my own protection. At the hospital, I was wheeled into a waiting room and left unattended. A few minutes later, another stretcher was wheeled in beside me. It was the lady who had crashed into our van. She was furious and vented her rage at me. She had apparently been at one of the local casinos with someone illicit, and would now be in big trouble when she got home.

With the shock of the crash over, the bronchitis had kicked back in. I couldn't afford to answer her, although some choice retorts came to mind; in fact, I was having trouble breathing and was in a gathering panic that I might cough and choke. We lay side by side for over twenty minutes in our angst and despair until an orderly discovered us and set me free. I then turned my full spite on my fellow detainee and lambasted her: threatening to tell her husband, boyfriend, or pet ram the real reason for her tardiness. I was coughing and spluttering to high heaven when the orderly finally prevailed on me to leave the poor woman to her injuries and allow myself to be X-rayed.

The doctor, who had seen it all and more, said my neck was just bruised, as were my ribs and hips, but that I was a lucky man. He told me I'd often think of Route 95 in the months to come, for the pain would be no laughing matter. Gazing at one of the X-rays, he showed me what looked like a white filmy cloud across my chest and said I was so riddled with bronchitis, it was a wonder I could even talk. He told me he could cure this or give me painkillers, but not both. I was already bent over from the soreness in my ribs, and every time I even contemplated coughing, the hurting would spread through my whole body. Reluctantly, I opted for the cure.

He gave me a shot in the butt with a needle the size of a turkey baster, and bade me swallow two pills the like of which my uncle used to give to any of his nags that might profit from a boost on race day. He said I'd be a new man in a week, although one in my own private purgatory. With that, he had a nurse call a taxi and I was removed to the nearest Con Rail station. There in the waiting room, I was reunited with my bandmates who were stretched out, to a man, on any available space, moaning and groaning, rubbing their innards and waiting for the first train to New York.

That was the end of Kevin Jenkins and Black 47. He was due to take a sabbatical anyway, oddly enough, to do a tour with Cyndi Lauper. He flew to Europe the next day and later told me that he had to sit in a cushioned chair for the first week of shows. His parting words to us were, "Later for you muthas and your luck of the Irish. I'm outa here while I'm still in one piece!"

That doctor was on the ball. I don't know what kind of horse pills he gave me, but the bronchitis fled from my chest and has never returned. He was also a bit of an optimist. The couple of months of pain stretched on, and it was the following September before I could breathe like a normal human being again. Life is never without irony, however, and for every down, rest assured that half an up is waiting around the corner. With the pain gone and the album recorded, I got a call from Danny Goldberg, who had recently become president of Mercury Records. He had received a copy of *Green Suede Shoes* from our lawyer, Richard Grabel, and had cried when he heard our recording of "Bobby Sands MP." I assured him I had been experiencing some pain myself of late, though more of a physical nature. He made no great promises, but told me that there would always be a home for Black 47 at Mercury as long as he was running the show. Would we be willing to sign with him? We were back—in black!

32

MARIA'S WEDDING

Oh Maria, I'm so sorry I wrecked your wedding
You just got to believe me
But just the thought of you taking your clothes off for that jerk
Ah, it got me drinking
And then suddenly I'm staggering into church and I'm
Dancing like Baryshnikov all across the high altar
Oh, I bet that you're still mortified
But just think, girl, no one's ever going to be forgetting
The day I wrecked your wedding.

Oh Maria, I'd get down on my knees, girl
You just got to believe me
But just the sight of you standing there in your brand-new wedding dress
Ah, it got me so upset
Then your father's screaming, "You no good lousy punk
I always knew you were an Irish drunk."
Your mother she is having
Her 19th nervous breakdown
But just think, girl, no one's ever going to be forgetting
The day I wrecked your wedding.

Oh Maria, I'd do anything you asked me to
Swear I'll change, I'll even give up drinking
Hanging out with the boys
'Cause I just can't live without your body and you.
I'll even sell my Strat

Give up the band
You better believe me, girl, this time it's true
Oh Maria, I'll even go out and get a job for you.

Oh, Maria, I'm so sorry I wrecked your wedding
You just got to believe me
But ten years from now this is all going to be one big happy memory
Oh, your old man is even gonna grow to love me
I'll give him six grandchildren
I'll be so respectable
I might even run for president
I'll be so electable
Keep you happy and expectable
Forever pregnant and that way you'll never be forgetting
The day I wrecked your wedding.

From Fire of Freedom, *EMI Records 1993*
Published by Starry Plough Records/EMI Blackwell Music (BMI)

PERFORMING ON ST. PATRICK'S Day in New York City is like riding a wild stallion. You may think you're in control, but if you're wise you just hang on and shape the energy as best you can. Coming from the puritanical commemoration I had been used to back in Wexford, the orgiastic nature of the city's celebration was shocking at first. The wholesale ebullience and cultural overload was even embarrassing to the nitpicker in me. But now I embrace it all, every plastic Paddy artifice: the leprechauns, flashing shamrocks, green beads, and even the green beer, though it reminds me of pea soup and I wouldn't drink it in a month of Sundays.

Why do I endorse the whole gloriously tribal affair? Because it's a day to salute those brave souls who made it out alive from the waterside slums of New York, the cellars of Boston, and the shanties of Philadelphia, Baltimore, and Savannah. They arrived here in their teeming thousands, sick, poor, and dispossessed; not only did they survive, they thrived. They were persecuted by the nativist Know-Nothing Party and endured generations of discrimination before they were accepted in this country. On the way, they revolted, formed the San Patricio Brigade, and helped change the U.S. Army into the nonsectarian equal-opportunity employer it is today; they built the roads and canals of this country; rose up through the ranks of the political machines to run the cities; and if they want to crow a little one day of the year, then so be it. I'll help them blow the hell out of some saloon, club or hall so that they can raise the rafters with their celebration. There are many places to be on St. Patrick's Day in New York City, but St. Patrick's Night belongs to Black 47.

So it was at the Academy. We were filming the show and general carry-on for a video of "Green Suede Shoes." I don't know where we'd come from the night before—probably Boston or D.C. We'd driven from that gig straight to a TV studio for a morning show. Then a couple of hours' sleep before sound check. You awake with that shivery feeling of exhaustion, soon to be mixed in a cocktail with two more measures of street energy, and a sprinkle of expectation of the night that's ahead of you. It doesn't matter how tired you are, you'll get your bump soon enough. Then tea, honey, and lemon for the pain in your throat from the last couple of weeks' madness. And during the day, no alcohol, though it's pouring like a river all around you. It's all about riding the wave now. You only have so much to give and who wants to let the crowd down? Black 47 people don't tend to have money to burn. Workers and students with the wherewithal for a couple of tickets, and enough left over to get smashed. So easy does it. Every ounce of energy will be called upon during the night's show. And even then it's not finished, off to Philadelphia in the morning for another manic parade; only then can you let go, if you're still able or interested enough.

I'm not even certain I heard it. A slight pop maybe, but how could you be sure with the whole place swinging to "Maria's Wedding"? That song had come to symbolize Brooklyn and the craziness of so many nationalities jammed together, with all the attendant clashes of culture and misunderstanding that happen in an Irish-Italian love affair. Italian girls marry Irish guys. I don't know why, the deep-seated Catholicism, perhaps; or the food, the sex, the shouting, the arguing, the breaking up, the making up? Some of that essence is captured in the four-odd minutes of the song and there's no better way to close a St. Patrick's Day show. Through it all, I caught a whiff of something odd—sharp and foreign—but couldn't quite place it. I shrugged it off—too busy remembering the original Maria and wondering if she'd recognize herself in the lyrics. I did notice a disturbance of sorts in the balcony, though; and then the first person was onstage shouting something in my ear. What was I supposed to say, "Excuse me? How can I be of service to you?"

It wasn't until my buddy, Josh Cheuse, appeared, bloodstains on his shirt, his eyes popping out on toothpicks, that I really knew something awful had happened. Josh is anything but an alarmist, had been close to the Clash and seen his fair share of havoc. By then, all the usual backstage hangers-on had bolted. There was no one up there but us, and I could read the worried looks in the eyes of the band. Was this the moment we'd been dreading? Had we become a target for some Loyalist or crackpot bullet? You suddenly realize just how alone and defenseless you are up under the lights of a bare stage.

Amazingly, the audience was still pumping and jumping, unaware of anything. I could catch glimpses of more tumult going on in the balcony and some kind of acrid smoke had now drifted down toward the stage, or was that the usual haze of cigarettes? Your mind plays tricks on you at times like that. But there was no mistaking the fact that not one street or emergency door had yet been opened. All the old Elvis Murphy conditioning kicked in. Stay calm, and whatever you do, keep playing. Remember the nights of aggro down at the CYMS. Chairs flying through the air. Teeth knocked out. A bunch of teds dragging some poor culchie by the collar, while simultaneously kicking his face in. How did Elvis handle it back then? He didn't down instruments and run away. No, he kept playing until security woke up and did their job. And that's what we did onstage at the Academy. Besides, there had been no further shots and we were all still standing. Couldn't have been much of a marksman, I reasoned between beats.

Eventually, the doors did open, the house lights came up, and we finished on a big noisy drawn-out chord. We took our bows as normally as possible and trooped off into a screaming match with some stressed-out, panic-to-the-eyebrows Ron Delsner flunky. At the same time, Josh was trying to tell me his side of the story: at first he thought it was a terrorist taking potshots, but it turned out someone had shot himself. Geoff's wife then arrived in tears. Their eldest had been just outside the line of fire. But through all the panic, it was hard to get a total sense of what had just transpired.

And as more people crowded into the dressing room, each one jabbering and screaming with shock, the facts grew dimmer. I was still jittery and on fire from the show. I knew I just needed to take that inner couple of moments to decompress. Guys do it in different ways. My method is a long slug of cold beer that reaches all the way down to my toes before surging up into my brain. I was searching for a beer when I noticed a guy from Delsner's office approaching through the crowd. We'd done a number of shows together and had a good rapport. He was calm but I could tell that beneath his professional mien he had something important to say. Some problem with the check, no doubt. He asked to speak privately and led me out the door. Then he took me by the shoulder and whispered, "Your wife's been shot. We've got her in an ambulance."

He said more on the way downstairs, but I'm not sure I heard him. A moment before I had been trying to decompress. Now my world was turning inside out. People were running up past me, some panicked, others merely looking for the party. They were trying to kiss me and slap me on the back, talking about the gig, the songs, but it all seemed distant. Lots of voices, but muffled as if they were coming from underwater, and would this goddamn stairs never end?

Then I was out in the cold March air and I didn't have a coat. There was an ambulance parked outside the theater; I fought my way over to it and opened the door, but it was empty. Where was she? I tried to remember where our kids were but couldn't quite figure it out. Were they home with the babysitter? It was hard to concentrate. I recognized a cop on duty trying to deal with the crowd. But before I could get to him, I had become entangled with a bunch of Bronx boys who were out of their heads from drink. They recognized me and tried to lift me into the air and carry me down the street. One of them, a little soberer than the rest, saw something in my eyes; he was big and gathered me in his arms to shield me from his friends. "What's up?" he whispered. I just pointed at the cop. He nodded, then wrenched me free and waltzed me over.

The cop had been notified I was on my way and was looking for me. "They've taken her to Bellevue. I'll call for a car." But at that moment, a great flood of people surged out the doors and we were separated. I saw a patrol car cruising by, its lights flashing. To hell with waiting! I worked my way through the crowd and raced after it. There was a red light up ahead; it would surely stop and I'd climb in. But it picked up speed and sailed right through. I looked behind but the whole street was awash with people now, spilling out from the gig. I'd have to find a cab. But it was Times Square and the theaters had let out, too. Not a taxi for love or money. I ran madly, zeroing in on the familiarity of the Deuce, and made a left toward the library.

I was amazed at how fast I could run and still dodge around the groups of dawdling tourists. I was electric, panicky, and clear-headed all at once. I knew these streets intimately: each crack on the pavement was like a familiar smile. Every few seconds, I'd hop onto one foot and swivel my head backward to see if a cab might be coming from behind. Then I saw one and ran out into the street: other cars swerved to miss me, but just when I reached it, the driver accelerated away and flashed his "off duty" light. I can't remember much else except beating some Japanese people in a sprint and gazing out the window, at their surprised but polite faces, from a cab somewhere on Fifth Avenue.

Bellevue. Eleven o'clock, St. Patrick's Night. Oh sweet Jesus, what a scene! Carnage and despair everywhere. Junkies, battered women, drunks getting stomachs pumped, the mugged, the plugged, the barely standing, the whole messy debris of the city leaking out into the hallways. No security. Just walk right in. My wife is conscious and wounded, but can only think about the children. Have I called the babysitter yet? No, I haven't, I have to admit. Why shouldn't they be okay? They're sleeping. What's the point of waking them, I think.

Will she make it? I ask the young doctor, privately. The bullet has entered her left thigh, he tells me, passed clean through and out the other side, up through her pelvis, and is lodged in her right side. There will be three operations. They have to go in and see what's happened, make sure everything is working, and then get the bullet out. I tell him that she's a dancer. He frowns and sighs. They'll do what they can. Are the operations serious? They're not life-threatening, he says. Will she dance again? We'll do the best we can; he shrugs and strolls off. On this night, there are many demands on his time.

The hallway is now jammed with police, off duty, on duty, the PBA. From a few fractured sentences, I get some of the picture. A young cop's gun has gone off, hit himself and two other parties. Over in the corner, the brother of the young cop is dazed and surrounded by his buddies. I recognize him from somewhere—Reilly's probably, maybe Long Island. His face is as white as a sheet. I go back in to my wife. Tell her that the operations are not that serious—she'll be dancing again in a couple of weeks. She knows I'm lying but says nothing. Just points at a curtain. "He's in there."

I go outside looking for a doctor. It seems incredible that they'd have her in the same room as a dead man. Someone says emphatically that he's not dead. Then I hear an orderly mention Wormworth. Nico—our road manager—is here, too? But I'd just seen him onstage at the Academy about to break down the gear. No, it's his wife. The bullet had gone through the young cop's head on a trajectory up the balcony. It caught her in the hand and shattered it, ricocheted down some yards, and hit my wife. Is this coincidence or madness? I go back in to my wife. She had no idea. Didn't even know she was shot herself until she felt the dampness of the blood. Didn't know the seriousness until she collapsed while standing. The pain came later. The young doctor comes in again, smiling. He takes her hand and reassures her that she'll be home with her children tomorrow and that they're being well looked after. I realize I haven't as yet called. I rush outside. Our babysitter thinks I'm joking until she recognizes the edge in my voice. But of course she'll sleep over and look after the kids. No problem.

On the way in from the public phone, the corridor is buzzing with cops. "The mayor's on the way. He's on the FDR!" Giuliani is not popular with the NYPD, but they appreciate the support for one of their own in a moment of trial. PBA officials are all over the place now. Some are leery of me. They don't know what way I'm leaning. Will I make a big case out of this? One of them slips his arm around me and whispers, "He didn't mean it. Just one of those things." I don't know what to think, but there's no point in freaking out. It's a tragedy whatever way you look at it. I stand there against a wall and listen to the soft drone of the overhead lights, all of these big burly figures swirling around me. I begin to wonder if I'm dreaming.

"Scumbag!" The voice carries down the hallway and everyone looks around. There is a long silence, but I'm the only one who doesn't get the message: the mayor's car has turned around. His Honor, Rudy Giuliani, has gone home to bed. Someone apparently got the word to him that drinking had been involved. Possible suicide. Not quite politically correct. And then everyone speaks at once, as anger sweeps up and down the halls astride a chorus of "I told you so!" and "The sonofabitch!" and much more. I really don't know what to think. Many of these guys want to believe the worst anyway. I don't care. Who needs him? Then someone sneers, "Goddamn Mussolini! Hope he finds his balcony!"

The door opens. It's Chris, George, and Brian McCabe come to support me. They mix right in. This is a Brooklyn, Queens, Long Island scene right in the heart of Manhattan. They take over. Run the show. Allow me to relax. Cry if I want to. But no tears to spare right now. They check in with the cops, PBA, nurses, doctors. They have experiences of these things. Make sure we'll get updates on the surgery. Everything's under control, they tell me, time to let the professionals do their thing. No point in clogging up the corridor.

Chris and George take me outside. They have that great Brooklyn common sense. What would I need now more than anything? A drink. On the way, they'd picked up a couple of six-packs of Bass. We sit in the car. Nico arrives. He's only just found out about his wife. No one had told him. No one knew, I suppose. An unidentified black woman at a St. Patrick's Night hooley? He seems disoriented. We take him inside and get him set up with the doctors. He disappears into a side room. My wife is gone. Off for the first of her operations. Nothing to do but go back to the car. Drink some beers. Let the booze sink in, eat away the shock and adrenaline.

The night drags on in the parking lot. We listen to the news on the car radio. And the word is out. Shooting at a Black 47 show. Cop in serious condition. No details yet. Stay tuned. And then, a line of patrol cars arrives. The young cop's family whisked in from Long Island. What are they thinking? How can they possibly deal with this? As it is, they're almost swamped by a tide of other emergencies: the psychotic affairs and violent troubles of the whole city arriving here to be patched up and put back together again; or if all else fails, hefted off in sacks to the morgue. And then with a sickening finality, the word seeps out that the young cop is dead for definite. Some of his brother's friends come out for a smoke. They're silent, shell-shocked, how could such a thing have happened—on this of all nights? It was so sudden. He'd been partying with them only hours before. Now gone forever. A family wrecked. How can they ever celebrate St. Patrick's Day again?

We knew both him and his brother but, no matter how hard I try, I can't bring his face to mind. Chris and George rattle off some nights when we might have met. We get deep into detail. His age, what he looked like, friends of ours that he might have hung out with. It's a way to pass the hours and gain some perspective on what's happening. I feel like I know him, but can't reconcile any image I might have with his broken brother now across the parking lot, out for his own breath of fresh air. So many young men come to see us. Faces fresh, delighted to meet the boys behind their favorite songs. What was his favorite, I wonder? Everyone who comes to see us has one, and it's often an unlikely choice. There's the party animal who won't go home unless we play the solemn "Vinegar Hill," or the very serious young man ready to shoot the moon if we won't play "Czechoslovakia"; he even swears he met the original Gerty while in Prague last summer. And on it goes. . . .

Word comes out that the first and second operations on my wife have gone well. The shell has made a clean pass through the flesh. It's a miracle. They're going in after the bullet now. And then someone mentions AIDS and we all freeze. Where has the bullet been? Whose blood has it touched? The Curse is back in all aching grimness. And I lose it and say, He was a goddamn cop from Long Island—he wasn't a junky, didn't go out with guys. And everyone agrees, but we all go silent, nonetheless. And the city peers in over our shoulders. The city knows, but says nothing. The city knows everything, but we won't be sure until the tests are done. Then Nico comes out for a smoke and a whole new element arises. White cop shoots black woman. He's frazzled and can't think straight from the paranoia, and we reassure him that we're all in this together: my wife is white and she's been shot, too. The city shrugs: these things happen, and tomorrow will be another day.

Still the night goes on forever. More cops arrive. And we talk to the PBA and the story is being pieced together, but who knows, it's early days yet. Someone says he was depressed—a girlfriend had just left. Another says that was total bullshit. He didn't even have a girlfriend—the guy was never down a day in his life. The stories are tumbling in on top of one another. But from what we can gather, he'd been drinking. Who hadn't? The gun was new, he wasn't used to it, he was grooving to "Maria's Wedding," the gun showing. A security guard asked him to keep it covered. He'd answered politely, "Sure thing, but don't worry, it's not loaded." Put it to his head and . . . Those bullets are unforgiving, and it was lucky the whole balcony wasn't taken out. And the city sighs and nods, and if we'd listened closely enough, we'd have heard it whisper, "Makes sense." And it did make sense, and it still does. And all these years later, I still feel for his family.

Then I was called back in. The third operation had been a success. She was resting now, but wanted me to go home and make sure the children were okay. I had one last beer and the guys dropped me off. They wanted to come in, but I said I'd be okay. The kids were sleeping soundly, arms and tousled hair all over their Disney pillows—no idea of the drama that had been swirling around them and the awful tomorrow they might have awoken to. The operations were a miracle and before the scars had even settled, she was dancing again. But do such scars ever heal?

33

THOSE SAINTS

Seventeenth of March, year of '96
Outside the Academy it's a hundred bucks a ticket
Up onstage playing up a storm
"Maria's Wedding"
Keep your cool, get out the door
Three people lying on a balcony floor
One little bullet change so many lives
When you play in a band you can run
But you can't hide.

Back in the van we're all counting the cost
Big Murph comatose in New Orleans
Friends dropping off like proverbial flies
But hey, no time to cry
'Til one night we're rockin' Columbus, Ohio
Johnny Byrne partyin' back in the East Villageio
Phone ring at 4 A.M.—"What that you say
Johnny just fell off a fire escape?"

This could be the straw that breaks the camel's back
Till Geoff and Freddie mount a brass attack
The pipes scream out defiance
"This show don't stop until after the last dance!"

So come on, baby, get up off your ass
This ain't no dress rehearsal rag

No matter what you say or do
Life's just gonna make a fool out of you.
Makes no difference if you're green, white, orange, or blue
Those saints just gonna keep on marchin' through.

So we go to Ireland sing about Bobby Sands
But they think we're just a crowd of dumb Yanks
"Em . . . you don't understand the political culture"
If you don't know your past forget about the future!
Go on home to New York City
The drummer wake up hummin' "Smoke Gets in Your Eyes"
This ain't no Broadway musical, babe, your building's on fire.

Get back in the van and lick your wounds
Gotta make a new record write some tunes
When a man from the Mets says, "Are yez available
Come out and play for us in Shea Stadium
33 years to the day since the Beatles were here
Try your hand at bein' John Lennon
Kick-start the band into the next millennium!"
Shea is rockin' no time for regrets
The rhythm section starts kickin' in
Chris comes out rappin' "Time to Go"
Banish misfortune, get on with the show.

So come on, baby, get up off your ass
This ain't no dress rehearsal rag
No matter what you say or do
Life's just gonna make a fool out of you.
Makes no difference if you're green, white, orange, or blue
Those saints just gonna keep on marchin' through . . .

From Trouble in the Land, *Shanachie Records 2000*
Published by Starry Plough Music (BMI)

ONE MORNING, COPERNICUS and I decided to hit off to Paris for a long weekend. In our respective cups from a night's carousing, we hailed a taxi for Kennedy. To our surprise, the next plane to Paris was not until later that same evening. Although we had a fifth of Smirnoff for the preservation of spirits, we felt that the humor might be long gone off us by then. We told the somewhat surprised clerk that we'd take the next plane out wherever. That happened to be Port-au-Prince in Haiti. Done, said we, a little bit of voodoo would not go astray!

The weekend strayed into an adventuresome week, and while crossing the mountains from Cap-Haitien back to Port-au-Prince we ran into one of those great Caribbean storms. Although it was only late afternoon, the sky turned totally dark. The heavens were riven with great streaks of forked lightning and the wind howled like a cornered banshee. Our rented car trembled and shook from the drenching gale, while large rocks cascaded down the mountains in front and behind us. We were of two minds whether to push on or pull over for shelter, but the hills above us were in motion, with torrents of rain sweeping through the loosened rubble. Our only chance was to keep moving and pray. That's how it now felt for Black 47 with one thing after another cascading toward us. All we could do was keep our heads down and hope that the storm would eventually abate, as it did in Haiti. There the clouds had finally broken and we witnessed the most glorious of sunsets, with the earth cleansed and redemption in the air.

Good things were happening, too. The reviews of *Green Suede Shoes* were strong and Mercury had serviced everyone and their mothers. That album brought us a whole new legion of listeners and swelled our audiences. There was no Top Forty hit, but the songs became favorites with our new following. And regeneration is the name of the game with Black 47. More than most, we depend on a vibrant live audience, since we make our living from touring. Our audiences often come of age in front of the stage: they get drunk, laid, hooked, engaged, married, have children, and then return with the kids at festivals. If we fail to turn on new people every night, the wheels eventually stop turning. *Green Suede Shoes* added some major axle grease, especially in colleges.

As for Mercury Records? They seemed to think that we'd dropped straight from the skies, a bunch of fully formed aliens with odd accents. Danny Goldberg has very eclectic tastes and we fit right into his scheme of things, but one could almost see his lieutenants scratch their heads at both our sound and our songs. I've never been one to complain about record companies. They are what they are: incompetent and incapable at the best of times. Nonetheless, most of their employees do their best, and there have been hard workers at the various labels we've been associated with. The problem is, few have any overview of the industry—they tend to work in one department and have little meaningful contact with either their coworkers or the real world of the musician. Added to that, they have no mentors to guide them. The vision-aries of the '50s and '60s have long passed on or been kicked upstairs. The young in-the-trenches workers are lucky to retain the same boss in the course of a calendar year, for the attrition rate is absurd. At EMI, we had eleven product managers in less than three years, some to whom I was never even introduced, such was the brevity of their tenure.

Mostly now, companies throw money at a project and if it doesn't catch on within two or three weeks, then it's on to the next one. There's not even any point in complaining. Deal with it or get a real job. As Philip Glass once said to me, "There's only one rule in this business, get a good advance—there won't be anything else." My friend, Suzzy Roche, has another point of view. She thinks that companies actually give tour support to get the artists out of New York during the pivotal first four weeks of an album's release, thus preventing them from asking awkward questions.

She might have a point. We were two weeks out on a tour to support *Green Suede Shoes* when a check we were promised didn't arrive. I called persistently, but no one would respond to my ever more frantic messages—the interns wouldn't even pick up, for Christ's sake. Finally, there was a message on my machine from some assistant of an assistant asking me to desist: Danny was no longer president and tour support had been suspended. I wasn't even surprised, barely disappointed. But we still had two weeks to go on the tour. Two weeks of gigs and promotion that we'd have to pay for ourselves. The alternative was to let people down. Record companies can do that with impunity, but not a band that values its word. And so, we were label-less again. No panic on the Titanic—more where that came from.

The music was fine, the gigs great, but life itself was catching up with us. When a band like ours rolls through town, it picks up hangers-on, helpers, enablers, liggers, giggers, and those who just want to be close to the bright lights for the night. Most of them come and go; eventually, they return to their jobs and significant others, reliving the memories through CDs. But there are also people to whom the music itself gives direction and focus. Some of these become close friends. John Murphy (Big Murph from the above song) was a case in point. Strangely enough he was from County Wexford, but I first met him in the early Reilly's days. He was tall, redheaded, often silent, with a shy smile in his eyes that beguiled the ladies and made them want to protect him. There is a peculiar quietness, nay even a stillness, that comes from a brush with tragedy. I recognize it instantly now. Back then I didn't. He never told me himself, but his best friend had been killed in a motorcycle accident. It didn't keep John away from bikes.

He moved fluidly between New York and New Orleans where he did promotion for us. Over the course of years, we grew close. He had put some problems behind him and was due to move back to New York. He never made it. One foggy night in the Quarter, he took off helmetless and crashed. He was in a coma for some years and was finally moved home to New Ross in County Wexford. He regained consciousness, but it was all over. Parts of his body had atrophied from the inactivity. It was hard to tell where his mind was at.

I took to visiting him in the hospital on my visits home. He was so well looked after. As always, everyone loved John. Even in his beaten-up state, his beautiful nature shone through. The staff encouraged visits: they felt that if something from his past intruded, it might shake him back into awareness. When we toured Ireland in 1996, they brought him to our show in Wexford. It was a bizarre situation. There was John in a corner of the ballroom, propped up in his hospital bed, just gazing at us, unfortunately, with no great sign of recognition. I remember little else from the gig.

My visits were draining. John would alternate between staring at me or out the window, as I'd carry on an hourlong monologue on the news from New York and New Orleans. I could never tell if anything was getting through. Eventually, I'd run out of steam, give him a hug, and totter out of there, emotionally spent. One day, however, when leaving for Shannon, I called in to say a quick goodbye. Usually I would notify the staff and they'd prepare John for my arrival. But there was no one at the desk and, pressed for time, I literally ran into his room. He looked at me and this time there was no mask. I'd caught him unawares. He burst out crying. He knew he was trapped. That most independent of persons would have to be looked after hand and foot for the rest of his life. He didn't want to see me. I was a reminder of what he had been. He passed away soon after and I was glad for him. He was finally free.

It wasn't just John; Ireland was slipping away. Or, at least, the Ireland that I had locked in my mind. Whereas before, I would just head down to the pub and by the time I had downed a couple of pints of Smithwicks, I would be firmly tuned in to the Eire wavelength, now it took me days to set aside preconceptions and ease back into the life over there. This was nobody's fault but my own. My friends, for the most part, treated me as if I had only left a couple of months previously, instead of the decades that now separated us. I suppose I wasn't ready to flush out enough of the past to make room for the present and the future. My parents were a constant source of worry. Nothing immediate. Just that nagging feeling that time was speeding up and racing by. Whereas before, I would love to travel over to the West Coast of Ireland and immerse myself in the landscape, light, and the more native ways, now I stayed close to Wexford so that I could be a presence to them.

Perhaps it was because I couldn't imagine my own children moving to another country and only seeing them for a couple of weeks a year. Or was it that I could finally see the years catching up with the deep-sea sailor? He now had a touch of Parkinson's and his hand was unsteady while grasping his glass of Jameson's. Still, the old salts continued to meet in their pub and laugh at the Holy Marys and any vestige of religious hypocrisy. Many of them were still vital, and they delighted in their own company, but no younger sailors joined them. Wexford had become landlocked. The town had fallen from grace with the sea. The harbor was silted; nothing afloat but fishing boats. Young men from the Faythe and John Street got what jobs they could in factories, instead of setting out oceanward. Just the old men now and their talk of Rio and Santos and Montevideo. I noticed that my Father would get a very faraway look in his eyes when the talk turned to Buenos Aires and Argentina. What was he missing there? He would lapse into silence, as if he had gotten off at the great Avenida Libertador and wasn't quite ready to move on. There was something that always drew him back to that country, something deep that was now causing him sadness or regret. I very much wanted to find out what it was.

And then the boulder did drop on the band. Johnny Byrne's death sent me into a tailspin that lasted for over a year. It wasn't just that he was a close friend, it was the sheer needlessness of his passing. We had recently assembled a studio in my home, and worked there every day on a project called *Keltic Kids.* I usually like to keep my home life separate, but Johnny was one of those people who could blend in anywhere, blend out, too, when the circumstances demanded. We had both enjoyed recording *Keltic Kids.* There wasn't the stress that often comes with doing sessions for a record company, or even a band. Johnny understood that I felt guilty about being on the road and away from my children on so many occasions. I wanted to write an album that they could listen to—perhaps later on in life—to show them that I cared. Added to that, I had been driven round the bend by many of their awfully patronizing kiddy CDs. I wanted to try and capture some of the real magic of childhood for kids of all ages—including me and other less sugary parents.

It was great to hang out with Johnny again. He had been with us through many of the ups and downs of Black 47, knew all the personalities, and was able to bring events into a focus that I could no longer do. We invited guest musicians and singers. One of Johnny's favorites was Rosanne Cash, who regaled us with wonderful and bittersweet tales of her father, a hero to both of us. She came to do one song and stayed for two, we were all having such a good time. That general warmth still sparkles off many of the tracks. We even prolonged the recording, taking our time with various mixes; but in the end, I had to go back on the road and we pronounced *Keltic Kids* finished. Johnny was to fix two small glitches and then have the recording mastered.

The band was playing the Dublin, Ohio, Irish Festival that weekend and I flew off. The gig was a blast; it felt like half of Ohio was there to see us. The party after—as is often the case where musicians run into one another—was rip-roaring. I managed to sneak away around 3 A.M. I can't have been asleep more than an hour when I got a phone call from Steve Duggan in New York. Johnny had fallen off a fire escape and was clinging to life in the hospital. Did I have his mother's number? I could barely remember my own. I'd heard a lot about his mother and how close they were, but I didn't even know what part of Dublin they came from. It was the old immigrant story: you know so much about someone, but you often really know so little. I knew everything about where he had fallen from, however, because he was subleasing my old apartment on B and Third.

Steve Duggan is a good man under pressure. He insisted that I make some coffee, then sit down and comb my mind for ways of contacting Johnny's family. There's a dread that comes over you at times like that. And yet, the picture of Johnny naked and bleeding on the pavement wouldn't allow me to sink into depression. That was the same pavement Carlita had strode down. Boris and Gerty had argued on its flagstones. I'd tried to persuade Josie to go clean there and instead watched her go walkin' away with her God. Real people, real songs, there had to be some way of contacting Johnny's family. And then it came to me, as things often do, through music. I'd had lunch with Johnny and his friend, Phil Chevron of the Pogues, some months previously. On impulse, I called Phil. He didn't know Johnny's home address either, but had a number for a mutual friend in Dublin. Phil put in a call to him; he went around to Johnny's mother's house and waited until she returned from Sunday Mass to tell her the news.

I took the early morning flight back to New York. Johnny's blood was still on the sidewalk. It all seemed so deadening and even inevitable. In the early morning, East Third Street was still hot from the night before and Johnny's mattress was hanging from the fire escape. I knew what had happened. The bedroom was like an oven; he'd pulled the mattress through the window to catch the night breeze. Then, he'd either tripped on the lip of the windowsill or slipped off the mattress while sleeping. How could he have been so stupid? It was four stories up, and even in my wildest days in that apartment, I was cautious about sitting on the fire escape, let alone dragging a mattress out onto it and sleeping there naked.

Johnny must have been drinking. He was a guy who should have run a mile from booze. His specific type of alcoholism was the same as my grandfather's, though a little less severe; Thomas Hughes only needed one whiskey before it took over. Johnny's addiction kicked in somewhere between three and four drinks. My grandfather had no choice in the matter. Just a sip and he was on a spiral to nowhere. Johnny's was more unpredictable. If he limited himself—which he usually did—he could function. He was very conscientious about his work and would never drink during a project. He knew better. He had just finished *Keltic Kids* and a CD for the Táin, another New York band. A double whammy. I knew the feeling well. Have a few drinks, let off some steam. But alcoholism is an illness. Unfortunately, it's one that we overlook in the music business, probably because it's so prevalent.

We all knew Johnny had a problem. We even used to laugh about it—in a kindly way: "Oh, there goes Johnny again." You could even tell visually he was "happenin'," as we called it; his glasses would slip down and perch sideways on his nose. He would lose all self-awareness and call you up in the middle of the night for long meandering conversations that made little sense. Other times, he would stumble around Avenue B, get mugged, beaten, and robbed of the little money he'd have on him. There were many times when I was about to speak up, but I didn't—the lack of time or energy, perhaps, or did something more insidious prevent me? The music world is an unforgiving environment. Excess is a given. We'd all had our moments with it. There was a code. You don't say anything about me and I won't about you. We're all tough cookies and we can work ourselves out of this. Besides, the common wisdom is that alcoholics will never get better until they face up to the fact themselves. So, lay off. I'll plough my furrow, you plough yours!

But on that sick, sad, sorry morning I had to come face-to-face with my own betrayal of a friend. In the months that we'd been working on *Keltic Kids,* Johnny and I had talked through acres of our own history, loves, losses, and all manner of other things. He had confided in me and I in him. I'd had many opportunities to bring up his drinking. And he would have listened. He respected what I'd done in life and measured some of his own failings against a number of my insignificant, but to his mind major, successes. He had got himself on track and his life was turning around. Since our early days, he'd always owed me money but he'd finally paid me back. Ironically, because of his work on *Keltic Kids,* I now owed him. He was terribly pleased about this. It might have seemed like a small thing to others, but to Johnny it was a major triumph. On our last meeting, I was about to pay him, but he brushed me off, said we'd settle after the mastering of *Keltic Kids.* It was the first time he'd had a little one up on me, and I smiled to myself after he'd gone. I'm not sure that Johnny would have given up the drink at that point, though, from some of his ancillary conversations, I felt he was close to it. A little extra prodding from someone he respected would not have hurt. I just hadn't gone that extra mile for a friend.

Johnny lingered on for some time. There was no hope but we needed to get his family over from Ireland and they had to make the decision. It was painful all around. Some of his friends were angry in the end. They had hoped for a miracle, as if all the longing in the world could bring him back to us. I seethed at the funeral tributes in the chapel at Bellevue. I couldn't even bring myself to talk. All was cake, roses, regret, and glowing memories—and maybe that's the way those things should be. But many of us there were suffering from some form of the same illness that killed our friend. No one brought that up. And when it was over, we all went over to Reilly's, got smashed, and told our favorite Johnny stories.

His family came to the apartment and took a few small keepsakes. Then I invited his friends over—each one took whatever meant most to them. Everyone said I should keep his torn leather jacket. I did and it hangs in my closet, still not mended. I settled up his affairs, praying that his bills would come in under the amount that I owed him—if even by pennies. It would have meant so much to him. When all was done, I searched his hiding places, but there was little of consequence: a couple of joints and a packet of condoms. And that was it, his CDs and cassettes, some paperback novels, an address book—the remains of a life. I filled a couple of garbage bags and left them down on the sidewalk. After that, I folded his best clothes—his women charmers, as he called them—and took them to the Salvation Army. Then I went back to my old apartment for the last time, sat on the empty floor, and remembered the night we finished the mix on "Her Dear Old Donegal." Johnny had turned off the overhead lights of the studio, and in the warm red glow of the mixing board we listened to a song that meant so much to both of us. When it was finished, we both had sat there in the silence, each lost in his own thoughts. That same silence seemed to cross over the years and the space and inhabit the apartment on Third Street. When I finally stood up to go, I swore that I'd never be silent again when there was a need to speak out.

34

FANATIC HEART

I remember your eyes from the 12th of July
When the sirens were screaming and the flames lit the sky
You held me so tight, thought you'd never let go
'Til the bullets exploded in the pavement below
Then I laid you down next to a burnt-out car
Screamed out for help but you were gone too far
Still got that picture of you locked away from the start
Developing inside my fanatic heart.

I went around in a daze for a couple of years
With the blood in my veins frozen over with tears
I did anything that they asked me to
All I could see was that picture of you.
The young ones passing by say, "How about you, real hard man?"
But deep down inside I was just a castle of sand
Still got that picture of you wrapped away from the start
Developing inside my fanatic heart.

Then they took me inside, threw me up against a wall
They put electric prods on my chest and my balls
They told me to sign things I knew weren't true
In the end I did what they told me to do
Then they locked me up threw away the key
Left me there with just your memory.

Now I walk through New York like a grey silhouette
Trying hard to remember what I'm supposed to forget,
That look in your eyes on the 12th of July
When the sirens were screaming and the flames lit the sky
I sleep with other women, hold them through the night
All I want to do is get on with my life.
Still got that picture of you locked away from the start
It's frozen inside my fanatic heart.

From Black 47, *independent 1991, and* Fire of Freedom, *EMI Records 1993*
Published by Starry Plough Music/EMI Blackwell Music

ONE DAY IN the mid-'90s there was a cease-fire in the North of Ireland. The peace process had kicked in and the guns went silent. But had the fanatic heart finally stopped beating? Hardly. With all the best will in the world, a chain of events that stretched all the way back to Strongbow leaping ashore in Wexford back in 1169 would not come to a conclusion overnight. "Much hatred—little room": Mister Yeats, as usual, hit the nail on the head. Someday there will be a settlement agreeable to all, but it will take generations for the pain and memory to settle and subside.

What would my grandfather make of it? Still no united Ireland? Or would he, too, have tired of the endless cycle of violence? I definitely had. So had most Irish-American activists of my acquaintance. What had begun in another era as a peaceful spin-off from the American civil rights movement had over an almost thirty-year period degenerated into a military standoff, with a measure of sectarianism institutionalized on both sides. It was time for change, time to rebuild.

From my own point of view, Black 47 had given back heroes and icons to Irish-American youth. They could use these as portals through which they might discover their history and heritage. Had the songs also played a part in sending young men out to die—as Yeats feared his poems might have done—and as an occasional observer has suggested in our case? I don't think so and they definitely weren't written in that spirit. But words and music when combined in a charged atmosphere can become dangerous symbols and even catalysts. What they had done was to help awaken Irish feeling in America, and to politicize people on a grass-roots level. I had always felt that the solution to the problems in the North of Ireland would come from America. And now an American president—rather amazingly with the consent of both the British and Irish governments—had his envoy working full-time on a treaty that might bridge the gap between all sides.

I asked my grandfather once when Irish unity would come. He had taken a long time before finally sighing, "When Ireland forgets and England remembers." It wasn't his usual ideologically bound answer, but it contained the seeds of wisdom. I was never going to forget Ireland and the problems we had inherited. I would always remember and reflect on its troubled, inspiring history. After all, what songs there still are to write! But like many people who had devoted some part of their lives to the struggle for civil and economic rights in the North, I was heartened by the unruly peace that was spreading over that part of the country. The people on the ground were picking up the pieces and creating a new and, hopefully, more tolerant society. What then did Bobby Sands and his comrades die for? Another Stormont government, this time one with fair representation for Nationalists? That's a question that cannot be swept under the carpet; it should be dealt with by ongoing discussion and reflection. Otherwise it will fester and young men in future generations will be forced to deal with it.

Will there ever be a united Ireland? Of course there will, although, ironically, it will come when no one really cares anymore, and more than likely within a European context. It will be a long and tedious process fraught with pain, for peace does come dropping slow and is always harder to maintain than war.

Like many other Irish-Americans, I was eager to turn back to the problems we have in this country. Although a part of me would always look homeward at Ireland, I had finally come to terms with the fact that I would not be returning. My life was here and I had a stake in the United States. My children were growing up. If anything, I wanted to make this country a better place for them to live in. Like many immigrants, I had always thought of the United States as something separate, apart from myself. Oh, I identified with the streets and the people and the city; but even though I was political, in some abstract way I always felt that those who were born here were ultimately responsible for what went on in D.C. Surely that was shirking—taking an easy way out.

So I became a citizen. And for the first time I started to use the word *we* when I spoke of the United States. It felt strange and a little self-conscious, and I didn't use it around other Irish-born people for a while. But that, too, was hypocritical. So to hell with it! I'm no flag waver. I grew up around intense blinkered nationalism and can readily differentiate it from patriotism—a far more wholesome and mentally healthy sentiment. For in the end, what is a country but a collection of the various people who live there? I've always exulted in the sheer vitality of the many races and nationalities that combine to make up the population of the United States. That was one of the reasons I came to multicultural New York: to experience life to the fullest. And it was out of this roiling gumbo that Black 47 came to be formed.

We wanted to capture that feeling on a CD, and so decided to record one of the live shows at Wetlands with Stewart Lerman producing. People had always claimed that we were much better in performance than on CD. That was fine by me. I always felt the same about Springsteen, Marley, the Clash, and any other number of the great performers. There's a fire that unites a band onstage that is rarely stoked in the clinical setting of a studio, where you're more centered on capturing the essence of a batch of songs early in their life. Onstage is very different; there you can explore the oft-performed song, feel it out, expand and contract it, and feed off the sparks kindled by the other band members. That's what we did with *Live in New York City.* Stewart, who is a fine musician himself and who can empathize with each member of Black 47, captured a sweat-soaked night at the turn of the century with the band and the audience totally united. I was glad we got it down right because that CD will always bring back the essence of so many other wild nights since our first faltering evening in the Bronx. It captures all the heart and defiance of Black 47. It also reminds me of Chris and the times we had together.

It had been coming for a while, but Chris had decided to leave and pursue his own music. He had developed his brand of Irish hip-hop under the name Seanchai and the Unity Squad. Although he was able to introduce some of this onstage with us, to develop it to the perfection that it deserved, he had to strike out on his own. A band like Black 47 is too encompassing—smothering even—if only from the time it absorbs and the sheer fatigue it induces from the endless traveling. With no weekends off, it's hard to get an alternate career jump-started. I know that well, from the opportunities I've had to forgo as a playwright. But the bottom line is: when you're not doing exactly what you want, there's nothing quite as deadening as heading off on some relentless slog to Buffalo or Boston and coming home drained in the dawn light. Chris stayed to record *Trouble in the Land* and then went the extra mile promoting the CD before having a hand in picking his replacement, Joseph Mulvanerty. Although they were sometimes a blur, I'm proud of the years we put in together. We started with one innocent jam before sixty people in Reilly's and went on to play before over sixty thousand people at Farm Aid. Some of my best memories of Black 47 will always be playing guitar behind Chris as he blew away any amount of people while performing "Walk All the Days" or "Time to Go." But now it was time to go.

There was an evening I remembered out in Queens in the early days. It had been snowing and there was a small crowd in the bar, gathered more for company in the storm than to see us. There was no stage and we set up on the floor at the back of the room, right between the ladies' and gents' bathrooms. A number of the patrons were very drunk, including one Irish head-the-ball who had just arrived in from London, jet-lagged to the eyebrows. In fact, he was so out of it that even though he passed us on his way to the bathroom a number of times, he never quite comprehended that we were playing music. After our first break, we found that the men's bathroom had been destroyed. The bartender, who was also the owner, inspected the mess very gravely with much shaking of the head. Oh well, it was his problem, we figured, and if we quit now, we wouldn't get paid. However, we were a bit on the uneasy side, with this random violence having taken place literally behind our backs.

After our second break, when we returned to play, we found a trickle of water coming from under the ladies' bathroom. We had seen head-the-ball staggering around in the general vicinity and since there were no ladies present, we were now convinced that he had a hand in the matter. After a couple of songs, we looked over: the trickle had turned into a flood and was pouring over our electric cables. Just at that moment, the drunken bastard picked up a bar stool and roared out, "That fuckin' music is drivin' me mad!" With that, he swung out at the silent, but lit, jukebox and smashed in its glass face. He must have felt he had the right idea, for we both stopped playing instantly and a silence descended on the bar. His friends now alerted this London cowboy that we were the actual cause of his torment, not the jukebox. There was a moment's stand off where the big lug turned to face us, raised bar stool above his head, while we stood transfixed in the rising water. He began to advance toward us, the fire glowing in his eyes. Chris bent down, opened his pipes case, and felt for the gun inside. Then he said to me, calmly but determinedly, "If he lays a finger on us, I'll shoot him."

As it happened, calmer minds prevailed. The owner intervened. "Ah, come on now, Paddy, it's about time for you to go home." Perhaps the jet lag, or what little sense he had left, kicked in, but moments later his friends managed to bustle him out the door. Chris closed his pipes case—the situation, if not under control, at least defused. We stood amid the damp carnage, the place now pretty much deserted, blankets of snow on the windows blacking out the night. We still had two sets to play, but there didn't seem like a lot of point. As we packed up to go, the owner came up to us and observed in one of the great understatements, "That man has a lot of problems."

We were involved in many more glorious and triumphant incidents in the ten years we played together, but for some reason that one came to mind when Chris was finally leaving. Perhaps it summed up our relationship: close, intense, humorous, and very much on edge. I learned a lot musically from Chris, but I learned even more about life.

I'd been feeling the need to spread my own wings. I had the playwriting outlet, but this particular urge seemed to call for expression through music, though of a different nature than Black 47. I had been in the habit of taking my family down to Riverrun, a restaurant in Tribeca, on Sunday afternoons. After being on the road and out late for a couple of nights running, it was a good setting in which to unwind and relax. Two or three pints would go down easily, and while walking home scraps of lyrics and melodies began coming to mind. These felt very different than what I'd been writing for Black 47. Some of them were almost like shards of memory in the form of sounds or rhymes. Later that night, I'd write them down or sing them into a tape recorder, then forget all about them until the next Sunday when a new sequence would begin. At first, many were connected with growing up in Wexford: sights and sounds that I remembered, scenes from my boyhood, memories of my mother and father when I was a child and they were a lot younger than I was now. With the experience of living, I was better able to understand their earlier and more vibrant selves, and could place myself in situations that I had observed as a child.

In my head, on those walks home, I could hear three instruments playing the melodies: trumpet, violin, and double bass. There was even a sound to the plangent arrangements that suggested a melancholic sense of time and place. I'd heard echoes of it before in the tango music that the deep-sea sailor used to listen to on his time spent at home. From those Sundays over one autumn and winter I collected many individual pieces and began to assemble them. Sometimes it was hard to combine cadences, rhymes, and rhythms, but I decided to just go with the inner spine or feeling as best I could. There was no need to beat these fragments into shape like a pop song. They would be what they were—pieces of memory stitched together.

The first song that I worked on had four very divergent verses, and yet there was the shade of an inner schematic within them that I was able to follow. The first verse was inspired by a vague sexual memory, and yet the verbal images had little to do with sex—more those of a returned traveler arriving in New York City on a foggy nineteenth-century night. It had a spectral feel that was not entirely comfortable or comforting. Gradually the song began to unfold in my mind, until I could hear the interplay of the instruments and see the events transform into lyrics. Everything felt familiar, preordained in an odd way, until eventually to my chilled surprise, I realized that the song was about a spirit returning to the city and trying to reunite with someone that he had once loved. I called it "Kilroy Was Here" after a ghostly sign painted on the wall of a laneway back in Wexford. As a boy, I used to stare at it and wonder. Even then, I knew that it would have some significance for me off in the future.

I told Stewart about this and other songs and the instruments I was hearing. He was excited at the prospect of doing an album based on these ideas, with no thought of commerciality. He called a bunch of players, some of whom I knew and others who I had heard of. Fred arranged the strings and horns; we got together and jammed, like the old jazz combos. Then we recorded the songs live over two long evenings. We gave little instruction to the musicians—just the names of two CDs that might provide some signposts: *Sketches of Spain* by Miles and *Astral Weeks* by Van. *Kilroy Was Here* is also the title of the album that came out of those sessions. I felt a great weight off my mind. It was as though I had been freed of a certain baggage of memory. I was also glad to turn the recollections of my mother and father into songs. Within months I knew why.

I got the phone call every emigrant dreads. My mother had cancer. Although it was pretty advanced, there was no immediate reason for concern. Things would take their course. I was going home the following week and would be able to spend time with her. At that moment, the very word *time* had a bitter edge to it. Where had it all gone? What had been so important that I'd been able to put my good intentions on some kind of career long finger?

But there would still be time, wouldn't there? I needed to know that. It was midsummer and we had a heavy schedule of gigs. *Trouble in the Land* was still current and the band had obligations. Then I'd have a month's vacation to spend with her, and maybe I'd just stay on in Wexford, and finally take the fabled time that I'd been meaning to for years.

We still had two gigs to go when I got the next call. There had been a relapse and she was in the hospital. Still, no cause for immediate alarm. But it was the height of the summer season. Aer Lingus couldn't change my reservation, they had no open seats to Dublin or Shannon the next day, Friday; but there was a chance that I could get a standby flight to London, then get over to Dublin on Saturday morning. In the meantime, my brother and nephew managed to get Aer Lingus flights out with me on Saturday night. I put in a call to Wexford. Things were bad but not immediate. Should I cancel the gigs, just head out to Kennedy, and try to get to London? I wanted to see her alive—after all the absence, I needed to hold her hand that one last time. I had missed my grandfather's passing by days. I didn't want a reprise of that. And then I thought of her. How horrified she'd be at the idea of letting people down for her sake. That old Wexford practicality. How were the guys in the band doing for money? Would it put them out? I knew that's what she'd be thinking. I called again. My sister said to wait until my scheduled flight. My mother was asleep and comfortable. I didn't go to Kennedy but bought a dark suit at J. Crew.

We played the Jersey Shore on the Friday night. I managed to keep it together; I even did an interview for the *Irish Voice*. The years of professionalism kicked in. The crowd was raucous and loving in that hardscrabble Jersey manner. It was a relief to flow with the energy, but every song was charged with emotion and "Fanatic Heart" almost ripped me apart. I wasn't sure I could do an encore, but Hammy said, "You've got to. I've got a surprise for you." With that he took off his pants and shirt, wiggled suggestively back onstage to the roars of the crowd, and began playing "I Got Laid on James Joyce's Grave."

She had made it through the night. There was just one afternoon gig to get through on Long Island and then the band dropped me at the airport. I checked in my bags, keeping the new dark suit with me so that it wouldn't get creased. Then I found Jemmy and my nephew Chris in, where else, the bar? It was good to be with them and a hard-drinking Donegal crowd of our acquaintance who were also heading home. None of us paid any attention to the increasingly frantic Aer Lingus announcements. The pints were flowing. We were old hands and knew the drill. No need to line up. Just go on board at the last minute. Save a lot of hassle.

There was consternation when we all barreled up to the check-in. They had been looking for me for an hour. The earlier flight to Belfast had been delayed and passengers taken off. Due to some mistake my ticket had been issued for that flight—because of the stress, I had never checked. My bag was already on board. But no sign of me. It could have been a bomb planted; after all, I was connected with Black 47, it was snootily explained. The mistake had not been mine and I was in no mood to put up with that kind of profiling. But eventually a supervisor intervened and my situation explained.

When we got to Dublin, my bag was missing but there was no time to wait around. My mother had taken a turn for the worse, and it was now a race against time all the way to Wexford. Her hand was still warm, but we were thirty minutes late getting there.

35

KILROY WAS HERE

Watch the mist like a blanket bleed on the town
Muffling the streets—damp eiderdown
Step down the gangway onto the pier
Off the tramp steamer that took you all the way here
A shot in a tavern, resurrect your old bones
Then it's out in the street in search of lost souls
Approached by a lady of dubious charm
She takes you by the arm
Upstairs into a frozen room
She undresses 'neath an alabaster moon
Saying, "Sweetheart, what would you like me to do?
I'll do anything that you want me to."
But I can't tell her 'cause someone might hear
So I whisper politely, Kilroy was here.

Up on Christopher, the shadows of sad young men
New York cowboys every one
Lost innocents, some are even sweet
But straight as crooked arrows down the foggy winding street
With looks so searching, penetrating and cruel
Hot lasers piercing right down to the cockles of your soul.
One of them inquires silently: "Hey stranger, how about a gift?"
No, I'm only here to see Montgomery Clift.
"But he's a long time gone, you know what I'm talking about, my dear,
And we all know what you're looking for down here."

The next time you see Monty, you stick your tongue in his ear
And tell him that Kilroy was here.

Up on 57th, a street of bitter tears
A prophet is celebrating the Jewish New Year
And the ghosts of all those Christmases past
Troop by like broken mirrors made of Presbyterian glass.
A brokenhearted Jesus steps down off his cross
Bolts out the door of St. Malachy's Church.
"I came to resurrect you but no one gave a damn
So I'm out of here, you go tell your novenas to some other man"
"Won't you consider your options?" Cry two ladies in trade.
"No, I'm sick of being mistaken for the Marquis De Sade."
"We're so sorry to disappoint you," but he doesn't want to hear
The cock crowing in the distance
So I kiss away his tears and buy him 30 silver dollars' worth of beer
And reassure him that Kilroy was here.

Back on board the First Mate is fulminating,
"Don't you never get tired of your little-boy escaping
Why don't you take all your memories go store them in a locket
Seal them with a kiss then go drown them in a bottle"
On the quayside she waits, her face cold and ashen
Shivering with fear we used to call it passion.
The tide is rising but the fog has grown deeper
The First Mate says, "She can't come but you can keep her
Locked in a drawer next to the cross of your Redeemer
That's the only place for love on this phantom tramp steamer"
You reach out to hold her but she's starting to disappear
So you say, "Wait for me, I am coming my dear."
But you've lost her forever, 'cause now Jesus has her ear
And he's whispering that Kilroy was here . . .

From Kilroy Was Here, *Gadfly Records 2001*
Published Starry Plough Music (BMI)

THE DEEP-SEA sailor was shattered. The tears streaming down his face—the first time any of us had seen him cry. It wasn't supposed to be like this. He was to go first. He had been the one with the ailments. She had done yoga, kept herself in shape, always seemingly in control, except for a patch of depression over my Down's syndrome sister; but she'd managed to come to terms with that. It had even renewed her faith. She never missed a Mass on a Sunday and other days, too, not like the rest of us. And now that she'd gone, with the whole center of the family caving in, I realized just how much we'd all depended on her.

The sun was splitting the rocks when we reeled out of the hospital and made our uncertain way back home. Everything becalmed, so unlike Wexford, more like Sunday morning on the Saragosa. Not even a hint of the usual blustery southeast sea breeze. The deep green summer leaves on the old trees of Wexford beamed with health from last week's rainfalls. Her garden was ablaze with flowers, the bees out in force, thrilled as ever with her nectar-filled haven.

I couldn't bear to be in the house after the young priest stopped by. At first, he had been a comforting presence, taking the weight off our stumbling conversation. It gave my sister, Mary, a chance to bustle around and make tea while he wrapped the rest of us atheists, gnostics, couldn't-give-a-damns, and born-agains in the sonorous certitude of Mother Church. My sister had already stepped from out of my mother's shadow and was attempting to marshal us back into some semblance of a family. She would have a tough job ahead of her in the years to come. But now, in the blazing morning, her tea revived us, while the young man in black ran us through the ritual that would break the back of the next few days: the reading of her name at the remaining Sunday Masses, the removal to the funeral home up in the Faythe, the visitation hours, the final closing of the coffin, the funeral Mass on Tuesday, the procession out to the graveyard in Crosstown, and then the interment. My sister was unexpectedly firm, and it was a marvel to see one who had deferred so often now take charge, while the rest of us sipped our tea in silence. The coffin would remain closed, she said; there would be no viewing of the corpse. The priest immediately nodded his understanding. My mother had been quiet and unassuming, my sister stated, but she had not been without a degree of vanity. She would not have cared to be seen in such a manner. How right she was, we were all quick to agree.

And then the priest turned to me and asked if there were something I would want him to say at the Mass, apart from the fact that she was obviously such a good family woman. Not a word or thought would come to mind. I sat there like a dummy. A wonderful lifetime in which she had given of herself, time and again, to everyone; and I couldn't even dredge up a sentence to expand on the Catholic catchall, "a good family woman." My younger brother, Brendan, mentioned that she loved her garden, spent pucks of time mucking around in it, even read books on the matter. She had indeed; a couple of those books were scattered on the floor next to her chair. I happened to be sitting in it, and now could take in her view. Odd that I'd never noticed it before. She'd often look up from studying some picture of a plant and visualize it out there among the teeming flowers, finding just the right spot for it, or dismissing it as foolishness. I'd never known the names of her flowers; in one ear and out the other, she'd say, when I would ask her the same questions year in, year out.

I never totally understood her fascination with her garden, although I liked the end result well enough. But now as I gazed out at it, in an abstract way, I recognized the peace she must have gained from its contemplation and study. And then I remembered, all in a rush, that I had never known anyone with as sound a judgment when it came to people, while at the same time, she was probably the least judgmental of anyone in my experience. If she had deemed someone untrustworthy, she would never come outright and say it. It was more like she would introduce little questions or doubts so that we might be warned, yet always reach our own conclusions. The priest struggled for a moment with that conundrum, but then licked the top of his pencil and wrote some words in his little book. He closed it, nodding in satisfaction, and you knew he felt he had captured her essence with these bare facts. And that was that. He stood up to go and carefully placed his book inside his jacket. How many lives were summed up within and stored away in a couple of sentences.

In the garden, the lilies seemed to mock me with their cloying, overpowering sweetness. Why hadn't I made it in time? What, in the name of Christ, had I been thinking of? I should have bolted for London at the first phone call. All my life, I'd managed to man-ufacture second chances—opportunities to make amends—but that was out of the question now. There would be no redemption this time. I'd blown it, plain and simple, and I cursed at myself and at the priest's Sunday morning God, if indeed there was one. I moved around the little path of paving stones, dry-eyed and desert bare, and really saw her flowers as if for the first time. And how beautiful, yet almost feral, they were. They were alive in a way that I no longer was. Just as that thought crossed my mind, a deep despair rose up from inside me and almost swamped my senses. I'd never felt such pain or loss before. Yet, even through the black-ness, I could feel that this despair was wrong.

The bitterness either consumed itself or washed away over the next days, as I looked into the sad eyes of so many people who had been touched by this quiet woman. She had meant worlds to her friends, neighbors, and relatives. She had her place in life, had traveled and come to the end of her road. If I wanted to be bitter about my own shortcomings in not partaking more in that life, then that was my problem. The young priest put it best at her funeral Mass. She had tended to her garden with love and atten-tion, and the seeds from her plants and flowers had been carried outward and were now giving bloom in other gardens and coun-tries. If her own seed had passed on, then it had done so in its own good time and in order to give more life. This was the way of God and of the world. What more could one ask for?

What more, indeed? Bitterness had often cursed my family: mostly through politics, though occasionally through inheritance of land. My grandfather's family had split over Parnell and not spoken for generations; the old man himself had held an ongoing and terrible grudge over the lost civil war. This was what he had warned me to beware of back on tramp's heartbreak: "Don't ever get stuck on a road such as this. You'll know what I mean in good time." I could see now why he turned to alcohol once or twice a year: to drown out this hopeless anger and put it behind him for at least one evening, though he would regret his conduct in the morning. My mother had refused all her life to allow any of this familial turmoil to consume her. She had won her own great battle with it on the birth of my younger sister, Anne, and even in her passing, she was sending me this subtle message.

If I'd been slipping away from Wexford over the last years, now the town enveloped me and claimed me once again as one of its own. Old school-friends, musicians, girlfriends, even people I had not particularly cared for, called by the house or stopped me in the streets and embraced me or shook my hand. They made no big point that I'd been gone for decades or had given my allegiance to the city. I was born among them, I was one of them, and despite any self-induced distance I might put between us, there would always be a place for me within the mossy-backed walls of Wexford.

After the funeral, the deep-sea sailor held his own at the hotel bar. He was surrounded by friends and family. An occasional old salt would stop by and murmur a word of encouragement in his ear. He would brighten up, nod an assent, and murmur something back. They still had their codes and their ways, different from the rest of us. And when they'd gone, that faraway look would creep back into his eyes again. But he looked frail and his hand shook very noticeably now when he poured water into his Jameson's, so much so that I would take the glass jug and pour it myself to save him the embarrassment. And as I looked at him, I remembered the summer mornings, so long ago, when my young and beautiful mother and I would wait for his boat train to arrive at the North Station and he'd step off in his trench coat, battered suitcase in hand, home again from the Argentines and reunited with us. And I knew that the next time the phone rang in New York, I would not be late.

36

ORPHAN OF THE STORM

Get off the plane at Kennedy
Got a dream in your heart though it's down in your boots
Got a hundred quid in your pocket
And a couple of addresses in Woodside and the Bronx.
And you fit in like a fist in a glove
With the other hard chaws in the gang
Some are running from themselves
Some are running from God and man.
And you drink to dull the memory of why you strayed from home
To the concrete fields of New York City
An orphan of the storm.

The gangerman looks at you
Respect in his eyes
He knows you'd work until you drop
'Cause there's a black rage eating away inside of you
You'd walk though walls, son, before you'd ever give up
And at nights you're like a phantom
Nailing every young one you can
It's better than lying awake in the dark
Thinking of her with another man
But she'll never take your dreams away
That's not why you've come
To the canyoned streets of New York City
An orphan of the storm.

You only went back once
You just had to be sure
Kindness in her eyes
You saw only pity there
So drink up your Jameson's whiskey
Wash it down with pints,
Obliteration on the rocks
Then out of here in the dawn's hungover light.

So you put her far behind you
You hardly think of her anymore
Well, maybe on a rainy Sunday night.
You're the gangerman yourself now
Got a new job down the Trades
Every little thing's going to be all right.
Then they blew you to sweet Jesus
On that grand September day
Not a cloud on your horizon
Your heart finally okay.
But they'll never take your dreams away
They were not for sale or loan,
On the shattered streets of New York City
This orphan has finally come home.

From New York Town, *Gadfly Records 2004*
Published by Starry Plough Music (BMI)

I DID MANAGE to spend more time in Wexford from then on. It's funny, when you really set your mind to something, it happens. The world doesn't collapse. You just mark out a couple of extra weeks in a year, book a ticket, and before you know it, there you are. My father looked forward to the visits. We'd sit around and read the papers in the morning, then drive to some seaside village in the afternoon, always careful to have a quiet pub in mind, where no one cared if his hand shook when he raised his glass. The loss was still heavy on his mind, but the tears were drying up, as tears always do.

I had something new in common with him. I had traveled with the band to Argentina to play some dates. The visit had given me an understanding of the man that I had only guessed at before. I had strolled the streets of Buenos Aires, met some of his old friends, and seen him through their eyes. I had wandered across the Pampas and exulted in the sheer beauty of their wide-open spaces and instinctively knew how a man of my father's type and generation could feel free and full of hope in such a gorgeously lush country. And I had gone up the river to his beloved Rosario and played in its old opera house. There were times that I wished to ask him flat out for the intimate details of his long visits to this country, but he was in such deep grief I was afraid to upset him any further. And so I held my peace and figured that time and whiskey would provide an opportunity when I would get him to reveal his secrets. The nights were long for me while he watched television. I sat in her chair, gazed out at her garden slowly going to seed, or fiddled with my laptop.

One night, I happened upon seventy pages of an old novelized version of *Liverpool Fantasy* that had been mistakenly filed. For want of something better to do, I began to read and, without thinking much of it, corrected various errors as I went along. By the time I got to the end, I realized that I was also adding and deleting sentences and paragraphs. So, I continued on with this story of a band called the Beatles who broke up in 1962 and never made it out of Liverpool. Unlike the play, the novel wasn't just about the main characters: it was about all rock 'n' roll bands and the music we make: what it's like to be onstage, how the players see, feel, and hear the music, and how it changes us and ultimately sets us apart, for better and worse.

Around eleven at night, the deep-sea sailor would turn to me, point at the clock, and say, "If you're going out for a drink, you better get movin'." I'd almost be reluctant, now that I was so caught up in the novel, but then he'd add almost plaintively, "Go on now, I'll be all right." And I knew it meant something to him that life should continue as normal and that he not be treated like an invalid. So I'd close the computer and head down the hill

toward the town, couched around the solemn floodlit steeples of
the twin churches. The soft, sooty smell of Wexford would comfort me as I walked down ancient John's Gate Street, wishing that
the old sailor was well enough to handle Mary's Pub. And inside
the old establishment, the fire would be glowing in the grate, the
faces ripe and red. Joss Kielty might be playing his harmonica, and
the pints would flow as free as the Slaney River only a couple of
hundred yards away. It was always a comfort to go there, for it
wasn't much more than a stone's throw from my grandfather's
house on George's Street—long ago converted into seedy flats.
The very decor of Mary's summoned up memories of the old
area that I'd grown up in. It had been a tinker's bar back then—
one of the few places in town the traveling people were allowed to
congregate in. Occasionally, as I came through the churchyard
gate from school, a group of them, mad with drink, would be settling their differences with bare fists and curses outside in the
street. No violence anymore, but inside there was still a fading
flavor of the Wexford of my childhood. Some of the older patrons
recognized me as the boy who used to race to early Mass in the
friary on gale-force Tuesday mornings, scared out of my wits by
the slates careening off the rooftops and smashing into
smithereens on old Abbey Street, now alas a parking lot and a
ridiculous high-rise. Some of the younger customers even knew
the Black 47 songs, for it's a bar where republicans are also welcome. Not that people in Wexford think too much of politics
when they're having a few drinks, but I've always felt welcomed
there and my pint would be pulled before I'd even order it.

Before I knew it, I'd be back in the house and my father would be
inquiring what news. And I'd relate some piece of gossip that I'd
overheard. Then he'd ask that his whiskey be replenished and we'd
sit there watching British television get progressively more sug-
gestive as the night wore on. It was a strange feeling at first, to
come home and watch soft porn with your old man. Bonding of a
sort, I suppose. One night, during a particularly lurid scene, I was
moved to say, "Jesus, that's hot stuff." Without taking his eyes off
the screen, he raised his drink to his mouth, coughed a little from

the bitterness, then whispered, "Ah, sure you wouldn't believe
some of the things you'd be watchin' here at night." And he was
right. But it never stopped him tuning in. And why not, when
you're a lone widower? Though his flesh had grown weak, the
deep-sea sailor's spirit appeared to be more than willing.

One night, I stayed late in Mary's talking to some Sinn Fein
men and drank a little more than usual. When I got back to the
house, I was in the best of good spirits. My father barely noticed
me entering. I think he had been dozing with the television running; as was his habit, however, he picked right up where he had
left off. The screen action was literally eye-popping and would
have sent the Christian Right into convulsions. I can't remember
much of a plot, but a cleric of some creed was administering a dis-
ciplinary spanking to some obviously deserving young woman.
My father was taking all this in with great gravitas, and I considered the reaction of my republican grandfather, were he to see the
two of us sitting there enthralled by this "auld English smut," as
he called even the most innocuous of kissing scenes. For this had
his comrades sacrificed their lives.

"God bless the Brits," I murmured.

"They have their moments," my father whispered. I had to
listen closely now because the Parkinson's had ravaged his once
commanding voice.

"You know what?" said I.

"What's that?" He didn't take his eyes from the screen. Neither
did I, for the cleric now had the young lady over his knee and was
giving her what-ho.

"We should invite that young priest up for a drink."

He appeared to consider this for a moment, before inquiring,
"Your man from the funeral?"

"Yeah, he's probably sitting on his ownio down in the presbytery. Wouldn't he be far better off up here slummin' with the boys,
a bottle of beer in his fist?"

"That fellah'd drink it off a sore knee," my father stated nonchalantly. Then he took a long draft himself and shuddered, but
his eyes remained peeled to the screen.

"What do you think?" The idea was very plausible to me. In fact, it seemed the only right thing to do.

"Whatever you like," my father sighed, "as long as he doesn't want to turn off the television and say the feckin' rosary, or some such nonsense." Parkinson's notwithstanding, he was pretty emphatic on that point.

"Hail Mary full of grace, little Johnny won the race?" I didn't look at him when I spoke. But I caught his secret smile in the mirror; he was happy that I remembered the old line.

But I had a bee in my bonnet. "I'm sure he's seen worse," I said, getting back to the serious business. I suppose my father thought I was joking. And I was, somewhat. But when I looked at the phone, the priest's number was there right alongside the undertaker, the doctor, and other functionaries from the funeral. The television cleric now had produced a table tennis bat and was administering discipline with abandon. The whole scene was just too funny. I took a slug, picked up the receiver, and dialed the priest's number. My father didn't appear to give a damn. He had taken off his reading glasses and was now fully honed in on the screen.

The phone was ringing down in the presbytery. I had been there many times as a boy and could visualize it blaring through the big old drafty house on School Street. The onscreen bishop—for such he was, as I now caught a glimpse of his purple shirt—had removed his leather belt and was working himself into a frenzy. The young woman was squealing at the top of her lungs. "I deserve everything," she repeated with every lash of the belt on her silken buttocks. This was going to make a great story for the band on our next long road trip. Be good for at least fifty miles. Things were obviously coming to some kind of a climax on the screen when a familiar voice tentatively inquired from the phone, "Hello?"

"Hello," said I back, caught somewhere between the bishop and the curate, as it were.

"Can I help you?" Contrary to what I had imagined, the young priest had been sleeping but was solicitous, and obviously girding himself for any emergency.

Now that I had him on the line, I wasn't quite sure how to

phrase the invitation, especially with the howls of the damsel renting the room. I looked over at my father, but he was bent over examining his Jameson's. "You better tell him to bring his own bottle," he croaked. "We're gettin' low."

"I'm sorry," I blurted out. "I think I have the wrong number."

"Are you sure?" the young priest asked. "Is there something I can help you with?"

The squealing stopped. The spanking had ended, the scene had changed, and the bishop was back in church giving a sermon. The young lady, now very sensibly dressed, was demurely staring up at him. In the silence, I was lost for words and a bit disoriented. I could sense the young priest's concern on the other end of the line. "No problem, Father, everything's under control," I finally said.

"That's good." He paused for a moment before hanging up and added, "Good night so, and a safe journey."

Jesus, I thought. Had he recognized my voice? His words rang in my ear for some time. Then my father noted with the barest of grins on his face, "If that fellah had waltzed in here this time of night, the whole street would have thought I was dead."

"We could have said it was a social call." I sighed, regretting that I hadn't the courage to ask him.

"Yeah!" my father's voice suddenly came back in a blast, discarding its usual whisper. "We could have said he was droppin' by to see the bishop."

His grip seemed firmer, his hand less shaky, when he topped up our glasses. "I don't want that fellah standin' over me until after the Tralee Races. There's a young horse I've been watchin' this two years," he said with some conviction, then held up his glass in a toast. When I clinked it, he added matter-of-factly, "After that he can do what the hell he wants. I won't have to listen anyway."

Now that the subject had been raised, it didn't seem out of place to inquire if, after all the years of atheism, he might not sooner have the more worldly Protestant rector dispatch him to the great blue yonder. By this time, the bishop had managed to get rid of his tweedy wife and had lured the damsel back once more into the sacristy, so the deep-sea sailor's mind was on more important matters.

He reluctantly delivered this last enigmatic thought on the subject. "When a dog is howlin' at the moon, it doesn't matter a damn if he's on the left side of the road or the right."

Words of wisdom that might also have applied to the band. With Chris gone, everyone stepped forward. Instead of trying to put a stamp on what should happen, I let matters take their own course. Young Mister Mulvanerty introduced a new musicality into the arrangements. He had come to the uilleann pipes late, having begun his musical career as a jazz drummer in his high school band. He brought this experience to bear on his new love for Irish music; it was stirring to hear traces of Hendrix and Brubeck merge with O'Riada and O'Carolan, and on those sacrosanct pipes, too, no less. His dueling duets with Geoff on soprano sax now became a highlight of the night; listening to Fred, he was able to ingest the whole range of the bone player's style and knowledge. Andrew Goodsight, who had joined after the van accident, stepped to the front also and began to showcase his own impressive free-form bass chops, often setting the table for the improvs with fluid harmonic lines. He dug deep into the grooves and swept the dust from the walls on his solo in "Rockin' the Bronx," thereby enabling us to reinvent and bring new life to old standards. The ladies sighed their approval while their boyfriends were forced to give him grudging nods of approval. But Hammy was the revelation. He was again firing on all fours: always first to show up at the gigs now, tuning his drums, staking out his position onstage, and psyching himself up for the night ahead. It was like being back in Max's or CB's playing with the young powerhouse of the '80s all over again, except that now he had all the wily moves of the veteran at his beck and call.

The songs will always speak for themselves with Black 47, but to me music can say things that words can only dream of. With so many songs being requested, our shows were rarely under two hours, and I took to leaving the stage a couple of times a night, as much to enjoy what the musicians were cooking up as to take a breath. On the long journeys home, with Nico—and later P2—laughing and driving and John Murray taciturnly analyzing the PA system, we were like a family, usually dysfunctional, but always united against the world outside. John's Dublin accent and his North Side stories would often transport me back to the wild days in Rathmines with my brother and the Atlantic College crew, and cause me to wonder what my life would have been like if I'd stayed and married Bridie. But only for an instant, because the craic in the van is always lively and excitable after a gig, with much mimicry and banter of whom we'd seen, talked to, and many another thing, too.

Gradually, however, the laughter and talk would trail off, and guys would drift into sleep; then Nico would put on a Miles CD and there'd just be the two of us and the many miles ahead: he driving, and I staring out at the white lines being steadily swallowed up beneath us. A calmness would descend as we allowed Miles and his golden horn to envelop the van in a wave of well-being; and from out of that warmth many people that I'd loved and played with would step forth in kaleidoscopic cameos. After a good gig, there's a peace and contentedness that seeps from your bones; this essence of goodness ensures that most of these memories are joyful, if often humorous. For our world of rock 'n' roll changes daily. There's always a new cast of characters and you can pick and choose just whom you wish to deal with or walk away from. And on nights like that, you realize how lucky you are to be doing what you've always wanted to do. And on one of those nights, I remember thinking that my dark angel would always smile down on me and that life would continue like that and then . . .

I can't overestimate what a beautiful day it was. Clear blue with just the barest hint of fall in the air. January is New Year for much of the world, but the first two weeks after Labor Day signal the beginning for New York. People come back from the shore and the mountains full of new resolutions, and for some reason there was even more hope in the air than usual. Maybe there was even time for the Mets to turn it around.

I was reading about the Amazin's at breakfast when I heard it coming in the distance. For the first moments, I paid no heed, far more interested in Mike Piazza's batting average. But the sound grew exponentially until it was roaring toward my back. I ducked my head onto the table, suddenly sure the plane, missile, whatever, would come right through the walls; then with a whoosh it had passed over. Before I could even question its nature, I heard the most sickening thud—very unlike the screech and tearing of plane crashes in movies—more like the sound of a sledgehammer connecting with thick concrete. Then a silence, much the same as when a shot has been fired and the echoes have finally ceased. When there was no further sound, I ran up onto the roof of my building. The door was ajar; some of my upstairs neighbors had beaten me to it. At first I saw nothing. I hardly knew what to expect anyway. I followed the outstretched arm of a neighbor. It was, indeed, hard to take in the sight, much less process it: a gaping hole about two thirds of the way up the westward tower of the World Trade Center, ugly black smoke pouring out, and within, small tongues of flame licking away quietly at the darkness.

No one spoke. It was too much. We live just north of Canal Street and the view of the Trades had always been spectacular. I don't know why it sprang to mind, but my first real sight of them was toward the end of the movie *Carnal Knowledge*, when Jack and Artie are having their last conversation. But that was just an instant flash. Suddenly, everyone was talking and shouting and you could hear the cries echoing from the surrounding rooftops. It was an accident, of course. How could the bloody pilot have gone so off course and hit one of our lovely towers? The utter stupidity of it all! Hadn't he ever seen the old pictures of the crash into the Empire State?

And then the second plane hit the eastward tower. We didn't see it and the sound was muted, for the plane came from the south and was blocked from our view. But we felt the impact; the tower itself seemed to buckle from the shock. There were no flames from our angle, just another gaping, smoky hole and then a confetti of glass and paper exploded outward and seemed to hang in the air around the two buildings. Jesus Christ! It dawned on us all that we were being attacked, but by whom? I ran downstairs for a pair of old binoculars and trained these on the eastward building. Large black pieces of debris were sailing right through the glassy confetti. I instinctively knew that bodies were hurtling down but on no account did I wish to see them. Luckily a neighbor asked for a look. Better him than me, I thought, as I handed them over.

He never got to use them for suddenly a cloud of brown smoke and dust erupted and the building wavered and collapsed to the ground in an almost orderly, but totally surreal, manner. It was hard to trust the eyes, but this was no mirage. The building had disintegrated downward in a couple of awful seconds and a great cloud of smoke and dust arose, to my mind, almost like a shroud. People were now yelling and screaming from all the rooftops. A number of women around me cried hysterically, while the men cursed loudly in anger and disbelief. It was as if time stood still during those awful seconds while comprehension sought to reassert itself. The general consensus was that the tower had been blown up by bombs previously placed in the basement; and the feeling, though generally unspoken, was that these unidentified bombers were invincible and could now do as they wished with the city.

I stayed on the roof for another couple of minutes trying to piece together any thoughts and emotions that I might have had, but everything seemed utterly changed, and I don't mean just the purely physical. The westward building was still standing but it looked violated. I got the distinct, sickening feeling that the gaping hole in that tower was like an ugly smoking wound that would never be healed. Now a general panic swept across the rooftops and the screams merged with the howl of many sirens heading south on Broadway. The loudest scream, though silent, was, "What's coming next?"

I took back my binoculars and trained them on the standing tower; it seemed so close and we on the rooftops particularly vulnerable, being less than a mile away. I had no hope; it was just a matter of time until the second tower fell, and I didn't think for a moment that the orderly collapse of its sister would be repeated. No, this one would surely explode outward and shower us with the glassy confetti, the dark beams, and God knows what else. Many others felt the same way and there was an exodus off the rooftops. I ran downstairs, just in time to turn on the TV and watch the second tower disintegrate in the same sickeningly neat manner.

It's very hard to put into words the feeling of vulnerability in the next hours as rumors swept the city: new planes were headed in for more attacks, the tunnels had been booby-trapped, the "bombs" that had brought down the Trades contained biological and germ warfare devices. And then soon after, two screaming air force jets banked over the city, causing widespread panic, before they were identified. Where the hell had they been, we screamed back skyward? But there was no reply, nor has there been a satisfactory one to this day.

I headed down to Canal Street and decided to walk toward the WTC area, knowing that it would soon be blocked off. People were streaming up Broadway, dazed and glassy-eyed, some formally dressed, some in casual attire, but most dusted over with a fine white powder. After five or six blocks, however, the smoke and dust became too dense and I was forced to halt. With my back against a wall, I watched emergency vehicles speed down Broadway, shoving the escapees up onto the sidewalk. All was chaos, but there was remarkably little panic. Just shock—silent for the most part—with no hysteria or tears, only a dazed, bitter uncertainty. One man stood out, an African-American: his shirt had been either blown off or removed. He must have been about six foot four and he was covered from head to toe with that same fine white dust with which we would all soon be familiar. He was moving up Broadway with a purposeful stride. I looked in his eyes as he passed me. There was no shock or fear there, just a fierce but calm determination to get home, get out of that area, get back to some kind of sanity. I watched him until he faded off into the smoky distance of Broadway. He took a large measure of our past with him.

37

MYCHAL

In New York City I made my home
I loved the streets, the very stones,
Cared for my comrades, cherished my friends
Loved all beginnings, had no time for ends.
A city's streets are full of woe
I saw suffering where e'er I'd go,
I did my best to console and heal
Treat each human with full dignity.

I never saw a reason to
Hate someone who thinks different than you
Each one has their anointed place
In the love reflected in their God's face.
We all have sorrows our share of trials
We all are sinners in each other's eyes
Love alone can ease the pain
God bestows love in so many ways.

I have my failings and I have tried
To look them squarely in the eye,
To be there when someone might call
For I know cruel well how hard it is to fall.
I love the company of friends
The fire and the music sparkling in their eyes
But I achieved my heart's desire
When I rode beside the ones who fight the fires.

As I arise on this September morn
The sun is beaming down the streets are warm
God's in his heaven and all is well
I will go forth and do His will.

From New York Town, *Gadfly Records 2004*
Published by Starry Plough Music/BMI

WE MOVED BACK into Connolly's on Saturday nights soon after
the attack. We hadn't meant to. As part of a new design, I was
trying to limit our appearances in the city—make the band less
accessible. But all plans were out the window now. Everyone
was doing their part to get the city up and moving again and it
was imperative that Midtown climb back to its feet as quickly as
possible. That was the idea during the blitz in London, and we
were now facing our own test.

It was a strange time. Scars had not even managed to form and
all wounds were exposed. There was an odd feeling abroad on Saturday nights. Times Square was empty. Lone people hurried across
Broadway, their heads down, collars up even in the mild weather.
It was like a shadow had descended on the city. One could almost
sense a shiver of apprehension ripple through the streets; and
always the thought of that still smoldering mass graveyard a
couple of miles south. The resolute, the cussed, and many rescue
workers descended on Connolly's for relief, a bit of normality, and
the promise of some kind of catharsis with Black 47. After a couple
of drinks, we all managed to re-create the old scene, at least to
some degree. There was a fervor to the partying, an almost maniacal refusal to leave the bar until the last glass was drained.
Everyone had been hurt, and it was good to be transported, in
some manner or other, from the awful reality. But the atmosphere was so charged, almost hysterical, it often took the band
well into the set before we'd manage to break through this
rearranged psychic fourth wall and unite with the audience. It
wasn't unusual to have a stranger just break down crying at the
bar, or for a friend to slip off pale-faced and trembling into the
night, unable to cope with memories and the absence of familiar

faces. There was also a niggling fear that the madmen might strike again. Yet there was a fierce determination that life must go on.

The loss was staggering. At the time, we weren't even sure how many people had been killed; the numbers quoted varied widely. And then the estimates hardened into a round three thousand. But it felt like more than that. Because every day word would come through that some friend, acquaintance, or even a person you just knew by sight had perished. As the weeks and months passed and we traveled around the tristate area playing gigs or occasional benefits, people would show up with pictures of the departed. It was usually the same story. We would stare at the young faces and be told that their favorite song was "Banks of the Hudson" or "Danny Boy" or some number that the speakers couldn't identify, and could you please dedicate it because they would have been here in the front row if they could, and it would mean so much to the family. It was wrenching when you recognized the pictures, but far worse when you didn't. To think that they had invested so much in you, and you couldn't even recognize them.

There was something missing in the city and it was hard to fathom exactly what it was. Even though all New Yorkers were trying their utmost to bring life back to normal, it was sometimes hard to remember exactly what normal was anymore. The island seemed to be skewered eastward, now that the towers had slid away into the west. Add to that the fact that Canal Street was like an armed camp with barricades across Broadway, Church Street, and all the natural thoroughfares south into ground zero, as it was now called. The National Guard ruled the streets: edgy young men, often in from country areas, with fingers on cocked triggers, looking lost in the unfamiliar urban setting. How could they be otherwise? Even those of us used to the edgy streets felt uneasy in the new order.

And don't even mention that smell. Christ, it lingered for the better part of six months: burning, rubbery, and acrid with some awful other component that you didn't even dare speculate on. For days it would hang over everything and then suddenly disappear. You'd open your window, mad for a breath of fresh air, and then the wind would change and there it was in your face again, or even worse, back in your apartment. Once it gained entry, there was no getting rid of it. We were all coughing. Not major bronchial barks, but tiny catches between your breastbone and your throat that caused a shallow nagging itch. But even worse was the awful ephemeral emptiness. It was like you had been drained of some essence of yourself. You weren't even sure what it was, and to make it worse, you had no idea if it would ever return.

For a long time, I thought about it. Tried to give words to it and the situation around us, capture it in song; but it always came out as something banal and unpoetic, cloyingly sentimental and tasteless. I knew I was way beyond any kind of creative fertile ground and, after a couple of futile attempts, threw my hat at it. I wrote very little in the way of music during that first strange year. It wasn't laziness either. I just didn't trust my instincts. For the first time as a songwriter, I didn't really care anymore. There were more important things. If the Bobby Sands maxim, "no one can do everything, but everyone has their part to play" was ever true, then this was its time. Black 47's task was to get on with the job and play, hopefully bring back some small bit of light, or even normalcy, back into people's eyes. Still, it nagged me that I couldn't put my finger on what was missing.

It took nine months or more before the obvious hit me. We were physically and psychically missing the presence and spirits of the people who had been slaughtered. They weren't just digits in some round figure that could be replaced instantly. They were part and parcel of our lives; the very pulse of the city beat just a little slower without them. We knew that New York would eventually regenerate; new people would arrive to fill the empty spaces. All great cities do that. But in the meantime, we had lost the life force and inspiration of three thousand very vibrant citizens. Three thousand spirits that had contributed mightily to the light and life of our times had evaporated. It would take time and turmoil for them to reconstitute and find their way back home.

Father Mychal Judge was one of those and, oddly enough, he came to represent and personalize the lives we had led previously. Odd, because who would have thought that a Franciscan priest would, in a largely secular and diverse city, come to be recognized as a figurehead for so many? But tragedy makes for strange bedfellows and throws up the most unlikely of heroes.

Mayor Giuliani is a hero, too. He did a remarkable job along with thousands of other New Yorkers. With our president out of commission, flying around the country like a blue-arsed fly, there was a void to be filled; and in his absence Rudy stepped forward and became a man for the moment. Not that the city missed Mr. Bush. Despite all that happened, I never witnessed one act of panic. I remember well that awful afternoon, standing in the Broome Street Bar with a large group, watching television for some kind of word from D.C., some sign of leadership, and marveling at just how well this bunch of New Yorkers was adapting to the situation. That's the nature of the city, and the mayor on that day, and in the coming months, personalized the grit and fortitude of its many inhabitants. But his elevation to Valhalla has also been a disservice to us, for, with his customary arrogance, he brooks no dissent on the lessons to be learned and has at times shamefully politicized the event for partisan gain. No one in the immediate aftermath of the disaster and few to this day have held him accountable for placing the city's emergency headquarters down by the World Trades, even though they had been the target of our worst previous attack back in 1993. He is the key to many answers and yet, because of his fame and haughtiness, no one dares ask him more than the most rudimentary and flattering of questions.

Perhaps it's more water under the bridge, but there's a bitterness still festering around the city, and in the commuter towns of New York State, New Jersey, Pennsylvania, and Connecticut, that won't go away until the full story of this disaster is looked at in the light of day. People who have suffered and lost family and friends wish to know the whole truth, no matter how it reflects on us all. They resent the fact that the event has been and continues to be politicized and that the deaths of their loved ones are being used to justify a vanity war in Iraq. There would not have even been an investigating commission if the families, and especially the widows of those who perished, had not raised their voices. And why, in an age when no one trusts or respects politicians or their venal parties, should Republicans and Democrats have been the only voices on the investigating commission?

No one doubts that when the necessary amount of lip service has been paid and enough dust gathered, most of the commission's recommendations will be conveniently ignored, or implemented but not enforced. We were all caught unawares by what happened. But there were agencies and people who were paid to protect us and keep an eye on the security of the country all the way from the president, through the mayor, down to the lowest gumshoe in the FBI. It's a rare one of them who has accepted any measure of blame and owned up to their responsibility; consequently, there's not a person I know in New York City who doesn't think that the same type of tragedy or, God forbid, an even worse one can happen again.

That's why people have turned to Mychal. Who knows if he was a saint and who cares? He was the better part of us all. I barely knew the man; to me, he was another punter who came to Connolly's to let off a little steam. It was hard to ignore him, though, even when he wasn't in his robes. For he was a mirror into which you looked and saw the good side of yourself. When you spoke to him, the conversation was all about you. It wasn't just that he was interested, he knew that each human has a need to be the center of attention for even a couple of minutes. He could sense the sorrow that's at the heart of us all, and he could identify its manifestation in each person. He couldn't walk away without ministering to that pain or hurt in some way.

I knew one small side of him, the music fan who liked to be at the center of things. He adored the buzz and the bright lights. I suppose it took his mind off the cares of so many others that he so willingly bore on his shoulders. I was stunned when I read his obituary. There were so many other facets to the man that I couldn't have even imagined. He's public property now and he's already slipping away from us. But I cherish a number of small things about him. He had an endearingly vain side. In the tumult and heat of our gigs, he was always immaculate with every hair on his head plastered into place. There was almost a shine off him—not the spiritual one that's so often mentioned now—but the physical. Rarely was a man so well shaved, scrubbed, and tastefully cologned. But that was just the outside, a façade, as it were. If you looked closely enough, you could feel the inner loneliness that enabled him to empathize with the private pain he saw in everyone else.

One night, I mentioned to him that I had been a Franciscan altar boy back in Wexford. He was familiar with our friary and we talked about it and the relics of little St. Adjutor ensconced in the side altar. I wondered what had become of Father Justin, the friar who wasn't in his box on the day of my triple confession. I may have even given him a brief account of my adolescent moral debacle, for Mychal had a grand sense of humor and would have enjoyed the absurdity of it all. He did take a mental note of my question and told me he'd find out about my old confessor. Months, perhaps even a year later, he approached me and said he had the information I requested. I had no idea what he was talking about; people in bars are forever making idle promises. Why should he have been any different? But he was. And that's why we all love Father Mychal Judge, OFM, and why the city and so many of us will never be quite the same without him.

38

THE FAR SIDE OF THE WALL

We've done some things, terrible but true
Across the blazing years, letters of fire
Politicians smile, they shake hands for the camera
But some things never change, no wonder that I'm angry at
The voices that I hear with every sigh and call
Thinking of you holding him
On the far side of the wall
I wish I could reach out
Save you from each and every fall
That I know you're going through
On the far side of the wall.

Remember August days, an ecstasy of blue
Floating through that seaside town
Bodies burning, me and you
Fast forward to the streets
Orange shades of paranoia
We'd go our separate ways
Couldn't even admit to knowing you.

Think of me now and say a silent prayer
When other hands are touching you
Remember, I still care.
And in that bleary dawn
A tiny spark of blue

So hold on, my darling
Tonight I'm going to break on through
The voices that I hear with every sigh and call
Thinking of you holding him
On the far side of the wall.
I wish I could reach out
Save you from each and every fall
That I know you're going through
On the far side of the wall.

From Elvis Murphy's Green Suede Shoes, *Gadfly Records, 2005*
Published by Starry Plough Music (BMI)

DOWNTOWN BAGHDAD BLUES

Got a buddy in Najaf, he's playing it straight
Prays to the Lord Jesus Christ every night
Got a homey in Samarra goin' up the walls
Every time he hear an Islamic prayer call
Me, I don't care much for Jesus or Mohammed
They don't stop bullets to the best of my knowledge
Later for the both of you, catch you in eternity
Hopefully, toward the end of this century

I didn't want to come here, I didn't get to choose
I got the hup, two, three, four Downtown Baghdad Blues.

I wish I was back home rootin' for the Padres
'Stead of dodgin' bullets from Mookie El Sadr
I wish I was back in the land of Guiliani
Instead of takin' heat from Ayatollah Sistani
Don't know what I'm doin,' but one thing is clear
Twenty years old, I can kill but I can't buy a beer
Keep your head down, don't get your brain cells fried
You'll be home by Christmas, dead or alive.

I wish I was back in the US of A
Instead of dodgin' rockets in Fallujiay
There's a lady with my tattoo on her so special
Dream of her and me out in the desert
She ridin' round in her Daddy's Ford Explorer
I'm kickin' in doors, hey, I thought this war was over
Got sand in my nose, sand in my eyes
But the sand can't cover up the sights of a
Sniper with my number, got his finger on the trigger
Hope my baby's okay, I'm still waitin' for a letter
All I get are emails, so much left unsaid
It's hot here, baby, but it's so cold inside my head.

Mission accomplished, yeah, up on deck
Got no armor for my Humvee, I'm left facin' this train wreck
Shia don't like me, want Islamic Revolution
Sunni say civil war is part of the solution
Maybe someday there'll be peace in Fallujah
McDonald's on the boulevard, Cadillac cruisin'
I'm tryin' hard to keep this whole thing straight
But will someone tell me what am I doin' here in the first place?

From Elvis Murphy's Green Suede Shoes, *Gadfly Records 2005*
Published by Starry Plough Music (BMI)

PEOPLE ASK ME, were I sixteen now would I take up a career in music? I think not. This is another age, and popular music plays a far different role within it. It's not that musicians are less committed, and God knows, they are much more technically proficient than we were; kids in garages knock off whole Hendrix symphonies with little bother, some are even pyrotechnically as accomplished. Do they have the man's soul and feeling? Well that's another matter. Artists are products of their time and Jimi was a giant of a freer and more adventurous era. To me, modern rock 'n' roll has been institutionalized and become so part of the system, it has lost much of its appeal. When I first picked up a guitar the music was still fresh and finding its way. Now most of its considerable landscape has been explored and mapped out, and is illuminated by the bright unflinching floodlight of self-awareness. In short, it has become another victim of the age of irony. To make great rock music, you need a certain amount of innocence curried with blind faith, both of which are in short supply these days.

We're in the midst of an information age; songs such as "Blowin' in the Wind," "What's Goin' On," "Biko," or "The Message" are no longer as crucial to get the word out. Music has become a luxury, a nonessential one at that. This is not the view of some disgruntled veteran. I would be delighted to be proved wrong, for the traveling has always been more important to me than the actual arrival. No, it's that of an interested observer and fan who has watched rock music's evolution from the vantage points of garages, pubs, clubs, stadiums, board rooms, and political arenas, but most important, from the street. There will always be popular music, great music at that, and each generation will, and should, find its own. But it's the place the music occupies in society that interests me now.

We are firmly entrenched in an age of celebrity. We manufacture these figureheads and discard them by the day. They are titillating to us, though they rarely mean much: we have so little invested in them, mostly because of their fatuousness and the brevity with which they inhabit our landscape. An occasional one has a degree of substance and may even stand for some principle or other, but those few tend to get boring and tendentious, as complexity doesn't sit well with our attention spans, overdriven lives, or the present system. And there is a system—a funnel—through which these stars are delivered to us. I know it well because I was part of the process back around 1994. In fact, I had a longer run, and more opportunities for "greatness," than most are granted. But I wasn't really suitable material, being too diffident, jealous of my privacy, too much in love with the actual creative process, and unwilling to hang out and spend precious time with idiots. The image-makers at EMI and Mercury, no doubt, could rattle off many other reasons for my anemic fizzle in the starry firmament, including, perhaps, an insufficiency of talent. But I recognized my own shortcomings many years ago when measuring myself against Cyndi; when all was said and done, though, I just didn't have the same hunger or desire for celebrity.

The process itself did fascinate me, however, and I was able to appreciate the attention I received while taking note of it all with some humor. The most important lesson I learned was that once you passed through that narrow portal down the chute of stardom, very few ever managed to get back in line for another turn. This had nothing to do with the talent of the applicant. It's just that the gate-keepers abide by two very strict rules: keep it fresh and move it right along, babe! So, don't blame that band or performer who scores their one big hit and then promptly disappears. It's not their fault that they were not chosen for the second go-around. It is their fault, however, if they have believed their own publicity; it's even more their problem if they can't sustain a career in the field they love because their record-company support has been withdrawn and they no longer have the heart or perseverance to go right back to scratch and start all over again. Life's tough; wear a helmet if you want to be an artist. Which reminds me: Isn't that the most overabused of modern words? Back in Wexford, *artist* was a title conferred upon you by popular acclaim. To this day, I wouldn't dare describe myself as such, for fear of people back home in the pub cracking up at my presumption.

No, I wouldn't become a professional musician again. I'd enter the field of television—a veritable wasteland, it's true—but one that is actually effecting social change, no matter how stultifying or perni-cious. Walk down any street in America, and you'll see its steely blue hypnosis at work behind every window. Books, theater, music, the things that I love, are all well and good, but they have a minimal impact on our lives compared to the old dummy box in the corner. I'll bet there are few houses in the United States with more toilets than TV sets. That's how much a part of the fabric of our lives it has become. Its influence is all pervasive, usually overt, but often sublim-inal, too. Every night onstage, I can feel the audience flagging at around twenty-seven minutes and again at fifty-five. It puzzled me for years until the penny dropped. Their attentions spans are demanding the accustomed time slots and ad breaks.

"But excuse me!" I used to scream. "I'm alive up here. I'm not television. Don't you dare blank out on me!" But in the end, I got a pain in my arse gazing out at the slack-jawed stares of incomprehension. Now we just pump up the volume or jolt the tempo to help Mister and Missus Joe and Joanne TV get over their addictive hump. Pathetic, merely sad, or frightening? Maybe it's all three, but that mountain is far too formidable to be climbing night in, night out. So I take Father Jim's advice and walk around it. Although, strangely, after you break through the hour barrier, the problem dissipates and you can hold the audience in the palm of your hand until the balls fall off the Christmas tree. I'll leave that conundrum for better minds to solve.

Hannah Arendt wrote about the banality of evil in the attitudes of the Nazi functionaries responsible for the concentration camps. But I think that the evil of banality is the new threat. Most of us are so enmeshed in a tawdry consumer-driven society, we no longer have the energy to rise up from our couches and make a difference in the world around us. The Roman patricians recognized that "bread and circus" was the way to control their plebeian underlings. I don't claim that there is any like-minded conspiracy afoot today: most politicians and modern patricians don't have enough cop-on to get laid in a brothel, let alone come up with such a complicated plan or its application. But I do know that most people in the United States are so worn out keeping their economic heads above water that they readily surrender hours a night to the mind-deadening reassurance of our modern-day circus beaming at us from the corner.

Jesus Christ on a bike! At least the plebeians got to watch the Christians being thrown real-life to the lions. Now we settle for gaping at a crowd of digitized morons spouting inanities at one another over canned laughter. If that were all, then it wouldn't be so bad. But with the sheer amount of sludge that's being excreted on us, we're losing the ability to think and discern for ourselves. The one-liner and the sound bite rule. All complexity is frowned upon. Instead of cherishing our myriad shades of gray, we adore the bald black-and-white statement. But the world is a complex

and crazily quilted place where the simple truths of the funda-
mentalist and the fool, while often comforting, lead only to more
chaos and human suffering.

Back in 1984 we worried that Orwell's awful world was at hand,
but to me, the threat seemed exaggerated and unlikely. I still
think it's a ways off, but getting ever closer, for television supplies
an alternate universe that, with repeated viewing, becomes more
real and glamorous than the reality we are experiencing. It
reminds me of something Lester Bangs said to me twenty-five
years ago, when noting that the United States didn't have an influ-
ential musical press to match that of the United Kingdom: "If
Melody Maker stated on a Friday that the next craze would be
Moroccan punky reggae from Newcastle, then by Monday every
city in Britain would have its own Moroccan punky reggae band
singing with a Geordie accent." The United States still doesn't
have a strong musical press, but the world has MTV. The minute
Black 47 hits a hip-hop beat, every milquetoast homey in the
crowd salutes us with ghetto moves and motions that he's aped
from $50,000 videos paid for by international corporations. These
same white-assed 'hood imitators would drop dead at the mere
thought of actually taking a stroll through East New York or Bed-
Stuy, where their much more economically challenged brothers
ape the same moves from the hipper *106th and Park*. That's why I feel
that television and its more active sister—the Internet—are the
new frontiers. That's where complacency, indoctrination, and
rigid uniformity must be challenged in order that real social
change can be effected and spread outward.

All that being said, there is still a role, even a compelling need,
for musicians in our less-than-brave new world. For music and the
right songs, if played with conviction, can still galvanize large and
small audiences and propel them toward activism. And what a
need the United States has for a broader-based opposition to this
disastrous war in Iraq. What a reflection on our society and skewered values that we may have already slaughtered more than thirty
times as many people in Iraq in the name of freedom as were murdered down in the World Trade Center, and to what end? Are we so

hoodwinked by the insidious sound bite and the sheer weight of xenophobic propaganda that we are unable to grasp the moral and practical consequences of this carnage? God only knows the seeds of hatred that have already been sown in Fallujah and Baghdad, eventually to be harvested in our own cities. Black 47 has always had a considerable body of its fans in the armed services; we support them wholeheartedly, yet question why they have been sent halfway around the world to get trapped in this quagmire. And we refuse to be browbeaten into silence by chicken hawks and armchair patriots who cry treason at the first sign of dissent. Our troops have been betrayed by a bunch of grasping politicians who have cast them into this morally indefensible, vanity war. We've spoken out against this travesty from the beginning, and suffered the loss of many a fan and friend as a consequence. That's as it should be. The purpose of a band like ours is to speak its mind, regardless. Iraq is the defining issue of our time. The appropriation of the media, in particular television, in support of this debacle is a far greater threat to our freedom than Al Qaeda or the many unjustly profiled hardworking Muslim immigrants. Popular music is a waning force but with a bit of effort, and less focus on celebrity, it can still circumvent the power and reach of the idiot box. For rock musicians this war may well be a last chance to redeem our particular art form and grant it some needed relevance and credibility. And if we shoot our bolt in the process, then better to go out with a bang than a whimper.

And what of Black 47? We've been on the road for fifteen years now. Almost an accomplishment in itself, seeing that we formed to fulfill a couple of gigs. Most musicians never get to experience the life we lead or the thrill of transforming ourselves and an audience night after night. Despite some mishaps, we've been privileged and very lucky. Besides, consider the alternatives. Playing in a rock 'n' roll band is a hell of a lot easier than being under someone's thumb in an office, or mixing cement for forty hours a week. Sometimes you're tired and wonder why you've driven all the way to Chicago or Holyoke, D.C., or Cleveland. And it wouldn't be worth the hassle if you didn't feel that what you're doing has some small importance, especially to the young people who look around them and know that things could be better. Some of those will wake up the morning after a gig and we will have added a pinch of spice to their conviction that they should do something about the world. Perhaps we will have only infected a couple of them with Bobby Sands's maxim. But if we can continue to do that one hundred and more nights of the year, we'll be playing our part.

Then again, that's something you rarely have the time or energy to reflect upon. Because you have a job to do and it's staring right back at you in the form of a sea of faces who have shelled out their ten or twenty bucks and are depending on you to deliver. Hammy will shout out, "One, two, three, four!" and you hit that first guitar chord, and what was dim and cloudy only seconds before jumps into amazingly sharp relief; so much so that two intense and exhilarating hours later when you're signing autographs for bright and excited eyes, it all makes perfect sense, and you don't even think of all the miles you still have to travel that night, or all the other nights down all the days ahead.

I was ready for the phone call this time. Bag packed, suit pressed, ticket in hand, I was on the way to Kennedy before I'd put the receiver down. The deep-sea sailor was waiting for me in the hospital. He couldn't speak but I could tell that he had been counting the hours it would take us to get from the airport down to Wexford. He began to cry and I held his hand. He was the child now waiting at the station, and I was the man. They left us alone. There were so many questions I wanted to ask him: Was he torpedoed once or twice—just hadn't bothered to mention the second time, considering it redundant in that off-handed Wexford manner? Did I have a stepbrother or -sister in Argentina as was rumored in family lore? Had I lived up to his hopes and dreams for me or did he even have any? All of the unanswered mysteries of the deep-sea sailor. But it was too late. His voice was gone and his hand shook violently. And then my family came in and the boys told him that they had learned to sail that summer; he studied their faces for traces of himself and my mother. The younger one declared that on their small training vessel he was "master of the jib"; that brought a smile to the face of the old mariner. The older boy said nothing, just stared intently at his grandfather's face, and I could tell from his eyes that he had what the old people used to call "a touch of the sight." It would be lost on him in the broadness of American life, and maybe that was for the better. It was a troubling gift at best. The deep-sea sailor nodded. He saw the same thing, but had no words left to express it.

As the day wore on, he grew more agitated and kept pointing to the top of a newspaper where he'd scribbled in pencil the barely legible words: "40—Harrington." My sister, Mary, raised her eyes heavenward; he'd been returning to this time and again over the last days.

"It must be Harrington's of Dublin, the headstone suppliers. Do you owe them money?" I ventured. No, he shook his head emphatically, and his eyes signaled that he considered himself a sorry man to have sired such a dope.

"Is it someone else that we don't know?" my sister inquired resignedly. He was even more emphatically negative. His eyes blazed with the seaman's old impatience at the landlubber's lack of understanding of anything worthwhile under the starry heavens.

"Can you write it down?" I asked.

I didn't have to hear his voice to know his reply. "Don't you think that if I was able to write the damn thing down, I'd have done it days ago instead of lyin' here on me bloody back lookin' out at a crowd of jackasses without a brain between them?"

Eventually, he appeared to come to the conclusion that he had been saddled with idiots all his life and, in this his darkest hour, things were unlikely to change. With an abject nod of resignation, he closed his eyes for a bit of rest. The nurse looked in and suggested that we let the man be. Women had always been attracted to him and fiercely protective—nothing had changed. We all filed out into the August evening, scratching our collective heads, the mystery of "40—Harrington" unsolved.

The phone rang at four in the morning. He had already

slipped away by the time I got over to the hospital. But that was okay. It had been a peaceful casting off, according to the nurse. After we'd made the arrangements, I drove back to his house and stood for a long time looking down the hill past the twin steeples. A red sailor's dawn was breaking over the harbor and all was well with the world. He was finally free and I knew that he had already gone.

The young priest did him proud at the funeral. I thought of mentioning the incident of the on-screen bishop and my phone call, but it hardly seemed the time or the place. I read some lines from Ecclesiastes, but kept a weather eye on the coffin for fear his corpse might rise up and accuse me of hypocrisy in front of the whole town. They sang the Mariner's Hymn for him, but it was leaden and syrupy—just the kind of thing he hated. I felt like kicking in some kind of South American rhythm behind it. But maybe it was as well I didn't. For it wouldn't have been seemly to have him leap from the coffin, tango down the aisle, hop into the hearse, drive out full tilt to the graveyard, and "get this bloody show on the road so people can go to the pub," as he would have put it.

Later on, when we were saluting him with his trademark round of Jameson's, one of his old friends solved the penciled mystery. It was all to do with the young horse he'd had his eye on for two years. It was trained by Jessica Harrington and running in the upcoming Tralee Races. The word spread like wildfire about Jem Kirwan's wish to bet forty final Euros on a pony, and there was much debate and argument among the old salts about the reliability of his other tips down through the years.

On the last night, when we were packed and ready for the early morning trip to Dublin Airport, I bade my time and waited until all were safely in bed. It was midnight and quiet as I headed out across the laneways of Wexford. I went back to a place I had known as a boy. It was dark down there and deserted, in its own pool of silence. I hesitated for a moment, my instinct telling me to beware of such isolation. But then I shrugged. Hadn't I trolled the very depths of the Deuce in my time and come out unscathed? What fear then of some Wexford laneway? It smelled of age and innocence, of neglect, and a different time. I moved amid its silky darkness and felt for familiar landmarks. Here a brick that stuck out, there a tangle of ivy that dropped from a rooftop; a drainpipe, new when I was a boy, was now rusted and brittle. Then on a brick wall, in ghostly faded letters: *Kilroy Was Here,* barely glowing after all the years. I traced out its letters against the rude stone. Then I put my back to its message and waited.

My eyes grew used to the darkness and my ears sensitive to the sounds of the night. I was still for a long time, before I felt the first hint of their rustling presence. At first, that's all they were: sensations. But when I relaxed sufficiently their outlines became more apparent. A Crusader home from afar, his eyes skimming the laneway for the sight of some loved one. He looked right through me, but I recognized his concern that all had died while he was away. He was followed by a Cromwellian Roundhead, thin-lipped, dour, and convinced of his own righteousness. A Croppy boy, his hair tight against his skull, hurried toward me, then stopped, as if listening for pursuers. He turned backward and crouched before moving on again, this time in a panic. Wave after wave of history rolled by, until the whole laneway was full of them; and then I saw my grandfather leaning against a doorway, watching a procession of black-suited workers led by Larkin and Connolly.

All was still for a moment, and then the familiar figure of a beautiful young woman passed me. She had dark hair and wore a flowered print dress just below her knees; she could not have been more than eighteen. Three men, dressed in the suit jackets and wide trousers of the forties, stood in a doorway and watched her approach. It was easy to tell that the youngest of them had been overseas, for he was dressed a little more stylishly and was more confident about himself. He stepped forward as she passed, murmured something, and smiled at her. She did not smile back. Even so, I could tell that she was pleased with the attention. The young man bade his companions good-bye and followed her down the laneway. I watched them for the longest time and knew that when they passed out of sight I would be free, and would not see them again until I took my own place in the laneways of Wexford. Until then . . .

In conjunction with this book, Black 47 has released *Elvis Murphy's Green Suede Shoes* on Gadfly Records. This complementary CD contains twelve of the songs referred to in *Green Suede Shoes*. It can be purchased in any record store or at all the usual online outlets. The band's official online distributor is www.cdbaby.com, where you can also buy *Black 47 Independent, Live In New York City, On Fire, Trouble in the Land, New York Town, Elvis Murphy's Green Suede Shoes,* and Larry Kirwan's solo CDs, *Kilroy Was Here* and *Keltic Kids.*

For a complete history of Black 47, band tour schedule, fan forum, free downloads, and newsletter, go to www.black47.com

For bookings, call Jeremy Holgersen at 212-581-3100, or write to blk47@aol.com

To listen to the band's 24-hour online radio station, go to: http://www.live365.com/stations/black_47

Feb 5th 2006

"Satisfaction" was released
in 1965 - R. Sts -
Super Bowl 40
Steelers - Seattle Seahawks
Jerome Bettis
#36 Steelers   330# "The Bus"
Hines Ward - MVP
#84 Roethesberger
Youngest Quarterback
ever in a Super Bowl

Bill Cowker (Coach)
Dan Rooney (owner)
5th win - last win 1980
21-10 Score - Super
                    Bowl
Broadcast to   Champions
      230
Countries!

Shaun's hands
name is Advantage!

Permissions